Henry Hastings Sibley

Henry Hastings Sibley

DIVIDED HEART

Rhoda R. Gilman

MINNESOTA HISTORICAL SOCIETY PRESS

www.mnhs.org/mhspress

The Minnesota Historical Society Press is a member of the
Association of American University Presses.

Manufactured in the United States of America

10 9 8 7 6 5 4 3 2 1

Portions of chapter 2 originally appeared in Jennifer S. H. Brown et al., *The Fur Trade Revisited* (East Lansing: Michigan State University Press, 1944).

An earlier version of chapter 3 originally appeared as "How Henry Sibley Took the Road to New Hope" in *Minnesota History* 52:6 (summer 1991).

♾ The paper used in this publication meets the minimum requirements of the American National Standard for Information Sciences—Permanence for Printed Library materials, ANSI Z39.48-1984.

International Standard Book Number 0-87351-484-X (cloth)

Library of Congress Cataloging-in-Publication Data
Gilman, Rhoda R.
    Henry Hastings Sibley : divided heart / Rhoda R. Gilman.
        p. cm.
    Includes bibliographical references and index.
    ISBN 0-87351-484-X (alk. paper)
    1. Sibley, Henry Hastings, 1811–1891.
    2. Governors—Minnesota—Biography.
    3. Minnesota—Politics and government—To 1858.
    4. Minnesota—Politics and government—1858–1950.
    5. Legislators—Minnesota—Biography.
    6. Fur traders—Minnesota—Biography.
    7. Frontier and pioneer life—Minnesota.
    8. Generals—United States—Biography.
    9. United States. Army—Biography.
    10. Legislators—United States—Biography.
    I. Title.
F606.S56G55 2004
977.6′04′092—dc22
[B]

2003026997

Printed by Thomson-Shore, Inc., Dexter, Michigan.
The paper is EcoBook 100, manufactured entirely of recycled post-consumer waste.

Contents

Preface

As businessman, territorial representative, treaty negotiator, state governor, military leader, writer, and elder statesman, Henry Hastings Sibley played a more varied and influential role in shaping the character of the Upper Mississippi valley than any other individual. He had opportunities to become a national figure, yet he invariably chose to remain with the place he loved and had helped to name "Minnesota."

Historians have written of him mainly in relation to Frederick Jackson Turner's theory of the frontier experience. Sibley's long life lent itself to tracing the stages of that experience over time, and since the region where he lived was the same from which Turner drew the defining elements of his theory, Sibley's career seems on the surface to bear it out. As the frontier thesis came under attack for oversimplification, Turner himself admitted regional variations and in his later work turned toward the study of sectionalism. In today's thinking, the immense complexity of cultural transition and mutual accommodation is recognized, and the study of frontiers has become largely one of how that process has played out among multiple groups and in specific regions.

When Sibley's life is closely followed, the complexity of his own story becomes more apparent. Although heir to the New England tradition of his family, Henry himself grew up in the culturally diverse, bilingual community of Detroit. His lifelong fluency in French was an essential part of the role he played, not only in politics but also in business and personal relations. French was the common language of the fur trade, and the tradition was tenacious. In the 1850s, when Sibley sought to exert direct personal influence on Pierre Chouteau, Jr., he wrote in French, although normal business correspondence with the firm was in English. During his years on the Upper Mississippi Sibley gained at least a working knowledge of the Dakota language, too, and he took a keen interest in the publication of the first Dakota dictionary. He came by request to the deathbed of Little Crow's father and witnessed the old chief's advice to his son, Taoyateduta, that the younger man lead his people in accommodating to the ways of Europeans.

Sibley was a bridging figure between the Indian/French/Métis world of the Upper Mississippi River valley and the Anglo/northern European world that became the states of Iowa, Wisconsin, and Minnesota. In coming to the frontier, he brought along the class distinctions of an older society, and those were shared not only by the military hierarchy that controlled the region but also by the French-Canadian workforce that he employed. The latter regarded their *bourgeois* as a patron and protector and had little use for the rough egalitarianism common to America's western border. Viewed from this perspective, Sibley's aloof stance toward partisan politics, his self-righteous public poses, and the intensity of the abuse later directed at him by political opponents become more understandable. It also becomes easier to understand his somewhat tortured efforts to describe the earlier society in terms acceptable to the prejudices of Minnesotans in the 1880s.

On the broader stage of national history Sibley's life spanned nineteenth-century America. Rooted in the political and social establishment of the old Northwest Territory, he witnessed the colonizing of a continent and its people, the closing of the frontier, the agony of civil war, and the explosive birth of an urban, industrial society. He was keenly conscious of what he conceived to be the nation's destiny, and he identified closely with it. An heir to the Indian policy of Lewis Cass, who had managed to dispossess the Great Lakes tribes without war, Sibley belonged to the generation that was left to pay the final price of that betrayal. And unlike Cass, he had personal ties to the Dakota people that placed him in a deeply ambiguous position.

This is a book of regional history and biography. But it is also a story of a place on earth and of a human life lived there and, as such, has a dignity and integrity of its own. Sibley's life was not an unexamined one. In writing of it, I have felt at times as if I were in a hall of mirrors. I have had to deal with Sibley's own evolving view of himself and his carefully constructed historical images. In his early articles on frontier adventure, in his nostalgic reminiscences, and in his unfinished autobiography I have found differing reflections, none of which matches the face I saw in contemporary documents. I have felt his awareness of this and have sensed a silent admission that there were things he could not say. Is that why he abruptly abandoned his own attempt to write his life story? Like the rest of the country, he never questioned the moral superiority of European civilization and he saw assimilation with it as uplifting the "savage." Yet this easy justification for conquest, when contrasted with the reality of the Indians' fate, left an unhealed wound upon both man and nation.

Part of Sibley's image as well as his importance to history rests on the mountain of papers he left to the Minnesota Historical Society, which he had helped to found and served as president for many years. Those papers contain, firsthand and unvarnished, the record of the public man, but one looks in vain for the private person. Apparently the papers were given to the Society with instructions from Sibley himself that all domestic items be weeded out and returned. Presumably destroyed was family correspondence, not only with his Dakota daughter, Helen, but also with his wife Sarah and his other children. For glimpses of the human being behind the reserved façade, I relied on letters in other collections and on private notes buried in business correspondence. Of particular importance are letters to the Solomon Sibley family in Detroit, preserved in the Burton Historical Collection of the Detroit Public Library, and, for Henry's later years, the Crawford Livingston Papers recently acquired by the Ramsey County Historical Society in St. Paul. Livingston married Sibley's niece, Mary Potts, and the papers include correspondence of Mary's mother, Abbie Steele Potts, with her sister Sarah as well as with Sibley himself, for whom she kept house during his last twenty years.

As I have tried to tease out from hints and fragments the stories of the women who influenced Sibley's life, I have also tried to lay to rest some of the many myths and misunderstandings that have gathered around him in the absence of published facts and a complete biography. I have included his full name in the book's title to avoid confusion with his contemporary, Henry Hopkins Sibley, who was also a Civil War general (Confederate), also an Indian fighter, and well known as the inventor of the Sibley tent.

My work has been immensely aided by others, but since it has extended over a period of more than thirty years, it is impossible to name all of those to whom I owe thanks. A few are indicated in the endnotes. In general, I can say that without the support and generous help I have received from the staff of the Minnesota Historical Society, this would be a far poorer book. (I think, for example, of John Dougherty, who regularly noted for me items on Sibley as he prepared newspapers for microfilming—items, like needles in a haystack, that I might never have found otherwise.)

Special mention must be made also of the Sibley House Association and the people who have worked there. In recent years the former director, Lisa Krahn, and David Grabitske (now with the Minnesota Historical Society) have assisted me in the search for elusive materials. Several of Sibley's descendants have also been generous in their efforts to help me determine if there was a surviving cache of personal papers. As those in any field of scholarship and study know, there is no substitute for a community of research. Whether colleagues, students, or simply friends and family, the insights of others and the exchange of ideas and enthusiasm are essential to the vitality of one's work.

Preface

As businessman, territorial representative, treaty negotiator, state governor, military leader, writer, and elder statesman, Henry Hastings Sibley played a more varied and influential role in shaping the character of the Upper Mississippi valley than any other individual. He had opportunities to become a national figure, yet he invariably chose to remain with the place he loved and had helped to name "Minnesota."

Historians have written of him mainly in relation to Frederick Jackson Turner's theory of the frontier experience. Sibley's long life lent itself to tracing the stages of that experience over time, and since the region where he lived was the same from which Turner drew the defining elements of his theory, Sibley's career seems on the surface to bear it out. As the frontier thesis came under attack for oversimplification, Turner himself admitted regional variations and in his later work turned toward the study of sectionalism. In today's thinking, the immense complexity of cultural transition and mutual accommodation is recognized, and the study of frontiers has become largely one of how that process has played out among multiple groups and in specific regions.

When Sibley's life is closely followed, the complexity of his own story becomes more apparent. Although heir to the New England tradition of his family, Henry himself grew up in the culturally diverse, bilingual community of Detroit. His lifelong fluency in French was an essential part of the role he played, not only in politics but also in business and personal relations. French was the common language of the fur trade, and the tradition was tenacious. In the 1850s, when Sibley sought to exert direct personal influence on Pierre Chouteau, Jr., he wrote in French, although normal business correspondence with the firm was in English. During his years on the Upper Mississippi Sibley gained at least a working knowledge of the Dakota language, too, and he took a keen interest in the publication of the first Dakota dictionary. He came by request to the deathbed of Little Crow's father and witnessed the old chief's advice to his son, Taoyateduta, that the younger man lead his people in accommodating to the ways of Europeans.

Sibley was a bridging figure between the Indian/French/Métis world of the Upper Mississippi River valley and the Anglo/northern European world that became the states of Iowa, Wisconsin, and Minnesota. In coming to the frontier, he brought along the class distinctions of an older society, and those were shared not only by the military hierarchy that controlled the region but also by the French-Canadian workforce that he employed. The latter regarded their *bourgeois* as a patron and protector and had little use for the rough egalitarianism common to America's western border. Viewed from this perspective, Sibley's aloof stance toward partisan politics, his self-righteous public poses, and the intensity of the abuse later directed at him by political opponents become more understandable. It also becomes easier to understand his somewhat tortured efforts to describe the earlier society in terms acceptable to the prejudices of Minnesotans in the 1880s.

On the broader stage of national history Sibley's life spanned nineteenth-century America. Rooted in the political and social establishment of the old Northwest Territory, he witnessed the colonizing of a continent and its people, the closing of the frontier, the agony of civil war, and the explosive birth of an urban, industrial society. He was keenly conscious of what he conceived to be the nation's destiny, and he identified closely with it. An heir to the Indian policy of Lewis Cass, who had managed to dispossess the Great Lakes tribes without war, Sibley belonged to the generation that was left to pay the final price of that betrayal. And unlike Cass, he had personal ties to the Dakota people that placed him in a deeply ambiguous position.

This is a book of regional history and biography. But it is also a story of a place on earth and of a human life lived there and, as such, has a dignity and integrity of its own. Sibley's life was not an unexamined one. In writing of it, I have felt at times as if I were in a hall of mirrors. I have had to deal with Sibley's own evolving view of himself and his carefully constructed historical images. In his early articles on frontier adventure, in his nostalgic reminiscences, and in his unfinished autobiography I have found differing reflections, none of which matches the face I saw in contemporary documents. I have felt his awareness of this and have sensed a silent admission that there were things he could not say. Is that why he abruptly abandoned his own attempt to write his life story? Like the rest of the country, he never questioned the moral superiority of European civilization and he saw assimilation with it as uplifting the "savage." Yet this easy justification for conquest, when contrasted with the reality of the Indians' fate, left an unhealed wound upon both man and nation.

Part of Sibley's image as well as his importance to history rests on the mountain of papers he left to the Minnesota Historical Society, which he had helped to found and served as president for many years. Those papers contain, firsthand and unvarnished, the record of the public man, but one looks in vain for the private person. Apparently the papers were given to the Soci-

Henry Hastings Sibley

◦ 1 ◦

The General Begins an Autobiography

IT WAS A WARM FEBRUARY DAY IN 1884 at Kittrell in the northern low-lands of North Carolina, where General Henry Hastings Sibley had taken refuge from the long and icy winters of Minnesota. The arrival of his seventy-third birthday on the twentieth of the month set him to thinking about the passage of time. How quickly was a man's short journey accomplished!—And how much more swiftly even did the world he had known change and vanish. Not many years remained, he reflected, to set down firsthand the whole sweeping story of his life, as he had often been urged to do.

The general was no stranger to pen and paper. As a young man he had published a number of elegantly written articles for eastern readers who were eager for a vicarious experience of the wild frontier. In more recent years he had poured out memoirs, recording for reverent posterity his recollections of a world that had come and gone between the morning and afternoon of a single lifetime.

His own eyes had seen Minnesota change from a land of wild grass and tall timber, the ancestral home of the Dakota and Ojibwe, to the breadbasket and milling center of the world. He himself had stood before Congress to urge the forming of the territory with its six thousand people, and he had sat as its first spokesman in the House of Representatives. More than any other man he had pressured the reluctant Dakota to hand over to the white man one of the world's richest agricultural empires. A state had been built from that empire, and he had presided over the convention that framed its constitution and served as its first governor. Finally, when the dams of retribution broke and the torrents of Indian anger and despair threatened to sweep away the very foundations of the new commonwealth, he had led a hastily gathered band of citizens and soldiers to its defense. The title of "general," which he prized more than any other, had been earned in anxious marches across the plains, in the hot confusion of unexpected battles, in the horror of blood-soaked grass, and in the slow swinging of thirty-eight Dakota corpses from a scaffold in Mankato.

Like Minnesota, he himself had changed. As a sinewy youth on Mackinac

Island he had vaulted across the counter of the American Fur Company store to throw out an offensive voyageur, and had stood tall in the mission church to proclaim his faith in Christ. Years on the prairies of Minnesota turned that youth into a mature man. They were years touched with loneliness, sickness, and disappointment that left both outer and inner scars, but also produced the resolve that saw him through political and military battles more ugly than he could have imagined. Those battles had bequeathed the bitterest lesson of all—the quandary of a righteous man who becomes the tool of injustice.

Surely the story should be told, but every story must have a beginning, and that is often the hardest part. He took up the pen, but he may have paused for a while as he let his eyes rest on the green hues of the early Carolina spring and wondered how to reawaken the memories of so many years. Perhaps he wondered also how far to penetrate the layers of myth that gather when people have recounted old events a hundred times with the benefit of hindsight and the nagging need for self-justification. In time the myth becomes official legend and the legend itself becomes a symbol. Would he in fact be able to write the story of that ardent young man who had been so prone to hasty decisions and sometimes to searing regrets? Or did he sense that try as he might to be true to himself and the times he had lived in, he would write instead the story of Minnesota's First Citizen and Noblest Pioneer, a myth that embodied the pride of state and nation? At last he drew the paper toward him and put down the first sentence:

---

*I was born in Detroit, Territory of Michigan, February 20th, 1811....
My father was one of the only two lawyers established there....*[1]

He could clearly recall his father's stout body, broad shoulders, and massive head, cocked a little to one side in an effort to overcome the deafness of advancing age. Long gray hair and an equally long beard framed his father's deep-set eyes and craggy eyebrows. Solomon Sibley, Chief Justice of the Michigan Territorial Court, had been the very picture of a venerable judge. And his manner matched his appearance. "No man would have slapped him on the shoulder any more than he would Washington," one young member of the Michigan bar had recalled. "Any lawyer who had to address him would involuntarily take his feet from the table, his hand from his pocket, eject his quid of tobacco, and address him as 'Your Honor.'"[2]

But that was in his later years. Solomon Sibley was just twenty-eight in June 1797 when his horse picked and slipped its way over the rough Allegheny traces toward Pittsburgh. Tucked carefully in the inner recesses of his saddlebag was a sheaf of documents and letters recommending him "to the friendly nature and patronage of all good men wheresoever Providence may cast his Lot." They testified that he hailed from Sutton, Massachusetts, held a bachelor of arts degree from Rhode Island College, had read law for the required term, and sustained "a fair and unblemished character." He had been admitted to the Rhode Island bar at Providence on April 11 of that very year and now contemplated establishing himself as an attorney in the Northwest Territory.[3]

The world must have seemed young that June when Solomon climbed the towering green ridges that lay across Pennsylvania like folds in a mammoth carpet. Beyond them to the west was the Ohio country and miles of forest and prairie that faded into inconceivable depths of time as they did of space. Already five generations of Sibleys had been born in North America since John Sibley had left Middlesex to cross the ocean. Five generations had cut and burned, plowed and planted, built, surveyed, staked, deeded, and fenced until the expanse of forested hills had been carved into farms and looked to Europeans at least faintly like the land of their ancestors. Yet before Solomon, the son of Reuben and Ruth Sibley, none of the family had moved farther than New England.[4] How many more generations of fathers and sons, mothers and daughters, would be needed to transform the forests that lay beyond the great mountain chain no one could guess.

When the last ridge was crossed and his eyes rested on the jumble of wooded hills descending toward the Ohio River, Solomon undoubtedly perceived it as an empty land, new and untouched by man. However, the Ohio valley had been dotted for centuries with the towns and fields of settled, semiagricultural people, and thousands of tombs and ceremonial earthworks testified to their instinct for building, their yearning for immortality, and their antiquity in the land. Yet the myth that North America was a virgin wilderness had already sunk deep into the minds of European colonists. It was a soothing fantasy, and even when the dispossessed Native Americans made their presence inescapably felt, they could be put out of mind by the newcomers as unreasoning creatures without past or future, whose fleeting moccasins hardly disturbed nature's carpet of leaves. The Indians seemed

Solomon Sibley

to Solomon no more a part of his world than the dangerous animals lurking in the forests along the trail ahead.

His first destination was Marietta, at the mouth of the Muskingum River, some two days' journey down the Ohio from Pittsburgh. The choice was inevitable for a young Yankee lawyer. Not only was Marietta the oldest Anglo-American settlement and seat of government in the Northwest Territory, it was also the center of New England influence and of Federalist politics. There Solomon was cordially received and made a number of friends, among them a fellow lawyer, Paul Fearing; Sheriff Ebenezer Sproat; and Judge Joseph Gilman, who certified him as duly qualified to practice law in the territory. Marietta, however, was already well supplied with legal talent, and for some months young Sibley remained undecided about where to settle. At length in June 1798, having considered and rejected the hustling western towns of Cincinnati and Chillicothe, he set out for Detroit, which had been evacuated by the British army only two years earlier.[5]

The move had been suggested by the territorial judges, who in May held the first general session of a U.S. court there. Legal business was "very considerable" in the distant outpost, Judge Return J. Meigs told Solomon, and there was only one American lawyer in the town.[6] Moreover, a glance at the map revealed its key position on the strait that connected the upper and lower Great Lakes. Since its establishment by the French in 1701, Detroit had been the funnel through which Indian trade from the West had poured into Canada.

Sibley found Detroit in 1798 far different from the raw, stump-filled Ohio settlements built of green logs and mud chinking. The fruit trees in Detroit's orchards had matured and reproduced, its houses were weathered and vine-covered, and some of its families had been there for three generations. The hundred or so buildings of the town proper were huddled within a wooden stockade that kept them from spilling over the sharp edge of the riverbank in front and tied them like apron strings to the ramparts of Fort Lernoult, which stood on higher ground a few hundred yards back from the river. An American flag waved over the fort, but in the narrow streets of the village, topped by the slender cross above St. Anne's Church, and in the line of gabled farmhouses, gardens, and orchards that clustered along the river, was a French world.[7]

Most of Detroit's commerce still came and went through Montreal, and most of it had to do with the fur trade. So on the streets Sibley found at times nearly as many Indians as white men, and he heard not only the lilting lisp of French, but also the unfamiliar rhythms of Ojibwe, Ottawa, and Potawatomi, and often a Scottish burr. Americans, he soon determined, numbered fewer than two dozen outside the garrison of the fort. The young Yankee had little liking for the town's cosmopolitan society, but as Meigs had prophesied, its legal business was plentiful, and Gilman had assured him that "neither Judge Meigs nor I were wanting in our recommendations to the Gentlemen with whom we were acquainted." Sibley's Federalist connections helped even further, when he received an appointment as deputy attorney general for Wayne County only a few days after his arrival.[8]

Aided by this introduction, and even more, perhaps, by his own hard work and deliberate, conscientious temperament, young Solomon soon established himself as a trusted attorney, not only with the small group of American newcomers but among French and British businessmen as well. Within five months he was elected Wayne County's representative to the first legislature of the Northwest Territory, and he continued to hold the office until 1802 when the county was transferred to the new territory of Indiana.[9]

Those were tumultuous years on the Ohio frontier. Federalist control, established with the election of John Adams as president, was eroding. In the Northwest Territory the Federalist governor, Arthur St. Clair, struggled against a flood of settlers pouring across the Ohio from Virginia. These new arrivals, voting Republican and demanding more local control, along with more access to Indian land and more rapid development of the western territories, sent one of their own as a representative to Congress in 1799. The following year the Republican tide rising in the West swept the entire country, and the inauguration of Thomas Jefferson as president in the spring of 1801 set the stage for carving the state of Ohio from the Northwest Territory.

Throughout his legislative career Solomon Sibley stood firm on Federalist principles. He supported the autocratic St. Clair and opposed the Jeffersonianism that was finding some support even among New England elements. To his old friend and legal mentor, Congressman Seth Hastings of Massachusetts, he expressed wonder that anyone with the "cool investigating spirit" of New England should be snared by "the wild and fashionable frenzy of modern Republican philosophy."[10]

But the currents of national politics had not yet reached Detroit. There voting was determined by local questions, and the community liked the representation it was getting. Sibley spoke out on such parochial issues as control of drunkenness among U.S. troops, clearing of French and British land titles, and better mail service. His grateful fellow citizens voted him the "freedom of the corporation" after he pushed through a bill for the incorporation of Detroit in 1801. Even in this, however, were echoes of New England: the law sponsored by Sibley provided for an annual town meeting to elect a board of trustees and to review all ordinances passed by them.[11]

So it had happened that Solomon Sibley's life and work became permanently identified with the city of Detroit and the territory of Michigan, although for many years he resisted the association and yearned to leave at the earliest opportunity. His greatest objection to the place was his difficulty in finding a wife. The entire female population was French, but though other American bachelors were often charmed by the vivacious *habitantes*, Solomon found "no pleasure in listening to their French nonsense—They speak no English & I speak no French."[12]

His thirtieth birthday loomed before him like a watershed, but it came and went and still he bemoaned his loneliness in "a country of savages and frenchmen."[13] He thought that if he could make a trip to New England he might find someone willing to be a frontier bride on short notice, but the opportunity never came. When legislative business took him to Cincinnati, he tried a hasty courtship there but was rejected. At last the treasure appeared under his very nose. On a visit to Marietta, he found that Sally Sproat, the long-legged, tomboyish daughter of his old friend Colonel Ebenezer Sproat, had turned from horseback riding to piano playing and had grown from the awkward sixteen-year-old he had known during his Marietta days into an accomplished young lady of nineteen. Inquiring with great trepidation through Paul Fearing and another friend, Solomon, now thirty-one years old, learned that the colonel approved of him "both for his honesty & for his politicks," and that Sarah herself was not unwilling. They were married in October 1802.[14]

My mother was a noble specimen of a pioneer woman.[15]

The words the general wrote were stilted and pompous. But how to describe the spirited and unwavering Sarah to a generation for which propriety was paramount and to people who had never known her world? He had been keenly disappointed years before when he had read proof sheets of a cloying, milk-and-water sketch of her to be published in a book on pioneer women—and he had told its author that "'Sarah Sibley' if alive, would be tempted to smile at the picture drawn of her earthly pilgrimage."[16] But now he himself seemed unable to do better.

No one had ever claimed that Sarah was beautiful, and she herself had often made jokes about her size, but her vigorous, big-boned body had borne ten children without complaint, and the cares of a family had never drained her energy or her spirit. She had been an only child—the pet and joy not alone of her parents but also of her grandparents during the years when all of them had shared a single log cabin within the stockade at Marietta. Lacking a son,

Sarah's father had taught her to be an expert rider and had encouraged her independence and her love of the forests and hills.[17]

Her father was Colonel Ebenezer Sproat a distinguished officer of the continental forces during the revolutionary war.... Her mother was a daughter of Abraham Whipple the oldest Commodore of the revolutionary navy, and noted for his successful daring while in the service. Both of these officers emigrated at the close of the war, with their families, to Marietta....[18]

The Whipple-Sproat clan was among the earliest settlers on the Muskingum, and like many other members of the colonizing Ohio Company, they had been driven west by financial necessity. Commodore Whipple made and lost several fortunes during his long career as a sea captain and privateer, but at the end of the war he was nearly destitute after spending most of his savings in the Continental cause. He was still a tough seaman at the age of fifty-six, and chose to join his daughter and son-in-law in their venture beyond the mountains rather than endure an old age of genteel poverty in his native Providence.[19]

Sproat was in much the same financial condition, having failed dismally in a short-lived postwar try at the mercantile business. His thorough schooling brought him a commission as captain when he entered the Continental army, and his natural aptitude as a soldier and leader of men helped him rise quickly to the rank of colonel. Towering to a powerful and well-built six foot four, he commanded not only respect but also loyalty. He was a gregarious man who seemed at ease with every kind and class of people, always ready with a humorous quip. But he had an impulsive generosity that did not prove an asset in business.[20]

After losing his own and his wife's inheritances, Sproat accepted the hazardous job of government surveyor for one of the seven easternmost ranges beyond the Ohio River. This first step in charting the mathematical grid that would parcel off the hills and forests into convenient units of private ownership was fiercely opposed by the Indian people living there. But the country and the occupation suited Sproat, and the danger was, if anything, an added attraction. When the Ohio Company was organized, he quickly joined it, moving his family to Marietta in 1789.[21]

Indian opposition escalated into war between 1791 and 1795, and the new settlement was under intermittent siege until the battle of Fallen Timbers established American control and began the inexorable process of dispossessing and driving out both the native tribes and those from farther east who had found refuge in the Ohio valley. During the time of hostilities at Marietta, Colonel Sproat was a natural choice for commander of the settlement's militia, and thereafter he served as sheriff of the county. He loved the outdoors, kept fine horses, and was usually followed by one or two of his favorite dogs. The Delaware Indians of the Muskingum valley, who were always apt with a descriptive nickname, called him Hetuck, or Buckeye, because his height reminded them of the towering horse-chestnut tree.[22]

Sarah idolized her father. Together they rode horseback across the mountains when she was ten years old and on her way to be enrolled in the Bethlehem Female Seminary, a Pennsylvania girls' school kept by the sisters of the Moravian church. When she returned five years later, he bought her a piano to liven the lonely hours in the isolated western settlement. It was the first such instrument to be carried to the Upper Ohio. Two years after Sarah's marriage to Solomon Sibley, in the late summer of 1804, the still active colonel rode across Ohio to Detroit, taking with him Sarah's favorite horse, and the two had shared another wilderness journey together when she returned with him for a visit to Marietta. While she was there the tall Buckeye suffered a sudden stroke and was felled without warning. Sarah stayed on with her widowed mother through the spring of 1805, and when her first son was born on June 5 of that year, she named him Ebenezer Sproat.[23]

The colonel's estate consisted of many debts and many empty Ohio acres, but his legacy of independence and resilience served Sarah well during the years that followed. In 1812 war engulfed Detroit. Like most American civilians, the Sibley family took to the fort when a British army threatened the city, and they along with the other occupants endured the noise, the terror, and the uncertainty of a daylong bombardment. After Detroit was surrendered, most of the town's citizens remained where they were under British occupation. Solomon, however, was among those who asked for permission to leave. He and Sarah with their three children—seven-year-old Sproat, three-year-old Catherine, and the baby Henry—fled as refugees back to Marietta, where they stayed until they received news of the decisive British defeat at the battle of the Thames River in the fall of 1813. Another daughter had been added to the family by the time they wearily headed north, only to find themselves stranded for the winter in Cleveland when early ice closed navigation on Lake Erie.[24]

Settled in Detroit again, Sarah watched her brood increase and mature while Solomon's legal practice expanded and his involvement in public affairs deepened. In 1820 he was elected delegate to Congress from Michigan Territory, and during the three years that followed he spent many months away in Washington. With brisk efficiency Sarah meanwhile took over the management of both the household and the farming operations on his land outside Detroit.

"You express a wish to know how I make out to manage the Boys, farming &c &c," she wrote to her husband. "I have had no difficulty in getting the Boys to comply with my directions as yet, nor do I expect to have any. . . . I have disposed of all the hay out in the field, except two stacks, at ten dollars per ton. I have received but little money for it, but it is sold to people that you are indebted to, and that answers the purpose equally as well." Or again, "I hired Leonard to take my wheat to mill. Burr Stones are in operation but water is rather too low to grind with both. I shall discharge my Irishman tomorrow. I have hired John Burgess, who understands driving and taking care of horses. I received today four hogs from Hosmer, the whole weighing little more than 500 lbs."[25]

When seventeen-year-old Sproat broke his nose in an accident felling trees for firewood, she wrote: "He was covered with blood, and dreadfully disfigured. . . . You may suppose that I was very much frightened. I however exerted all the fortitude I possessed, and held his head while the Doctor examined and dressed the hurt." And she added, with clinical interest, "It is strange that altho' the bone of the nose was broken and forced through the division or gristle in the middle, the skin remained entire."[26]

Having waited many weeks for the slow and irregular mail, she scolded Solomon for his laconic letters: "I was almost angry, and thought I would not write to you again, but you know I am apt to retract, when I form resolutions hastily." Yet she frankly longed for him: "I feel as if my patience would be entirely exhausted before I see you. Whenever anything either pleases or vexes me, I think I would give almost any thing to fly to you to participate in my feelings." And, again, she told him archly: "You direct me to apply to Captain McCloskey to supply my pecuniary wants. You need not fear my calling on him or any one else to meet those that you alone are authorized to gratify and which I hope in a few weeks to have the pleasure of receiving."[27]

Brimming with indignation or sympathy, Sarah reported in full the town's gossip, political and personal: Elizabeth Cass had given birth to a baby girl two days after Governor Lewis Cass had returned from Washington. Sheriff Austin E. Wing and Doctor Ebenezer Hurd had engaged in a fistfight. "It was a private quarrel, something about a cow," she told Solomon, adding, "It is the first time they have spoken to each other since the election."[28] William Brewster had married Maria Farley and had left immediately for New York without his bride. Sarah thought "she had better have remained at school until his return, but I suppose he was afraid some one else would carry off the prize in his absence."[29]

Solomon also received a full budget of family news. Baby Sarah "sings and dances and tries to talk" and "will call Papa, and look to the door to see if you are coming." Four-year-old Alexander was doing well in school, although "they are all older than him." Catherine had attended several of Detroit's unceasing balls and parties and "has had attention enough ... to turn the head of a girl of fourteen." But her sympathetic teacher, Eliza Trowbridge, told Sarah that Catherine "pursues her studies with as much diligence as ever she did." And Sproat, writing to Solomon from Schenectady, New York, where he had begun attending Union College, observed with manly concern, "I am very glad to hear that Henry is so useful to mama, now that we are both away from home."[30]

My early youth was in no manner distinguished unless it was that I was more given to mischief than my fellows. So many were my exploits in that direction, that my dear mother often declared me incorrigible, and the black sheep of the family.[31]

Sharply etched in the general's memory was the rambling one-and-a-half-story house at the corner of Jefferson and Randolph streets in Detroit where he had grown up as the third member and second son in the noisy, active tribe of Sibley children. It had been a farmhouse on the outskirts of the town when Solomon bought it following a disastrous fire in 1805 that had leveled Detroit. Over the years it had been remodeled, and additions had been built on as the family had grown. The front lawn, facing Randolph, was shaded by a small orchard of pear trees—a tall, sturdy variety of uncertain origin unique to the French settlements of southern Michigan. Solomon's pride was unbounded when one of them produced a mammoth pear seven-and-a-half inches long and fourteen inches around. A flower bed bloomed on the corner, and the vegetable garden and stables were on the other side, along Jefferson.[32]

From Jefferson Street it was only a few hundred yards to the riverbank, where the town's busy wharves were crowded with craft of all kinds, from the canoes of Indians and traders and the *bateaux* of French farmers to tall-masted sailing ships. In 1818 "Walk-in-the-Water," the first awkward-looking steamer, had belched its black smoke over the Detroit River, and by 1826 six steamships were operating on Lake Erie.[33]

The Detroit of Henry's boyhood was a place of many arrivals and departures. Only when the Erie Canal was opened in 1825 did immigration from the East begin to turn toward Michigan. Until then Detroit had remained a city with neither important industry nor an agricultural hinterland. But its com-

Alexander Macomb, Detroit as Seen from the Canadian Shore in 1821

merce still reached along the waterways to the far interior, as it had done since the days of French dominance. After the War of 1812 the American Fur Company moved into the territory formerly occupied by Canadian traders south of the Great Lakes and along the Upper Mississippi River, and Detroit was second only to Michilimackinac as a center for the company's business. The town also became the government administrative headquarters for great stretches of unmapped country when Illinois achieved statehood in 1818 and all that remained of the original Northwest Territory was annexed to Michigan.[34]

Administration in those years was largely concerned with implementing the national postwar policy of ringing the northwestern frontier with forts. Therefore the most memorable comings and goings that Henry witnessed as a boy were military—troops embarking or returning from Mackinac, from Fort Dearborn at Chicago, Fort Howard at Green Bay, or Fort Crawford at Prairie du Chien. He was only eight years old when the U.S. Fifth Infantry left Detroit in May 1819, under orders to extend the line even farther up the Mississippi with a new fort at the mouth of the St. Peter's, or Minnesota, River.

A year later, in May 1820, a great expedition headed by Governor Cass started for Lake Superior and the headwaters of the Mississippi to tighten U.S. control over those dimly known regions. Three thirty-foot canoes had been loaded in front of the governor's house and, each flying a U.S. flag from its stern, had raced up the river, while most of Detroit followed in carts and on horseback along the bank as far as Grosse Pointe to see them off. The expedition returned successfully but with less fanfare after four months of exploration and treaty-making.[35] Two years later more troops departed to build Fort Brady at Sault Ste. Marie on land the governor had bought in 1820 from the Ojibwe there.

Soldiers were a daily sight in Detroit, for they were stationed there until 1826, occupying the rebuilt and renamed Fort Shelby and also at various times the nearby posts of Fort Meigs and Saginaw. Indians also were still frequently seen in their customary dress, and the French continued to give Detroit a foreign flavor. It could be heard in snatches of song from the boatmen on the river and in conversations on any street corner; it could be seen in the bright toques and sashes of voyageurs from Mackinac, in the two-wheeled carts or *charettes* that crowded the streets, in the ornate headdress of a nun, or in the outline of a wooden windmill against the sky.

The international border was another vital presence in the life of the town. Commerce and social life passed freely over it, especially in the winter when a bridge of ice united Detroit with the community of Sandwich facing it across the river. The same ice suspended the busy stream of lake traffic that tied each village to its separate country. Isolated by miles of snow-filled forest and swamp on every side, the international neighbors clung together and shared the cheer of parties, social visits, winter sports, and infrequent news from the outside world. Yet beneath this friendly intercourse, as beneath the frozen surface of the river, ran deep currents of remembered fear and national rivalry.

For some the ties were even stronger. Elijah Brush, who had been the sole American lawyer ahead of Solomon Sibley in Detroit, had married Adelaide Askin, daughter of a leading British fur trader. Old John Askin had moved across to British soil when Detroit became American, and after Elijah died in 1814 his widowed wife rejoined her father. But the Brush children remained Americans. Edmund, the oldest, lived for a while in the Sibley household and read law under Solomon. A younger brother, Alfred Brush, had been Henry's closest boyhood friend, and the general had named his own youngest son for him.[36]

Another family with strong international ties was the Abbotts, whose roots were deep in Detroit and the fur trade and whose members were divided between British and American allegiance. During the War of 1812 James Abbott and his brother Samuel had opted for the American side, but James found himself in trouble with Ohio authorities who suspected him of harboring British sympathies. From his refuge in Marietta, Solomon Sibley came to the aid of his neighbor and testified staunchly to Abbott's loyalty. Later, as a commission merchant, as a leading supplier of the northwestern military posts, and as Detroit agent for the American Fur Company, Abbott accumulated a fortune. His solid, two-story wooden house on Woodward Avenue, with its great brass knocker and dormer windows, its cellar stocked with fine liquor, and its reputation for hospitality as genuine as the sterling on its table was a landmark for those who knew Detroit and the inner circles of the territory's business and governmental establishment.[37]

That powerful establishment consisted of a tight little community of friends, neighbors, and interconnected families. Nearly all were Anglo-American, and those who had not come from New England or upper New York had filtered across the line from Canada. The Sibley family knew all more or less intimately. Included in the circle were a number of names that then or later loomed large in the northwestern country tributary to Detroit—the country that in time became Wisconsin and Minnesota.

There was Robert A. Forsyth, the governor's personal secretary, whose brother Thomas was an Indian agent at Rock Island, Illinois. Thomas Forsyth had accompanied the troops of the Fifth Infantry in 1819 on their way to build the fort at the mouth of the Minnesota. He had gained the tardy consent of the Dakota chiefs in the area by the government's usual combination of bribes, whiskey, and threats. The Forsyths' half-brother, John Kinzie, served the Indian department at Chicago, and his two sons, Robert and John, formed lasting friendships with the young Sibleys while attending school in Detroit. Among the general's papers were still a few stilted schoolboy letters from them.[38]

Robert Forsyth accompanied Governor Cass's expedition of 1820. Another member of the same party, whose destiny was thus joined to that of the Northwest and its people, was Henry Rowe Schoolcraft. Resourceful, ambitious, and a talented publicist, Schoolcraft had ended in bankruptcy after a ten-year career in the New York glassmaking industry. His persistent literary efforts brought him no more success. But in 1819 he produced a book on the Missouri lead mines that had attracted the attention of Secretary of War John C. Calhoun and won him the commission to accompany Cass and explore the copper deposits of Lake Superior. He did much more, however. His *Narrative Journal* of the expedition, hurried into print in 1821, called widespread attention to the journey and aroused public curiosity about the mystery of the Mississippi's still unknown source.[39]

In 1822 Schoolcraft received through Cass's influence an appointment as agent to the Lake Superior Ojibwe at Sault Ste. Marie, and a year later he married a mixed-blood daughter of John Johnston, who had for many years been a trader at the Sault. Jane Johnston had been carefully educated in Montreal and Ireland, but through her and her mother Schoolcraft was also united to a

remarkable family of Ojibwe leaders. Schoolcraft took advantage of the connection to study and write about Ojibwe customs and legends, and in time
made himself an accepted authority on the culture and languages of the Great
Lakes tribes. In 1832 he headed another government expedition that reached
the source of the Mississippi at Lake Itasca. Meanwhile, he retained his position with the Indian department and dabbled in Michigan politics.

The Cass expedition also included a pair of promising twenty-year-old
youths from upstate New York: James Duane Doty and Charles Christopher
Trowbridge. Trowbridge was a scholarly store clerk with a knack for languages and an interest in Indians. Cass had given him the post of assistant
topographer and encouraged him to learn all he could of the Algonquian di-
alects. Trowbridge put this knowledge to use over the next four years in negotiating treaties and in administering Michigan's Indian affairs. In 1825,
however, he shifted to banking, becoming first the cashier and eventually
the president of the Bank of Michigan. In 1826 he also became a close and
valued member of the Sibley family, when he married Catherine, the oldest
daughter and the former pupil of his sister Eliza.[40]

Doty was another sort. He had arrived in Detroit at the age of eighteen,
commenced studying law, and within three months was admitted to the bar.
His charm, his energy, and his facile schemes had quickly marked him as a
young man on the way up. At the age of twenty-three he became "Judge
Doty," after successfully promoting with the governor and Congress a plan to
create a separate territorial court for the remote western section of Michigan
and getting himself appointed its sole judge. Solomon Sibley, then serving as
congressional delegate, opposed the measure, but the agile Doty outmaneu-

vered him. In the years that followed,
Doty's energies were devoted to the area
that eventually became the Territory of
Wisconsin.[41]

The man around whom this circle re-
volved was Lewis Cass. Described by one
official visitor as "portly and altogether
governorlike," and by the Indians simply
as "Big-belly," he was a popular paternal
figure among his Detroit neighbors. Cass,
homely, heavy-joweled, and wearing his
customary red-brown wig, was a familiar
sight as he drove his family to church in
their high-wheeled *charette,* greeted

Lewis Cass   guests in front of his spacious old French-era farmhouse, or dutifully danced with each lady at the innumerable balls and parties that helped to pass the long winter season. Politically, the chief source of his success can be attributed to a lack of enemies or longstanding rivals. As Territorial Secretary William Woodbridge once shrewdly put it: "He has originated and kept in operation here a system of political machinery which few . . . could have devised. . . . While he has no one warm and disinterested friend, he certainly has no one enemy. All about him present the same smooth uniformity of surface."[42]

For seventeen years the system worked smoothly—partly, no doubt, because Cass was an efficient executive and an ardent and effective booster of Michigan. Like Sibley, Woodbridge, and several other territorial officeholders, Cass had come from New England by way of Marietta. Although he was a wholehearted convert to frontier democracy, factionalism was alien to his temperament, and he had a keen eye for competence and an ability to use the talents of men, even though they might not wholly share his political views. Such a man was Solomon Sibley, who had grudgingly made the transition from the Federalist to the Whig persuasion. Under Cass, Sibley occupied a long succession of public offices, resigning at last from active politics in 1823, when Cass secured him a well-earned seat on the territorial bench.[43]

As governor of Michigan Territory, Cass was ex-officio superintendent of Indian affairs for the entire Great Lakes and Upper Mississippi region, and it was there that his career had its most far-reaching importance. He did more than any other man to fix the pattern of U.S. Indian policy on the northwestern frontier. The first test of a successful western politician was whether he could keep the rate of land acquisition ahead of the advancing line of white settlement. Lewis Cass did so. In the course of negotiating more than twenty separate treaties, he appropriated for the white man vast areas of northern Ohio, Indiana, and southern Michigan and also laid the basis for future acquisition of northern Michigan, Wisconsin, and much of Minnesota. He checkmated the stiff economic competition of British traders along the border and surmounted opposition from the powerful and long-dreaded Ojibwe, the most numerous tribe then left in the Great Lakes region. Moreover, he accomplished all this without the immense cost of war. From the point of view of the United States, it was a brilliant record.[44]

Elements of force, strategy, deceit, and compromise entered into Cass's success, but its keystone was the effective threat of force. He both urged and vigorously supported the policy of building frontier forts. The primary purpose of the forts was defense against the British, but they also served to encircle the Ojibwe and were strategically situated to block the main trade routes by which goods from Canada might reach tribes like the Menominee, Winnebago, Sac, Fox, and Dakota.

To further ensure the economic dependence of these groups as well as the Ojibwe upon the United States, Cass did what he could politically to push the fortunes of the American Fur Company. The fragmented, highly competitive trade of Yankee merchants before the war had suffered when pitted against British titans like the North West and Michilimackinac Companies. Many of Cass's fellow borderers saw American Fur as only one more Canadian-run monopoly, but he defended the new company as the most effective instrument of American trade policy and repeatedly vouched for the patriotism of its British-accented managers like Ramsay Crooks, Robert Stuart, and Samuel and James Abbott. In return they supported his treaty policy among the Indians—support that became more effective as American Fur gradually choked off pockets of competition throughout the Northwest.[45]

At its best, treaty-making was no job for a sensitive and fair conscience, yet Cass, whose sense of honor would not permit him to personally appropriate so much as a pen or paper from government supplies, was a master of the art. The rationalization lay in his view of the Indian. He once wrote:

> Like the bear, and deer, and buffalo of his own forests an Indian lives as his father lived, and dies as his father died. He never attempts to imitate the arts of his civilized neighbors. His life passes away in a succession of listless indolence, and of vigorous exertion to provide for his animal wants, or to gratify his baleful passions. . . . Under such circumstances, what ignorance, or folly, or morbid jealousy of our national progress does it not argue, to expect that our civilized border would become stationary, and some of the fairest portions of the globe be abandoned to hopeless sterility. That a few naked wandering barbarians should stay the march of cultivation and improvement, and hold in a state of perpetual unproductiveness, immense regions formed by Providence to support millions of human beings?[46]

He spoke not for the American frontier alone but for the expansionist tradition of all Western Europe.

From this viewpoint any measure that forced the owners of the soil toward a "civilized" life would be justified morally. Appropriating their hunting grounds by whatever means would not only fulfill God's obvious program for fertile acres; it would contribute ultimately to the Indians' own good by forcing them to turn to agriculture. The feelings of Native Americans on the subject were irrelevant. Cass wrote: "We must frequently promote their interest against their inclination, and no plan for the improvement of their condition will ever be practicable or efficacious, to the promotion of which their consent must in the first instance be obtained."[47]

Yet perhaps there was something in this too-easy justification of self-interest that Cass's New England conscience silently balked at. Like nearly all Europeans of his time he denied that Western civilization could learn anything significant from Native American cultures. Nevertheless he seemed fascinated by them. He collected their artifacts and encouraged scholars like Trowbridge and Schoolcraft to study the Indians' languages and record their legends. When a scheme was proposed in 1820 for an exclusively Indian territory in Wisconsin where Christianized and educated tribes from upper New York and other northeastern states could gather, together with the Great Lakes tribes, into a self-sufficient community—perhaps eventually an all-Indian state—Cass supported the idea. Repeatedly in his writings occurred the vague and disquieting phrase: "our great moral debt to the Indian."[48]

Later, from his comfortable perch in Washington as Andrew Jackson's secretary of war, Cass would preside over the tragic removal of the southern tribes to Oklahoma, but it was in the Northwest that he set his personal stamp upon the course of Indian affairs. There his influence was carried westward by the generation of younger men who had grown up under him. They carried not only the outlines of his program, but also the expediency, the ambivalence, and the unanswered questions. And when events reached their inevitable conclusion, those men, of whom Henry Sibley was one, were faced with a reckoning in blood and shame that Cass himself had managed to avoid.

· 2 ·

The Call of Adventure

I was educated in the Academy at Detroit, which was equivalent to the High School of the present day, supplemented by two years tuition in Latin, and Greek, under Revd. Richard H. Cadle, an Episcopal Minister, and an accomplished classical scholar, and thereafter by the study of law of two years duration. My father intended me to follow his profession, but after the time indicated had elapsed, I frankly told him that the study was irksome to me, and I longed for a more active and stirring life.[1]

SARAH SIBLEY MUST HAVE REFLECTED OFTEN that her two eldest boys were named in reverse. Sproat, serious, hardworking, and touchingly eager to please, resembled Solomon. His college training was interrupted by ill health brought on, his father feared, by excessive study, and when he resumed his schooling as a cadet at West Point he quickly established himself at the head of his class.[2] But early in life her second son Henry began to show the unmistakable signs of his inheritance from Sarah's own father, the tall, adventurous Buckeye. As the years passed, his frame stretched out to a long, lean six feet, and his boyhood bent toward pranks and mischief developed into a passion for the open air and a restless impatience with sedentary occupations similar to that of his grandfather.

With one son already launched on a military career, Solomon had indeed hoped that the second would join him in the law, but in 1826 and again a year later he tried, probably with some feeling of resignation, to get Henry into West Point as well. Despite support from Delegate Austin Wing, the appointment was not made. News of the second failure, which came in the spring of 1828, must have been a keen disappointment to young Sibley, and it brought on a family crisis over his next step in life.[3]

Henry was in the habit of confiding his hopes and frustrations to Charles Trowbridge, with whom he had developed a warm friendship that lasted a lifetime. Trowbridge in turn was a close friend of Henry Schoolcraft, who spent the spring of 1828 in Detroit attending the territorial legislature.[4] It was probably through the Indian agent Schoolcraft that Sibley was offered a chance to go to the far northern outpost of Fort Brady at Sault Ste. Marie, Michigan. A position was open as clerk in the store of army sutler John Hulbert, who was Schoolcraft's brother-in-law. Henry appealed to his father for permission to accept the job. The general recalled:

After long consultation with my mother, they wisely concluded to allow me to follow the bent of my own inclinations, and on the 20th day of June, 1828, being then in my eighteenth year, I left my home never to return to it, except as a transient visitor.[5]

Sault Ste. Marie was a tough little border post in 1828, with a white and mixed-blood population that numbered less than five hundred, including the garrison. The cedar log stockade of Fort Brady reached down to the riverbank, along which stood an irregular line of one-story log houses in various stages of disrepair. Only the newly constructed Indian agency and the long, low house of the principal trader, John Johnston, showed signs of comfort or permanence. Across on the Canadian side was another and smaller trading settlement that had clearly seen better days.[6]

There was also a sizable Ojibwe community that had been located beside the thundering rapids as long as anyone—Indian, French, or English—could remember. It was the ancestral gathering place of the tribe, but its antiquity was not recognizable to European eyes. The history and traditions that could be heard in old peoples' tales, rich in symbolism and metaphor, or traced in inscrutable figures on illuminated birchbark scrolls, or expressed in the motions of a dance or veneration for a certain rocky headland were too subtle to be caught by those whose past was marked by monuments of masonry or heavy volumes full of words. Seeing none of these, most white men dismissed the collection of fragile bark dwellings and the ancient, tenacious life within them as an ephemeral thing—a curious glimpse into mankind's primitive and ignorant past.

Henry Sibley found "civilization" at the Sault represented by the officers of the fort,

Henry Rowe Schoolcraft

by the Schoolcraft and Johnston families, and, soon after his own arrival, by the Reverend Abel Bingham, a Baptist missionary. The Johnstons were a unique blend of white and Indian aristocracy. Trader John Johnston was an educated man and the scion of a genteel Belfast family, with whose members he maintained close ties throughout his life. His wife, The Woman of the Green Valley, whose less poetic baptismal name was Susan, came from a long line of revered Ojibwe statesmen and orators and was herself a power in the tribe.

Tall and commanding, Susan Johnston knew English but seldom deigned to speak it. Cass credited her with having saved the day for him when negotiations broke down during his effort to buy land for the site of Fort Brady in 1820. Several leaders of the Sault band, whose kinsmen had died beside their patriot hero Tecumseh only seven years before, reacted with fury to the American proposal. Others were overawed by their anger, but The Woman of the Green Valley, calmly and with unanswerable pragmatism, pointed out the suicidal folly of war.[7]

Sibley saw little of the Johnstons at first, for through the summer he spent long hours in the post store. Neither the work nor the business atmosphere appealed to him, and he began to think longingly of going home. "I have seen so much deception practiced here ... that I hardly know whom to trust," he wrote to Trowbridge, indicating in the same letter that he hoped to get a position with a Detroit merchant. In mid-September, however, John Johnston returned from a trip to New York mortally ill, and within a few days he died. His widow needed temporary help with the trader's business, which she continued to operate herself for a number of years. Possibly again at Schoolcraft's suggestion, she hired Sibley, and he stayed on at the Sault through the fall and winter as a member of the family circle.[8]

Vivid images may have crowded into the general's mind as his pen hovered above the page of his memoir—images of the eager, awkward seventeen-year-old, away from home for the first time, learning about the world from soldiers at the fort or cutting his teeth in the Indian trade under the direction of the formidable Susan Johnston. But the appraising eye of posterity looked over his shoulder, and he wrote:

> *I remained in charge of her affairs during the fall and winter succeeding, and as the family of my employer embraced three educated, and lady-like daughters, the home sickness from which I had previously suffered, was very much alleviated by their company.*[9]

Of those daughters, twenty-six-year-old Eliza, dark-skinned and quiet, re-sembled her mother. Charlotte, four years younger, was lively and outgoing and unmistakably the sister of the cultivated Mrs. Schoolcraft. But it was fif-teen-year-old Anna Maria, with her soft way of saying "Hen-ry," and her ra-diant blushes when she did so, that intrigued him the most. All three were subjects of great interest also to the young officers at the fort, who eyed the newcomer from Detroit with considerable envy.[10]

Among the army men Sibley had a chance to observe a less delicate aspect of Indian-white relations than he found in the Johnston family. Winter was long and isolated in the squalid little settlement, and Indian and mixed-blood women were looked upon as fair game. The next summer, after Sibley had left for Mackinac, Schoolcraft's ne'er-do-well younger brother James informed him that "Things go on in the same way at the Sault. If the census were rightly taken, there is now 10 children in Embryo whose legitimacy may be doubted." Apparently young Henry was not entirely naive, for another corre-spondent inquired: "Did Josette return with you to Mackinac? Or have you found some other fair one to undo?"[11]

In April 1829, at age eighteen, Sibley said farewell to the isolation of the Sault, as well as to the Johnstons, and presumably to Josette. The relatively short trip down the St. Mary's River past St. Joseph and Drummond Islands and through the upper corner of Lake Huron to the Strait of Mackinac proved unexpectedly treacherous, as it had to many other travelers. The small schooner in which he sailed was trapped by ice for eight days in a widening of the river known as Lake George. Supplies ran out, and Sibley was among those who went ashore to hunt for game. Warm winds that broke up the ice brought more danger as they entered Lake Huron, but the ship arrived safely at Mackinac Island about the first of May.[12]

Mackinac was far different from the Sault. For over half a century under both British and American rule the rugged little island had been the nerve center and gathering point for all of the fur trade south of Lake Superior and west of Lake Michigan as far as the Missouri River. In 1829 it was still operating headquarters of the American Fur Company and next to Detroit the busiest commercial center in Michigan. It had a fort, an Indian agency, a Presbyter-ian mission, a Catholic church, and an organized county government. From June to August the island was the scene of feverish activity as boatloads of furs came in from Fond du Lac and La Pointe at the far end of Lake Superior, from the distant plains of the Dakota country by way of Prairie du Chien and Green Bay, from Milwaukee, Chicago, and the Grand River around Lake Michigan, and from the nearby forests of the Upper and Lower Peninsulas.

In the American Fur Company warehouses the furs were sorted, graded, and packed for shipment on to New York. At the same time accounts were settled and new outfits were formed, manned, and supplied for the next winter's trade. Meanwhile, the crews enjoyed a brief spree before returning to the lonely woods. Wages were spent, old friendships renewed, and sometimes old grudges settled.

Sibley's first move on arriving was to present himself at the office of Robert Stuart, the company's manager on Mackinac. Sibley had apparently been promised employment for the summer, but Stuart told him that he would not be needed for another month. Finding that his friend John Kinzie was on the island and about to leave for a visit to his parents in Chicago, Sibley agreed to go along, and the two young men boarded a sailing ship for the trip down Lake Michigan. Kinzie had worked for Stuart, and during the leisurely voyage he probably briefed Henry on the habits of his new employer.[13]

Stuart was undoubtedly known to Sibley, at least by reputation, for he had many business and personal connections in Detroit, and already an aura of legend had gathered around the adventurous early life of the tall, rugged Scotsman. Fresh from Perthshire by way of Montreal, Stuart had become a member of Astor's ill-fated expedition to the mouth of the Columbia River. He had sailed around Cape Horn to Oregon and had been the leader of those who trekked back across the Rockies in the years 1812–13. Enduring awesome hardships, they were the first band of Americans after Lewis and Clark to cross the continent. Since 1817 Stuart had directed the company's business at

The American Fur Company warehouse (left) and the office and residence of Robert Stuart directly beside it (right) on Mackinac Island today, little altered since the 1830s

Mackinac, second in command only to Ramsay Crooks and John Jacob Astor himself.[14]

To these well-known facts Kinzie could add stories of Stuart's exacting demands on his employees and his terrible temper—of how he had once nearly brained a defiant voyageur and with quick repentance had stayed by the man's bedside and nursed him until he was out of danger. Kinzie could also tell ruefully of the boisterous, sometimes cruel sense of humor that led Stuart on one occasion to set up a fight between the cocky young clerk and a sour old house servant. Stuart, Kinzie recalled, had watched through a window and roared with laughter as the youth and the old man threw awkward punches at each other. Yet just as the Scotsman's rage was matched by equally deep wells of kindness, so his crude practical jokes were offset on occasion by a gorgeous and expressive flow of language and a perceptive sense of humor.[15]

Kinzie could also tell of how Robert's wife Betsy Stuart, motherly and devout, sometimes interposed to soften her husband's discipline and had insisted that Kinzie improve his sketchy education by reading aloud and reciting to her in the evenings. It was Betsy's energetic Christianity that led the Stuarts to encourage and support the establishment of the mission on Mackinac in 1823, and a school opened there for mixed-blood children. Most of those who attended were the offspring of traders, some from as far away as the Mississippi headwaters and the Minnesota valley. Through them the mission and its school exerted widespread influence, and in time it sent new missionary offshoots deep into the upper lakes country.[16]

During the past winter, Sibley learned, a religious revival had swept the island, adding many souls to the small Presbyterian congregation centered around the mission. One of the converts had been crusty Robert Stuart himself. His employees became convinced of the change of heart when they heard him mildly tell a careless voyageur to retrieve a pack of furs the employee had dropped into the lake. The old Stuart, they agreed, would have knocked the fellow in after it. Since Sibley, like John Kinzie, was to be a member of his employer's family, he could well conclude that life on Mackinac would be different from the free-living, careless days at the Sault.[17]

It was indeed. The summer season of 1829 soon came into full swing, but although Mackinac was at its liveliest, Sibley had little chance to observe it from his clerk's desk. "All the Lake Superior & Fond du Lac traders have arrived," he wrote to Trowbridge in July, "and you may well suppose that I am now much more pressed than ever, in making out Outfits &c. for the interior. . . . Yesterday I rose from bed at 4 o'clock and stopped writing at half past eight in the evening, not having left my desk except to go to my meals, & it is now 4 o'clock in the morning of the 21st."[18]

He returned to Detroit in the fall, since American Fur had no immediate openings in sight. But he planned to keep trying, for "I think I shall have Mr. Stuart's influence in my favor, if there is any such thing in the book." During the winter of 1829–30 he worked at the Bank of Michigan in Detroit, where Trowbridge was cashier. American Fur probably had every intention of recruiting Solomon Sibley's son, but if any additional influence was needed, it appeared in a warm testimonial letter to Stuart commending the young man's "zeal and industry." It was signed by the bank's directors, including James Abbott and Trowbridge himself.[19]

Thus in September 1830, after another summer's work for Stuart, Sibley signed a five-year contract to serve as clerk and storekeeper at Mackinac. The terms were $350 for the first year, $450 for the second, and $550 thereafter,

The harbor and town on Mackinac Island as drawn by Seth Eastman

with room, board, and laundry supplied. Apparently Stuart had some special assignments in mind also, for he added that an additional $50 would be paid if Sibley's services were needed at any other place than Mackinac.[20]

I was domiciled in this sequestered spot for the most part of five years.[21]

What more could the general say about his life on Mackinac? It had held more religion than romance and more hard work than adventure.

Under the guidance of the Reverend William M. Ferry, who had founded the mission and school, the island's first Protestant congregation continued to thrive. Stuart's conversion brought in the rest of the fur company employees (those who were not French Catholics) like the members of a highland clan following their chief. A new church was built in 1830, and the number of attendees was swelled by members of the town's Anglo-American business community, by officers and men from the fort, and after 1833, by the School-craft family, for in that year the Indian agent was transferred to Mackinac. Schoolcraft, who had found himself "saved" in 1831, quickly became an elder of the church along with Stuart.[22]

The devout group of teachers from the mission school included at various times Frederick and Elizabeth Ayer, Hester Crooks, William T. Boutwell, and the Jedediah Stevens family, all of whom Sibley encountered again farther west. One of the teachers, Eunice O. Osmer, wrote several delicately yearning letters to her "beloved brother in Christ" after Sibley had left Mackinac, but there is no sign that he returned her sentiments.[23]

In 1830 Sibley made a public profession of faith and joined the church. Religion in his family had tended toward the socially respectable rather than the enthusiastic, but the spasm of evangelical fervor that gripped the country in the 1830s and his continuing association with the missionaries had a lasting influence. As years passed, however, he became increasingly outspoken in his dislike for the sectarian rivalries and theological disputes that "for ages, have been prolific of dissension and intolerance, disgraceful in the eyes of the outside world, and in direct and irrepressible conflict with the teachings of the Prince of Peace."[24]

What Sibley saw on Mackinac may have sowed the seeds of this feeling. The missionaries sought to save not only the heathen but also the Catholics. Nor were they above using their hold over the business and governmental seats of power on the island to advance their cause. French Catholicism had been established at the Strait of Mackinac since 1671, and when challenged, it found eager defenders. Prominent among these was Madeline Laframboise, an Ottawa-French woman who for fifteen years had operated a highly profitable trading business on Michigan's Grand River. Retired in an impressive home on Mackinac, she devoted herself to the church. The conflict resulted in what one resident recalled as "a religious war," which bitterly divided the small community and in time undermined the mission.[25]

Meanwhile, Sibley's work for the company brought him into contact with all groups on the island and with a broadly colorful collection of traders who had made their livelihoods for varying numbers of years or, in many cases, generations in the fur business. The European names that were oldest in the Great Lakes country belonged to Frenchmen, for it was under France that trade with the western tribes had begun in the seventeenth century. In the next hundred years French traders—some of them illegal migrants to Indian country, others licensed by the French crown—traveled west, following a network of waterways as far as the northern plains and the Upper Missouri River.

In 1763 the Treaty of Paris gave the French possessions in the St. Lawrence valley to Britain, and within a decade control of the fur business passed into the hands of new entrepreneurs, mostly Scottish, although sprinkled with a few Yankees from New England. With abundant supplies of British manufactured goods, they moved swiftly to take over the French trading network. Loosely united in partnerships, the largest of which was the North West Company, these Montreal-based traders reached into the heart of the continent and gave keen competition to the English Hudson's Bay Company. War and a new international boundary cutting through the Great Lakes eventually brought the formation of the American Fur Company in U.S. territory.

Whether owners and managers were British or American, however, their work force, along with a number of minor traders and hired clerks, remained French. Sibley had heard some of the family names around Detroit: Beaubien, Reaume, Coté, and Campau. Others like Grignon, Roussain, Dube, Chaboillez, Gautier, and Brisbois had survived changing times and several flags in the Mississippi River valley. Nearly all who bore these names were bound with strong ties of ancestry or kinship to one or more Native American tribes. Like the fur trade itself they drew from both worlds and formed a living bridge or middle ground between the cultures.

Even as late as the 1830s the St. Lawrence valley continued to supply new voyageurs, as the common laborers of the trade were called. They signed "engagements" of three to five years and worked their way to Mackinac, bringing shipments of goods. There they were parceled out among the various traders whose contracts with American Fur generally called for the company to supply them with hands as needed. It was an occupation that absorbed the surplus sons of French-Canadian working families for more than a century.[26]

Over the long span of years the general had known and employed many of these voyageurs and their heirs. Now most of them were gone, but in contrast to the carefully measured words about himself, this was a subject his pen could warm to freely. He wrote:

> *They were a hardy, cheerful, and courageous race submitting uncomplainingly to labors and exposures, which no other people could have endured.... They were unrivalled as canoe, and boat-men, extremely skillful in their management in the stormy waters of Lake Huron, Michigan, and Superior, and in navigating the numerous rivers and their tributaries on their way, with valuable cargoes, to the distant interior posts.... The muscular carriers vied with each [other] in their powers of endurance, and their capacity to transport heavy weights.... Notwithstanding ... the men as a rule, were merry, good natured, and obedient to the orders of their superiors.*

Then, touched by another wave of nostalgia, he added:

> *It affords me pleasure to bear witness to the fidelity and honesty of the Canadian French voyageurs ... [which] I found abundant occasion to prove.... In fact, the whole theory of the fur trade was based upon good faith between employers, and employed.*[27]

Not everyone had seen it that way. James Lockwood, a Prairie du Chien trader of the same period, recalled that the men were "transferable like cattle to any one who wanted them." Their wages were low and the single outfit of clothing furnished them was grossly inadequate. For anything further they had to pay their employer whatever he chose to charge, and since it was to his interest to keep them from leaving the country, most traders saw to it that by the end of their "engagement" the men were deeply in debt. As to honesty, Lockwood pointed out that any goods that disappeared from carelessness or theft were charged in full to the entire crew of the boat that had carried them. He acknowledged that voyageurs "are very easily governed by a person who understands something of their nature and disposition, but their *bourgeois* or employer must be what they consider a gentleman, or superior to themselves, as they never feel much respect for a man who has, from an engagee, risen to the rank of a clerk."[28]

Perhaps at the age of twenty-one Henry Sibley's own touch of romantic enthusiasm evoked a matching response in the men under him. In any case, his ability to command the devoted loyalty of a crew of voyageurs became apparent in the summer of 1832. Stuart had entrusted him with an urgent request to Governor George B. Porter at Detroit for certain needed trade licenses, and he set out down Lake Huron in an express canoe paddled by nine picked men.[29]

The trip was stormy. After nearly foundering, they lay windbound for three days near Saginaw Bay—long enough for Sibley to discover that his voyageurs were as improvident as they were lighthearted. He found that the supplies for the whole trip had already been eaten. Finally, safe but hungry, they arrived at the first settlement only to learn that a cholera epidemic was raging in Detroit. They pushed on, nevertheless, the men insisting on braving the risk of disease along with their young commander. Half a century later Sibley could still recall with a thrill of pride the fine show they made as they dashed singing down the river, past a wide-eyed crowd on the Detroit wharves, the voyageurs bedecked in their gayest finery, and plumes waving gracefully at the bow and stern of the canoe.[30]

When they pulled into the quarantine center at the end of town Sibley was relieved to learn that the only cholera victim in his family had been his grandmother, the aged Katherine Sproat, who had lived with Sarah and Solomon in Detroit since the death of her own parents in 1819. Henry's business with the governor was quickly done, and he left the next day, returning safely to Mackinac, a seasoned young *bourgeois*, deeply imbued with the color and romance of the fur trade.[31]

In reality the fur trade's romance, along with its economic and diplomatic importance, was already becoming a thing of the past. Long gone was the time when control over commerce with Indian people and therefore of their allegiance was a matter of concern in the councils of Europe. And after a brief bonanza when white trappers slaughtered the beaver of the Rocky Mountains in the 1820s, the brutal, risky, smelly, and often unprofitable business of collecting and selling animal skins had lapsed into a minor industry, important only in areas where there was as yet no other. The Great Lakes and Upper Mississippi River valley, like western British America, were still such an area, and there the commanding image of the fur trade remained strong, even as the substance itself faded.

In 1830 the American Fur Company held a nearly complete monopoly in the region. Small-scale individual traders continued in business here and there, but there were no other major suppliers of trade goods. In 1822 Astor succeeded through a major lobbying effort in eliminating the competition of the government-operated stores ("factories"), which had been created originally to counter the Canadian trade and had persisted in offering Indians an alternative source of supply. In this effort the company received all-out support from Cass, Doty, Solomon Sibley, and other Michigan politicians. To the west, American Fur merged in 1827 with Bernard Pratte & Company of St. Louis. The latter firm, operating as Astor's Western Department, had absorbed an upstart rival on the northern plains known as the Columbia Fur Company and had mounted an aggressive campaign to acquire the trade of the upper Missouri River and the northern Rockies. Thus from Detroit to the mouth of the Yellowstone and from the banks of the Wabash to the British boundary, the American Fur Company was not only the dominant, but almost the only large commercial enterprise.[32]

Only along the international boundary west of Lake Superior was there still active competition. An epic struggle between the Montreal-based North West Company and the English Hudson's Bay Company resulted in a merger in 1821. For a decade after that the two remaining colossi of the North American fur trade—the American Fur Company and the Hudson's Bay Company—sparred across the border. By 1831, however, tentative negotiations had begun, and in 1833 the two firms reached an extralegal accommodation by which international competition ceased between Lake Superior and the Red River.[33]

By 1830 the Indian tribes of the Great Lakes and Upper Mississippi River valley, as well as those of the northern plains, were hemmed in on all sides. Their territory was dotted with U.S. forts and occupation forces; their population was decimated by epidemic diseases; the most valuable animal species had been hunted nearly to extinction; and their food resources were shrinking before the onslaught of illegal prospectors, timber cruisers, and farmers. In material terms two centuries of trade had made them dependent upon European technology, yet in other respects their cultures remained vital, and the seasonal rhythm of their lives in the forest and on the prairie was little changed. They clung to the fur trade as the only means by which that pattern of life and with it their cultural identity could be preserved.[34]

Every band had its own trader, and the barter that had formerly been conducted by the band as a whole was now the business of each individual hunter. The trader advanced on credit from the company store ammunition and a meager stock of supplies for the hunter and his family through the winter, to be paid in pelts with the coming of spring. Sometimes he furnished traps, guns, or muskrat spears on loan, with the understanding that these would be turned in at the end of the season and repaired for use again the next year. It was essentially piecework—but piecework in which there was no guaranteed price for the product. For the fiction of independent trade continued, and if the winter's catch did not cover the credit received at the going price of furs, then a debt was recorded in the trader's book.[35]

The smaller traders were caught in the same system. Most considered themselves independent businessmen, buying their yearly "outfits" from larger operators on credit. If a series of bad seasons or a slump in the fur market drove the trader out of business, he assigned to his creditor such assets as he had. The principal one was usually the book of debts owed by his band of hunters.[36]

From Mackinac, headquarters of the Northern Department of American Fur, the various districts and dependencies fanned out to the west and south. Most were defined by tribes or bands rather than strictly by geographic area. The westernmost and largest district was that of the Upper Mississippi Outfit, with headquarters at Prairie du Chien. It included the Sac, Fox, and Winnebago in southern and central Wisconsin and northeastern Iowa, and the Dakota of the Mississippi, Minnesota, and Upper Des Moines River valleys. Its territory reached north along the Mississippi from Dubuque to the shifting buffer zone between the Dakota and Ojibwe.

In 1827 an agreement between Astor and Bernard Pratte & Company of St. Louis merged the interests of the two firms and gave control of the Western Department of American Fur to the St. Louis company. The same agreement created the Upper Missouri Outfit from the remains of the once independent Columbia Fur Company. Supplied from St. Louis, this new outfit's territory formed the western boundary of the Upper Mississippi Outfit. Sandwiched between the two on the northwest was the small fiefdom of Joseph Renville at the headwaters of the Minnesota and Red Rivers. Renville, a founder of Columbia Fur, was the head of a powerful mixed-blood family, partly French but predominantly Dakota. He controlled trade not only on the watershed between the two great river systems but in the remote country reaching toward Devils Lake and the British boundary. Renville owed a loose fealty to American Fur and was supplied through Prairie du Chien.

The sprawling Upper Mississippi Outfit was commanded by Jean Joseph Rolette, whose reputation as a tough, unscrupulous operator extended from St. Louis to Montreal. It was rumored that he had once been a theology student and a novice among the Jesuits; more definitely known was his skill at running whiskey past an Indian agent or quietly roughing up a competitor.

After several years of ruinous competition with Rolette, American Fur made overtures that brought him into the fold of its subsidiary traders. There he continued to be a perpetual headache to the company's management. In 1827 Astor and Crooks commissioned a talented young clerk named Hercules

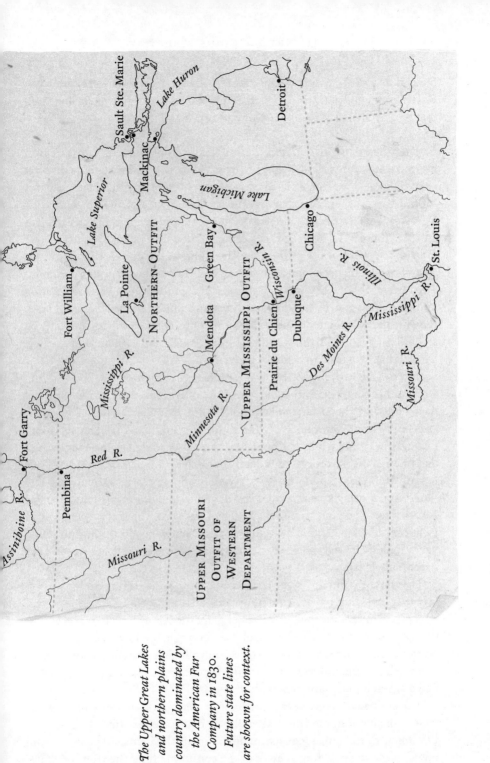

The Upper Great Lakes and northern plains country dominated by the American Fur Company in 1830. Future state lines are shown for context.

Dousman, son of Mackinac merchant Michael Dousman, to straighten out Rolette's tangled accounts. Dousman proved so useful in Prairie du Chien that he stayed on as Rolette's junior partner.[37]

During the era of British domination, trade goods for this entire region poured from Montreal through the Great Lakes. By the time Americans took over the trade, however, St. Louis was already becoming a major supply point for the Missouri and Mississippi valleys. As early as 1821 the American Fur Company sent Samuel Abbott to St. Louis to survey the market and establish an office there.[38] In 1823 the first steamer climbed the Mississippi to the new fort at the mouth of the Minnesota River, and in the decade that followed, steamboat traffic between St. Louis and Prairie du Chien became common. The lead mines of northwestern Illinois and southwestern Wisconsin, long known and worked by Indian people, were occupied by white miners, and in the mid-1820s Rolette's Upper Mississippi Outfit was supplying not only itself but the whole Northern Department at Mackinac with most of the bullets and bar lead used in trade.[39]

Meanwhile to the east, Ohio was rapidly becoming the breadbasket of the Great Lakes fur trade. Pork, flour, corn, and other foodstuffs that in the early days had rarely been carried beyond Mackinac or Grand Portage grew increasingly important, not only for supplying the many traders scattered through the country, but also for sale to army posts, Indian agencies, missions, and often to the hard-pressed Indians themselves. By 1830 the rich, level valleys of the Scioto and Miami Rivers were producing large agricultural surpluses. Purchasing these supplies was a tedious and time-consuming job, for sellers were small and scattered and travel was slow. Some of it was handled by James Abbott in Detroit, but the company also sent buyers through the Ohio valley looking for bargains in items like flour, bacon, lard, cheese, candles, tobacco, and whiskey.

During the winter of 1832–33 and again in 1833–34, Henry Sibley was assigned to this duty, working on horseback out of Cleveland. It was for him a new phase of the business and a relief from the winter's isolation at Mackinac. Although the change was welcome enough, the long weeks he spent crisscrossing rural Ohio and western Pennsylvania, haggling with farmers and small manufacturers and arranging for transportation and storage, whittled away at his enchantment with the fur trade.[40]

The early 1830s were years of rising prosperity, and in Cleveland itself as well as throughout the Ohio valley, Sibley could see the stirring of new developments—turnpikes, canals, manufacturing, the increasing use of steam power—and the bursting growth of the country behind the frontier. Statehood for Michigan was on the horizon, and the population of Detroit had more than doubled since 1830. By contrast the fur trade, even with its veil of remembered glory, could only seem a static and declining business. And no doubt his family and Detroit friends were quick to point this out, urging him, now that he had tasted life in the north for nearly five years, to turn to something with more of a future.

Meanwhile, the American Fur Company was in the midst of great changes. It had been an open secret that Astor wanted to retire, and in 1832 negotiations had begun, looking toward the reorganization of the business. By early 1834 the lines of the future were growing clear. The Western Department was to become independent under the name of Pratte, Chouteau & Company of St. Louis. The Northern Department, retaining the name of American Fur, would become a partnership, with Ramsay Crooks as president and senior partner. Among the other major investors were several Detroit merchants, including the Abbotts and William F. Brewster. Districts and outfits within the territory were reorganized, but most of the subsidiary traders remained undisturbed. However, for Sibley's immediate superior, Robert Stuart, there proved to be no place in the new company.[41]

These developments coincided with Sibley's own readiness for more responsibility and advancement. Although touched at times with glamour, his five years at Mackinac had brought little of the wilderness adventure he may have dreamed about. What they had brought was intimate contact with the workings of a continent-wide business and confidence in his own ability to manage men and the commerce of a growing country. His contract with Astor ran until 1835, but he was ready for a change. In the summer of 1834 he determined to discuss the matter with Crooks himself.

I sought him out, and told him frankly, that my parents were strongly opposed to my longer sojourn in what was little better than a wild Indian country, that I had been offered the position of cashier in two banks, one in Detroit, Michigan, and the other in Huron, Ohio, with a liberal salary for so young a man as I was, and while I did not recognize the right of the new company to insist upon my remaining to fulfil the old contract, I preferred out of respect to him as an old friend of my father, and myself, that he would voluntarily release me from my engagement, [and] in consideration thereof I would pay the new corporation $1,000.[42]

· 3 ·

To the Mississippi

*T*HE GENERAL MAY HAVE PAUSED at this point in his writing to reflect on the boldness he had to summon in confronting Ramsay Crooks. He may also have called to mind vivid memories of the man who became to him a business mentor and a longtime friend.

Next to John Jacob Astor, Ramsay Crooks was the most powerful figure in the American fur trade for many years. His early career closely paralleled that of Robert Stuart, and he had known fully as many perils and adventures, yet Crooks was not the kind of person that legends gathered around. In a curious way the two men embodied the twin traditions of Scotland: Stuart the temperamental, swashbuckling highlander, born to equal shares of poverty and pride; Crooks the canny, frugal lowlander of humble family (he was a shoemaker's son), with a single-minded dedication to business.[1]

In Crooks that dedication was no simple passion for amassing money. He was from the generation of men that saw the narrow, feudal traditions of a class-conscious mercantilist world finally shattered by the explosive energy of industrial capitalism. He belonged to the newly liberated middle class that had found at last a channel for its own creativity and genius through the medium of business enterprise. Whatever the overtones of greed, whatever the moral compromises that competition might demand, men like Crooks held the conviction that by maintaining the integrity of the credit system and hewing to the practice of sound business principles they were knitting the very fabric of the good society.

Ramsay Crooks

Personally Crooks was a quiet and kindly man. In Britain he might have seemed like the benevolent father figure in a Dickens novel; in the seedy, cutthroat world of the American fur trade, where survival often called for ruthless tactics, he was regarded with deep ambivalence. The one thing no one ever questioned was his almost religious devotion to the advancement of the business under his direction.

Crooks had kept an eye on Judge Sibley's promising son at Mackinac and had been responsible for broadening the fledgling clerk's training in the business by assigning him to the job of provision buyer. There he had proved sharp and reliable. Now the new president had further plans for him.

Studying ways to promote and keep Sibley, Crooks marshaled those powers of persuasion that had put together Astor's rambling fur trade empire from half a dozen warring elements and had brought into line men ranging from the merchant prince Pierre Chouteau, Jr., to the slippery, combative Joe Rolette. He had long been aware, no doubt, of Solomon's objections to his son's choice of a career and he sensed the young man's prickly pride and need to prove himself. So Crooks first applied flattery, speaking in the warmest terms of Sibley's record with the company and implying that the firm would suffer a significant loss if he should refuse the new responsibilities that awaited him.[2]

What Crooks had to offer was in fact tempting. It consisted of a junior partnership with Rolette and Dousman and independent management of the entire Dakota trade north of Lake Pepin and up the Minnesota River valley. Next, to reinforce his own arguments, Crooks called in Hercules Dousman. It was a shrewd move, for although Dousman at thirty-four was eleven years older than Henry Sibley, the two men had developed a warm rapport during the years the young clerk had spent at Mackinac.

Sibley also knew Dousman's family. Old Michael had established himself on Mackinac long before the War of 1812. His warehouse and farm, mills and schooners made him an economic force on the island, and his home was a center of informal hospitality. It was he who had administered Sibley's oath when Henry became a justice of the peace for Mackinac County in 1832, and the young man had often called at the Dousman house to pass the time with Hercules' sisters Nancy and Kate. So whatever reservations Sibley might understandably have about an association with Rolette, he could have no doubt about working with Hercules Dousman.[3]

Still Sibley hesitated. He had promised his parents that he would return to the Detroit area, and he knew that the distant assignment on the Upper Mississippi would be greeted with anything but enthusiasm. It was

Hercules Dousman

Dousman who sensed the weak point in Henry's defenses. Here at last was the wild country and the adventure that had eluded Sibley at Mackinac and the Sault. The Minnesota River valley was the final stronghold of the old fur trade. Dousman painted glowing pictures of the high, rolling plains, the herds of buffalo and elk, and the thousands of lakes alive with waterfowl. It was this, Sibley always maintained, that brought him around:

I was finally won over by his repeated and persistent appeals, and assented to the agreement, whereby I became for the remainder of my life, a denizen of what is now the magnificent state of Minnesota.[4]

The contract agreed upon on August 15, 1834, was to run for six years, and created a partnership that was to be known as the Western Outfit. Crooks's new American Fur Company, headquartered in New York, would supply the capital and hold a half interest in the business. The remaining half was divided among Rolette, Dousman, and Sibley on a 5-3-2 basis. The partners would draw no salary, but Dousman was guaranteed $1,500 per year and Sibley $1,200 before any further distribution of profits.[5]

The Western Outfit would be headquartered at Prairie du Chien, and American Fur undertook to deliver all goods there, rather than at Mackinac, receiving its usual 5 percent commission on cost and transportation charges. Implicit in this arrangement was a major change in shipping routes. Goods formerly sent through the Great Lakes now came up the Mississippi. Another new factor was the increasing supply of provisions available from Illinois farmers. All purchases made in the Mississippi River valley were to be handled directly by the western partners themselves. Furs and skins, however, were still to be funneled through Mackinac, where they would be sorted, graded, and repacked for shipment farther east. American Fur would make a flat offer for the season's catch, and if the partners refused it, the furs would be sold on commission in either New York or Europe and the receipts credited in due time to the Western Outfit.

The partners had full control over hiring of employees and contracts with subsidiary traders, although American Fur had access to the books at all times and the business was subject to Crooks's general supervision. Rolette and Dousman were stationed at Prairie du Chien and Sibley at the mouth of the Minnesota River, opposite Fort Snelling. The partners would meet each summer in Prairie du Chien and the books would be closed on August 1.

Numerous other details were spelled out in the long contract, including the outfit's trading area, which was to be the same as that of Rolette's old Upper Mississippi Outfit, extending from the lead mines of Dubuque on the south to the Falls of St. Anthony—or as far above as was necessary in dealing with the Dakota. All trade with the Ojibwe was specifically forbidden, for they were the preserve of the Northern Outfit, headquartered at La Pointe on Madeline Island. Those along the Upper Mississippi traded with William A. Aitken, an old employee of the North West Company who had been in the headwaters country since the early 1800s. He managed the Northern Outfit's Fond du Lac Department. Business with the Ojibwe along the St. Croix River and farther east belonged to a former New Englander named Lyman Warren, who operated directly from La Pointe.

One matter not mentioned in the contract was the question of Alexis Bailly. Since 1823, with a brief hiatus in 1831, Bailly had traded for the American Fur Company and Rolette in the territory now slated for Sibley. Bailly was not a party to the new arrangement, and his contract with the old company had still a year to run. Both Crooks and Rolette were anxious to get rid of him. He was an energetic and competent trader, whose string of posts along the Upper Mississippi and up the Minnesota River valley had grossed some $20,000 during the previous year. But he had quarreled with Rolette, and an unsuccessful attempt in 1831 to break away and establish himself as a competitor had marked him as unreliable. An even greater objection was his long-standing feud with Indian agent Lawrence Taliaferro at Fort Snelling.[6]

Unlike Schoolcraft and most of the other agents in the northwestern region, Taliaferro was no friend of the American Fur Company, which he saw as an exploitive monopoly. Nor did he owe his appointment to Lewis Cass. A stubborn, patriotic, and intensely self-righteous Virginia aristocrat, he had political connections in the Old Dominion that had enabled him to hang onto the agency at Fort Snelling for fifteen years. During every one of them he had been a thorn in the side of Rolette and the company. As the company trader stationed nearest to the agency, Bailly had borne the brunt of this antagonism, and he had returned it with interest. The enmity escalated through several incidents of illegal whiskey confiscated from Bailly and resulting lawsuits. It culminated in a threatened duel between Taliaferro and Bailly. Little as Crooks liked Taliaferro, he knew that such extremes of bitterness, especially when they involved a government official, were bad for business. Having failed in repeated efforts to get Taliaferro removed, he was eager to replace Bailly with someone more conciliatory.[7]

The decision to do so had obviously been made before Bailly's district was offered to Sibley, but carrying it out was left to the devices of Rolette and

Dousman. They feared that Bailly, if simply cut loose, would remain in the country and compete against the new outfit. Bailly himself made their course easier by attempting once more to run whiskey past the watchful Taliaferro that summer. When Rolette returned from Mackinac to Prairie du Chien in August, he learned that the liquor had again been seized.

Heading immediately for Fort Snelling, Rolette engaged in a wary interview with Taliaferro in which each man professed his goodwill and desire to cooperate. Instead of defending Bailly, Rolette maintained that the trader had acted against company policy. With a show of resignation he accepted Taliaferro's edict to deny Bailly a trading license on consideration that the whiskey be returned and the company not be prosecuted. Back at Prairie du Chien, Rolette wrote gleefully to Crooks: "—of this last arrangement between Mr. Taliaferro and myself I was satisfied as it will give us a chance of getting rid easily of Mr. Bailly."[8]

It proved more difficult than he thought, however. Taliaferro departed for a winter's leave in the East, and Bailly promptly applied for a license to Major John Bliss, the army commander at Fort Snelling. Bliss was aware of Taliaferro's decision, but after some hesitation he granted Bailly permission to continue trading through the winter and wind up his affairs without loss. Armed with this trump card, Bailly appeared at Prairie du Chien in late October to meet his would-be successor and confer with his former associates.[9]

Sibley, meanwhile, had traveled from Mackinac to Green Bay and up the Fox River to the point where a two-mile portage trail connected with the westward-flowing Wisconsin River. It was the well-established route to the Upper Mississippi followed by Marquette and Joliet in 1673 and used by most travelers and traders since that time. The portage in 1834 was a major trading point and the site of a military post and an Indian agency. Between 1830 and 1833 Sibley's friend John Kinzie had served as government agent there. On the Wisconsin River Sibley found a tiny sternwheeler about to head downstream, and five days of dodging snags and pushing the boat off sandbars brought them to Prairie du Chien.[10]

The Prairie of the Dog—so named, tradition said, for an old Fox chief who had established his village as a neutral trading ground there—lay a mile or two above the actual mouth of the Wisconsin. Here the majestic flood of the Mississippi was broken into a maze of islands and channels. Along the eastern bank the bluffs swung back from the river, leaving a broad, level plain that had been the site of trading rendezvous and treaty councils for more than a century.

When Sibley arrived, the business center of the town was still on a low-lying island separated from the eastern shore by a narrow lagoon. Dominating the scene were the crumbling stockades of old Fort Crawford, built when the United States reoccupied the country after the War of 1812. Beside them stood a row of cabins and houses, the largest of which, along with an assortment of log warehouses and outbuildings, belonged to Rolette. Others served as hotels, taverns, an Indian agency, a sutler's store, and the homes and businesses of several of the older French settlers. Here and there abandoned chimneys and empty foundations were testaments to the flight by some of the community to higher ground away from the Mississippi's periodic floods. High and dry also, well back from the river, stood the new Fort Crawford, built of stone and nearly completed by 1834.[11]

Sibley, like most other visiting traders, was probably made comfortable in Rolette's home, for hospitality and expansive generosity were the other side of the tough little Frenchman's complex character. In the years since 1804, when he came west as a junior partner of the trader Murdoch Cameron, Joseph Rolette had become Prairie du Chien's leading citizen. It was not only that he owned a good share of the town (he was said at one time to have paid seven-eighths of the real estate taxes); he was a driving force, an innovator, and a seizer of opportunities. He had several farms, had imported the first hogs and sheep, and had built the first sawmill in the country. He was vain and on occasion gullible, but he had a probing, active mind that moved like quicksilver. No one, it was said, could calculate sums as fast as he. Nor could anyone move faster, once a decision had been taken.[12]

The hostess who welcomed Sibley to Rolette's modest mansion was not

Farms at Prairie du Chien in the 1840s

the least of the trader's valued possessions. In 1819, when she was barely fifteen, Jane Fisher had become the bride of the forty-year-old Rolette. Her mother had died at an early age, and her father had taken his sons and his trading business to the British possessions after the War of 1812. Jane was left in Prairie du Chien to the care of her aunt and uncle, Domitelle and Michael Brisbois. Educated in a Cincinnati convent, Jane was beautiful, cultured, lively, and strong-willed enough to prove herself in time a match for her formidable husband.[13]

From John Kinzie's wife Juliette, Sibley might already have heard the story of how some travelers had met Rolette once as he was returning to Prairie du Chien after a number of weeks' absence. Several of the party had just come from the Prairie, and the trader inquired eagerly about his crops, his mill, and his favorite horse. As they were paddling away, he turned back and called as an afterthought: "Wait a minute—how are Madame Rolette and the children?" Yet Rolette was not without family feeling. He maintained contact with relatives in Quebec and St. Louis and for years financed a luckless, alcoholic brother in the fur trade. His son and daughter were sent east in 1833 for schooling under the paternal eye of Ramsay Crooks, who visited the children periodically and reported on their progress.[14]

Stories collected around Rolette, and Sibley no doubt heard many of them as he waited in Prairie du Chien for the arrival of Bailly. Rolette's fear of water was legendary. When riding in a canoe he tied his pocket handkerchief to one of the ribs and never ceased to clutch it. Dousman may have told Sibley of the time when he and "Don José" (as the two privately called their senior partner) had been threatened by floating ice on the Mississippi. Terrified, Rolette crossed himself and solemnly declared that he would build a church in Prairie du Chien if only God would spare them. They reached the shore, and with one foot on land Rolette gestured toward heaven. "Collect it if you can," he called. "You haven't got my note for it!" But there was a witness, and Dousman gave him no rest until he paid.[15]

There were other tales of his cowardice and bravado. One early trader recalled a fracas with the Dakota at the mouth of the Minnesota River during which Rolette at first refused to come out of his room, then trembled so hard that he broke the ramrod in his gun. His military career in the British cause during the War of 1812 climaxed when he carried to Mackinac news of the capture of Prairie du Chien. Asked for the tidings, he announced in a solemn tone that there had been "A great battle—a sanguinary contest." When his hearers anxiously demanded to know how many were killed, he answered "None." Nor had any been wounded. With cheers and laughter they welcomed him ashore. Yet despite all this, men feared Rolette. When fire threatened his warehouse, he succeeded in bullying a crew of voyageurs into carrying his powder kegs to safety while never approaching the building himself.[16]

Bailly refused to give up the business until his contract expired the following summer, but he did agree to take Sibley with him to the mouth of the Minnesota and introduce him to the people, the country, and the far-flung operations of the Dakota trade. It was not what the partners had wanted, but they had to settle for it.[17]

Here, again, the general must have hesitated in his task of writing. As a young newcomer he himself had scarcely been consulted in the plan, and time had long since healed the wounds, but the treatment given Bailly would perhaps reflect no credit on the others involved. Were not private business transactions outside the legitimate scope of history? At last he drew a curtain across the whole episode, writing:

I was fortunate enough to fall in with Alexis Bailly Esquire, a gentleman who was in charge of four trading stations, that were within my district. ... Mr. Bailly's destination being the same with my own, we formed a party of five.... [18]

It was on a cold day in late October that Sibley and Bailly, accompanied by two voyageurs, a sixteen-year-old boy who wanted to rejoin his relatives near Fort Snelling, and a Winnebago guide, set out by horseback on the three-hundred-mile trip upriver. The first day brought near disaster and a dismal ducking in the Mississippi. As they crossed to the west bank a little above Prairie du Chien, their clumsy dugout canoe overturned. All reached shore safely, but the rest of the day was spent drying out their baggage and themselves and retrieving their horses.

Bad luck continued, for three days later the guide disappeared, leaving them lost on the Iowa prairies. So they backtracked toward the Mississippi, which they knew had to be east of them, losing nearly two days by the detour. Though longer, the route up the Mississippi followed well-established trails and was marked at each stage by picturesque bluffs and hazy autumn vistas of water and islands. Their only break in the journey was at the house of old Augustin Rocque, located on a broad prairie just below Lake Pepin. For many years Rocque had traded with the nearby Dakota, who were known as the Wabasha band after a long line of chiefs bearing that name. Sibley remembered that Rocque had comfortable beds, plenty of provisions, and a pretty sixteen-year-old daughter.[19]

In the course of the journey he also got to know the man with whom he was to spend the next six months. Alexis Bailly, like so many others in the country, was a son of the fur trade. His father, Joseph Bailly, who had traded for years in Mackinac, Lower Michigan, and Indiana, could claim descent from the colonial aristocracy of New France; his part-Ottawa mother was connected with a tribe that for generations had controlled the trade between the Upper Great Lakes and lower Canada. Bailly was stocky, handsome, a bit of a dandy, and disconcertingly well educated. He was informed on current affairs, had a nodding acquaintance with the law, spoke (and wrote) faultless English—although his native tongue was French—and was fluent in several Indian languages as well as Latin.[20]

But it was no doubt his stories of the northwestern country that interested Sibley most. As a romantic nineteen-year-old student in Montreal, Bailly had volunteered to carry dispatches for Jean Douglas, Countess of Selkirk, to her husband, who was isolated during the winter of 1816–17 at Fort William on the far shore of Lake Superior. Returning from the perilous thousand-mile journey, the young courier received, he said, a kiss from the valiant and beautiful lady herself. In 1821 he had again served the interests of the Selkirks, as well as his new employer Joe Rolette, when he drove a herd of cattle from Prairie du Chien up the Mississippi and Minnesota River valleys and down the Red River to the disaster-stricken colony founded by the Earl in the territories of the Hudson's Bay Company. There the animals sold at a legendary price.[21]

Four years later, in 1825, Bailly located a post at the mouth of the Minnesota River across from Fort Snelling on a point of land that had been the first encampment site of the troops who built the fort in 1819. They called it "New Hope"—a name touched with bitter irony after nearly a third of them died in the first winter.[22]

In 1826 Bailly married Lucy Faribault, who, like himself, was the child of a French trader and a mixed-blood mother. Her father, Jean Baptiste Faribault, had traded for years among the Dakota, and with the marriage Bailly acquired deep roots in the country—roots that now resisted transplanting. He talked freely with young Sibley—what had he to lose?—recounting his grievances against Rolette and pointing out the way in which the American Fur Company squeezed its small traders dry then dropped them like useless rinds. He had, he estimated, cleared some $200,000 for the company in his ten years at New Hope, and now he was a ruined man.[23]

On October 28 the party arrived at its destination. Sibley first saw the broad valley of the Minnesota River at its junction with the Mississippi from the crest of a bluff known as Pilot Knob. The unforgettable grandeur of the view and his own conscious sense of history combined to keep the moment fresh in his memory:

> *When I reached the brink of the hill overlooking the surrounding country, I was struck with the picturesque beauty of the scene. From that outlook the course of the Mississippi River from the north, suddenly turning eastward to where St. Paul now stands, the Minnesota River from the west, the principal tributary of the main stream and at the junction, rose the military post of Fort Snelling perched upon a high and commanding point, with its stone walls, and blockhouses, bidding defiance to any attempt at capture.*[24]

Riding down the steep trail into the valley, he found that the post of New Hope, or St. Peters, as it was more often called, consisted of a collection of sagging log huts clustered along the southeastern shore of the Minnesota. This rickety collection faced a broad, sandy island that divided the mouth of the stream into two channels and hid from view the swifter flowing current of the Mississippi on the other side. The valley was nearly bare of trees, and the walls of Fort Snelling could be plainly seen on the far bluff, directly across from the trading station.

The largest of the log houses belonged to Bailly, and another was occupied by the family of his father-in-law, the trader Faribault, who had already left

Lithograph of Fort Snelling by Seth Eastman in 1833

for his wintering post at Little Rapids, some forty miles up the Minnesota. The rest of the buildings included cabins for a blacksmith and a carpenter and for the voyageurs employed by Bailly, as well as storehouses for goods and furs. The house to which Lucy Bailly welcomed Sibley was so dilapidated that he made a mental note to replace it as soon as possible and included an urgent request for new buildings in his first letters to New York and Prairie du Chien.[25]

Within a few days Bailly seemingly changed his mind about selling and asked Sibley to make him an offer. Unwilling to act without the consent of his senior partners, Sibley immediately wrote to Rolette and Dousman. He also told Crooks, who replied with enthusiasm, hoping that the bargain would be promptly closed. Crooks in turn urged Rolette and Dousman to make terms immediately with Bailly, for "we never can consider ourselves safe so long as he has any control over the trade of any of our people."[26]

The suspicious Rolette, however, saw only trickery in Bailly's proposition. He noted that the trader had come around only after he had advanced goods to his Indian customers on credit for the winter. "After mature reflection of Mr. Dousman and myself," Rolette told Crooks, "we wrote to Mr. Sibly [sic] to decline purchasing Mr. Bailly who refused to sell last fall—previous to the credits being made.—You well know that the Indians will not pay well any other person but the one who trusted them. As to binding him by contract I considered that no instrument would bind him as he had nothing to pay." And nursing his old grudges, Rolette concluded that had Bailly's motive "not been a bad one he never would have proposed to sell out to Mr. Sibly—I know him too well."[27]

Crooks was philosophical about the partners' decision on Bailly. "Your passing the winter together I deem of great advantage to you," he told Sibley, "for by observing closely his system of management you may learn to adopt what is really useful, and avoid the errors of his practice." Then, pontificating a bit, he advised the younger man: "Be just and firm in all your dealings, and you will soon obtain the confidence of everybody, and the attachment of your people will soon follow.—Conciliate the good will of the officers of government, especially the Indian Agent; and your situation will soon be free from much of the trouble which has heretofore beset the incumbent of New Hope." Meanwhile, writing to Samuel Abbott, Crooks observed with satisfaction that "Mr. Sibley seems quite 'au fait' already and will prove I daresay a first rate man for our business."[28]

· 4 ·

The Sioux Outfit

*T*HE WINTER SPENT WITH BAILLY was an unusually long and severe one, during which snow piled deep, cattle starved, and the main diet, as Sibley recalled it, was salt pork and bread. Nevertheless, it allowed the young trader a time of relative leisure in which he became acquainted with the rigors of the country, the Dakota people, and the lively military community across the river. He was also able to observe the structure and personnel of the sprawling business for which he would soon be responsible.

Central to that business was the store at St. Peters itself, which served five Dakota villages in the immediate vicinity, as well as the small mixed-blood community around the fort and visiting groups of Dakota from the Cannon and Cedar River valleys to the southwest. It was under the direct eye of the trader, who also managed three distant posts through hired clerks. One of those was at Traverse des Sioux, some seventy miles up the Minnesota River. Another was beside Lake Traverse at the headwaters of the Red River, and the third was a post among the Sisseton Dakota whose wintering location varied from year to year but was generally between the headwaters of the Des Moines and Big Sioux Rivers. Also within the Sioux Outfit were two independent subsidiary traders. One was Faribault, Bailly's father-in-law, and the other was Joseph Renville, whose post was at Lac qui Parle on the Upper Minnesota River.

Until the winter of 1834 there had been a third: Joseph R. Brown, a soldier turned fur trader, had located in 1832 at Oliver's Grove on the Mississippi opposite the mouth of the St. Croix River. Supplied by Bailly and Rolette, he had traded up the St. Croix and on the east bank of the Mississippi. It was also common knowledge that from this point barrels of whiskey

Lawrence Taliaferro

were often hauled in carts across the prairie to the Minnesota River above Fort Snelling, thus avoiding government authorities. Like Bailly, Brown had quarreled with Taliaferro, but with even more disastrous results, for the Indian agent had refused to renew Brown's license in 1834 and left him with a substantial investment in a business he could neither operate nor sell.[1]

One reason that Taliaferro alleged for his action was the opening in 1834 of a third trading station in the general vicinity of Fort Snelling. This store, located at a spot known as Coldwater, just to the north of the fort, represented competition for the American Fur Company—a principle that Taliaferro enthusiastically favored. It was owned by an independent operator named Benjamin F. Baker, a Virginia schoolteacher who had come to the fort as a civilian employee in 1822 and had soon taken to trading with the Ojibwe up the Mississippi. Baker's move to Coldwater threatened to overcrowd the trading business between the Falls of St. Anthony and the head of Lake Pepin.[2]

The Dakota communities clustered within this area all belonged to the division of the tribe known as the Mdewakanton. When first encountered by Europeans in the mid-seventeenth century, they lived near Lake Mille Lacs. During the next hundred years, pressed by the Ojibwe from the north and drawn toward better trading opportunities on the Mississippi, they had moved below the Falls of St. Anthony and were now centered in the lower Minnesota and Mississippi River valleys. There they lived in permanent villages beneath the sheltering bluffs, where wood and water were close at hand, and where the rich, sandy soil of the bottomlands could be loosened easily by a hoe and coaxed to produce corn and other vegetables. Their large, rectangular houses of poles and bark, many of which accommodated three or four related families, were often empty, however, for the ancient round of seasonal activities took entire bands away for weeks at a time, hunting, fishing, wild-ricing, or sugar-making.[3]

More than a century earlier another such activity had been added—the annual or semiannual journey to secure ammunition, tools, cloth, and other trade goods. At first this took them as far as Prairie du Chien or even Green Bay. But for at least the last two generations, white traders had come nearly every year to winter near the mouth of the Minnesota, reducing the need for travel by the Dakota living there. Since the building of the fort, one or two permanent stores had been opened in the vicinity.

Nearly within sight of the fort on the bank of the Minnesota was the Black Dog village, whose people were said to have split off a generation earlier from a band located four or five miles farther up the river at a place called by white men "Long Avenue" or Nine-Mile Creek. Twenty-five miles above the fort on the Minnesota was a larger group known by the name of its leader as

Shakopee, or The Six. Nine miles below the fort, where the Mississippi made a sweeping bend to the southeast, was a village called Kaposia, or "light-footed"—probably in reference to its championship at the game of lacrosse. East of the river near the mouth of the St. Croix was a smaller group whose head man was known as the Big Soldier, and farther south along the Mississippi was the band of Wacouta or The Red Wing, located some six miles above the head of Lake Pepin on the west bank. A large band headed by Wabasha and located below Lake Pepin was served by the trader Augustin Roque, who was supplied from Prairie du Chien.[4]

Leadership of the bands was generally hereditary, but there were often exceptions. One such was Cloud Man, a member of the Nine-Mile village, whose experience of near starvation while on a winter buffalo hunt led him to consider the urgings of Taliaferro that the Dakota turn to farming. At last he volunteered to learn, and at the suggestion of the Indian agent, he moved with his own and several other families to a spot between two small lakes some six miles north of the fort. The agent had supplied seed, advice, and a man with a team of oxen to plow some of the prairie sod. By 1834 the little settlement (called Eatonville by Taliaferro in honor of his superior, the secretary of war) had grown to number some 130 Dakota.[5]

These tentative beginnings of agriculture were only one sign of the great changes Sibley may have noticed occurring among the people to whom his life would henceforth be connected. Several months before his own arrival, two young Connecticut farmers had appeared at the fort, spurred by the wave of evangelical revivalism to spend their lives in the service of God and the heathen. Taliaferro suggested they build a cabin on the shore of Lake Cal-

A Dakota village near Fort Snelling

houn near Eatonville. An officially sponsored effort came at about the same time from the American Board of Commissioners for Foreign Missions, which surveyed the field in the summer of 1834 and sent missionaries in 1835.[6]

The presence of the government was also being directly felt for the first time among the Dakota. The purchase of the Fort Snelling military reservation in 1819 had been paid for in the time-honored fashion of gifts and bribes to the tribe's leaders. Under Taliaferro's more paternalistic administration, however, a treaty in 1830 that designated strips of land to serve as buffer zones among the tribes of the Upper Mississippi valley included compensation in the form of small annuities and government services. Among these were farming tools and draft animals; a blacksmith to mend traps, guns, and muskrat spears; and also a limited fund for education. Another provision of the same treaty set aside a tract of land on the west side of Lake Pepin for mixed-blood relatives of the tribe, whom Taliaferro hoped would take up farming there.[7]

The generation of leadership that had agreed to these treaties and seen the building of the fort was also in a state of change. The people of the Nine-Mile village were already becoming known as Good Road's band after the vigorous young man who had assumed leadership there in 1833. At Kaposia an old chief called Little Crow had died early in 1834 and had been succeeded by his son Big Thunder, whom Sibley would come to know as a mildly "progressive" headman, willing to see his people take up the plow and listen to the missionaries. At Black Dog's village the aged chief, who was also called Big Eagle, was growing more feeble as the days passed, and it was clear that his son Grey Iron would soon replace him.[8]

Most of the Mdewakanton communities ranged in population between a hundred and two hundred members, although the Indian agent counted 368 at Shakopee. The number of potential regular customers for the store at St. Peters was thus in the neighborhood of 1,300 people. This was increased to around 2,000 by frequent visits from a division of the Dakota known as Wahpekute, who lived along the headwaters of the Cannon and Cedar Rivers, and who had no resident traders among them.[9]

The fort in clear view across the river from New Hope was to be a constant presence in Sibley's life, both business and social. The Indian agency buildings and the house occupied by Taliaferro stood just outside the walls and opposite the main gate. Like other such officials, Taliaferro bore the courtesy title of "Major" and worked closely with the military authorities, although he was a civilian employee of the War Department. Other circumstances, too, soon linked Sibley intimately to the life within the fort's limestone walls, for a few months after his arrival he and his partners began looking into the possibility of operating the army sutler's store there.

The American Fur Company sought to maintain a monopoly in the fur trade at nearly any cost. Having through political influence eliminated the government-run stores that competed with it in the 1820s, the company now found that as army posts sprang up throughout the West, Indians had the option of patronizing the sutlers' stores. No law or regulation forbade sutlers from accepting furs in payment for goods, although Crooks did his best to get one adopted. The implications for the company's business at St. Peters were clear, and control of this potential competition was a prime objective.[10]

The position of post sutler, often a profitable one, was a political plum, usually awarded to a loyal supporter of the party in power. In the spring of 1835 the appointment at Fort Snelling was given to Samuel C. Stambaugh, a newspaper editor and Democratic Party hack from Pennsylvania. But Stambaugh, who had formerly done a stint as an Indian agent in Wisconsin, had no desire to move again to the Northwest and was willing to subcontract the business. After nearly a year of dickering, the company secured a partnership agreement by which Sibley would manage the store and Stambaugh would collect a percentage of the profits. The traders were confident that any losses to them would be more than offset by their ability to set higher prices in dealing with the Dakota.

For Sibley the venture would prove a headache from beginning to end. Stambaugh was a difficult man to deal with, and mutual distrust soon developed. Moreover, bad luck plagued them. Profits of a sutler varied in proportion to the number of troops served. Within a year the garrison at Fort Snelling was drastically reduced by the needs of the Seminole War in Florida. Worse yet, the men of the First Infantry, who had been stationed at the fort, steamed off down the river just before payday, leaving the sutler with a good many unpaid credits. The next year, lands east of the Mississippi were opened to settlement, and there was an inrush of independent traders and whiskey sellers, thus making control of the sutling far less advantageous to American Fur. It was not until early 1839, however, that Sibley was at last able to close out the partnership with Stambaugh.

Another tie to the fort was Sibley's involvement with the mail service, previously handled by the army along with its dispatches. As early as 1835 Sibley used his Michigan political connections to urge the establishment of a post office at the fort with regular service from Prairie du Chien. He was successful, and in 1837 the Western Outfit secured the contract for carrying the mail, which it held until 1839. In summer, steamboats were the carriers, but during the long winter freeze, runners had to be hired. The partners divided the route into two sections, the midpoint being the trading post of Augustin Roque at the southern end of Lake Pepin. A carrier hired by Dousman delivered the mail there, and it was picked up by Sibley's man. Even with this arrangement, keeping the mail on time was a constant struggle.[11]

These experiments with government contracts were part of a flurry of expansion undertaken by the ambitious young trader in the first three years after his arrival. The investment in larger buildings at New Hope—a project to which Crooks, Rolette, and Dousman had all quickly agreed—was part of this initiative, and Sibley soon took steps to open two new posts—one on the Sheyenne River, north and west of Lake Traverse, and one at Little Rock on the Minnesota River. He also sought to consolidate his monopoly of the Dakota trade, complaining angrily when William Aitken of the Northern Outfit opened a post at Otter Tail Lake, close enough to draw trade away from the Sioux Outfit's post at Lake Traverse. Crooks promptly ordered Aitken to back off.[12]

Immediately after reaching St. Peters, Sibley had planned to make the round of his new district accompanied by Bailly. They had actually set out on December 1, 1834, going up the Minnesota River, as far as Traverse des Sioux. Winter was already closing in, however, and they found the snow so deep on the plains that they were forced to turn back. Sibley hoped to go in the spring, but the season proved too busy for travel. In May Bailly's family left for Prairie du Chien, where Bailly had bought a house and farm, and he himself soon followed.[13]

Rolette arrived at St. Peters in time to meet with the various clerks and traders of the district when they brought in their winter's catch of furs, and he joined Sibley in negotiating new arrangements and signing new contracts for the Western Outfit. Sibley himself then made a three-week journey to Prairie du Chien, returning in time to see construction begun on the new stone warehouse and store. Thus it was early in the autumn of 1835 before the head of the Sioux Outfit was able to start again on his tour of inspection.[14]

His own curiosity about the country was no doubt one motive for the long trip, but there were business reasons also. Firsthand acquaintance with places and people was essential within the ever-fluctuating intertribal, interracial, and intercultural milieu of the fur trade. There was no such thing as a standard contract; each agreement depended on the needs and bargaining power of those negotiating it. Family ties were crucial; old band rivalries and intertribal tensions played a role; the new influence of missionaries on subsistence patterns and the loyalties of respected individuals must all be factored in. Knowledge of personal history was power, and a canny trader would be informed beforehand of where the pitfalls lay. What Sibley learned on this trip and in the years ahead would produce the fine-tuned diplomacy that later made him indispensable in negotiating treaties with the Dakota.

The first post on Sibley's route belonged to Faribault at Little Rapids. Jean Baptiste Faribault was born in the province of Quebec and was the educated son of a former French official. After half a dozen years in the mercantile trade, he, like Sibley, had opted for a more adventurous occupation, and taking employment with a fur trader, had arrived at Mackinac in 1798. The next twenty years of his life followed the usual fur trader's story: a series of isolated wintering posts, several close brushes with death, marriage to a mixed-blood woman, and graduation from the status of hired clerk to that of small independent operator.[15]

Living at Prairie du Chien in 1819, he made the acquaintance of Colonel Henry M. Leavenworth, who commanded the troops assigned to build a fort at the mouth of the Minnesota. Leavenworth was impressed by the industrious Frenchman and urged him to locate near the new fort, promising protection and assistance. The area was familiar to Faribault, for he had traded previously at the Little Rapids, where, in fact, he had met Pelagie Ainse, his wife. Accordingly, the trader moved his family, establishing a store and an extensive farm just below the fort, on the sandy island to which Lieutenant Zebulon M. Pike had bequeathed his name. In 1820 Leavenworth saw to it that the island itself was bequeathed by treaty to Pelagie and her children, inserting an article to that effect in an unratified agreement to purchase additional land for the military reservation. Leavenworth's successor, Colonel Josiah Snelling, took a less favorable view of the establishment and forced Faribault to relocate his home alongside that of Bailly on the southeast bank of the Minnesota. Faribault then reopened his business at Little Rapids, spending the winters there and the summers with his wife and family at the mouth or "entry" of the river.[16]

The five-year contract that Sibley and Rolette signed with Faribault in June 1835, was the usual arrangement with an independent subsidiary trader. Faribault agreed to buy all his goods and supplies from American Fur and to sell his furs exclusively to the company. He was charged a one-third markup on the original cost plus transportation of all eastern and European goods delivered at Prairie du Chien. The company agreed to secure three voyageurs, whom Faribault would employ, and who would be allowed to buy goods only through him, thus enabling the trader to collect an additional markup on any

purchases made by his men. Faribault bound himself to trade only with Indians to whom he had previously given credit and "not to interfere directly
or indirectly with the Indians belonging to any other of the outfits" of the
American Fur Company.[17]

At Traverse des Sioux, the next stop on Sibley's tour, the post was the property of the company, purchased from Bailly, and was operated by a hired clerk
on a contract renewable each year at a salary of $550. Louis Provençalle, nick-
named Le Blanc, who had been stationed there for nearly ten years, was a rare
example of a voyageur who had risen to the rank of clerk. Like most men of
his class, Provençalle was illiterate. He was capable and ingenious, however,
and he had devised a system of hieroglyphics, understandable only to himself, by which he kept accurate records of the trade. He had a working relationship with a nearby band of Sisseton Dakota who were notable for their
general antagonism to traders and missionaries.[18]

Beneath a jovial and even gentle exterior, Provençalle carried a touch of
almost insane temper. When a crowd of young Sisseton bullies had started
to pillage his store, he seized a blazing stick from the fire and in a reckless
rage waved it over an open keg of gunpowder, threatening to blow the whole
concern to glory if they touched a thing. After that, and after hearing tales of
how with seething fury he had flayed alive a wolf that molested his chick-
ens, they treated *Skadan* or The Little White Man, as they called him, with
wary respect.[19]

Sibley's other wintering clerk, also inherited from Bailly, was Joseph
Laframboise, a son of Madeline Laframboise, the Mackinac matriarch. Joseph
received approximately the same salary as Louis Provençalle, but with
Laframboise, Sibley and Rolette had signed a three-year contract "to winter
at such station as shall be designated." The location chosen in 1835 was on the
Crooked or Big Sioux River.[20]

After Traverse des Sioux, Sibley and the voyageur who accompanied him
left behind the broad tongue of deciduous forest that spread southward
through central and southern Minnesota, dividing the prairie land and oak
openings along the Mississippi from the treeless plains that reached westward to the Missouri and beyond. Traverse des Sioux, or The Place Where the
Sioux Cross, took its name from an ancient trail that led directly west at that
point, forming a shortcut across the great southern bend of the Minnesota
River.

The valley of the Upper Minnesota River, like that along the river's lower
stretches, had been carved out by glacial torrents in past ages and dwarfed
the narrow stream that meandered down it. Cutting a majestic two- or three-

mile swath between abrupt bluffs, the valley descended slowly over successive shelves of granite from the wide range of high land known as the Coteau
des Prairies that divided the waters of the Mississippi from the Missouri. At
a place where the Minnesota, dammed by a ridge of glacial gravel, backed up
to fill its spacious valley with the shimmering waters of Lac qui Parle, stood
the palisaded fort of Joseph Renville.

The quantum of Renville's European blood was uncertain. Rainville was
a common Canadian name, and he might have been fathered by an obscure
voyageur who carried it to the Upper Mississippi. When among the Dakota,
however, Renville himself claimed to be wholly Indian, and his appearance
supported this. His full brother Ohiya (Victor) had been a noted Dakota war
chief who died in battle against the Ojibwe. But neither did Joseph contradict
the assumption of white men that he carried French genes along with a
French name. Somewhere he had acquired a fluent command of the French
language, although he read and wrote it only with difficulty, and he had also
become a Catholic.[21]

The swarthy lad started in the fur trade some time in the 1790s as the interpreter and protégé of Robert Dickson, a tall, red-headed Scot who for
twenty years dominated the British trade in what was then Spanish territory
west of the Mississippi. When Dickson moved north of the British boundary
after the War of 1812 and became an agent for Lord Selkirk, Renville accom-

The valley of the Minnesota River

panied him and began trading for the Hudson's Bay Company in what was then assumed to be British territory on the Upper Red River. In 1821 he was a leader in the formation of the Columbia Fur Company, and when that band of independents merged with American Fur in 1827, Renville remained at his post by Lac qui Parle and extracted from Rolette an agreement to supply goods and to market furs without undue interference.

Renville's influence among the Dakota was considerable, and Rolette was shrewd enough to continue the hands-off policy, although he fumed from time to time at the trader's gross extravagance in supporting a band of armed followers and an extended web of dependents and kin. A number of these were not western Dakota but members of the Mdewakanton band, to whom Renville was allied by both blood and marriage. They had migrated west from the Mississippi River valley at Renville's invitation and in search of better game.[22] The five-year contract that Rolette and Sibley signed with Renville in the summer of 1835 was generally similar to that with Faribault, although the terms given Renville were somewhat more favorable.[23] Later in the same summer, several months before Sibley's first arrival at Lac qui Parle, Renville had welcomed the group of Presbyterian missionaries sent by the American Board and headed by Dr. Thomas S. Williamson. The trader's early Catholicism had apparently yielded to the prospect of religious training, education, and medical care for his family and associated band.

Sixty miles beyond Lac qui Parle, on the eastern shore of Lake Traverse, was Sibley's farthest post. It stood a short distance to the north of the low, swampy valley that divided Big Stone Lake, the source of the Minnesota River, from Lake Traverse, whose outlet joined the Red River and ultimately flowed into Hudson Bay. The watershed had been a favorite trading site for years. Dickson's major post had been located there, as had the headquarters of the Columbia Fur Company. In a business sense, both had faced westward toward the low, hazy line on the horizon that marked the summit of the Coteau des Prairies. Trade at Lake Traverse came from the western plains, brought by mounted bands of Sisseton and Yankton Dakota who followed the buffalo herds and sometimes exchanged goods and pelts with their Teton tribesmen even farther west along the upper Missouri.

The abandoned buildings of the Columbia Fur Company had been taken over by Bailly, who maintained a small station there under the management of Hazen Mooers, a native of New York state and a longtime trader in the Minnesota River valley. When Bailly departed, however, Mooers quit the service of American Fur and moved down the Minnesota to open an independent post at a place called Petite Roche, or the Little Rock, between Traverse des Sioux and Lac qui Parle.[24]

To operate the orphaned post at Lake Traverse, Rolette and Sibley tried a novel experiment. Joseph Brown, as a result of his misfortune with Talia-ferro, found himself in debt to Rolette and the Western Outfit for more than $2,400. Scrappy and assertive, he also claimed that he had grievances against Rolette. Perhaps through the mediation of Sibley and Dousman, the matter was settled in the summer of 1835 by a contract in which Brown agreed to four years of virtual indentured servitude in return for the cancellation of his debt. For his services as clerk and trader he would receive $150 a year, plus specified quantities of pork, flour, tea, sugar, coffee, lard, and tobacco.[25]

Rolette mistrusted the mercurial Brown, and instead of placing him in charge at Lake Traverse he made an agreement with Renville to manage the trade there with the help of his son, Joseph, Jr. Their compensation would be half the profit—or half the loss. Brown was to keep the books and also, since he was known for his skill at farming, he was instructed to rebuild the dilapi-dated post buildings and to sow crops and raise cattle in hope of supplying a substantial share of the food required by the western posts. He was formally cautioned not to interfere in any way with the trade itself, yet at the same time

Looking west across Lake Traverse. A burial scaffold in the foreground overlooks a Dakota village and the stockaded trading post.

Sibley seems to have told him quietly to see to it that the post did not lose money. Brown found it entirely impossible to follow both instructions.[26]

Before Sibley arrived at Lake Traverse on his tour of inspection, he had already received a long, exasperated letter from Brown, and he probably guessed that it would be the first of many. Brown clearly resented the authority given Renville and felt hampered at every turn by the decisions of "the Squire." Not only was he accustomed to operating independently; he no doubt also nursed a certain sense of his own superiority as a white man. He admitted to Sibley that Renville "is going the entire animal to give a profit to this business," yet he continued to pour out endless examples of what he saw as inefficiency and poor management.[27]

The Renvilles, it seemed, could never quite understand that for businessmen every sentiment and tradition must give way to the overriding necessity of making as much profit as possible. The Renvilles moved to a different rhythm. When the season opened, they gave goods on credit to all the hunters alike until nothing was left. They saw no reason to discriminate against those who had failed to pay credits before nor to hold back a part of the stock for rewarding and resupplying those who returned early with a good catch. All were members of the band; all contributed and had similar needs; therefore all should be treated alike. By such evenhandedness they avoided jealousy and resentment among the Indians and avoided reprisals, which usually took the form of killing cattle or stealing horses. Brown interpreted this as "paying for protection." He acknowledged, however, that not an animal had been lost except one horse which "old age toted off."[28]

If Sibley, following Crooks's urging, passed on the word that the Indians should be discouraged from using premium-priced buffalo robes to make tipis, the Renvilles were apt to shrug.[29] The Dakota always made their lodges from precious buffalo hides. Why should they give up the handsome, weather-tight dwellings in which they took such pride simply to buy more goods from the trader? Although old Joseph Renville knew the fur trade as well as any man in the Minnesota River valley and knew that changes were coming fast, he never accepted what seemed so plain to men like Brown and Sibley—that the attitudes and communal customs of the Dakota were inherently inferior to those of "civilization" and must be replaced as speedily as possible by a proper sense of acquisitiveness and competition.

To the clash of cultures was added a clash of personalities. Brown, left alone in charge of the post during most of the winter, often went beyond his instructions and took authority into his own hands. His close rapport with Sibley and his frequent reports to St. Peters were resented by the Renvilles.

They in turn resorted to harassing him in small ways, until in May 1836, Brown wrote: "If ever I am caught to pass another year as I have done this, I believe you will catch a weasel asleep.... No, Mr. Sibley,... send me anywhere else, to Petite Roche, to Devils Lake, to hell if you will, and I will not murmur, ... but never, while I have legs to escape, will I pass one month in the same fort with one of that [Renville] family."[30]

Brown, too, could be exasperating. When the quality of tobacco furnished under his contract did not suit him, he wrote huffily to Sibley: "If the comp'y cannot afford to furnish me Cavendish tobacco, I would thank you to send me 8 lbs on my acct."[31] In business he was apt to produce either a brilliant coup or a spectacular failure. This and his incorrigible independence kept him from being the kind of steady trader to be relied on year after year. Yet there was an engaging quality about the man that Sibley like many others found irresistible. His keen sense of the absurd accompanied a mind of remarkable depth, and his rancor would usually dissolve in humor, often at his own expense. His weakness for women was widely talked of, even in the free and easy Fort Snelling community that, like Sault Ste. Marie, took for granted exploitation of Indian and mixed-blood females. He had been legally married twice, once to a daughter of the trader Dickson, and later to a mixed-blood Ojibwe woman named Margaret McCoy. Brown had accepted the second marriage in order to gain for his daughter a small inheritance that had been left in trust at the death of his uncle. "I took into consideration that I had helped bring her into the world," he told Sibley, "and by very little sacrifice could give her $1,000 at least if she lived." He cautioned Sibley, however, not to let the mother charge anything to his account, for "I can never acknowledge her as my wife."[32]

When Sibley, accompanied by Renville, arrived at the closely palisaded post on the eastern shore of Lake Traverse, he must have quickly observed that Brown was preparing for yet another entanglement. The twice-widowed wife of Renville's brother, a handsome mixed-blood woman, was staying at the post. According to Dakota custom she had become Renville's responsibility when his brother was slain, and the trader had taken her into his family. Perhaps for convenience, perhaps from fear of scandalizing the missionaries, Renville had sent her that autumn to Lake Traverse, where she kept house for Brown. With her was her daughter by a first marriage, a young girl named Susan Frenier. Brown's attentiveness to Susan and her studied aloofness were both plain to see.[33]

Susan was among a group of bystanders who gathered one day to watch some pistol target practice. Renville, who was using a new weapon with a hair trigger, accidentally fired into the crowd, and Sibley recalled:

The report was followed by a piercing shriek from the sixteen year old girl, and she was seized by the older women, and placed on a bed in the nearest building. I followed to ascertain the extent of the injury inflicted, and found the bed surrounded by wailing females, who were doing nothing for the sufferer. I pushed them rudely aside, for it was no time for ceremony, and found that the girl had been shot in the groin, the ball passing through that portion of the body. I was soon satisfied that no artery, or other important blood vessel had been severed, as there was but little hemorrhage.[34]

Feeling awkward and helpless in spite of his assumption of authority, Sibley suggested washing the wound with cold water and told Renville that they should leave immediately to get medical aid from Dr. Williamson at Lac qui Parle. Their frantic all-night ride was slowed by a sudden storm on the prairie, but when they at last arrived, the missionary doctor left promptly for the sixty-mile journey back to Lake Traverse. Susan recovered to become in time the third (and permanent) wife of Joe Brown.[35]

In the meantime Sibley continued on his return to the mouth of the St. Peters. An early snowstorm overtook him soon after he left Lac qui Parle and held him for a day in the shelter of a poplar grove. His pace quickened by this warning, he passed the new house that Mooers had built at Little Rock and cut away from the river along the faint trace across the prairie marking the way to Traverse des Sioux.[36]

Ruts made by cart wheels could be seen in some places, for ten years earlier the Canadian traders of the Columbia Fur Company had introduced a Red River version of the two-wheeled French *charette* to haul their furs and supplies during times of low water on the Minnesota. Made entirely of wood, the Red River carts were easy to repair or replace along the trail and had quickly become a trademark of the large French-Indian mixed-blood community near the British border. Renville still used carts regularly to bypass the shallow upper reaches of the Minnesota River, and after a slow and painful ascent by canoe that fall, Brown vowed never again to carry goods by water above Traverse des Sioux.[37]

During the long, silent journey Sibley's thoughts must have gone back now and again to Brown and the Renvilles, and to the long shadow cast by the choices a man made on the lonely frontier. Before leaving St. Peters he wrote jokingly to his mother about the difficulties of his bachelor life and had added: "In truth, I begin to think seriously of taking unto myself a wife, and I give you fair warning that I shall not hesitate to make propositions to the first fair lady I meet with, who pleases me, and who will deign to look with a favorable eye on one of that contemned but slandered class of men called Indian traders."[38]

An opportunity soon arrived. He had been back in his house only a few nights when his sleep was interrupted by an elderly Indian who brought his daughter, offering to leave the girl under the trader's protection for the winter. The incident had stayed vivid in Sibley's memory down the years, and of it he wrote:

The poor girl meantime, stood there awaiting my reply, having covered her head with the blanket she wore. I excused myself to the father, telling him it would be wrong in me to comply with his offer, that I had no intention of taking to myself an Indian maiden for a wife, for many reasons I could not explain to him, except one which he could comprehend, and that was, it would make the other Indians, and their families, dissatisfied and jealous.

Then, choosing words carefully for a generation of readers that worshiped propriety, the general added:

It must not be supposed, that from an Indian point of view, there was anything savoring of immodesty in the proceeding I have narrated. . . . I shall have more to write on this subject farther on, when I will demonstrate, that female virtue was held in as high estimation among the Sioux bands in their wild state, as by the whites, and the line between the chaste, and the demimonde, quite as well defined.[39]

But these were to be the last words Sibley wrote in his autobiography. It was never finished. Perhaps memories even more poignant crowded forward, and he laid down the pen, realizing that to tell the story of his own life was a far more complex undertaking than he had imagined.

· 5 ·

Hal, a Dacotah

*T*HE CONTRACT THAT ESTABLISHED THE Western Outfit was to have ended in 1840. Those first six years in the Minnesota country, which brought Henry Sibley to the age of twenty-nine, had not been easy ones, although as the general reminisced, memory softened them with the glow of nostalgia.

The forces that tugged at the young man's sense of self were often in conflict—just as were the forces that struggled to shape the nation's own identity in Jacksonian America. Repeating his maternal grandfather's trek beyond the edge of settlement, he recreated the image of the bold frontiersman—the guns, the horses, the dogs, the hunting prowess, and the camaraderie with Indian people who were still proudly independent in their own land. Yet the Upper Mississippi frontier of the 1830s was far different from that of the Ohio valley in the 1790s. So also, the expectations that Henry Sibley shouldered were more complex than those of Ebenezer Sproat.

To be a benevolent landholder and provide leadership to a growing community of farmers and craftsmen was no longer enough. At Mackinac Sibley had served an apprenticeship in a continent-wide business, and now he faced the test of managing his own part of the enterprise along with the opportunity to make a fortune. In this he had formidable role models. Ramsay Crooks and Hercules Dousman were both self-made men in the pattern of an expanding capitalist world. Dousman especially—shrewd, blunt, and with a single eye to making money—coached him, prodded him, and confided in him like an older brother.

Nevertheless, Sibley's position in the isolated community around Fort Snelling demanded different roles also. The world of class distinctions and gentility, and the paternalistic stance that went with it, were ever present. The officers at the fort, mostly graduates of West Point, maintained an island of gentlemanly conviviality, divided by a wide chasm from the life of the common soldiers. The younger set welcomed Sibley with enthusiasm, although his sense of propriety held him apart from their wilder doings.[1]

Voyageurs and small traders, on the other hand, along with their mixed-blood families, looked to Sibley as their intermediary in dealing with the imponderable powers of the War Department and the American Fur Company. And the fort, a relatively safe and easy destination by steamboat, yet still in the heart of the fabled North American wilderness, was a magnet for distinguished visitors of scientific, scholarly, and literary note. Many of these called on the agent of the American Fur Company for help in their travels, and Sibley became the involuntary benefactor and host of men like geologist George W. Featherstonhaugh, novelist Frederick Marryat, artist George Catlin, and geographer Joseph N. Nicollet.

Another source of ambivalence was the conflicting agenda for the American Indian held by trader and missionary. The wave of evangelical revival that Sibley had encountered at Mackinac was still washing westward, and it engulfed the Fort Snelling community just after his arrival there. Sibley had committed himself to it, earnestly if not wholeheartedly. Throughout his years on the Upper Mississippi he maintained cordial relationships with the bands of missionaries that came and went, helped them at times with transportation and supplies, and corresponded often with old friends from Mackinac like William Boutwell and Frederick and Elizabeth Ayer, who were working with the Ojibwe to the north. One of his first excursions after arriving at New Hope was to call upon the two young farmer-missionaries who had established themselves near the agricultural settlement of Cloud Man, several miles from the fort. There, accompanied by one of the more pious army officers, he joined in a short prayer meeting with Samuel and Gideon Pond in their log house overlooking Lake Calhoun.[2]

Homesickness was never far beneath the surface of his letters to Detroit, and he repeatedly bewailed the lack of mail. In 1835 he was indignant that the family "should allow me, a thousand or more miles from them, to remain from the 1 of May until the 1 of Sept. without receiving one letter from home." And by the spring of 1837, he was lamenting: "Go home I must this year, if I live and am not kept back by main strength, for it is now three years since I left home and I long to see you all once more. I cannot foresee the time when I shall leave here for good, but hope to do so one of these years." Early in 1838, after the promised visit, he wrote to his youngest brother Fred, who was away at school for the first time, "I must do as you do, that is stick it out bravely until the time comes round when we shall all meet once more at home, there to remain."[3]

His loneliness and anxiety were intensified by nagging illness. In the summer of 1835, he had been "quite unwell." He was ill again in the summer of 1838 and throughout the following winter he suffered from "an attack of the liver complaint which has reduced me much." That spring he told Fred of his plans for an extended hunting expedition, "should I live until fall." The doubt may have been a real one, for in January 1840 he reported that "the bilious fever came near finishing me last summer." Temporarily restored, he was ill again by the spring of that year, prompting Dousman to remark, "I am afraid you take too much medicine and do yourself more injury than good by it."[4]

Sibley's living conditions had improved with the construction of an impressive stone house in the years 1837 and 1838. The cooking and household chores that he described whimsically to his mother—"scarcely a day passes that the Agent of the Grand Co. is not seen with sleeves rolled up and towel in hand"—were soon taken over by hired help. The best remembered was a mulatto cook named Joe Robinson. In the early years cooking was done in a basement kitchen with a cavernous fireplace and glowing hearth. The rest of the house, like the buildings at Fort Snelling, was heated by wood-burning stoves. Guests, both Indian and white, were often present, and Sibley's "bachelor den" took on the character of a combined frontier hotel and hunting lodge.[5]

"I have six horses in my stables and I own about twelve dogs, all of which are of the best blood," he told Fred. "I have by far the best horse in the country. He paces a mile in 2 min. 50 sec. And I have already refused $200 for him repeatedly." The animals were, he admitted, "the principal part of my family." Young John Charles Fremont, who stayed at New Hope as a member of Nicollet's mapmaking expeditions in 1838 and again in 1839, recalled especially the two giant dogs, Lion and Boston. Lion, Sibley's pet, guard, and hunting companion, "had the run of the house." The animal was, according to his owner, "half Irish wolf-dog and half Scotch grey-hound ... 29 inches high and exceedingly fierce and fleet."[6]

Sibley's dog, Lion, painted by Charles Deas in 1841

Another guest, the English geologist Featherstonhaugh, chiefly remembered the cloud of tobacco smoke that permeated the trader's quarters. Sibley himself acknowledged "the comfort of my long pipe during the interminable winter evenings of this high latitude," and he also smoked "segars," of which he ordered liberal quantities from New York. The chess set and backgammon board that he sent for in the first winter were supplemented as time passed by a growing library of historical classics like Froisssart's *Chronicles* and Prescott's *Conquest of Mexico* and of popular fiction, including the works of James Fenimore Cooper and the novels of Walter Scott and Edward Bulwer-Lytton. He also subscribed to the *New York American* and later the *National Intelligencer* and read gentlemen's periodicals like the *Spirit of the Times*.[7]

In 1835 the garrison at Fort Snelling was entering upon a period of religious enthusiasm led by Major Gustavus A. Loomis, who had been assigned to the post in the summer of 1834. As Gideon Pond dryly observed: "I would say there was a revival of religion there, but there was none there to revive."[8] The cause was strengthened the following spring when two parties of missionaries appeared at St. Peters, both proposing to carry the gospel to the Dakota Indians. One group, headed by Dr. Williamson, had gone up the Minnesota River to Lac qui Parle at the earnest invitation of Renville. The Reverend Jedediah Stevens and his party stayed near the fort, intending to take over the work of the Pond brothers and start a mission and school at Lake Harriet, beside the village of Cloud Man.

Before they parted company, however, the missionaries, with the ardent support of Loomis and his converts, organized the first Presbyterian church in the area. On Sunday, June 11, 1835, some twenty people met in one of the fort's company rooms to "enter into church covenant." Henry Sibley was one of the four elders they chose. He also served the mission school, acting along with Taliaferro as a supervisory committee to handle admissions of all students and manage any difficult cases of discipline. Additional duties of the two men included conducting examinations and receiving funds. Like its predecessor on Mackinac, the short-lived Lake Harriet school mainly served the mixed-blood children of traders and army officers.[9]

Sibley no doubt attended some of the revival meetings held at the fort by the Bible-thumping Loomis, whom Featherstonhaugh scathingly described as "a long-legged, self-sanctified, unearthly-looking mortal." Whatever Sibley's opinion of the preaching, he found the Major's family "charming," and he maintained a warm and lasting friendship with Loomis's son-in-law, Lieutenant Edmund A. Ogden. Both Loomis and Ogden left Fort Snelling when the troops of the First U.S. Infantry were sent to Florida in the summer of 1837, although Loomis returned in the late 1840s and served briefly as the fort's commander. Sibley's friendship with the Pond brothers also continued, and when the high-handed actions of Stevens drove them to leave the Lake Harriet mission, he offered Samuel Pond a share in the business of the Sioux Outfit. Pond decided against involvement in the fur trade and instead went east to pursue ordination as a minister. After his return he met and married a sister of Mrs. Stevens, and Sibley acted as best man at the wedding.[10]

Sibley's own inner struggle is hinted at in letters to his family, which contain periodic references to his religious faith. Writing to his younger sister Mary in 1835, he concluded several paragraphs of brotherly advice with the words: "Do not say to me that I am always preaching, for I do not discharge half my duty toward any portion of my dear family.... Sinful & weak as I am,

I trust solely upon the grace of God to conduct me through this world of trouble, for my own resolutions are as the early dew which passeth away."[11]

In May 1837 the period of prosperity that had buoyed Sibley during his first years as head of the Sioux Outfit came to an abrupt close. A financial panic brought near collapse of the nation's banking and monetary system, followed by years of depression and stagnation. Along the Upper Mississippi, however, the first impact was cushioned by treaty money.

The summer and fall of 1837 saw the signing of three major treaties by which the Ojibwe, Dakota, and Winnebago tribes gave up all their land east of the Mississippi. The American Fur Company anticipated collecting substantial amounts in fulfillment of Indian debts accrued from earlier years. The Ojibwe treaty was signed at Fort Snelling on July 29; the Dakota and Winnebago treaties, both negotiated in Washington, were signed on September 29 and November 1. Taliaferro, infuriated by witnessing the influence of traders at the Ojibwe treaty council, managed adroitly to assemble a delegation of Mdewakanton chiefs (the only Dakota band involved) and embarked with them on a steamboat without prior announcement. He hoped thus to evade the traders, but Sibley, Bailly, Stambaugh, Brown, and half a dozen others arrived in Washington hot on his heels.[12]

The custom of government payoffs to traders as a part of Indian treaties was already becoming infamous. The fur trade, by its very organization and the fact that it operated entirely on credit, made business losses appear on the books as Indian debts. Although Indian people often challenged traders about the sums owed, they generally recognized the existence of tribal debts at the local level. As often as not the traders themselves were relatives by marriage and in some degree a part of the tribal community. Thus small traders and Indians united in demanding that the losses be compensated when treaties were signed. Larger firms exploited these demands to leverage government money. In the Dakota treaty of 1837 an amount of $90,000 was allowed to pay traders. This represented a little more than a third of the debts they had claimed.

The trip east—Sibley's first experience in Washington, as well as with treaty-making—gave him a chance also to pay his long-postponed visit to Detroit. He stayed with his family there until the end of February 1838. When he returned to St. Peters the three treaties were still before Congress, and times were growing harder in the Upper Mississippi country. Fur prices had fallen, and for muskrat—the staple of Sibley's trade—there was no market at all. The previous year's catch remained in a New York warehouse, and, as Crooks told him, "not even a nominal value can be named."[13]

Soon after his return Sibley also learned that trouble had exploded among the turbulent Sisseton on the far western edge of his trading area. Louis Provençalle, Jr., who had been hired the previous summer for work at Lake Traverse, had been slain while trading for the company near the James River, and Brown had been shot and wounded at the post itself. A number of the company's horses and oxen had also been killed or stolen. Sibley retaliated at once with a decision to close all posts west of Lac qui Parle. Dousman agreed emphatically. "Burn all of the buildings, fences, etc. immediately and withdraw everything from there and … establish no new post this year," Dousman wrote. "Besides punishing the dogs, no new post can pay the expense at the present rate of furs." By July Sibley had in fact closed all but three of his outlying stations.[14]

Word that the treaties had been ratified reached the Upper Mississippi that month. As Dousman remarked, "otherwise we were gone coons." Months dragged on, however, before they received payment, and the amounts remained uncertain. Special commissioners had to be appointed to allot the money, and the books of each claimant were examined. A divisive complication lay in the fact that some of the credits predated the reorganization of the American Fur Company and disputes developed between those whose interests lay with the "old" and the "new" firm. Sums assigned to Rolette's old Upper Missippi Outfit would go to him alone, while payment for Indian debts incurred after 1834 would go to the Western Outfit and be split among the partners. In September Dousman wrote to Sibley from Prairie du Chien, where the commissioners were deliberating: "I have my hands full in looking after all the little intrigues & log rolling which is going on." Elsewhere the same was true. Robert Stuart, by then living in Detroit, had a claim on payments to the old firm and, still smarting at his exclusion from the new partnership, complained loudly of sharp dealing.[15]

Crooks, meanwhile, took the opportunity to close the books and reach a current settlement with the various outfits. He also did some reorganizing, including a thorough shakeup in the management of the Northern Outfit, headquartered at La Pointe. In December 1838, he made a grueling cross-country trip from La Pointe to St. Peters, then he and Sibley traveled together on the river ice down to Prairie du Chien. From there Sibley wrote to his father, "I shall know in a few days how I stand in the world, which will gratify me much, for hitherto such has been the uncertainty of our securing our debts &c. that we could form no estimate of what would be the profits of our Outfit."[16]

The end was not yet in sight, however. Distribution under the Winnebago treaty (by far the most lucrative of the three) became mired in politics and

charges of corruption, and it seemed that payment would be held up indefinitely. Writing again in April to Solomon, who was apparently in financial
straits as a result of the hard times, Henry complained that "we shall suffer
much embarrassment ourselves, as we could not anticipate that the Govt.
would reject the decisions of its own agents." Then he added: "I think it prob-
able now that I shall leave this country next year, if I can arrange my affairs
satisfactorily, and sell out my investment without much sacrifice."[17]

Such was not to be the case. Hearings on the Winnebago claims dragged
on through the year and in November 1839 Crooks again attended to the uncertain affairs of the Western Outfit at Prairie du Chien. Since all plans had
to be made and orders placed a full year in advance, it was agreed to extend
the partners' original contract another year. Back at St. Peters, Sibley wrote
to his father: "I am to remain until 1 August 1841, when I promise you that if
I [am] alive I will go home for good and all. I would not have made any
arrangement of the kind if I had not become utterly discouraged from the dismal state of affairs in Michigan, from attempting to go into business next year
in Detroit as has always been my fixed determination."[18]

Payment of traders' debts was not the only advantage offered by treaties. It
was customary for tribes to demand special grants for mixed-blood relatives
who could not legally benefit from the main provisions of a treaty. This was
of keen interest to the American Fur Company, since nearly all its employees
and subsidiary traders were either of mixed blood themselves or had mixed-
blood families. And most of them owed the company money.

The three treaties of 1837 all included sizable grants for "half-breed" relatives of the tribes, and determining who was eligible to receive them and
how they were to be distributed was another lengthy process clouded with
ambiguities and fraud. Even as the Dakota treaty was being negotiated in
Washington, Sibley presented to the commissioner of Indian affairs a petition from more than a hundred mixed-bloods praying that the benefits
granted under a previous treaty "be equally divided between all connected by
blood with the Sioux and not those alone who are strictly half-breeds."[19] This
was an issue of particular importance to men like Bailly, Brown, and Faribault, whose wives were mixed-bloods and whose children had a quarter or
less Dakota heritage.

Already, Sibley had apparently forged bonds of trust that reached through
the little community that existed uneasily in the middle ground between Indian and Euro-American worlds. In the summer of 1838 he received nearly
twenty powers of attorney from mixed-blood families, enabling him to collect for them their share of the $110,000 allowed by the treaty to those "hav-

ing not less than one quarter Sioux blood." More personal friendships were formed also. In January 1837, Sibley hired Angus Anderson, one of several trusted mixed-blood clerks. Anderson served as bookkeeper-clerk and managed the household at New Hope during his employer's absence in the East from October 1837 to March 1838. In June 1838, Sibley signed a similar contract with Alexander Fairbault, son of Jean Baptiste, who would become a hunting companion, business associate, and lifelong friend. Another addition to the roster of clerks was William H. Forbes, the son of a Canadian trader who had retired to Montreal. Young Forbes was hired by the American Fur Company in 1837 and assigned to Sibley at St. Peters, where he remained for ten years. In 1846 Forbes married Agnes Faribault, a daughter of Alex, and the next year took charge of Sibley's store in St. Paul.[20]

Sibley acquired one more connection with the mixed-blood community at about the same time. It was with Joseph Jack Frazer, whose father had been a British trader and whose mother was a mixed-blood half sister of Wacouta, chief of the Red Wing band. Left with his mother, Frazer had been reared among his uncle's people, and by his early thirties he had become renowned as a killer of both men and animals. Then he decided to claim a place in his father's world. In the transition he was aided by another uncle, the Wabasha trader Augustin Roque.

While working for Roque in the summer of 1838, Frazer returned two of Sibley's horses that had strayed and been caught some distance down the Mississippi. At New Hope, he was interviewed through an interpreter by Sibley's guest, the English writer Marryat, who marveled at the record of twenty-eight scalps taken by this "fine intellectual-looking man." Marryat was also somewhat taken back by Frazer's desire to add the scalp of his father because of his anger at having been abandoned. Dousman had a particular interest in Frazer, and it may have been on his recommendation that Sibley engaged the mixed-blood the following year to accompany himself and Fremont on an extended hunting expedition. The association started then lasted until Frazer's death in 1869.[21]

Sibley's long and complex relationship with the Dakota people themselves began in frustration. In 1835, at the end of his first summer in their country, he wrote to his sister:

Jack Frazer

"My house is filled with Indians, each one pestering me for articles which I will or will not give them as the case may be.... Of all savages I believe the Sioux have the least reason in their composition, otherwise they would not attempt to drive a man mad as I believe they sometimes intend to do me."[22] As time passed his dealings with them eased. He became fluent in their language and familiar with their ways. There remained, however, the clash between the paternalism of the missionaries and of men like Taliaferro and the roughshod equality with which small traders and Indians faced one another—each trying to gain an advantage, yet each dependent on the other in a business that supported both.

To missionaries the Indian was a child to be educated and protected. It appeared to them, as it did to Lewis Cass, that any measure that destroyed the native culture and substituted that of Europe would ultimately benefit Indians themselves. No question existed in their minds as to the superiority of the European race—or at least of its civilization and religion. To traders the Indian was both an ally and an adversary, and in any case a being whose power must be respected and whose ways must be learned. When accused of cheating innocent Indians, most would have responded like old Joe Rolette, who snorted: "*Oui, monsieur,* I've spent my whole life trying to cheat an Indian and haven't yet succeeded."[23]

Defending the character of traders from the distance of fifty years and a transformed society, and conscious of the racial and cultural bigotry of the 1880s, the general had chosen his words with care. Even so, he placed himself at a distance from the image by writing in the third person:

> There was a peculiar fascination in such a career...What constituted that fascination would be difficult to describe, except upon the theory that the tendency of civilized man when under no restraint is towards savagery as the normal condition of the human race.... One was liberated from all trammels of society, independent, and free to act according to his own pleasure.... Moreover, he was regarded by the savages among whom he was thrown, as their superior, their counselor, and their friend. When sickness prevailed in their families, he prescribed for them, when hungry he fed them, and in all things he identified himself with their interests and became virtually their leader.[24]

Sibley's own passion for hunting and for the risks and majesty of unspoiled nature proved one of his strongest links with the Dakota. By 1839 he was preparing to spend more than two months on a fall hunt with a nearby village, sharing their camp life, their hardships, and their dangers. He had hoped to make such an expedition in 1838 in company with Captain Martin Scott, a noted hunter and sharpshooter stationed at the fort, but circumstances apparently prevented it. Business with treaty commissioners and Sibley's lingering "liver complaint" may have interfered. Moreover, his boyhood friend, Alfred Brush, whom he had hoped would join them, proved unable to leave Detroit.[25] The next summer, however, a ready companion appeared in the person of Fremont, the young lieutenant of topographical engineers assigned by the army as an aide to Joseph Nicollet.

Nicollet had made his headquarters at Fort Snelling for more than a year in 1836 and 1837, establishing warm friendships with both Taliaferro and Sibley. He returned again in 1838 with U.S. Army sponsorship to map western Minnesota, and in 1839 he and Fremont went up the Missouri River from St. Louis, exploring the country as far north as Devils Lake and descending the Minnesota River to Fort Snelling. They arrived in mid September, and Nicollet immediately departed by steamboat for St. Louis. Fremont and Sibley, meanwhile, made preparations for their adventure with the Dakota.[26]

They were to accompany the people of the Black Dog village to the upper reaches of the Cedar River (then called the Red Cedar), which was in a broad buffer zone of neutral ground that had been created by treaty in 1830 to reduce clashes with the Sac and Fox tribe to the south. Since no permanent settlements existed there, game tended to be plentiful, but venturing into it was risky. The Dakota welcomed the presence of the white party as potential protection against enemy attack, and Sibley tried without success to notify the Sac and Fox through their government agents that the expedition was a peaceful one. Faribault, Forbes, and Frazer accompanied Sibley and Fremont, and they brought along two Canadian voyageurs with carts to carry their gear and make their camps.[27]

It was almost the end of September when the long line of Indian families—men, women, children, horses, and dogs—headed toward what is now northern Iowa. Baggage and very young children were loaded on *travois*, and women led the horses that pulled them. They traveled nine or ten miles each day and made camp at a prearranged spot where wood and water were at hand. There they were met by the hunters of the band, who had fanned out on horseback, looking for game. Forty years later Fremont could recall the "bright fires, where fat venison was roasting on sticks before them, or stewing with corn or wild rice in pots hanging from tripods." Women tended to the fires and cooking, and children rolled about on the ground. The party of "gentlemen" shared a large buffalo-skin lodge, which, according to Sibley "was new and as white as snow."

After nearly two weeks Sibley and his party grew tired of the slow march and, leaving Forbes with the cart-drivers and the Indians at Pine Island on the Embarrass (now Zumbro) River, they turned west in search of buffalo.

Dakota Indians traveling with horses and travois

They found none, and other game also proved scarce. Two days later they encountered a near disaster. Awakened in the middle of the night, they saw a towering line of flames headed toward them across the prairie. "We had just time to secure our horses and encircle our camp with fire when the flames dashed by us with the speed of a race horse," Sibley recalled. "Nothing can surpass the magnificence of a prairie on fire at night when under the influence of a gale of wind. The entire horizon appears like one sheet of flame, and the maddened element, with its loud roar and fantastic shapes, leaping and bounding hither and thither, is well calculated to terrify the boldest man."

After another five days of hunting, the party rejoined the Indians near the headwaters of the Cedar River and found that nearly half the band had returned home. Although the rest declared that they would accompany Sibley into the contested ground, he feared for the safety of such a small party and with Fremont and Frazer, the carts, and the two drivers, left the expedition and headed southeast for Prairie du Chien. Fremont hoped to board a steamboat for St. Louis before the river froze, and Sibley was scheduled to meet there with Crooks and his business partners. After much wading of swollen streams and a close encounter with a war party of Sac and Fox, they reached the Mississippi just above Prairie du Chien on November 2.

Alarmed for the Dakota band as well as for his friends Faribault and Forbes still encamped on the Cedar River, Sibley immediately sent a messenger to warn them of the Sac and Fox. His worry only increased when word arrived that the latter had attacked a party of Winnebago and slain fourteen.

After the parley with Crooks, he with the two carts and drivers headed back to the Cedar River, where his friends, alarmed also for him, welcomed him with relief. Two or three days later they left the Dakota and started the two-hundred-mile trek to St. Peters over prairie that was alternately muddy and snow-covered. The carts were useless in both deep snow and mud, so they loaded their belongings on the horses and walked most of the way. They arrived after an absence of just seventy days.

As winter closed in and the year 1840 opened, Sibley wrote to Eliza Trowbridge, who, like her brother Charles, was one of his closest confidantes. It was a long, reflective letter, in which humor struggled with despondency.[28] Referring to his recent hunting trip, he told her that for details of it she would have to read a sketch he had agreed to write for a sporting magazine. The piece appeared two years later in the *Spirit of the Times* under the pen name "Hal, a Dacotah."

He told Eliza of the decision made at Prairie du Chien to stay one more year, and what it had cost him: "I have spent the flower of my life in the Indian country, in the hope of obtaining a competency. . . . I am fatigued almost to death by the vexation & trouble inseparable from the trade with the Indians." He returned also to the subject of a wife. Apparently he had courted and been refused during his visit in Detroit two years earlier, and "the monosyllable No! sounds so frightful to my ears, that I am half persuaded not to risk where even a possibility might exist of my hearing the hateful word again. . . . At New Hope we cannot boast of any but copper-colored beauties . . . and I have half a mind sometimes to take one to wife (as I would not meet with a refusal!) were it not that a certain Mrs. Sibley in your neighborhood might strenuously object to having a red daughter in law, be she never so pretty."

Concluding, he said: "You see that Henry Sibley is Henry Sibley still. Full of his nonsense and therefore by no means so ill as to require nursing. . . . I can say in all sincerity that my Red Cedar trip has cured me completely as far as my bodily health is concerned although the 'inner man' is somewhat worn down by a constant succession of cares and anxieties."

Care and anxiety continued through the spring, for, as Dousman said, "Times have never been so hard on this river since it was settled." For a while it looked as though Sibley's desire to leave might be fulfilled. When he and Stambaugh closed out the sutlership at Fort Snelling in the spring of 1839, they were succeeded by the trader Benjamin Baker. Within the year Baker died, and his creditors, the St. Louis commission house of Chouteau & Mackenzie, engaged Sibley to take inventory and protect their interests. The firm was apparently so well satisfied with his work that they offered to bring him to St. Louis as a partner in their business. Sibley immediately wrote to Crooks, who left to Rolette and Dousman the decision of whether to release him from his contract. They refused. The disappointment must have been bitter, for Sibley wrote to his father that it was "a most advantageous offer … with an almost certainty of making a fortune if my life was spared a few years." Added to his depression that summer was the return of illness in the form of ague and also a persistent eye infection.[29]

He had already laid plans for another hunting trip to the Cedar River in the fall, but this one proved to be far more than a sporting excursion. Turning his back on the frustrations of business and the demands of the civilized world, he lived for nearly four months with the Dakota, from October 1840 through part of January 1841. Forbes remained in charge at New Hope. Alex Faribault accompanied Sibley at first, but left to attend to a new post that he and Laframboise were opening on the Blue Earth River. A pair of Canadian voyageurs stayed with Sibley to handle a cart with his supplies, and as always he was followed by his two favorite dogs.[30]

Although still risky, the situation in the neutral ground had changed. Treaties with the Winnebago in 1832 and 1837 had called for their removal to that area. They were understandably reluctant to become a human buffer between the Sac and Fox and the Dakota, but at last in 1840 the army undertook to move them forcibly. The government assured them of its protection and was proceeding to build a fort on the Turkey River. Meanwhile, game was still plentiful, and Dousman urged Sibley to have his Indians take advantage of this and hunt on the Cedar River throughout the winter.[31]

About 150 men with their families from several villages agreed to take part in the venture. As customary, the expedition was organized in a quasi-military style, with fixed rules of conduct and a small group of "soldiers" delegated to enforce them. Infringement brought swift and certain punishment. Sibley was subject to the code like all others, and at one point along the journey south, he unwittingly broke the prime rule of remaining within the boundary defined for hunting. His fur cap was snatched away, and his fine buffalo-skin lodge was threatened with destruction. Too proud to incur the further disgrace of resisting the discipline of the march, he endured chilly ears for the rest of the day. His lodge was saved that night by making gifts of food and tobacco to the soldiers.[32]

Once arrived at the Cedar River, the Indians chose a site for a permanent camp and built a makeshift picket of poles and branches to fortify it. The women, children, and elderly stayed at the camp, cooking, collecting fuel, and attending to the endless chores of preserving meat and processing skins. The younger men scoured the surrounding country for deer, elk, bear, and whatever else they could take. Those less able-bodied set traps for beaver and otter. Successful hunters claimed the skin and choice parts of their kill; the rest was divided equally. Unlike some winters the Dakota could remember, when whole camps were reduced to starvation, it proved to be a season of plenty. Sibley estimated that more than two thousand deer and fifty or sixty elk were brought in, along with many bear and a few buffalo.

He himself hunted with the others, except on Sunday—or what he thought was the Sabbath. That he had lost count of the days became clear when he made a solitary trip to the Turkey River, some twenty miles away, to check on the progress of the new Fort Atkinson. Arriving there, he found an acquaintance who failed to recognize him as the long-haired, bearded huntsman emerging from the woods. Asking why the men were working on Sunday, he was told that it was in fact Thursday.

There was only one major alarm during the winter. It occurred when the leader, Little Crow, took all of the men with him on a quick foray to the forks of the Cedar, some forty miles away. Sibley, unaware of the plan, had been on a solitary hunt. Returning, he found himself and five old men left to guard the camp. A stranger had been seen skulking in the woods, and a night of preparedness followed. At one point some of the sharp-eyed women who were on watch reported figures moving, and all guns were fired in an effort to make the place seem well defended.

Apparently the strategy worked. Scouting the next day, Sibley found the tracks of a large group of men with horses who had withdrawn in the night. He at once sent a young boy from the camp to find the Dakota men and tell them to return immediately. When they arrived, he reproached Little Crow with disregard for safety of the camp. The leader acknowledged that he had probably taken an unjustified risk.

Some time in early January, Sibley and his two men left with the cart and headed for Prairie du Chien. From there they were able to travel on the frozen Mississippi back to St. Peters. The fall and winter had given Sibley a fund of memories and experiences that fueled further essays from the pen of Hal, a Dacotah, as well as later reminiscences by General Sibley.[33]

Although neither writer ever hinted at the fact, Sibley's relationship to the people whose name he appropriated had in fact deepened during the short days and snowy winter nights on the upper reaches of the Cedar River. To increased understanding was added the irrevocable bond of kinship, for in August 1841 a young woman of the Mdewakanton band bore him a child. Whether the liaison began during his long sojourn of the previous winter is uncertain, but it seems likely. Her name has been translated as Red Blanket Woman, and her father was Bad Hail, a headman of the Black Dog band, who, with his family, accompanied the expedition. Many stories have been told about Red Blanket Woman, but only two facts are clear—that her relationship with Sibley did not continue, and that she died only a few years after their daughter's birth.[34]

In February 1842, Forbes, again in charge at New Hope, wrote to Sibley, who was in Washington: "<u>She</u> is well and the <u>stranger</u> [emphasis in original]. I went out there the other day. They are camped about 4 miles back from this place by the side of a lake out there with Blk Dog's Band. She behaves well, only once she joined in the Scalp Dance, when I sent her word if she did so again I would act the soldier."[35]

The scalp dance, performed exclusively by women, was a ritual of mourning for those slain in battle and centered around the trophies that compensated for the loss of Dakota life. It often continued for days. Forbes's warning reflected Euro-American distaste for what was regarded as a particularly savage custom.

His concern apparently extended to having the child baptized, probably at some point during Sibley's long absence in the East that year. Father Augustin Ravoux noted in the record of St. Peters parish the baptism of "Helene," born August 28, 1841. No parents are named, but Forbes, who was a Catholic, served as her godfather. Sibley's own conviction of the need to give his daughter a Christian upbringing no doubt played a role in his decision at some point during the next three or four years to take Helen from her Dakota relatives and place her with the family of William R. Brown and his wife Martha. Brown was a farmer for the Methodist mission that had been established at Red Rock (now Newport). There Sibley provided for the child's support and continued to keep in touch with her. Whether this new tie influenced his decision to remain in the Minnesota country cannot be known, but after 1841 he made no further mention of intending to leave.[36]

· 6 ·

Turning Points

*T*HE YEARS 1841 AND 1842 were a pivotal time in the life of Henry Sibley. Not only did they bring the experience of fatherhood and with it a new dimension in his relationship to the Dakota, they also held out the flickering promise of a dramatically different future for the Upper Mississippi River country.

Ratification of the 1837 treaties, which extended white settlement to the east bank of the Mississippi, had set in motion a whole series of events. Iowa Territory, organized in 1838, took in the western part of what had been Wisconsin Territory. Thus Sibley's post became a part of Clayton County, Iowa, while the bluffs across the Mississippi were in Crawford County, Wisconsin. Distant and tenuous as it was, civil authority became for the first time a reality in the area. Sibley himself became a justice of the peace as he had been in earlier years at Mackinac. Across the river Joe Brown, returning east after the Lake Traverse post was closed in 1838, had established a farm and a small settlement on Grey Cloud Island. Early in 1839 Brown was commissioned a justice of the peace for Crawford County, and in 1840 he was elected to the Wisconsin territorial legislature.[1]

In 1839 Lawrence Taliaferro retired, ending his twenty-year tenure as Indian agent. Meanwhile, the military authorities at Fort Snelling were reacting to their decreased isolation. Captain Joseph Plympton, who became commander in 1837 with the arrival of the Fifth Infantry, had taken steps to clarify the boundaries of the military reservation and strengthen army control over it. A survey in 1839 extended the line eastward from the Falls of St. Anthony to include a wide swath of land opposite the fort, which, lying east of the Mississippi River, was now open to white settlement, including whiskey sellers who catered to the troops. Plympton also undertook the unpopular task of clearing out the sizable community of illegal settlers who had been tolerated on the reservation for years. In May 1840 they were forcibly expelled and, retreating downriver, formed the nucleus of the new town of St. Paul.

The 1839 survey line also included the American Fur Company buildings and the community of some fifty people clustered around them, which was by then coming to be called Mendota. The political power of American Fur prevented any immediate move by the Army to oust them, but Sibley himself quickly became aware of the high-handed nature of military authority. He wrote to the governor of Iowa, requesting clarification as to whether civilians living on the military reservation were subject to military or civilian rule. And at this time he became keenly interested in securing government recognition of the unratified agreement negotiated by the fort's first commander, Colonel Henry Leavenworth, which had given the island opposite Mendota to Pelagie Faribault.[2]

The year 1841 opened darkly with Sibley hearing a criminal case as a justice of the peace. It related to the brutal rape of a ten-year-old girl, and although it had actually occurred in Wisconsin, Sibley was called upon, since Brown, the only Wisconsin peace officer closer than Prairie du Chien, was away at the legislature in Madison. Legal trouble also continued over the settlement of Benjamin Baker's estate, although Sibley's part in it no longer involved him in the sutler's store.[3]

Immediately after Baker's death in late 1839 the post of sutler at Fort Snelling had gone to a young Pennsylvanian named Franklin Steele, who had come west to explore the timber business in the St. Croix valley but was open to any opportunity. He had potent political connections with the Democratic administration that was still entrenched in Washington, and he had already established a local reputation for initiative by staking the first claim to

Sibley with unidentified associates,
probably Joseph Rolette, Jr., (standing) and Franklin Steele (left)

the premier waterpower site at the Falls of St. Anthony. The sutling business had also drawn Henry M. Rice, another young opportunist. He had made his way to the Upper Mississippi River country from Vermont by way of Detroit and Sault Ste. Marie. Baker had hired him at Fort Snelling in 1839, and in 1840 Rice had secured the appointment of sutler at the new Fort Atkinson in Winnebago country. There he worked closely with Dousman.[4]

Despite an election that placed the Whigs in power, business conditions in the spring of 1841 did not improve, and it appeared that the contract of the Western Outfit would have to be extended for yet another year. Crooks, however, was negotiating with Pierre Chouteau, Jr., to take over the Upper Mississippi trade, and he was confident that an arrangement could be worked out if the partners themselves would meet with Chouteau. Sibley and Dousman agreed to go to St. Louis as soon as the spring business rush was over. Rolette, whose dominance had been undermined by illness and alcohol, was increasingly excluded from their decision making. Plans for the trip were abruptly cancelled, however, when the electrifying news arrived that the new governor of Wisconsin Territory was on his way to negotiate a treaty for the purchase of Dakota land.[5]

That governor was James Duane Doty, who had parlayed his post as sole judge in western Michigan into a prominent political career when that area became the territory of Wisconsin. He had already served as the territory's delegate to Congress and was appointed governor by William Henry Harrison in the month before the new president's early death. Sibley may have known Doty years before in Detroit and had undoubtedly met him again in Prairie du Chien. Although negotiating a treaty in Iowa would normally have fallen to the governor of that territory, Doty's long experience on the Upper Mississippi recommended him to the secretary of war, in whose department the Indian Office then rested. Doty himself, like his patron Lewis Cass, had been a firm friend of American Fur throughout his career.[6]

The treaty that Doty was chosen so abruptly to negotiate was the final flowering of a dream long held by missionaries and eastern "friends of the Indian." In 1820 the Reverend Jedidiah Morse, commissioned by secretary of war John C. Calhoun to propose a workable and enlightened Indian policy as the country moved west, championed the creation of an all-Indian territory, eventually to become a full-fledged state. The location suggested by Morse was the western part of Michigan, which eventually became Wisconsin. Cass, who was then still governor of Michigan Territory, at least tacitly supported his plan. In 1834, while Cass served as secretary of war, a territory had been created for the southern tribes, but it was far from what Morse had envi-

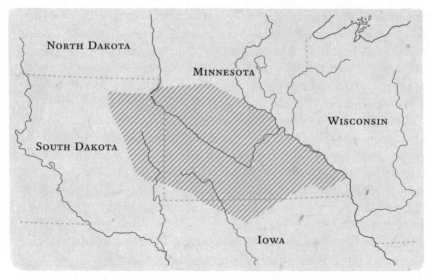

Approximate area (shaded) covered by the proposed Doty purchase

sioned since Congress had repeatedly refused to allow the tribes to form a government there on a par with other territories.

As the country turned its back on Jacksonian Democracy in the election of 1840, the time seemed ripe for carrying out Morse's plan. John Bell, the new secretary of war, had long favored it. Wisconsin, of course, already had thirty thousand white inhabitants, but the Dakota country across the Mississippi offered a feasible alternative. Apparently counting on speed and surprise to execute what amounted to a revolution in U.S. Indian policy, Bell immediately appointed Doty to buy the necessary land from the Dakota on terms that spelled out their settlement in farming communities and the early granting of citizenship. All white immigration was to be barred, and although no mention was made in the treaty of other tribes, Bell's clearly stated intention was to remove all Indians from the northeastern states to the Minnesota valley.[7]

The partners of the Western Outfit were no less taken by surprise than the rest of the country. Only a month elapsed between their first word of the treaty and Doty's arrival at Fort Snelling. Because of the uncertain prospects for the coming year, inventories had been cut to the bone, and goods for the gift-giving that always accompanied treaty ceremonies were not to be had anywhere on the Upper Mississippi. Nevertheless, the governor proceeded immediately to Traverse des Sioux, where the Indian agent had notified the western Dakota bands to assemble.

There, with Alexis Bailly pressed into service as secretary and attended by a handful of soldiers and a second lieutenant from the fort, he concluded a treaty with the Sisseton, Wahpeton, and Wahpekute on July 31, 1841. Sibley and a number of his subsidiary traders and employees were there to give what Doty testified was "indispensable aid" in securing the agreement of the Indians. Included in the aid was Sibley's promise to the Dakota that he would soon supply the goods worth $10,000 that Doty agreed to as gifts. Back at Mendota by August 4, the governor forged a similar treaty with the Mdewakanton and headed downriver, leaving Sibley and Dousman to secure the signatures of Wacouta and Wabasha, who had refused to attend the signing.[8]

The result of this whirlwind trip was an agreement to purchase some thirty million acres, reaching from the Mississippi on the east to the "western declivity" of the Coteau des Prairies, and from the neutral ground on the south to the Crow Wing River on the north. Written into the terms of the treaty was a sweeping scheme for government-assisted "civilization." In addition to providing that no Euro-Americans would be admitted to the territory except those specially authorized by the president, it promised that communities would be formed where roads, mills, schools, and other improvements would be supplied by the government, that each Dakota household would be assisted in establishing itself on a small farm, and that after two years of "settled living" full citizenship would be granted. Meanwhile, the president would appoint agents, a trader for each community, and a governor for the territory.[9]

Breathtaking as the package was in its implications for the country, the immediate interest of the American Fur Company lay with a provision for the payment of tribal debts. Doty's instructions specifically forbade such a clause, but he nevertheless included an amount up to $150,000 for compensating traders, pleading that this was absolutely necessary in persuading the Dakota to sign the treaty. For Dousman, who had bluntly urged Sibley "to have the interpreters and Indians as much under your thumb as you can," it was a gratifying result. He also gloated that Doty's inclusion of the so-called half-breed tract along Lake Pepin, which had been set aside by treaty in 1830, would call for paying off the mixed-bloods, many of whom owed sizable sums to the Western Outfit.[10]

Sibley himself took a broader view. Summing up the results in a letter to Crooks on August 26, he stated: "The provisions of this treaty, I consider to be better calculated for securing the interests of the Indians and of the people in the country than those of any treaty which has been made with the north-western Indians." His enthusiasm may have owed something to the fact that Doty took the liberty of recommending individuals for positions in

the new territory when the treaty should have been ratified. Of twelve
prospective agents and traders he named, nine belonged to the Sioux Outfit,
and regarding the post of superintendent or governor, Doty stated: "Mr.
Henry H. Sibley of this place is the most competent gentleman in every respect with whom I am acquainted, for this station." Nevertheless, Sibley's
long-standing sympathy with the missionary movement and his deepening
personal ties with the Dakota and mixed-blood communities no doubt
weighed heavily in his estimate of the treaty.[11]

Hopes that ratification would proceed as quickly as the negotiations
proved false. The death of President Harrison and the succession of John
Tyler threw the administration and the national Whig Party into disarray. By
the end of summer most of the cabinet had resigned, including the secretary
of war. One of Bell's last acts was to send the Doty treaty to the Senate with a
recommendation for speedy approval. Instead, it was tabled on the closing
night of the session.

The next day Missouri senator Thomas Hart Benton penned a steamy letter to President Tyler: "The whole scheme of the treaty, & the terms of it" he
wrote, "is in my own opinion the most unjustifiable & reprehensible thing of
the kind that has come before the Senate." The reasons for Benton's fury were
clear. He opposed the policy of "civilization" embodied in the treaty, and he
saw immediately that the measure sought to bypass the longstanding laws
and policies governing the formation of new territories. Even more funda-
mental, although never stated in the debates that followed, was the treaty's
threat of admitting racial and cultural pluralism to the governing institutions
of American society.[12]

With action on the treaty postponed until spring, the American Fur Company
turned again to its internal problems. Preceded by Rolette, Sibley and Dousman started for St. Louis in late September, but by the time they reached
Galena they learned that government money for the annuity payments under
the 1837 treaty was on its way. Presence at such payments was critical to the
fortunes of a trader. Therefore the partners hurried on to St. Louis, talked
briefly with Chouteau, and headed upriver again without a new contract, but
with Chouteau's promise to supply their goods for the coming year.[13]

Sibley had hoped to go directly on from St. Louis to Detroit, but it was November before he could get away from his post. Nevertheless, he spent Christ-
mas with his family, and then early in January headed for Washington. This
time he seems to have made no secret of the fact that he had more than Indian treaties on his mind. Emily Mason, sister of a former Michigan governor
and an acute observer of Detroit society, wrote to her father that Sibley "has

left his Indian home to look out for a wife." She had given him letters of introduction to several of her friends, for "He is a fine fellow. You know in what esteem his family are held here, and he is considered the flower of the flock."[14]

Indeed the tall, sober-eyed Sibley, with his gentlemanly manner and his aura of western adventure, found many admirers in Washington, both in political and social circles. By mid-January he was in the capital, lodged at Gadsby's Hotel. Robert Stuart, who was by then superintendent of Indian affairs for Michigan, was also staying there, and Sibley soon reestablished a friendship with his old boss from Mackinac. Stuart apparently took an interest in the social life of the "Dakota Sachem," as he teasingly called the dignified younger man. At one point Sibley protested to his father, "I have got so tired of everything and everybody that I eschew dinner parties, levees, &c and attend no more." Yet Stuart later assured him: "Some of our young ladies have been drooping since your exit [from Washington]. One of them said the other day that you were the finest man she ever saw."[15]

Stuart strongly favored the Dakota treaty despite his coolness to the new management of American Fur, and Sibley assured Crooks that "a perfect understanding exists between us." Crooks himself stayed in New York, mindful that his own presence might backfire in charges of self-serving influence by American Fur, and Doty, fully occupied with infighting among Wisconsin Democrats, remained in Madison. Even Dousman, who had little taste for politics, spent most of his time in the more congenial business milieu of New York. So Sibley became chief manager of the lobbying effort.[16]

The new secretary of war, John C. Spencer, was steadfast in his support of the treaty, and he leaned heavily on Sibley for information about the country and its Indians after being told by Michigan senator William Woodbridge that he could "rely most implicitly" on the trader's words. Benton's impassioned opposition remained the greatest single barrier to ratification, for the Missouri senator chaired the Committee on Indian Affairs, and the bill remained stalled throughout the spring. Even a visit from Chouteau, who, according to Sibley "has more personal influence with the Col. [Benton] than any other man in the country," failed to move the Missouri senator. Sibley apparently enlisted other connections also, including Joseph Nicollet, who was an intimate friend of the Benton family. John Fremont, Sibley's erstwhile hunting companion, had married Benton's daughter Jessie in October 1841 but there is no evidence that Sibley called on him for help. In any case, nothing changed Benton's mind.[17]

The two senators from Michigan favored the treaty, and Woodbridge was especially helpful. The other, Augustus S. Porter, was "uncivil," and Sibley observed to his father: "He is about as fit to be Senator as my Wolf-dog. The latter would be more respectable and would carry more weight." Lewis Cass, who might have wielded decisive influence, was at the time serving as U.S. ambassador in Paris and therefore played no part in the struggle.[18]

A brief break in Sibley's lobbying efforts occurred in late February when he and Dousman met in New York to negotiate at last a new four-year contract with the Chouteau Company. It was signed in the presence of Ramsay Crooks and was to take effect in August. On returning to Washington, Sibley took advantage of his standing with the secretary of war to launch an all-out struggle for securing recognition of the Faribault claim along with an appropriation to purchase it.[19]

The results on both the claim and the treaty effort were discouraging. Even major modifications of the treaty produced no breakthrough, and protests from several army officers stationed on the Mississippi swayed Congress against the Faribault claim. By late March Sibley was lamenting to his father that "I am stuck fast in this abominable place." Dousman had returned to Prairie du Chien, Stuart had left the hotel for other accommodations, and "I am completely alone."[20]

The arrival a few days later of a note from Franklin Steele may have come as a welcome change. Steele was in Pennsylvania on business connected with the sutler's store and also on a matrimonial mission similar to Sibley's. Regarding the latter he reported success and hastily invited Sibley to his wedding in Baltimore on April 14, 1842. With his new bride, Anna Barney, he planned to "leave immediately for the west, my youngest sister accompanying us." In closing, he jokingly reminded Sibley that "you are under obligations to have Mrs. Sibley at St. Peters upon the arrival of Mrs. Steele."[21]

Sibley attended the wedding and no doubt made a point of getting acquainted with Steele's sister, eighteen-year-old Sarah Jane, who would soon be his neighbor at Fort Snelling. Ten days later he was in New York, headed for Detroit, where he made a short stay before returning to the Upper Mississippi. He sent a final plea to the House and Senate on behalf of the Faribaults and left all further lobbying for the treaty in the hands of Stuart.[22]

On August 29, 1842, the Senate refused to ratify the Dakota treaty by a vote of 26 to 2. The overwhelming defeat buried all hopes for a northwestern territory to be governed eventually by Indian citizens. It also buried other hopes. Twelve days later the mighty American Fur Company closed its doors.

The partners of the Western Outfit were not carried under with the failure of the company, since on August 1 their firm had already become the Upper Mississippi Outfit of Pierre Chouteau, Jr., and Company. Returns for the previous year had yet to be settled, of course, and Rolette's real estate in

Prairie du Chien, most of it mortgaged to American Fur, was attached. The old trader may have been past caring, for he died on December 1. With characteristic pessimism, Dousman wailed: "My earnings of 18 years I can consider lost & I am used up root & branch," but he soon recovered his calm. He had done well at the Winnebago annuity payment, and he hastened to point out to Sibley that they were now free to trade with the Ojibwe as well as the Dakota.[23]

Trading with the Ojibwe was probably far from Sibley's mind at the time. He himself had scarcely returned from the east when he was suddenly pulled into a scene of bloody conflict. One June day a young Dakota boy mounted on a sweating horse came pounding down the hill to Mendota. Ojibwe, he shouted, had attacked the village at Kaposia, and a battle was under way. Then he was off to alert the people of Black Dog's village up the Minnesota valley.

Armed and mounted on his fastest horse, Sibley quickly covered the six miles to Kaposia. There he found that fighting was still going on across the river. Changing his horse for a canoe, he arrived at the house of a French-Canadian farmer on the east shore of the Mississippi. There a ghastly sight greeted him. The man's Dakota wife, brained and scalped, lay dying. Following the sound of gunshots, he met a trail of wounded and dead Dakota, along with others retreating from a disastrous encounter in which they had been cleverly ambushed by the enemy. Their loss, according to Sibley, "amounted to twelve or thirteen warriors killed, and nearly thirty wounded." No prisoners were taken, and the Dakota vented their rage and grief on the bodies of the five Ojibwe slain. All of the wounded were personally known to Sibley, who "exhausted my limited surgical skill in aid of the injured." At last, thoroughly sickened and appalled, he rode back to Mendota.[24]

While this was Sibley's first personal encounter with Indian warfare, hostilities had been heating up for some time in the Fort Snelling area. In 1839 vengeance for several murders escalated when young men from Cloud Man's farming village at Lake Calhoun had pursued and attacked a band of Ojibwe returning north to their homes. Fear of reprisal then forced the Dakota to abandon their tilled fields and move to a safer spot in the Minnesota valley. Although Sibley had not witnessed it himself, he talked with many who did, and he later wrote an account of the conflict for the *Spirit of the Times*.[25]

The new atmosphere of violence was a major setback for missionary efforts. With the Dakota gone, the school at Lake Harriet had to be closed, and a related incident brought an end to a mission among the Ojibwe at Pokegama Lake in the St. Croix valley. It seems possible that Sibley's own face-to-face experience with the scenes of killing at Kaposia may have influenced his decision—made shortly after this time—to take his daughter away from her Dakota family and ensure that she was reared as a white woman.

With this event and the summer trading activities behind him, Sibley set out early in October to hunt buffalo in the western country around Spirit Lake. The party consisted only of himself, Jack Frazer, Alexander and Oliver Faribault, and "eight horses and carts in charge of five Canadians and one American." They were gone for twenty-two days, returning earlier than expected.[26]

On the prairie, too, there were signs of change. In an account of the expedition published four years later, Sibley observed: "Where the Elk and Buffalo were to be found by hundreds and by thousands, the hunter may now roam for days together, without encountering a single herd." Accordingly, the party "abstained from useless slaughter" after they had at last come upon the game they sought. Sibley's own eagerness for the manly sport of killing may have been fading, for he described the pristine beauty of the country and wrote: "It seemed almost a sacrilege against Nature thus to invade her solitudes, only to carry with us dismay and death."

Although it gave Sibley inspiration for one of his best articles, the adventure nearly proved fatal. Having found a herd of several hundred buffalo, the hunters gave chase. Sibley, who had the fastest horse, outdistanced the others. He was in hot pursuit of a wounded bull that had left the herd when the animal turned unexpectedly, and the startled horse lunged to one side. Sibley was thrown to the ground almost at the feet of the buffalo "whose eyes glared through the long hair which garnished his frontlet like coals of fire—the blood streaming from his nostrils." For what seemed like an eternity they stared at each other, Sibley clutching his gun and the bull pawing and roaring. At last the animal turned away and Sibley dropped it with a final shot.

"I did not fail to render due homage," he wrote, "to that Almighty Being who had so wonderfully preserved my life. The frequenter of Nature's vast solitudes may be wild and reckless, but he cannot be essentially an irreligious man." Although spared, he still found himself in a bad situation, for one foot was broken, and his horse had followed the disappearing buffalo herd. At last, by repeatedly firing his gun he drew the attention of Jack Frazer, who retrieved the horse and helped him back to camp.

The accident cut short their expedition and left Sibley hobbling on crutches for several months. Despite the enforced inactivity, he spent an industrious winter at the fort courting Sarah Jane Steele. By March the news of his "Steeling" had reached as far as Prairie du Chien, and Dousman protested slyly: "You are a pretty fellow to get ahead of me without saying a word about it." He made no mention of his own romance with Jane Fisher Rolette, their partner's widow, whom he married within two years. Sibley's wedding to Sarah Jane took place at the fort on May 2, 1843, the ceremony performed by the post chaplain.[27]

This personal turning point in the trader's life coincided with trends that were much broader. The rejection of Doty's treaty made it clear that no barriers would ever be raised in the northwest to protect the rights of its native inhabitants, and the decade of the 1840s saw the United States exploding westward across the continent. War with Mexico revived the nation's economy and added vast new territories in the Southwest, while a steady trickle of settlers over the Oregon Trail established an American presence in the Pacific Northwest. Henceforth economic destinies in the Upper Mississippi country lay beyond doubt with steamboats, lumber, and land values, not with the livelihood of Indian and mixed-blood people. If Henry Sibley had fleetingly dreamed of himself as the paternalistic governor of an all-Indian territory, the color of that dream was now quite different.

‧ 7 ‧

The Squire of Mendota

*T*WO FACTORS CAME TOGETHER in the 1840s to change Henry Sibley's lifestyle abruptly. The nature of his business shifted in response to his own independence from American Fur and the new freedom of trade that came with the collapse of the company's monopoly on the Upper Mississippi. At the same time his marriage gave him not only a wife, but also a new circle of family ties that became steadily larger and more influential within the growing white community in the area. Sarah's brother Franklin Steele continued as sutler at Fort Snelling through the next decade, and his family remained close neighbors of the Sibleys. Steele already had plans for consolidating and developing his waterpower claim at the Falls of St. Anthony, but lack of capital delayed the enterprise until 1848. In the meantime he joined Sibley briefly as the trader reorganized the Sioux Outfit and expanded its reach to the west and north.

The business association proved short-lived, and although Frank remained a friend, it was the numerous Steele women who had a daily impact on Sibley's life. Sarah's father, General James Steele, died in 1845, leaving a widow and three unmarried daughters—Abbian (Abbie), Rachel, and Mary— all of whom eventually moved west. In 1847 the Sibley home at Mendota saw its first family wedding, when Abbie married Dr. Thomas Potts of Galena, Illinois. Both were sociable, outgoing people. Two years later they moved to St. Paul, where Potts became one of the town's first physicians and also a firm friend of Sibley. In 1848 Sarah's mother and her other sisters became part of the Sibley household at Mendota, and Sarah noted that she felt "quite like a new being since they came here." A second wedding was held in 1850 when Rachel Steele married Richard W. Johnson, a young lieutenant at Fort Snelling. Mary, who remained single, continued along with her mother to live with the Sibleys for many years.[1]

After the trading season had ended in the fall of 1843, Sibley took his new bride east to meet his family in Detroit and then on to New York, where he had business relating to the settlement of American Fur Company affairs. Time there was short, and Sibley had to leave the selection of a piano for

Sarah and the purchase of books for himself to the kind offices of Ramsay Crooks. All were to be shipped in the spring. The return trip was difficult. Bad weather and worse roads held them up for ten days on the way back to Detroit, and there they waited for travel to improve. The rest of the trip was little better, especially the final lap from Prairie du Chien. As Sibley told his brother, Fred: "It went rather hard with Sarah to be obliged on our way up to sleep in the same room with half a dozen men, and make her toilette in their presence, but she soon became accustomed to it, and even now speaks of her travels as not after all so very unpleasant."[2]

Sarah was by then pregnant with their first child, a daughter born in June 1844. They named her Augusta Ann. A son born early in 1846, whom they named for his father, died within a few months. In 1847 he was followed by a third child and second son, also christened Henry Hastings.

The marriage was on the whole a happy and affectionate one. Both clearly disliked the separations occasioned by Sibley's frequent travel on business and political affairs. While he was away on one such trip in the summer of 1848, Sarah wrote to her sister Abbie that she missed him very much, "the dear good soul," and added, "I love that man more and more every day I live." A few years later, when he was in Washington, she closed a lonely letter to him "hoping that you dream of me nightly."[3]

Meanwhile, Sibley's ties to Detroit were fading. Solomon Sibley died in April 1846. Henry made a trip east the next fall to see his mother and participate in the settlement of family business. Although he remained close to the Trowbridges, a certain coolness developed toward his brothers, Sproat and Alexander. But Henry continued to have a strong affection for his youngest brother Fred and by the end of the 1840s Fred came to Mendota to serve as a clerk and later to manage what remained of the fur business.[4]

Immediately after his marriage, Sibley began a series of alterations and additions to his house, and those continued on into the 1850s as the size of his family and the number of his dependents grew. The business office, noted for its shelves of books and massive oak safe, became a parlor graced by a Brussels carpet and the new piano. Female servants were hired. The dogs were banished to a kennel near the barn to join the horses and a pet elk that Sibley had adopted at some

Sarah Steele Sibley

point. The place was transformed from a hunting lodge into a gracious Victorian family home, bespeaking the social position and gentility of its owner.[5]

The setting in which the house stood was also changing. In 1839 the elder Faribault had built a home similar in style adjacent to Sibley's, and a permanent community was growing around the business buildings that made up the fur post. A Catholic chapel and missionary residence were erected by Father Lucien Galtier in 1842, and in 1847 Sibley financed the construction of a stone church "for Christian people of all denominations." Social life in the little village was knit to that at the fort, where officers and their wives came and went as before. Dakota visitors also continued to be a constant presence, sometimes in large numbers. During the summer of 1848 a solemn medicine ceremony that was held on the hill behind the Catholic church drew Indian families from many miles around for three days and nights of drumming, dancing, and healing.[6]

Although there had been no official resolution as yet of the questions hanging over the status of Mendota on the military reservation, tension between Sibley and the Fort Snelling authorities soon eased markedly. One reason may have been the presence from 1841 to 1848 of Captain Seth Eastman, who served several stints as the commanding officer. Eastman, already becoming a noted artist, and his wife Mary, an aspiring author, were both avid interpreters of Indian life in the West and held Sibley in great respect.[7]

Seth Eastman was a frequent hunting companion, and for Mary, Sibley was a friend and mentor, as well as the source of information and anecdotes about the Dakota. They shared sympathy for the effort of missionaries to pull the tribe away from its traditional way of life, and Mary Eastman developed friendships with a number of Dakota women. If she was aware that both Sibley and her own husband had Dakota daughters, the fact is not recorded. When her book, *Dahcotah; or, Life and Legends of the Sioux Around Fort Snelling,* was published in 1849, she dedicated it to Sibley. He reciprocated with an approving review published in one of the early issues of Minnesota's first newspaper.[8]

Sibley's own literary activity continued throughout the decade of the 1840s. He wrote eight articles and translated a ninth for the *Spirit of the Times,* which billed itself as "the only organ of the American Sporting World." They included both actual hunting exploits and the Indian lore that eastern readers hungered for. Mocking humor and a fashionable tone of self-deprecating superiority assured those readers that Hal, a Dacotah, had not "gone native." He almost never mentioned specific dates or places, giving the pieces a certain mythic quality that embodied the nineteenth-century white man's dream of bold adventure, native guides, big game, and the lovely precision of fine firearms. As a regular and valued contributor, Sibley became a friend of editor William T. Porter, who solicited both his writing and his support for subscriptions. When publishing with Porter he continued to use the pen name of Hal, although for later purposes he moved to the more dignified and romantic pseudonym "Walker In The Pines," conferred on him by an Indian friend.[9]

In "Hunting in the Western Prairies," published in 1847, Sibley returned with a touch of nostalgia to some events of the winter he had spent with the Dakota on the Cedar River. Among other recollections, he described how his dog Lion had attacked and without aid pulled down a large stag. In concluding, he wrote: "My noble Lion! Fleet, staunch, brave, and powerful! Your master will never look upon your like again." Demoted from his status as a household companion, Lion had left Mendota in disgust and spent his final years at Fort Snelling. A memento remained, however, in a life-sized portrait of the dog that his master had commissioned.[10]

Still an avid sportsman, Sibley regularly hunted birds and small game around Mendota, often taking Sarah and some of the other ladies along for an outing, but he made only one more extended expedition. That was in the autumn of 1847. He was accompanied by a party of seven, which included Oliver Faribault and another mixed-blood friend, plus four "voyageurs," a Dakota guide, and "one of my favorite black pointers." The trip took him northwest of Mendota up the valley of the Crow River and across to the Sauk, which he followed as far as Lake Osakis. This bordered an area that was slated to become the new home of the Winnebago tribe.[11]

Although the account he wrote for the *Spirit of the Times* included only hunting incidents, he acknowledged that the expedition was for business as well as pleasure. In addition to the proposed removal of the Winnebago, his business may have touched on the two cart trails the party encountered as they crossed the divide between the Crow and Sauk Rivers. The routes of those trails and the terrain they traversed were becoming important to Sibley, since the main thrust of his trade had already turned toward the northern plains.

The contract that created the Upper Mississippi Outfit in 1842 described its business as "trade with whites and Indians." This reflected the new realities of the country. Attempts at monopoly were futile, and there was also an abrupt loosening of control from above. To outsiders the change was not apparent, and along the Upper Mississippi the "company" continued for years to be known as American Fur. Nevertheless, the stern hand of Ramsay Crooks and the larger interests of the parent firm no longer restrained the traders.[12]

The old system had not been without benefits. When Crooks found it possible to do so, he had held to ethical business practices. Although liquor had always been an element in the fur trade, its excessive use was contrary to the interest of traders. They depended on Indian people as an effective labor force in gathering furs, and when monopoly existed, the pushing of liquor was usually kept to a minimum. Unrestrained competition and the demand for whiskey from a growing white population brought increasing pressure for traders to deal in what was still legally a contraband item. In other respects also, paternalistic elements in the business were crumbling fast.

With Rolette gone, Dousman had reorganized his half of the new outfit and had taken in Bernard Brisbois and Henry Rice as subordinates. Rice, already well acquainted with the Winnebago through his stint as sutler at Fort Atkinson, proved a valuable addition, and Dousman soon developed a friendship with the younger man not unlike his earlier mentorship of Sibley. In the Minnesota valley, Sibley also had acquired an important new associate in the person of Norman W. Kittson. Like Rice, Kittson was no newcomer to the country. Scion of an old Canadian fur trade family, he had signed on with American Fur at the age of sixteen in 1830. While he was delayed at Mackinac on the way west, he made the acquaintance of Sibley, and the trader's recollection of the lad's "sprightliness and intelligence" may have been a factor when Kittson left the company to become a clerk at the Fort Snelling sutler's store four years later. He worked there until 1838, then left for a year of travel and in 1839 returned to take charge of Baker's store at Coldwater. By 1841 he had become a trusted business partner of Franklin Steele.[13]

According to a short-lived arrangement made with Sibley in 1842, Steele and Kittson were to conduct trade on a cash basis at Coldwater and up the Minnesota River at Little Rapids, Traverse des Sioux, and Lac qui Parle. This put them into direct competition with several of Sibley's older traders, including Faribault and Renville. Kittson was to front for the enterprise, and the roles of Steele and Sibley were to be concealed. Chouteau approved the arrangement but was dubious that it could be kept "sub rosa."[14]

Whether secrecy was preserved is not clear, but in the spring of 1843 Steele withdrew and the other two entered into a very different partnership agreement. Under it Kittson was to run all of the Upper Mississippi Outfit's western business. This included supervising Renville at Lac qui Parle, building a new post at Big Stone Lake, and sending traders to locations on the Sheyenne River and the upper James River.[15]

This wholesale resumption of Sibley's trade on the Dakota plains was a response to the rising market for buffalo robes. But in the background lay more than that. Since 1833 American Fur had maintained an extralegal agreement with the British Hudson's Bay Company by which it received an annual payment in return for refraining from competition along the international border. No longer bound by that pact, Sibley was reaching boldly for trade with the large community of Métis (people of mixed French-Cree-Ojibwe ancestry) who made their headquarters at Pembina, where the Red River crossed the boundary.

The Métis, who considered themselves citizens of no country—*gens libre*—moved freely back and forth across the border. With well-organized seasonal buffalo hunts and a keen sense of commerce, they were a better source of robes than the independent bands of Sisseton and Wahpeton Dakota to the west. To the north also lay the rich fur territory of the Hudson's Bay Company, and more than a few Métis and Indian hunters were willing to make an illegal trip across the border to get higher prices for their pelts than the British monopoly would offer. Some of the bolder ones had even organized overland expeditions to the Mississippi, using wooden oxcarts to carry furs and hides, and driving along herds of horses and cattle for which there was no market in the Red River country. In addition to the Métis, there was a large group of Ojibwe at Pembina, an offshoot of the band at Red Lake. These, too, had formerly been off-limits for Sibley's Sioux Outfit, but with the new regime, all noninterference pacts were disregarded.

In the summer of 1844 Kittson started building a post at Pembina. It was a difficult year. The Dakota, already resentful of the wholesale slaughter of buffalo by the Métis, immediately saw through the new plan and threatened to stop any goods from going across their country to the north. In response, a party of Métis traders caught in St. Paul when hostilities erupted, undertook

Red River oxcarts on the prairie near Pembina

to carve out a new eastern trail to Pembina that went through territory controlled by the Ojibwe. Known as the "woods trail," it followed the east bank of the Mississippi to Crow Wing, then crossed and went up the Crow Wing River to Otter Tail Lake, where it turned north along the eastern edge of the Red River valley. Caught in early snowstorms, the exhausted party blazing the woods trail were near starvation when they reached Kittson's new post on the British border, but the Dakota had been successfully checkmated. Henceforth Kittson had little trouble sending his large and well-defended trains of carts along the easier route west of the Red River and down the Minnesota valley. Smaller trains and independent traders preferred to use the safer woods trail.

Through the rest of the 1840s the partners' Red River trade grew and prospered. At first Kittson's carts also collected pelts from the Sheyenne and James Rivers, and from Big Stone Lake, carrying them all to Traverse des Sioux, where they were put on keelboats for the last lap to Mendota. Meanwhile, Kittson's men repaired carts and packed up a new load of goods, also delivered by boat, for their return trip.

As the northern border trade expanded, Kittson found it impossible to manage both that and the Minnesota valley posts as well. Old Joseph Renville died in 1846, and thereafter responsibility for the trade at Lac qui Parle, Big Stone Lake, and farther west on the Dakota plains fell to Martin McLeod, an educated young Canadian who had come to the Minnesota country by way of the Red River settlement. Relieved of the need to collect furs from the Minnesota valley posts, Kittson was free to explore using a shorter route that was growing popular with independent Métis traders. It may have been to reconnoitre this "middle trail," which cut across country from the Upper Red River to Lake Minnewaska and then followed the Crow and Sauk Rivers to the Mississippi, that Sibley visited the area in 1847.[16]

While Kittson organized cart brigades, Sibley had to deal with the outrage of both Ramsay Crooks, who still controlled what was left of the old Northern Outfit of American Fur, and of the Hudson's Bay Company. Unable to stem the tide of trade to the south, the British company appealed to the Crown for troops to help police the border. It was a propitious time, for disputes over the Oregon boundary had produced international tensions. In August 1846, 350 British regulars arrived in the Red River settlement by way of Hudson Bay, prepared to put an end to the smuggling—and presumably to Kittson's business.

The effort backfired. Taken by surprise, the Hudson's Bay Company managers found themselves desperately short of provisions for the new occupying forces and hastily sent buyers overland to the Mississippi for help. One of them fell ill and was cared for at Fort Snelling, while the other went on to St.

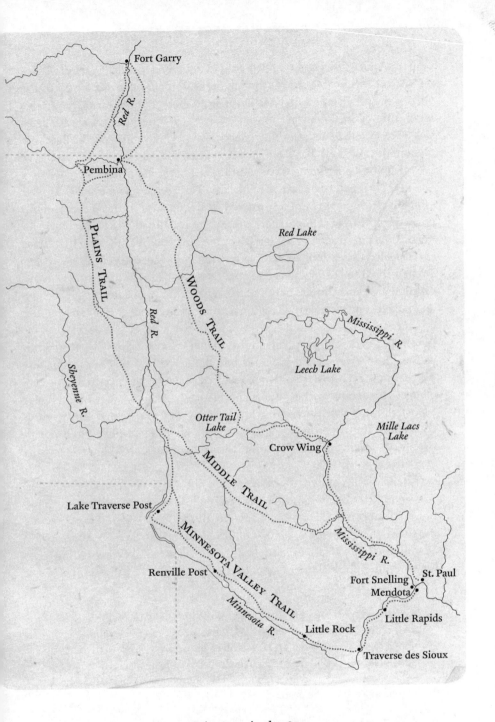

Western Minnesota in the 1840s,
showing major fur posts and routes of the main Red River trails

Louis and purchased supplies. The shipment upriver was delayed by low water, and for a while it looked as though the season might be too late for transporting the provisions to the Red River. With ironic but impeccable courtesy,
Sibley offered his own warehouse to store them if necessary. Other courte-
sies were extended also, and in general, Sibley's relations with the management of the Hudson's Bay Company remained cordial.[17]

At Kittson's post, antagonism continued, but the supply of smuggled furs
was quickly replaced by hard British cash. The Company's annual shipment
of goods through Hudson Bay proved inadequate for meeting the demand
created by the troops. Soon, therefore, Sibley and Kittson were doing a thriving business in supplying the British opposition, and the creaking Red River
carts headed north with everything from champagne to sheet iron stoves. As
at Detroit in the years between 1800 and 1820, so also in the Red River and
Columbia valley frontiers in the 1840s, the ties of Anglo culture, social class,
and business needs overrode national enmities in London and Washington.

In other parts of Sibley's small empire, matters were less hopeful. The condition of the western Dakota bands had deteriorated sharply through the
1840s. In 1844 a measles epidemic resulted in many deaths. Already the decline in population was becoming a problem for traders. In 1845 Laframboise
reported from Little Rock in the Minnesota valley that he had only twenty-
six Indians hunting for him, and four years later the number was down to
twenty. The decimation of elk, buffalo, and other game forced hunters to push
ever farther west.[18]

After a season or two of plenty in 1844 and 1845, when bad weather and
prairie fires to the north drove the buffalo into the James River valley, the
herds disappeared. Drought and a failure of the corn crop in 1846 worsened
the situation, and in the years that followed, hunger stalked the Sisseton and
Wahpeton. Mary Eastman, touched by tales relayed to Fort Snelling, portrayed in her book *Dahcotah* a pathetic but perhaps all-too-typical scene
among the Sisseton:

> Starvation forces the hunters to seek for the buffalo in the depth of winter.
> Their families must accompany them, for they have not the smallest portion
> of food to leave with them. . . . The children have hardly strength to stand; the
> father places one upon his back and goes forward; the mother wraps her dead
> child in her blanket, and lays it in the snow; another is clinging to her, she has
> no time to weep for the dead.

Traders like McLeod and Kittson had little choice but to extend credit in the
form of food. Simple humanity was only one reason; they had to do so if they
wanted hunters to bring in pelts the next year.[19]

Among the Mdewakanton, annuities from the 1837 treaty cushioned the decline of game. Some enterprising individuals found that trading with the western bands offered a profitable option, for the Mdewakanton could now obtain whiskey and other goods at St. Paul and elsewhere along the Mississippi's eastern bank. Being Dakota themselves, they were bound by no government regulations. Leadership continued to shift. The aging Cloud Man, who had refused to take part in war with the Ojibwe, lost influence in his village after it was moved to the Minnesota valley in 1839, and gradually the people merged with Good Road's band. Down the Mississippi, a younger Wabasha had succeeded his father in 1835, but the most dramatic change came at Kaposia. There the influential Big Thunder was killed in an accident in 1845.

Sibley, a longtime friend, brought the Fort Snelling surgeon to the chief's bedside as he lay dying. Together with Alex Faribault, Sibley and the doctor witnessed Big Thunder's charges to Taoyateduta, his oldest son and chosen successor to the title of Little Crow. Taoyateduta, a friend of Jack Frazer, was, like Frazer, known for a roving eye, prowess at hunting, and a disregard for the authority of tribal elders. Strong willed and restless, he had gone from Kaposia to live with the Wahpekute, and, leaving a family among them, had moved on to Lac qui Parle, where he joined the community around Renville's post and married into a prominent Wahpeton family. From the missionary Gideon Pond, Taoyateduta learned some English and how to read in the Dakota language, but he was no convert to Christianity. In 1845 he was still based at Lac qui Parle, although he had been one of those carrying on trade with Dakota groups as far west as the James and even the Missouri River.[20]

The father urged his son to abandon his wayward lifestyle and reckless habits and set an example for the tribe. He also urged the inevitable need for accommodating to the ways of Euro-Americans. However, when Taoyateduta returned from Lac qui Parle in the spring of 1846 to make good his succession as headman at Kaposia, his presence was immediately challenged by two of his half-brothers. A bloody confrontation followed. Although desperately wounded, Taoyateduta survived to take the ancestral name of Little Crow and see his rivals executed.[21]

One of the first initiatives of the new Little Crow was to invite the missionary, Dr. Thomas Williamson, to move from Lac qui Parle to Kaposia. Williamson complied and opened a school in the village, which Little Crow attended for a short time and to which he sent several of his children. The school faced deep-rooted opposition, however, among the village people, and controversy soon erupted as to whether it was being supported by education funds promised to the tribe in the 1837 treaty. The nonpayment of those funds had become a sore point among the Mdewakanton, and they were suspicious and resentful that the missionaries might be receiving the band's money directly from the government without Dakota consent. Seeing his popularity imperiled, Little Crow soon withdrew support from the mission school and turned again to competing with the established traders—a form of cultural accommodation that found little approval among his Euro-American neighbors.[22]

Sibley continued to be supportive of the missionaries and their efforts, although not always uncritical of their methods. On their part, they regularly sought his counsel and help. As for government Indian policy, Sibley's disgust with it had been festering since the defeat of the Doty treaty. Like most nineteenth-century reformers, he saw the future of Indian people as a stark choice between death and "civilization"—or what a later generation would call "acculturation." By the late 1840s he was advocating the extension of U.S. laws over the tribes of the Northwest "so as to secure them in life and property." The purpose was not only to foreclose intertribal warfare. Without legal rights to property, missionaries argued, the transition from an economy based on purely communal values to one based on individual ownership and land development was nearly impossible. At some point in these years Sibley contemplated publishing an article critical of U.S. Indian policy. He started to draft one, but it was never completed.[23]

Sibley's growing convictions led to a gradual parting of the ways with his partners over the role of traders in treaty-making and a definite cooling of his relationship with Dousman. This came to a head over the proposal for a second removal of the Winnebago. Political pressure to get rid of the tribe had been mounting in Iowa as the territory struggled toward statehood through the early 1840s. The "permanent" home to which the Winnebago had been moved from Wisconsin lay within the boundaries of the new state, and when these were finalized with the admission of Iowa in 1846, another treaty was already in the making. In October 1846, a few selected tribal leaders signed an agreement that their people would move north to an unspecified tract between the Dakota and Ojibwe. Both Rice and Dousman were active in engineering the treaty, and it confirmed the suspicions of those who charged traders with manipulating the process for their own benefit.[24]

The treaty was contingent on securing land from either the Dakota or Ojibwe tribes—a task that the Winnebago leaders entrusted to Henry Rice. Dousman must have counted on Sibley to persuade the Dakota. If so, he was disappointed, for Sibley opposed the placement of the Winnebago as a buffer between the two tribes and hoped to secure Lewis Cass's influence against it. In the course of his trip east that winter, following his father's death, Sibley went on to Washington. Dousman probably suspected his intention, for there was an unusually sharp tone in the letter he wrote urging Sibley to get back to Mendota in time to help Rice with negotiations for the land. Congress ratified the treaty in January. The Dakota remained firmly opposed to any sale, but Rice was able to persuade the Ojibwe to give up a tract west of the Mississippi between the Watab and Crow Wing Rivers.[25]

Sibley expressed his feelings on the Winnebago question in a letter to Trowbridge the following autumn: "These poor fellows will be thrust between the powerful contending tribes of Sioux and Chippewas, and I fear they will fare badly." Then he went on to say, "The whole policy pursued by the Govt. toward the Western Indians generally, has a tendency to destroy them, and that speedily. They dare not avow this as their object,... but by persisting in a course which they have been repeatedly warned must end in the extinction of these tribes, they show how little real regard they have for their welfare."[26]

Reluctantly, in the summer of 1848 the Winnebago began to make the move. Even with Rice's active persuasion, it took Eastman and a company of infantry from Fort Snelling to get most of them up the Mississippi. Much was at stake for the traders. The treaty allowed $40,000 for the payment of tribal debts and the location of a new home, plus another $40,000 for removal costs and subsistence during the first year. Most of that amount would eventually go to Dousman and Rice.

Dousman's principal business for years had been with the Winnebago, and since the partners' four-year contract with Chouteau expired in 1846, he had opted to withdraw from the fur trade and concentrate his attention on an expanding empire in steamboats, land, and eventually railroads. The Winnebago trade was to be taken over by Rice and Brisbois. Sibley made a separate two-year agreement with Chouteau for his Dakota and Red River trade.[27]

During the following year, while handling the affairs of the Winnebago, the energetic Rice laid the groundwork for controlling the Ojibwe trade of the Upper Mississippi and Lake Superior. In the early summer of 1848 he proposed to Sibley that they unite in one organization to be known as the Northern Outfit and to combine the Dakota, Winnebago, and Ojibwe trade. A new partner, Sylvanus B. Lowry, was added to handle the Winnebago under Rice's supervision, while Rice himself dealt with the Ojibwe. Brisbois was relegated to the dwindling trade in central Wisconsin and south of Lake Pepin. The Chouteau Company, which may have been the principal force behind the new arrangement, held a half interest in the firm and the others each a sixth. It was a move that Sibley had reason to regret.

The fact that profitable trade with the Indian tribes would soon end had been clear for some time, and Sibley had long since begun to extend his business activities into other areas. As early as 1837 he and traders William Aitken and Lyman Warren had made a contract with Ojibwe of the St. Croix valley to cut timber along the Upper St. Croix and Snake Rivers. When this was superseded by the treaty of 1837, the three joined with Dousman in building a sawmill at the falls of the Chippewa, although Aitken soon withdrew. The "Chippewa Mills" went into operation in 1840, but clearly none of the partners was adept at managing a lumber business. When Dousman finally negotiated its sale in 1845, he sighed: "Thank God it is off our hands."[28]

Steamboats were more rewarding. Until 1847 boats were individually owned and ran irregularly in response to the demands of business and the cargoes they carried. Profitability depended largely on the skill of the captain. Traders were among their chief customers and principal investors. Dousman became deeply interested in the business, and in the 1840s he often bought a share in boats on behalf of Sibley as well as himself. In 1847 he joined with Sibley, Rice, Brisbois, and several business associates from Galena to start a packet company, with boats running on a regular schedule. Their first boat, the "Argo," struck a snag and sank in October, but a new one, the "Dr. Franklin," began the 1848 season in triumph.[29]

Although undertaken in partnership, such business had been independent of American Fur and its subsidiary outfits. Under the new arrangements with the Chouteau Company in the 1840s, these personal ventures expanded to include land speculation, sometimes undertaken on joint account with the company. In 1844 Sibley contracted with David Faribault to open a retail outlet in St. Paul. This was for a time independent of the Outfit, since Chouteau was reluctant to get into general merchandising. Cash was scarce, however, and pelts were plentiful, so much of the business even with Euro-Americans involved payment in furs and deerskins. Managed after 1847 by William Forbes, Sibley's St. Paul store continued to grow along with the white population east of the Mississippi.[30]

A large element of that population was coming from New England, drawn west by the wealth of white pine in the St. Croix valley, which had been ceded in 1837. The 1840s saw lumbermen from Maine, New Hampshire, and other northeastern states cutting timber and building sawmills and settlements at St. Croix Falls, Marine, and Stillwater. They were joined from time to time by prospectors for metal, drawn by rumors of rich copper and iron deposits south of Lake Superior. Along with the newcomers came increased pressure for accessible government and legal services.

One of those eager to supply such civic needs was Joseph R. Brown. From his location on Grey Cloud Island he engaged in farming, townsite promotion, lumbering, and storekeeping. He also continued to be a justice of the peace, and as a personification of the frontier legal system he had rapidly become a legend, not only for his humor and wit—as keen as ever—but also for his unexpected ability to conduct official business. This homegrown facility soon extended to politics, and it was largely through his lobbying in Madison that in 1840 St. Croix County was established in the northwestern corner of Wisconsin Territory. During the winters of 1840–41 and 1841–42 he served in the Wisconsin legislature, and in the second session he worked hard to rally support for Doty's treaty with the Dakota. After its defeat, he turned again to trading on the western plains, where, in marrying Susan Frenier, he had acquired family ties with the Sisseton.[31]

Sibley's friendship for Brown persisted over the years, yet he must have found the man as much an enigma as ever. Although Brown had grown up from the age of fifteen in the frontier army, he used no profanity; a clever and incorrigible whiskey-seller, he was personally a teetotaler; and despite two divorces and his reputation as a philanderer, he was devoted to Susan and his family. From 1842 to 1846 Sibley, on his personal account, bought buffalo hides from Brown even as Brown competed with traders of the Upper Mississippi Outfit, and when Brown turned once more to townsite promotion and moved to the St. Croix valley, Sibley bought out Brown's western interests and assets on generous terms.[32]

The promise of statehood for Wisconsin had drawn Brown eastward again. That prospect held many questions and possibilities for what was coming to be known as the Minnesota country. As in Iowa, the struggle would prove to be a long one, with various influences, both local and national, pulling at cross-purposes. Brown was prepared to be one of those influences, and quite possibly he already knew that Henry Sibley, too, was contemplating a career in public affairs.

By his own measure Sibley had failed to become a self-made man on the model of Dousman or Crooks, but his experience and contacts in Washington surpassed those of anyone else on the Upper Mississippi. Writing to Trowbridge in 1847, he lamented his "want of success in business" and went on to observe: "It needs no prophet to foresee that things in this country are now in a transit state, and that the fur trade must ere long be brought to a close. What I shall then do, if my life is spared, remains to be seen; perhaps I may turn politician or office seeker, or apply myself to some equally mean occupation, perhaps not. *Nous verrons!* . . . 'Sufficient for the day is the evil thereof.'"[33]

∘ 8 ∘

Making a Territory

As Sibley pondered a future in politics, the entire configuration of the nation was changing, both on maps and in the minds of its citizens. While he wrote to Trowbridge, war with Mexico was going on, and although American forces had already entered Mexico City, news of the triumph had not yet reached the Upper Mississippi. Five months later, in February 1848, the Treaty of Guadalupe Hidalgo transferred to the United States the northern part of Mexico from Texas to California, and later in the same year Oregon Territory was formed from a region that until 1846 had been jointly occupied with Britain. Thus the country's future as a transcontinental power was sealed.

Already further expansion to the northwest had been trumpeted in the 1844 Democratic campaign slogan, "Fifty-four forty or fight!"—referring to the southern boundary of Russian claims on the Pacific slope—and it took no great imagination to chart the course of U.S. destiny across the rambling private domain of the Hudson's Bay Company to the crest of the Rockies. Key elements in this vision were the hamlet of St. Paul at the head of steamboat navigation on the Mississippi and the deep water port at the head of Lake Superior, little more than a hundred miles to the north. Adding to their significance was the growing commerce with the Red River settlement being opened by fur traders and Métis.

Thus expansionists dreamed of a territory and soon a state extending to the British boundary that would provide a launching pad for empire. Meanwhile promoters of both Iowa and Wisconsin had their eyes on the well-known waterpower at the Falls of St. Anthony and its potential for industry. With the Falls included in their own boundaries, development there would be tributary to the south. The miles of forest, swamp, and prairie reaching away to the north could wait indefinitely.

Among those with geopolitical vision and expansionist hopes was Stephen A. Douglas of Illinois. While still a congressman, he used his influence to rein in the ambitions of Iowa politicians and fix the boundary of that state well south of the Minnesota River. In the case of Wisconsin, too, Douglas played a key role, both as a congressman and later as a senator, in the lengthy jockeying that eventually set the state's northwestern boundary at the St. Croix River. Thus the nucleus of American settlement on the west bank of the St. Croix and from that river's mouth up the east bank of the Mississippi to the Falls of St. Anthony was preserved as the foundation for a new political entity to be formed from the remainder of Iowa and Wisconsin territories.

The need for such a territory was recognized as early as December 1846, when a bill for its organization was introduced in Congress after passage of the Wisconsin enabling act. At the time a state constitution had been drafted that placed Wisconsin's northwestern boundary east of the St. Croix River. The Wisconsin voters, heavily concentrated in the south and east part of the territory, rejected this constitution on issues unrelated to the boundary, and a second convention was called to try again in December 1847.[1]

Sibley played an active role as these events unfolded. His offhand words to Trowbridge in the autumn of 1847 had glossed over nearly a year of testing the political waters. During his visit to Washington in December 1846 to lobby against the Winnebago relocation, he also discussed the bill for the new territory with its author, Wisconsin delegate Morgan L. Martin. In the spring of 1847 he wrote to John McKusick, a prominent Stillwater lumberman, inquiring as to possible support in the St. Croix settlements if he should become a candidate for congressional delegate from the new territory. He also corresponded about his political prospects with Daniel G. Fenton, a lawyer and Democractic politician from Prairie du Chien.[2]

Any ties he might have had with Fenton were broken during the second constitutional convention, when the delegates undertook to change the boundary. Fenton led a drive for placing the Wisconsin line at the Rum and Mississippi Rivers, which would have annexed the St. Croix valley, the Falls of St. Anthony, and St. Paul. The convention adopted this, and the voters of southern Wisconsin approved it, with St. Croix County overwhelmingly opposed. The final decision, however, lay with Congress.

By early January 1848, St. Paul citizens were signing a petition to Congress furiously protesting the proposed boundary. Sibley supported the effort vigorously, and his position once more resulted in strained relations with Dousman. Never deeply into politics, and perhaps unaware of Sibley's new ambition, Dousman could not fathom his friend's reasoning. For his own part, he said, he had worked hard to promote the Rum River boundary. Dousman's letter was penned in his usual swift, clear, and strongly accented hand, with occasional underlining for emphasis. "I cannot see what interest you have in the matter," he said. "You are now sure to have the seat of Govt. of the new Territory fixed on your side of the [Mississippi] River. . . . The Govt. will be more anxious to treat for the country on the west than if the St. Croix had formed part of the new Territory & the sooner we can get a treaty with the Sioux, the better chance we have of getting something."[3]

More attuned to the realities of Washington than Dousman, Sibley could have replied that with the Rum River line adopted, it might well be years before there would be any new territory or Sioux treaty. Almost no American voters lived west of the Mississippi, and until the Dakota gave up the land, there could be none. Moreover, in shifting his sights from business to public office, Sibley made a subtle but important step away from Dousman's narrow focus on private economic advantage. As heir to his father's career in public affairs, Sibley's implicit assumptions gave more weight to long-range policy and influence over people than to immediate profit.

So in the spring of 1848 the tall trader from Mendota became a familiar presence at St. Paul political gatherings. With the French-speaking founders of the village, as with nearly all his own employees, Sibley was a revered and trusted figure. Newcomers from downriver, accustomed to the crude equality of the border settlements in Illinois and Missouri, may have been put off by his patrician manner. All, however, stood in awe of his experience in Washington and his influence with key national figures like Cass and Douglas. This balanced the suspicion held by some that he might be a spokesman for "the fur company" more than the community.[4] Along the St. Croix his genteel New England background was an advantage, and Franklin Steele served as a tie to fellow mill owners and lumbermen.

By 1847 Steele had succeeded in luring several Boston capitalists to invest in his development at the Falls of St. Anthony. They also had taken an interest in the boundary question. Thus the influence of men like Caleb Cushing and Benjamin H. Cheever added to the howls of protest from the Upper Mississippi in persuading Congress to modify the decision of Wisconsin voters. The new state was admitted in late May 1848, with its northwestern line at the St. Croix River.

Although a bill introduced by Douglas for the creation of Minnesota Territory failed to pass, no one felt that the measure would be long in coming. How to bring it about as soon as possible and to secure the coveted public offices and federal appointments became the focus of strategizing in the next months. There was much public wringing of hands by editors and local politicians over the supposed absence of law and government in the sliver of what had been Wisconsin Territory between the St. Croix and Mississippi. This was followed by suggestions that Congress could not have meant to deprive the citizens of their rights and that a residue of Wisconsin Territory still in fact existed. Plans were soon in motion to promote the idea and secure federal funding for officers in the remaining territory.

On this stage, Sibley had two principal supporting actors. One was Joe Brown, who had shifted his base of operations from Grey Cloud Island to a townsite just north of Stillwater. The other was a newcomer from Madison—David Lambert, a lawyer and sometime newspaper editor. He arrived in June with a letter of introduction to Sibley from Wisconsin Democrat Henry Dodge. Whatever private devils pursued Lambert, he became a resident of St. Paul and a friend and effective aide to Sibley until his suicide by drowning a year later.[5]

The other drama playing itself out that summer related to land titles. Surveying of public lands had begun west of the St. Croix in 1847. The citizens of St. Paul, still legally squatters, held valuable claims and had invested in buildings and other improvements. When an auction of federal lands was announced for August 28, 1848, at the land office in St. Croix Falls, they quickly organized, apprehensive of losing their property to speculators. Some were illiterate and others not fluent in English, so to avoid errors and confusion they agreed to have a single person represent them in the bidding. Their choice was Henry Sibley. They accompanied him in a body, some armed with large sticks, and there were no opposing bids. It cost considerable labor for Sibley to collect the deeds and convey each to its proper owner, and even then some hesitated to take the document, urging him to hold it in safekeeping for them. The incident, however, coming at a crucial time, solidified his image as a benign patron and protector of the humble French-Canadian and mixed-blood inhabitants.[6]

On August 26, while on his way to St. Croix Falls, Sibley attended a meeting—billed as a "convention"—held in Stillwater. It had been called by himself, Steele, Brown, and a few St. Croix valley citizens. The Stillwater convention brought together an undetermined number of self-appointed "delegates" from St. Paul and other places as well as the St. Croix to frame a memorial to the president, asking that he use his influence toward forming a new territory. The proceedings were clearly orchestrated by Brown, and Lambert served as one of the secretaries. With the petition drawn up, it was suggested that someone be appointed to carry it in person to Washington. Sibley made it known that he was willing to do so and to lobby for it at his own expense. He was chosen unanimously.

Whether or not Sibley and his friends had been aware of the schemes of John Catlin, former secretary of Wisconsin Territory, they along with the rest of the Minnesota country soon learned that he had assumed the role of acting governor of the territory's remaining fragment and was about to hold an election for a new territorial delegate. At a meeting hastily called on September 6, Sibley and his St. Paul supporters endorsed the idea but continued to urge the organization of Minnesota Territory. The election was set for Octo-

ber 30. Sibley, as choice of the Stillwater convention, was obviously the leading candidate.

Tension mounted when Sibley's new business partner Henry Rice announced himself a contender. Neither man was a resident of Wisconsin Territory, but the law did not require it, and the question was never raised. A
more divisive issue was that of party affiliation. Sibley had no formal ties to
either party and maintained his neutrality, focusing his platform on the organization of Minnesota Territory. Rice made a brief attempt to rally support
for himself among the region's overwhelming majority of Democrats. But a
more effective strategy was the outright buying of votes on election day,
which secured him a majority among the mill workers of St. Anthony Falls.
The short campaign ended with Sibley polling 236 votes, showing heavy mar-
gins in St. Paul and the St. Croix valley. Rice's 122 votes were largely from his
own employees and business associates at Crow Wing and from St. Anthony
Falls.

Almost unnoticed as the backdrop to this frontier election was the presidential contest between Lewis Cass, the senior statesman of the Democrats,
and General Zachary Taylor, a hero of the Mexican war nominated by the
Whigs. It became a three-way race when an upstart antislavery group who
called themselves Free Soilers nominated former president Martin Van Bu-
ren. Although they had no decisive effect on the election, their presence was
a portent of things to come. Had Cass won, Sibley would clearly have been a
leading prospect for governor of the new territory, a fact of which he and others were keenly aware. But with Taylor's election the vision of governorship
faded for a second time.

Thin ice formed on the river in early November 1848 as the Sibleys prepared
for the journey east and watched anxiously for the last steamboat. Finally Sibley hired a keelboat and pushed off downriver with Sarah, the two children,
and a small party of other late travelers, including Dousman, Alexis Bailly,
and Ellen Rice, who had been keeping house for her brother at Mendota. At
the mouth of the St. Croix they met the steamer "Dr. Franklin" and gratefully
climbed aboard. The rest of the trip was no easier—by stagecoach across Illinois, where mud alternated with burning prairies, by steamer across Lake
Michigan, and again by river to Niles, Michigan, the northwesternmost extension of the country's burgeoning railroad system.[7]

That winter in Washington was not only the beginning, but also in one
sense the high point of Sibley's political career. Certainly it was the most sat-
isfying part, for he became at once an agent of history and a symbol of the
new territory. The tale of how he rose, polished and urbane, before a Con-

gress that had expected a figure in buckskin and eloquently defended the right of pioneers to the protection of government and law became—almost immediately—Minnesota's most cherished founding legend. The speech was delivered on December 22 before the House committee on elections. It resulted in his being seated as a delegate, even though Congress never formally admitted the continued existence of Wisconsin Territory.[8]

His own success came as a surprise to Sibley, for he regarded his acceptance as quite unlikely. The real goal was securing a law to organize the new territory. He also planned, as he assured the missionary Gideon Pond, to push for a measure "extending the laws of the United States over the Indian tribes of the north west." In that effort he got no further than a resolution directing the House Committee on Indian Affairs to study the matter, but he did achieve two other measures that were close to the hearts of his constituents. He persuaded the postmaster general to order a weekly mail delivery to St. Paul and he secured the removal of the St. Croix Falls land office to Stillwater.[9]

In the struggle to organize the territory, Stephen Douglas proved an indispensable ally. Douglas opted to revive in the Senate his Minnesota bill that had died at the end of the session the previous spring. In the meantime he had journeyed up the Mississippi that summer and from Pilot Knob above Mendota had surveyed the same scene that impressed Sibley in 1834. It would be, he thought, a matchless setting for the future capital. Sibley was more practical. Land at Mendota was still unceded Indian territory, except for the small part that was within the military reservation. Moreover, Sibley's constituents lived in St. Paul, and they wanted the capital there. Douglas finally agreed, and Sibley also persuaded him that, following a precedent set in the case of Oregon Territory, Minnesota should receive twice the usual amount of federal land for public school purposes.[10]

Passage of the territorial bill in the Senate was a breeze, but the House was more difficult. Opposition came from a knot of Southerners who saw creating more northern territories as a threat to the careful balance of power between slave and free states. After long delay, the bill was reported out of the House Committee on Territories with several amendments attached. The most important amendment was a postponement in the effective date of the law, which thus preempted territorial patronage for the incoming Whig administration. With this proviso, the Whig majority in the House passed it. The Senate, however, refused to concur, and with time running out, it looked as if the act were doomed.

Douglas came to the rescue by threatening to kill the bill that would create a department of the interior if the House did not drop the amendment. Whether a bluff or not, the strategy worked, and Sibley maneuvered the Min-

*Painting of Sibley, commemorating his appeal to Congress
for the creation of Minnesota Territory, 1848*

nesota bill through a parliamentary thicket with only hours to spare. Thus on
March 3, 1849, the last day of the session, Minnesota became a territory. "I
walked that day," Sibley recalled, "with the highest head and the lightest
heart and the freest step and best face of any man in the crowd."[11]

News of the event did not reach St. Paul until more than a month later, carried by the first steamboat to arrive from downriver. In the words of David
Lambert: "One glad shout, resounding through the boat, taken up on shore,
and echoed from our beetling bluffs and rolling hills, proclaimed that the bill
for the organization of Minnesota Territory had become a law!" The delegate
himself arrived a few days later, weak from an illness picked up along the
river. Fortunately it was not the deadly cholera that appeared in St. Louis in
May, and his reception was, as a friend observed, "such as would go far to
make a sick man well."[12]

Sibley at once issued an address to the people of Minnesota, recounting
his various successes and failures in Washington. He also made it known that
he would be willing to serve as congressional delegate from the new territory

on a strictly nonpartisan basis. The neat flyer was facilitated by the presence of a printing press that had arrived in mid-April along with James M. Goodhue, publisher of the territory's first newspaper.[13]

Outgoing President Polk declined to appoint officers for Minnesota, leaving that perk to the new Whig administration. After two appointees had refused the post of governor for the remote territory, Taylor named Alexander Ramsey, a two-term congressman from Pennsylvania. Ramsey with his wife Anna and their young son set out immediately, traveling by steamer via the Great Lakes and by stagecoach across Wisconsin to Prairie du Chien, possibly to avoid the cholera in St. Louis.[14] Knowing there was no housing in St. Paul, Sibley at once invited them to stay at Mendota until a governor's residence was built. The party arrived on May 27 and remained with the Sibleys for nearly a month. Dousman meanwhile penned a note from Prairie du Chien: "I saw your Governor here a few days since and like him much— I think you can make a staunch friend of him."[15]

At age thirty-four, "Bluff Alec" Ramsey was already experienced in the realities of party politics. Disappointed in his hope for becoming collector of the Port of Philadelphia, he had accepted a post on the far frontier with a shrewd pragmatism that was part of his less-than-privileged Scottish and Pennsylvania Dutch background. In Minnesota he found a country poised for expansion in the 1850s and without entrenched political leadership. So unlike many carpetbagging federal appointees, he set about building a solid electoral base in his own territory and chased no distant prospects or promises.

"Our Governor takes well with the people," Sibley told Trowbridge six weeks after Ramsey's arrival. "He is a plain, unassuming man of popular manners and much good sense." The friendship that grew between them despite party rivalries and personal and social differences became one of Minnesota's enduring political legends. It was symbolic that while Sibley spoke French among the old *habitants,* Ramsey greeted crowds of newcomers from the *Deutschland* in German.[16]

Despite the flurry of congratulations and requests for favors, opening his home to the governor, and presiding at the ceremonial events of organizing a new territory, Sibley was preoccupied by deepening trouble in his uneasy partnership with Henry Rice. The two men could hardly have been more dif-

Alexander Ramsey with his young son, 1850

ferent. In contrast to the sober, reserved Sibley, Rice was charming, outgoing, and quick to inspire others with confidence in his soaring schemes. Yet beneath the charisma lay brooding doubts about human nature and the world. He moved between bursts of explosive energy and periods of depression often disguised as illness.

Throughout that winter and spring St. Paul had been abuzz with Rice's projects. In November the trader purchased a large tract of land adjacent to the settlement and immediately had it surveyed and platted. The existing village and this addition were together incorporated as the Town of St. Paul. Rice then contracted to build several warehouses and a large hotel near the upper steamboat landing and meanwhile cultivated popularity by lavish promises of civic improvements and gifts of land to his friends.[17]

As construction went forward on his buildings, Rice made a lightning trip east, allegedly to lobby for the territorial bill. That was apparently not his primary purpose, however, for on March 29 he married Matilda Whitall in Richmond, Virginia. He had been living in Mendota, where he had already begun building a new residence. When he returned with his bride, however, his plans had changed. In June the couple moved to St. Paul.[18]

Rice's new hotel, later named the American House, was the wonder of the Upper Mississippi country. Substantially completed in ten weeks, it was one of the largest establishments of its kind north of St. Louis. When Chouteau inquired about Rice's activities, Sibley replied guardedly, "I cannot say I am very well informed." He admitted that Rice had "purchased very extensively of property," but he denied any knowledge of their partner's accounts, adding significantly, "I gave you such hints as a fair construction of matters last fall would allow me."[19]

Clearly there was suspicion on both sides that Rice was using company money, but in a world of individual and partnership enterprises, the line between personal and business assets often became blurred. Investments in land and buildings had long been part of the fur trade, and as the frontier opened, speculative purchases were becoming accepted practice for the jointly owned outfits. Subsumed under "other business" in contracts, they rested on verbal agreements and the judgment of the partner who saw an opportunity. Nevertheless, spurred to action by Chouteau's questions, Sibley had an uneasy interview with Rice in which he sought to avoid confrontation but intimated that Chouteau was disturbed at how deeply Rice was plunging. In response a few days later, Rice offered his partners a half interest in his St. Paul properties, estimating the cost of the hotel at $13,000. Neither Sibley nor Chouteau had asked for this. Sibley suggested that a company representative come north to examine Rice's books, but Chouteau apparently saw no need for action.[20]

In July, Rice was in La Pointe, negotiating with Dr. Charles W. W. Borup, who ran the Northern Fur Company, a remnant of the old Northern Outfit of American Fur. Borup had been threatening to move to St. Paul, where he could compete, not only among the Ojibwe, but also in the much more profitable Winnebago trade. Early in August the two men appeared in St. Paul, and Rice informed Sibley that they had agreed to split the Ojibwe trade between them. Rice was still working to secure from Borup a promise of noninterference with the Dakota and Winnebago.[21]

Sibley immediately proposed to Chouteau that Borup be taken into their partnership "to devote his time to carry on the business, subject of course to the control of Mr. Rice." Since Borup had a shady reputation in the trade, Chouteau was dubious, but Sibley argued, "Whatever may be the other objections urged against him, it is admitted by all that [Borup] is a close business man, industrious and methodical." If Sibley's hidden purpose was to gain access to Rice's books through a sharp outside eye, Rice did not sense it. He quickly agreed and went to St. Louis to persuade Chouteau. Thus brought into Rice's Winnebago and Chippewa Outfit, Borup assumed management of all the Ojibwe trade.[22]

Only a few days later, early in September, Sibley's suspicions were confirmed. Having looked at Rice's books, Borup wrote a long letter listing scandalous irregularities and suggesting that they press Rice to return property from his own name to that of the outfit to make things look better. Sibley again urged Chouteau to send someone up, for "Dr. B. is absolutely horror-stricken at the way in which things are managed." At the same time, apparently judging that his new partner's loyalty might be for sale to the highest bidder, Sibley wrote to Borup, "*entre nous*," offering to share half of his own real estate investments in St. Paul. Rice apparently made an offer also, but Borup chose to wait until he knew how the wind blew with Chouteau.[23]

Maddeningly, Chouteau did nothing, and Sibley continued to pound him with urgent letters, each more insistent than the last. Meanwhile Rice warned that the Ewing brothers, Indiana traders who were Chouteau's chief rivals in the Indian trade, were making an approach to the Winnebago through their agent, David Olm-

Henry M. Rice, 1857

sted. On September 26 Rice and Olmsted reached an agreement through which they would split the Winnebago business, three-fifths going to Rice's outfit and two-fifths to Olmsted. It was the best he could do, Rice told Chouteau. Perhaps the name of Ewing rang an alarm bell with Chouteau. In any case, he at last dispatched Joseph A. Sire, one of the partners in his firm, to examine the outfit's books.[24]

Sire arrived early in October and immediately confirmed Borup's judgment. On October 9, at Sibley's urging, they applied to the district court at Stillwater for an injunction against Rice and his chief associates to restrain them from disposing of any property. The court order was issued, but no lawsuit followed, for on October 11 Rice met with Sibley and Sire, and the three men reached a settlement. It may have been engineered by Dousman, who was in St. Paul at the time and apparently played a backstage role in bringing them together. Under terms of the settlement the partnership was dissolved and Rice was cleared of all liabilities to Chouteau and Sibley, while they assumed all debts owed to others by the outfit and agreed to complete construction of two buildings in St. Paul that Rice had contracted for. Rice, on his part, was to turn over all business records and property belonging to the firm, including a long list of real estate holdings. He also gave up a claim on Chouteau for $4,500 in goods that Chouteau had failed to deliver and that Rice had been compelled to purchase from a Galena merchant.[25]

On the streets of St. Paul, news of the injunction against Rice was met with disbelief and shock. His friends immediately staged a testimonial dinner, and Rice himself put a good public face on the disaster. Privately, he wrote a chastened letter to Dousman. "I am unable to express my feelings toward you," Rice told his former partner, "but will say that I will do nothing to forfeit your friendship or confidence. I shall retire from all speculation, and give politics little heed."[26]

If turning his back on politics was Rice's intention, it did not last long. In the election for Minnesota's first congressional delegate, which had been held two months earlier, he had not opposed Sibley and Sibley had been chosen unanimously on a nonpartisan ticket. By October 20, however, Rice's friends, presumably with his support, held a meeting in the American House to organize a territorial Democratic Party in anticipation of local elections the following month. Although many of Sibley's friends were there, it was on Rice's turf and clearly controlled by the Rice faction. Sibley had anticipated the situation and warily steered clear of the convention, sending a letter instead. In it he declared himself a "Democrat of the Jeffersonian school" and repeated his argument that party alignment was contrary to the best interests of the territory.[27]

The handful of Whigs in Minnesota—mostly federal appointees—had nothing to gain by partisanship. Therefore they had formed a nominally non-partisan Territorial Party. In the November elections its candidates won with the help of Sibley Democrats. Meanwhile, Delegate Sibley and his family, this time accompanied on the journey by Governor Ramsey, had again left for Washington.[28]

Faced with the reality of long and regular absences in the East, Sibley had invited his brother Fred to join him in Minnesota and take charge of the books and correspondence of the Sioux Outfit. Until Fred's arrival in April, direction of the Dakota trade was left to Alex Faribault and Hypolite DuPuis. Borup and Chouteau had reorganized the trade with the Ojibwe and Winnebago into a new firm called the Minnesota Outfit, in which Sibley still had some financial interest. They now faced competition from Rice as well as from Olmsted, who continued to represent the Ewings. Sylvanus Lowry, who had great influence with the Winnebago, opted to stick with Rice, and merchants in Galena and St. Louis were supplying them. Borup was confidant, nevertheless, feeling that Rice's loose business methods would drag him down, and "Only one place can he injure us, that is in Washington."[29] Within a few months the doctor's judgment was confirmed.

Settling in for his second winter at the nation's capital, Sibley on his part began to feel both the power and the burdens of holding political office. Requests for favors rolled in, and old friends regularly turned up, seeking his influence. Every packet from Minnesota brought reams of opinions and gossip. Goodhue, the volatile editor of the *Pioneer,* who had approved of Sibley's nonpartisan stance, bombarded him with political advice and requests for government printing contracts. Sarah's brother-in-law, Tom Potts, loquacious and sociable as ever, offered news of family, friends, and politics, warning Sibley against Goodhue. Potts even kept a watchful eye on business affairs. Doctor Borup, he said, was detested in the community but was doing well with the trade. Forbes, who managed Sibley's store in St. Paul, was staying sober, and he, along with Faribault, DuPuis, and Borup's clerk, Joseph Mosher, was attending the Sons of Temperance. Forbes on his part informed Sibley that Potts was drinking less since Abbie and their baby, Mary, had joined him in St. Paul.[30]

Ramsey as governor was also superintendent of Indian affairs for Minnesota, and part of his business in Washington was to secure an order for the removal of all Ojibwe to unceded land in the northern part of the territory. This included the bands still living in Wisconsin. The political and economic benefits to Minnesota were clear: annuity goods, cash payments, and related trade would be funneled up the Mississippi through St. Paul, rather than going via Detroit and Lake Superior to La Pointe. On February 6, 1850, President Taylor issued a removal order, and Borup at once busied himself with keeping the prospective business away from Rice.[31]

Preoccupation with their own territorial affairs did not prevent either Ramsey or Sibley from watching the national drama over the extension of slavery being played out in Washington that winter as the aging moderates, Cass and Henry Clay, pleaded with extremists of both North and South. Clay, already ailing, delivered his last speech in February, and Cass, who had been again elected in 1849 as a senator from Michigan, warned openly of civil war. Then he set about patching together the stopgap Compromise of 1850. After Ramsey returned to Minnesota, Sibley continued to share by letter his forebodings about the clouds of disunion on the nation's horizon.[32]

In late March Sibley suffered from an eye inflammation, possibly a recurrence of the trouble that had afflicted him in 1840. When he emerged from his darkened room after several weeks, he found that he had been blindsided in more than one sense. Rice had spent the winter between Richmond and Washington, visiting his wife's family and lobbying for appointments and traders' claims. In this he was aided by Alexander M. Mitchell, an Ohio Whig who had been appointed marshal of Minnesota Territory and who had good connections with the Whig administration. Unknown to Sibley, in early April Rice secured for himself a government contract that promised to rebuild his fortunes.[33]

It was indeed a plum. The Winnebago Indians had never been reconciled to their new location at Long Prairie. Some, in fact, had eluded the army and remained in central Wisconsin at the time of the tribe's earlier removal to Iowa. Now many of their friends were rejoining them, and white settlers in Wisconsin resented their presence. One military effort to round up Indians in Iowa had already failed miserably, and through the winter and spring of 1850 complaints of Winnebago "depredations" in Wisconsin had continued to grow. So when Rice told the new commissioner of Indian affairs, Orlando Brown, that a carrot would do the job more effectively than a stick, Brown listened. Armed only with wagons, supplies, and a few gifts, Rice said, he would persuade his Winnebago friends to move back to Long Prairie at a cost to the government of seventy dollars each—far cheaper than sending troops. Brown agreed, and he also agreed to keep the matter quiet for a few days, since "enemies" of Rice would no doubt try to prevent the Winnebago from complying if they learned of his intentions.[34]

When Sibley discovered that both he and Ramsey had been bypassed, he was furious. He alerted Ramsey at once, but as the governor steamed off downriver to send an official protest to Washington from the nearest telegraph office at Galena, he met Rice on the way up. Blandly, Rice showed him the contract. There was nothing to be done, although nearly everyone in Minnesota agreed that the price was excessive.[35]

Still seething, Sibley called for a congressional investigation, and a committee was appointed to look into the matter. In Minnesota, Borup took precisely the course that Rice had predicted, dispatching several barrels of whiskey to La Crosse in hopes of intoxicating and scattering the Winnebago who had already gathered there for transportation up the Mississippi. When Sibley learned of it, he immediately wired his brother Fred, who was by then in charge at Mendota: "Have nothing to do with stopping Indians. Congress will settle matters."[36]

Eventually the heat generated by Sibley's protests led the Indian commissioner to resign, but the contract was honored and Rice went unscathed. Profitable as it might have been, however, Rice had no intention of spending his summer transporting Indians. After persuading some 350 of the Winnebago to return to Long Prairie, he struck a deal with Olmsted to take over the rest of the contract. Then he turned his attention to politics.[37]

The special election of 1849 had sent Sibley to Washington for a term of only one year, so he faced reelection in September 1850. Already in April, Rice's friends were circulating an anonymous broadside lampooning Sibley's dignified paternalism. Since the local elections in November had shown that Whigs held the balance of power between the warring Democratic factions, Rice attempted to turn the tables. His Whig friend Mitchell was nominated by a "Territorial" convention at the end of July. A few days later word reached Minnesota that Sibley would run on his record without the support of any party.[38]

The bitterly fought campaign turned on Rice's popularity as a developer of the territory and resentment for the power of "the fur company" felt by many citizens. Sibley was portrayed as a tool of Chouteau, and Rice as the "little man" trampled by a ruthless monopoly. Congress had been unable to get to its normal business because of the stalemate over slavery, so Sibley was stuck in Washington throughout the summer. With little taste for down and dirty politics, he may not have been sorry to leave his campaign in the capable hands of Joe Brown, who lined up Goodhue and other wavering supporters. The result was close but decisive, giving Sibley nearly 54 percent of the vote. The Rice faction's greatest inroads since the election of 1848 proved to be in St. Paul, where the two candidates were virtually tied. As before, Rice's candidate carried St. Anthony and the settlements above it on the Mississippi, while Sibley held his lead along the St. Croix and at Mendota. Everywhere the "French vote" added to Sibley's strength, and the missionaries stood behind him as a block.[39]

Thus Sibley successfully countered the first serious challenge to his political leadership. The victory not only assured him of two more years in office but also confirmed his dual and often contradictory role as a voice both for new arrivals eager to cash in on frontier development and for the deeply rooted community of Indians and Métis, whose two centuries of accommodation to white society faced abrupt destruction. Sibley had, in effect, put his shoulder to turning the wheel of change.

· 9 ·

Taking the Suland

*B*EHIND THE TALLY OF VOTES, the pronouncements of politicians and
editors, the eager questions of newcomers, and the calculations of investors there was one theme in the new territory—land. All of Minnesota west
of the Mississippi belonged to Indian people, but halting the tide of immigration at the river's edge seemed inconceivable. History had ordained that
the continent would become a clone of western Europe, and Indians must
give way or be eliminated. To raise doubts over that destiny was to be disloyal
to country and religion. The only questions were in the details: how and when
it would happen, and—most important—who would benefit.

Henry Sibley was no man to try sweeping back the tide of Western civilization. Like all of his generation, he believed in his deepest heart that it was
a force for good, set in motion by a Christian God. Still, he had misgivings
about its course. "I have pondered long and deeply," he told the missionary
Stephen Riggs, "as to the proper measures to be taken to save the remnants
of these tribes from destruction." A few days later, in September 1849, he outlined his opinions to the members of the American Board of Commissioners
for Foreign Missions, who were meeting in Minnesota to discuss the future
of the work there. He dismissed as unrealistic a renewed proposal for an all-
Indian territory in the Missouri River valley, instead favoring small, widely
separated reservations. Nevertheless, he defended the Indians' need for independence of action as well as education, and, above all, for hope in the future. "They are regarded," he feared, "as a damned race."[1]

Ramsey's first formal address as governor included a hardly needed urging that the new legislators memorialize Congress on acquiring all of the
Dakota homeland. Even earlier, in the spring of 1849, Sibley had prevailed
on the commissioner of Indian affairs to move toward negotiations with the
tribe. By early September rumors were flying that treaty talks would soon be
held.[2]

In a private note, Sibley urged Ramsey to wait, for the time was not right
"and I do not wish you to have any of the *onus* of the failure." Ten days later
he outlined to the governor what he then thought were the minimum neces-

sary conditions for a treaty: suitable reservations for the different bands in the Upper Minnesota River valley; a price for Dakota land of no less than ten cents an acre; payment of the $50,000 in education funds owed under the treaty of 1837; and a fair allowance for traders' claims.[3]

Armed with instructions from the Indian office, Ramsey nevertheless moved ahead along with his fellow treaty commissioner, Governor John Chambers of Iowa. But Sibley had been right. Little came of the effort. Only a handful of local Dakota leaders attended the council. They simply shrugged at the meager terms offered by the government—two cents an acre for all their land, no designated reservation, and no allowance for payment of debts to their traders. The sole achievement of the two commissioners was to negotiate a treaty with the Dakota mixed-bloods for purchase of the land along the Mississippi at Lake Pepin that had been set aside for them in 1830. Few had settled on it, and most were eager to turn it into cash.[4]

Indifferent as the Dakota may have seemed, they were well aware of the building pressures to force a treaty on them. That winter nature added another blow. Late autumn prairie fires burned over the entire Upper Minnesota valley and west as far as the James River. Blackened grasslands drove the buffalo to the Missouri River and beyond, leaving the Sisseton and Wahpeton once more facing hunger.[5]

At the beginning of January 1850, Martin McLeod wrote from Lac qui Parle that the season was worse than any previous one. By mid-February he and the other traders united with the missionaries in appealing to the Indian office to send relief for the western Dakota bands. None was to be had, and Sibley turned to Congress in a futile attempt to get a special appropriation. Meanwhile Ramsey, aware that he would soon be facing these very Indians across a treaty table, advanced a small amount of ammunition for hunting.[6]

Writing to Gideon Pond, Sibley complained that the struggle over slavery made it nearly impossible to draw attention to any other public issues. As for the Indian commissioner, Sibley was already at war with him over Rice's Winnebago contract. The delegate had earlier told Riggs that he intended to make a formal statement on Indian affairs, and to Pond also he declared: "I shall probably speak out my sentiments very freely as to the wretched policy of the Govt."[7]

The opportunity to do so did not come until midsummer. By then Washington was reeling over the sudden death of President Taylor and the attention of the nation was elsewhere. Nevertheless, it could well have been Sibley's last chance if defeated in the approaching Minnesota election. So on August 2, 1850, he rose before the House and poured out the indignation and foreboding that had been building in him for nearly a decade.[8]

The choice facing the country, Sibley declared, was civilization of the remaining Indian people or "their utter extermination." The policy of the United States had consistently led to extermination with a ruthlessness unmatched by the old empires of Europe or even the British in India. He predicted that history would in time "do justice to the heroic bands, who have struggled so fiercely to preserve their lands and the graves of their fathers from the grasping hand of the white man." As for the charade of treaty-making:

> If the act of making a treaty is not to be looked upon as a mere mockery or a farce, every stipulation and every pledge made ... should be scrupulously fulfilled.... On the contrary, ... the commissioners, by making promises which they know will never be performed, plume themselves upon having made a favorable treaty, leaving the poor victims to find out in due time that they have been betrayed and deceived.... I will venture the assertion that not one in ten of the treaties made will be found to have been carried out in good faith.

Turning to the future, he warned the congressmen:

> If anything is to be done, it must be done now.... Your pioneers are encircling the last home of the red man as with a wall of fire. Their encroachments are perceptible in the restlessness ... of the powerful bands who inhabit your remote western plains. You must approach these with terms of conciliation and of real friendship or you must very soon suffer the consequences of a bloody and remorseless Indian war ... What is to become of [them] ... when the buffalo and other game on which they now depend for subsistence are exhausted? Think you they will lie down and die without a struggle?

He clearly regarded this manifesto as an act of conscience. If the nation did not change its policy of oppression and genocide, "Minnesota shall at least be freed from any responsibility on that score."—But neither for Minnesota nor for Henry Sibley was it that easy.

Even as he spoke, Sibley faced the bitter dilemma of personal and political survival within the system he deplored. Not only did his reelection hang in the balance, but popular clamor for a treaty was building. Back in Minnesota, where he stayed for scarcely a month in October and early November, he found that thanks to Rice's machinations and the series of bad years on the plains, his own business was in a shambles. As the Chouteau Company dragged its feet over advancing more goods, Sire told Sibley: "The sums standing on the books to the debit of the several outfits up the Mississippi are really enormous—they exceed $400,000!!!"[9]

As Sibley looked at the previous year's accounts, he saw a dismal picture of losses on the real estate that Rice had turned over to them. Moreover, neither Rice nor Borup was making the hoped-for profits on the Ojibwe trade, thanks to gross mismanagement of the plan for removing all of the tribe to northern Minnesota. Told that their annuities would be paid that fall at Big Sandy Lake, Wisconsin Ojibwe—men and women, children and old people—had made the exhausting journey by canoe and on foot, only to find that neither supplies nor money would arrive for many weeks. As winter closed in, some two hundred died, either from hunger and exposure, or (as Ramsey officially claimed) from an outbreak of disease.[10]

It was also clear to Sibley that his own Sioux Outfit had again lost money in 1849–50. He remained outwardly hopeful about the approaching season, but reports from McLeod and Kittson grew less encouraging as winter drew on. Sire arrived from St. Louis in January to go over the books with Fred, who told his brother: "It certainly has a somewhat terrifying look." And Forbes wrote, "Our whole dependence is now a treaty. If that chance was not in perspective, Sioux O[utfit] would hardly be worth keeping together."[11]

In regard to that treaty, Sibley was the key figure in a tangle of conflicting interests. He could be confident of his influence with the Dakota, for however they might regard him, he had been a factor in their lives for seventeen years. Most of their mixed-blood relatives had either worked for him or traded under agreements with him; the prosperity of families like the Renvilles, the Faribaults, the Provençalles, the Freniers, and many others was aligned with his own; mixed-bloods and band members alike owed him money; and the missionaries, who had a recognized following in the tribe, viewed Sibley as a friend and benefactor. Even leaders like Little Crow and Wabasha were aware that it would be in the trader's own financial interest to help negotiate as large a payment for their country as possible.

In Washington, Delegate Sibley represented the white land-seekers of the territory and the expansionist ambitions of the United States, while at the same time he was identified with the declining business empires of American Fur and the Chouteau Company. Unlike his mentor Lewis Cass or his ally Ramsey, whose political and business careers rested unequivocally on clearing the way for white possession at the earliest time and least cost, Sibley's motives were divided, and he was never above suspicion on both sides of the issue.

In 1851, an additional factor complicated his situation. For years the Ewing brothers, a pair of Indiana-based traders, had conducted a trade war with American Fur in the Ohio River valley. Now, with nearly all tribes there removed to the southern plains, the Ewings were looking to the west and north. A few itinerant traders supplied by them had met with small success on the Upper Mississippi, but their presence and that of David Olmsted furnished the groundwork for claims against the Indians. The Ewings had a keen instinct for government money, and as with Rice, their real power was in Washington.[12]

While national events postponed movement on a treaty, Sibley and Ramsey maneuvered to control the process. By virtue of his office Ramsey was nearly certain to be one of the commissioners. He told Sibley that Hugh Tyler, a lawyer and political crony from Pennsylvania, was his first choice for the other. Sibley leaned hard on the Indian office, and by early summer in 1850 it seemed that Tyler would be appointed and that treaty negotiations might still be held later that season.[13]

The situation changed abruptly when President Taylor's death delayed government action and produced a new secretary of the Interior. A new commissioner of Indian Affairs had also taken office. Both listened to the Ewings, and by January it appeared that their chosen candidate, a congressman from Indiana, would be joining Ramsey at the treaty table instead of Tyler. Sibley was hard at work, however, and when the appropriation bill for the Indian office passed in February it contained a cost-cutting provision that required treaty commissioners to be officials of the department. He and Sarah stayed that winter at the same Washington boarding house with Luke Lea, the new head of Indian affairs, and the opportunity for close acquaintance proved valuable. In light of the changed law, and pressed by both Sibley and Ramsey, Lea agreed to become one of the commissioners himself.

Next to securing sympathetic commissioners, the instructions given them were all-important. Over these, Ramsey and Sibley came close to a falling out. In correspondence with Washington, the governor suggested that the instructions restrict payment of tribal debts, for traders would "exact the last penny." Sibley bristled immediately at the personal implications "while I am working for you individually as well as for the Territory, and bringing up all my forces to sustain you." Then in carefully measured phrases he excused Ramsey of meaning that "just debts" should not be paid, but added pointedly that obstacles to payment "would necessarily result in the failure of any attempt to treat." Ramsey heard the threat, and the final instructions left wide discretion to the commissioners.[14]

Back in Minnesota by mid-April, Sibley received several long letters from Martin McLeod. He had a close rapport with the square-faced, introspective Canadian Scot who had overseen trade with the western bands since 1845. McLeod described in detail the weak and starving condition of the Sisseton and their immediate dependence both on assistance from their traders and on the prospect of a treaty. He repeated what he had urged before—that negotiations be held first with them and the Wahpeton. Once the upper bands signed a treaty, the pressure on the Mdewakanton and Wahpekute would be almost irresistible. It was a shrewd strategy, and accordingly the first round of treaty-making was scheduled with the western bands at Traverse des Sioux in early July.[15]

By then prospects looked good for a treaty that would satisfy Minnesota promoters and politicians along with rescuing Sibley from financial ruin. Trying to reassure Chouteau as he reported their losses in November 1850, Sibley had declared: "The Indians are all prepared to make a treaty when we tell them to do so, and such a one as I may dictate.... I think I may safely promise you that no treaty can be made without our claims being first secured." He was not in fact that certain as he joined the commissioners and their mixed entourage on a Sunday in late June. But after their small steamboat had left Fort Snelling to churn its way up the flood-swollen Minnesota, the passengers assembled for Christian services and pondered on the text: "Thou shalt have the heathen for thy possession."[16]

Traverse des Sioux was the site of a Sisseton village, a series of trading posts, and a more recently established mission. These were located on a sloping prairie cradled in a curve of the Minnesota River some seventy-five miles above its mouth. The gathering held there that summer set a classic climax to the period of U.S. Indian treaties, as two cultures and a myriad of contending interests converged for nearly a month.

The government was represented not only by the commissioners and their official staff, but also by the local Indian agent, a crowd of commissaries, and a group of mixed-blood interpreters. A few dragoons from Fort Snelling added a military flourish. Missionaries present included Riggs and Williamson. Sibley and Dousman were there, along with most of their Minnesota agents. A few independent traders arrived, and a polished but unobtrusive presence was Richard Chute of Indiana, representing the Ewings. Chute's attractive and adventurous wife had come along to see the country and witness the pageantry. Other tourists and the press were there also, for Goodhue came to report the event for readers of the *Pioneer*, and a traveling artist named Frank Mayer soaked in the color and made hasty sketches in his notebook.[17]

Color there was. The occasional vivid costume of a Métis cart driver or voyageur, set off rakishly by knitted cap and sash, rivaled the fur, feathers, and beadwork of the Dakota. The most lavish finery belonged to Little Crow, who headed a delegation of Mdewakanton observers. More color was added as Sisseton and Wahpeton arrived from the upper country, the men on horseback with spears and rifles, the women leading ponies loaded with baggage and pulling carts or travois.

For three weeks the proceedings were delayed while scattered western bands kept coming, sometimes in large groups, sometimes as a few families. No exact count was made, but more than two thousand were expected, and the commissioners looked anxiously at their dwindling stock of provisions. The time was filled with feasting, drumming and songs, ceremonial dances, games, and contests. It may have seemed like an extended fair to the Euro-Americans and perhaps more like a wake to the Dakota. All knew it was a moment of passage.

The days were punctuated by death and marriage. One of the staff at the mission was drowned while taking a morning dip in the river, and his funeral was followed shortly by the gala wedding of a young mixed-blood couple. The sixteen-year-old bride was the daughter of a lieutenant of the First Infantry

Little Crow as he appeared at Traverse des Sioux in 1851

who had died in Florida. Like several other young officers with mixed-blood children, he had turned to his friend Henry Sibley to protect her interests after his transfer away from Fort Snelling.[18]

Sibley himself had little time for revelry. He made one hasty trip to Mendota to take care of business and visit the ailing Sarah, who had given birth to a baby girl in June. Back at the Traverse, he was occupied with circulating through the small city of tents and tipis, conferring with friends in all groups, advising, negotiating, and adding up accounts. One of the many gatherings in his tent was sketched by Frank Mayer as the trader, his long form stretched on the ground and his head propped on a bedroll, scanned some papers. Like smoke from the cigar between his fingers, reflections on the multiple ironies of the situation may have formed and dissipated as he read.

Scarcely anyone was too naive to see that the elaborate drama at the treaty table was a mask for naked conquest. If no treaty were signed, white men would swarm into the land anyway, and should the Dakota try to drive them out, some pretext would be found to send in troops. The pattern had been set a generation earlier in the Ohio valley and followed more recently in Illinois and Wisconsin with the Fox and Sauk. Elders of the tribe knew it, but the younger men were still defiant.

Whatever amount was offered would be a mere token and of little aid in Dakota survival. As missionaries insisted, an adequate land base along with schools, buildings, roads, and other improvements to help in the forced transition were of more value than cash. Yet Indians were quick to retort that the first (and often only) result of these government services was more employment for white men.

Sibley in his tent at Traverse des Sioux

Sibley, like most traders, had for years done business with individual hunters, giving each one credit and writing up purchases. Yet if the mountain of long-past debts were left to individual payment, not a fraction of the traders' losses could be retrieved. Therefore he would now insist on a lump sum from the tribe, appealing to the very sense of communal property and responsibility that he, like the missionaries, saw as the greatest barrier to civilizing the Indian.

The claims, calculated by compiling records and recollections back as far as the 1820s, amounted, by Sibley's estimate, to at least twice what money the commissioners were likely to allow. Fraud was unnecessary to account for the sum. The entire risk of the declining fur business had for years been borne by Indians. No provision existed for writing off their debts. If a trader failed or died, he passed on the Indian accounts receivable to his own creditors. If, like Sibley and Dousman, he managed to survive in business until the time for a treaty arrived, the accumulated losses—legitimate debts according to the structure and customs of the trade—might be recovered.[19]

Only ten years earlier Doty had not hesitated to include in his treaty special sums earmarked for traders' claims and for mixed-bloods, who could not by law participate in the treaty. Since then, however, political opposition to both practices had reached new heights. The indignant reaction of Congress and citizens to such subsidies was not a defense of Indians but of their own pocketbooks. By 1851 neither the commissioners nor Sibley could imagine that Congress would approve any item openly identified with either one. In reality there were subterfuges, and if legitimate traders did not use them, others, like the Ewings, were poised to do so.

After determining the extent of terms the commissioners would offer and Congress ratify, Sibley's task was to rally the traders and mixed-bloods into a united group and persuade the Dakota that it was the best bargain they could make. Beyond that were the problems of reaching some arrangement for recouping his losses and also for payments to the mixed-blood families. His two key associates were McLeod and Joe Brown, both of whom had years of acquaintance with the upper bands and family ties to them. Overcoming mutual distrust born of longstanding rivalry, they worked together for Sibley, and somewhere along the way, a plan of action emerged.[20]

Among the Dakota there were pockets of open opposition to any treaty, but they held only a minority. At the first formal session, on July 18, Lea outlined the government's initial offer, and the Sisseton chief Sleepy Eyes stalked out. After threats by the commissioners to end the council and depart, and after assurances from other Dakota leaders, the deliberations were resumed two days later. This time the terms were presented in writing, and Ramsey urged an immediate decision. On the next day the Dakota came back with a counteroffer, also in writing. The formal council was then adjourned and negotiations continued through the rest of the day and the entire night, with the Indians assembled on the upper terrace above the treaty grounds, and messengers shuttling back and forth.[21]

The terms finally reached yielded an annuity of approximately $68,000 to be paid for fifty years. An initial sum of $30,000 would be invested in schools, mills, blacksmith shops, plowing, fencing, and housing. In addition, a sum of $275,000 would be paid to the chiefs "in such manner as they, hereafter, in open council shall request." Words in the treaty implied that this was intended to pay the costs of removal to a reservation in the Upper Minnesota River valley and subsistence there until the annuities became effective; in fact, it was the loophole needed by the traders and mixed-bloods.[22]

By noon on July 23 formal copies of the treaty had been prepared, and the final ceremonies took place. After signing two copies of the treaty, each chief was directed to an upended barrel at which Joe Brown sat with a pen and a document that pledged them to pay their bands' debts and assigned approximately $210,000 of the "subsistence" money to traders and mixed-bloods as the chiefs "hereby in open council request." Some obviously knew what the paper was and approved; others were in the dark. It had been neither read nor explained during the council sessions, and when the Dakota agent, Nathaniel

The treaty signing at Traverse des Sioux, July 1851

McLean, requested that this be done, the commissioners brushed him aside. Actual names and amounts had not yet been attached to the paper.[23]

Since the cash sum was less than half the alleged debts, a committee of three—McLeod, Brown, and Louis Robert, an independent trader from St. Paul—met immediately after the treaty signing. They compared the claims and assigned a reduced amount to each one, setting apart $40,000 for payments to individual mixed-bloods. The traders listed had either been associated with Sibley or were well-known independents in the country. Pierre Chouteau, Jr. & Company was nowhere mentioned. Amounts owed to "the company" appeared under Sibley's name. The Ewing interests, represented by Chute, were given no hearing and apparently requested none, for, as Chute told his employer, Sibley "had his stakes pretty well set."[24]

Sibley himself, the largest and most powerful creditor, stood aside from the process, trusting his friends and giving an appearance of detachment. That same night, however, he was summoned to a meeting of Sisseton and Wahpeton chiefs, and "It being dark, I took a candle to enable me to write down what the Indians wanted me to do." As they called out the names of mixed-bloods, Sibley recorded them. This list, along with the names of traders and the amounts allowed to each, was later attached to the paper that had been signed by the chiefs at the treaty council.[25]

It was a neat piece of strategy. As the commissioners and their party along with the various guests and onlookers boarded a keelboat for the return trip to Fort Snelling, spirits were high. Liquor flowed; passengers accompanied the Canadian boatmen in French voyageur songs, and some volunteered to take a hand at the heavy sweeps. Sibley no doubt joined in the jubilation—but not too heartily. The river was still high and the water swift and treacherous. In their haste they traveled all night, and he was called on to pilot the craft, which arrived at the Mississippi only twenty-three hours after starting.[26]

The Mdewakanton and Wahpekute were already gathering, and the commissioners wasted no time. After an opening session, held on July 29 in Sibley's hot and crowded warehouse at Mendota, they adjourned to an arbor on the breezy heights of Pilot Knob.[27]

The Mdewakanton were the most sophisticated and prosperous of the Dakota bands. Their experience with the treaty of 1837 had not only furnished them with limited support in the form of annuities, but had also taught them bitter lessons in what to expect. Their principal spokesmen, Wabasha and Little Crow, were both wily negotiators who announced immediately that they would discuss no new treaty until the unpaid money owed under the former one was actually in their hands.

Sibley and Ramsey had anticipated the demand, and they had at Mendota

$30,000 in hard cash, loaned by the Chouteau Company. Armed with this bargaining chip, the commissioners felt confident. But the Mdewakanton were not easily bought. After three days the council adjourned, and for four more days informal negotiations proceeded. As with the western bands, the younger warriors were angry and belligerent, and some threatened that the first chief to sign would be slain. The leaders, on their part, recognized the truth of Ramsey's words—that with western Minnesota opened to settlement, they would be encircled by white communities and under crushing pressure.

At last, on August 5, with agreement reached on terms similar to those given the western bands, the formal council was reconvened. The chiefs demanded a reservation along the Minnesota River that extended from the lower end of the Sisseton-Wahpeton reserve down to Traverse des Sioux. The commissioners offered a compromise line at the Little Rock River and presented the treaty for signing. Still there was hesitation. Then Little Crow stepped forward and, turning to the young warriors gathered in the rear, announced that he would be the first to sign, even if he were shot before he laid down the pen. There was a stir of admiration for the bold gesture, and other chiefs lined up to follow him.

The Mendota treaty included a cash amount of $90,000 for each band, and Sibley again tried to secure written promises from the chiefs. The ploy did not work a second time, although the leaders of both bands assured him of their intention to pay debts to the traders. Two months later the Wahpekute signed a schedule of claims, allotting the entire amount, but the Mdewakanton adamantly refused. Meanwhile, the $30,000 paid to the Mdewakanton by agent McLean on behalf of the government led to a buying spree, and Sibley wrote hastily to Borup for help in rounding up "all the cheap horses" he could find in St. Paul and Little Canada.[28]

News that the treaties were concluded touched off a wave of celebration in the settlements east of the Mississippi. Writing in the *Pioneer*, Goodhue painted a white man's triumphant vision of "the red savages with their tipis, their horses, and their famished dogs, fading, vanishing, dissolving away, and in their place a thousand farms and white cottages and waving wheat fields . . . and cities crowned with spires and railroads with trains of cars." Even Daniel A. Robertson, the editor of the *Minnesota Democrat*, a political voice for Rice and no friend of either Sibley or Ramsey, rejoiced that "the magnificent valley of the Minnesota will soon furnish happy homes to thousands of our own progressive race."[29]

Acquisitive members of that race promptly swarmed across the river in search of land and promising townsites. "People are almost crazy to get claims on the west of the Mississippi," Sibley told a Washington friend in early September. The complaints of the Dakota to Agent McLean about this invasion somehow got lost in the bureaucratic wilderness, and—predictably—no response came from either the Interior or the War Department.[30]

Each illegal squatter on Indian land increased the pressure on Sibley to secure ratification of the treaties. To most Minnesotans it seemed inconceivable that Congress could reject them, but Sibley, after his years in Washington, was keenly aware of the divisive temper of the country and the sectional rivalries that might block expansion to the northwest. To Borup he had already observed wearily: "I would not go through with what I have endured for the last six weeks for $10,000. Nobody is satisfied of course. Everybody wanted everything." Yet he knew an even more bitter struggle lay ahead.[31]

Adding to his burdens that fall was a crushing personal sorrow. The new baby was doing well, and Sarah had regained her strength, but early in September four-year-old Harry developed pneumonia. For two weeks the parents sat helplessly at the child's bedside. Then, as Sibley described the end in a letter to his brother Sproat: "Only a few hours before his death, in the silent watches of the night, he broke out suddenly with the air and words of the little hymn 'There is a happy land, far far away.' ... God save me from a repetition of the anguished feelings which I then and since have experienced." In the weeks that followed, Sibley quite uncharacteristically shared his emotion even with old business associates. To Kittson in distant Pembina he wrote: "The depth of our affliction has almost rendered us careless of existence."[32]

Existence went on, nevertheless. As soon as the Mendota treaty was concluded, Ramsey departed for the Red River valley to negotiate yet another land purchase, this one with the Ojibwe. Meanwhile word spread of trouble brewing among the Dakota, stirred by traders who had been shut out from the claims settlement. Sibley, with an anxious eye on how this might interfere in Washington, appealed to Chouteau to put pressure on the Ewings and to Dousman for help in controlling Rice.[33]

On November 10 he was ready again to leave for the East. It was a family expedition. In the winter of 1850–51 he and Sarah had left the children at Mendota, but this time seven-year-old Gussie and the baby, whom they had named Sarah Jane, went with them. Sarah's mother and sister also boarded the steamer, for the older woman wanted to visit her family in Pennsylvania while she still had strength to travel. Only Fred Sibley remained at Mendota, entrusted with the slow process of winding down the business of the Sioux Outfit and keeping an eye on his own and his brother's land claims.[34]

The steamboat was hardly out of sight when Fred received a letter from McLeod at Traverse des Sioux, reporting his first conversation with a new trader there named Madison Sweetser. Although Sweetser was a brother-in-law of the Ewings, it was well known that he had quarreled with them, and the Ewings steadily denied any connection with his activities. They were lying. A partnership agreement had been signed in September by which the House of Ewing was to receive two-thirds of any profit made. They and Sweetser hoped for a repudiation of the traders paper by the Dakota and a re-assignment of treaty money from Sibley's group to themselves.[35]

Sweetser immediately sought out Sleepy Eyes and others like him who had opposed any treaty and were still unhappy with the results. With plausible promises and generous gifts he persuaded them to make him their attorney and revoke the traders paper. He even succeeded in gaining support from some of Sibley's own mixed-blood traders, who were disappointed at the amounts allotted to them by Brown and McLeod and felt "the company" was taking too much. The treaties had not yet been sent to the Senate when Sweetser appeared before Ramsey in St. Paul with a delegation of Sisseton and Wahpeton. They claimed that the agreement on debts had been secured through fraud. Shrugging, the governor observed that the debts were a matter between traders and Indians, not part of the treaty, and no concern of his.

The Ewings were apparently convinced that Ramsey was expecting a payoff from Sibley and Chouteau. Therefore they took the matter directly to Washington, where their influence was still strong. Through Sweetser they sent an allegation of fraud signed by the Dakota to the Indian Office.

Nasty as the situation seemed, it had less impact than Sibley had feared. The treaties faced far more important barriers from southern influence in the Senate. After months of delay, discussion of them began in April. Ironically, one of the principal opponents was John Bell of Tennessee, who as secretary of war in 1841 had been the main force behind the Doty treaty. In fact, he was not inconsistent. Whereas the Doty treaty would have raised a barrier to further white settlement in the Northwest, the 1851 treaty did the opposite. Bell was dedicated to preventing anything that threatened the delicate balance of power between North and South; settlement and early statehood for Minnesota was one such threat.

Against this Sibley could marshal impressive power. His old friends in the Senate, Cass and Douglas, stood by him along with a number of others including James Shields of Illinois and the Dodges—father and son—of Wisconsin and Iowa. Behind the scenes he was also aided by Ramsey's friend Hugh Tyler, who had served the commissioners as commissary officer during the treaty-making, and who had been retained by Sibley and the other traders to lobby the Senate. No record was kept of Tyler's activities, but his expenses were considerable.[36]

Meanwhile, with spring arriving Ramsey complained that the delay had set back development of Minnesota a full year, yet he marveled at the scale of settlement across the river: "We have grown quite familiar already with the names of some half dozen embryo towns on that side." To this Sibley responded that the country could now never revert to the Indians, whatever happened to the treaties. At the same time he warned the senators in Washington that failure to ratify might lead to a full-scale Indian war, and in private he told his friend Augustus Dodge that if the traders' claims were a decisive barrier, they would have to be dropped. "All private interests must be disregarded," he wrote. "Save the treaties I repeat at whatever cost to all concerned."[37]

At last, on June 23 two of the three treaties were adopted, the one with the Ojibwe being rejected. Unable to defeat the Dakota treaties, the opposition sought to amend them to death and nearly succeeded. The most nearly fatal change was striking out the provision for reservations. This left the Dakota facing exile to some unnamed place, yet to be chosen by the President.

What to do? Sibley, still in Washington, was sick at heart. He had already told Ramsey that the work, the compromises, and the mortification had been more "than any consideration would induce me to undergo again." Yet his frustration and that of Ramsey were no match for the anger and despair of the Dakota. They, too, knew that the changes they saw around them were irreversible. When Wabasha heard of the amendments to the treaty, he said to the missionary Stephen Riggs, "There is one thing more which our great father can do, that is, gather us all together on the prairie and surround us with soldiers and shoot us down."[38]

Ramsey realized that he was sitting on a powder keg as tension built between the white squatters and the Mdewakanton. So he appealed through Lea to the president, asking that the Dakota be allowed temporarily to occupy the unassigned reservation lands. Confident of permission, he then looked for a way to persuade the tribe to accept the rewritten treaty.

It was Dousman who provided an answer. In a conversation with Rice, he had heard the latter say offhandedly that for ten thousand dollars he could convince the Indians. Dousman leaped at the deal, perhaps to Rice's surprise. No one had ever questioned Rice's ability as a diplomat and persuader, but Sibley's distrust had kept him at arm's length from the treaty negotiations. Bluntly, Dousman told Sibley to deal with Rice face to face and not stand on etiquette. Nevertheless, Sibley turned the task over to Borup. Ramsey, on his part, found money for expenses and gifts, ultimately taking it from the subsistence funds in the treaty, and Rice met with the Dakota at Mendota and again at Traverse des Sioux. Exactly what he promised them and what he was paid by the traders was never recorded, but reluctantly the Dakota agreed to the amendments.[39]

No friend of the Ewings, Rice also succeeded in checkmating Sweetser. As part of their agreement, the Sisseton and Wahpeton signed a paper giving Ramsey power of attorney to collect and disburse according to their wishes the entire $275,000 granted for subsistence, removal, and to "settle their affairs." That most of them understood this to revoke the original traders paper as well as Sweetser's power of attorney was almost certain.

With the way cleared for actual payment of the treaty money, the pressure shifted from Sibley to Ramsey. He faced a thorny situation. Not only was there fierce rivalry among the traders, but the Dakota themselves were divided. Only the Wahpekute presented no difficulty. Honoring the paper they had signed the year before, they instructed the governor to pay $90,000 directly to their traders. With the Mdewakanton a number of stormy sessions resulted only in repeated demands that $90,000 be handed in cash to the seven chiefs of the band. This Ramsey refused to do, and he brought added pressure by withholding the annuities due the band under the treaty of 1837. At last, with Sibley's help, a compromise was reached by which the chiefs got $20,000 in cash for distribution to their mixed-blood relatives and Ramsey could pay the traders $70,000.[40]

The governor experienced even more trouble with the Sisseton and Wahpeton. In what threatened to become a violent confrontation at Traverse des Sioux, he chose to treat the original traders paper as a binding agreement. Most of the chiefs refused to accept this or to sign a receipt for the money and presented a new schedule of payments that reduced the traders' claims to $70,000, of which $10,000 was assigned to Sweetser. At last, with the help of troops summoned from Fort Snelling, Ramsey resorted to the time-honored ruse of arresting the main dissidents and appointing new chiefs who would agree to what he wanted.[41]

Still another difficulty remained. To secure Tyler's help in Washington, Sibley had promised him a percentage of the traders' claims. In lobbying the senators, however, Tyler's "expenses" (no one called them bribes) had been far greater than the amount settled on. Some objected, but Sibley held firm. Ramsey agreed, and probably for this reason named Tyler as his agent to take the money and pay the individual traders. Thus Tyler deducted his percentage in advance.[42]

Sweetser had been with the Indians during the fracas at Traverse des

Sioux. Still hoping to trace some of the money from Tyler back to Ramsey's pockets, or even to secure a new appropriation to reimburse those creditors who had been "cheated," he carried the battle to Washington.[43] Meanwhile in St. Paul he had found a new ally.

While Minnesotans had been mesmerized by treaties and land claims, a presidential election had taken place, and the Whig administration had been replaced by that of Democrat Franklin Pierce. A new governor for the territory would therefore soon be named, and Daniel G. Robertson, editor of the *Minnesota Democrat*, hoped it would be him. Sibley was without question the leading local candidate, but his involvement with the treaties and all the controversy attending them looked to Robertson like the makings of a convenient scandal. Thus with Sweetser supplying allegations of fraud and the *Democrat* serving as a vehicle for publicity, Minnesota was soon a subject of conversation in both New York and Washington.[44]

Sibley, back in Congress, immediately demanded an investigation to clear his own and Ramsey's reputation, and after Sweetser had filed charges, the Senate directed the president to conduct an inquiry. The change of administrations slowed the process, and the need to interrogate many witnesses, including a number of Indians, made it necessary to shift the investigation to St. Paul. Thus by the time the hearings opened on July 6, 1853, Ramsey was no longer a public official. Sibley also would soon be a private citizen, for Pierce had felt that his appointment as governor would be too controversial, and Sibley had announced that he was not a candidate for reelection as congressional delegate.[45]

The investigation dragged on into October. It was conducted by the new governor of the territory, Willis A. Gorman, and by Richard M. Young, a former clerk of the U.S. House of Representatives. Both were strangers to Minnesota. In all, forty-seven witnesses were examined by the government, and ten were called by the defense. The report of the commissioners, written by Young, was careful and even-handed. No evidence of bribery or of a conspiracy to cheat legitimate creditors was found, but they judged that Ramsey had indeed both violated the treaty and broken his implied promises to the Indians when he insisted on enforcing the terms of the traders paper. They concluded: "Now, whether this money would have been squandered or not, if paid directly to the Indians—still, if such were our treaty engagements with them, we were bound in justice and in honor to have paid the money according to our contracts."[46]

Sibley had only attended the hearings when summoned, but he was far from inactive. He made two brief trips to Washington in the summer and returned again in November for the opening of Congress, meanwhile writing urgent letters in defense of Ramsey. The President sent the report of the investigation to the Senate in February 1854. Whether through Sibley's efforts, through the abrupt withdrawal of all charges by Robertson, or—more likely—through the general attitude of the lawmakers toward Indians, the Senators dismissed the findings of the commissioners and declared that "the conduct of Governor Ramsey was not only free from blame, but highly commendable and meritorious."[47]

Thus southern Minnesota was taken from the Dakota under duress and in a cloud of deceit and broken promises. The Upper Mississippi traders, uniting in the end against a raid by outsiders, and backed by Ramsey, had secured their claims, but as Dousman observed with more prescience than he knew: "The Sioux treaty will hang like a curse over our heads the balance of our lives." Sibley himself maintained a conspicuous silence about it in later years, crucial as the event had been for both him and Minnesota.[48]

· 10 ·

A New Era

*I*IBLEY HAD OFTEN PROTESTED, both publicly and privately, that he had no personal desire for election as the territory's delegate to Congress. Part of this reluctance was the political fashion of the time, and part of it may have been his own pose of genteel aloofness. But by the spring of 1853 his weariness was genuine. Repeated travel across the country and months in Washington boardinghouses had taken a toll on both himself and his family. He had spent that winter alone in the East, for in 1852–53 Sarah, pregnant again, stayed at Mendota with the children.

The long agony of the Dakota treaties had still not ended, and Sibley's business affairs were in desperate need of attention. So it was no doubt with relief that he stepped aside that summer and in fact advised his friends to vote for Henry Rice. Tension between the two men had temporarily eased since Rice's help with the treaties, and Rice was far preferable to the candidate backed by Robertson, who had become the current archenemy of both Sibley and Ramsey.

In June 1853 carpenters and masons were busy making improvements to the house at Mendota, and on August 1 Henry and Sarah welcomed a "bouncing boy," whom they named for his uncle, Franklin Steele. Nine-year-old Gussie, who had been repeatedly troubled with inflammation of her eyes, seemed to be outgrowing the ailment, and although two-year-old Sallie was dangerously ill that fall, she soon recovered. In 1855 a third daughter, Mary Steele, would be added to the family. Sibley's mother had died late in 1850, severing one more of his ties to Detroit, but as railroads reached across Indiana and Illinois the new ease of travel made visits there more frequent.[1]

Encounters between Sibley and his first daughter probably increased at this time. Helen, by then reaching adolescence, continued to live with the William Brown family, but early in the 1850s they moved from Newport to St. Paul. Sibley continued to pay for her living expenses and also provided for her future, investing her money from the 1851 treaty in railroad bonds and keeping for her a separate account. An addition to it came in 1857 with the issuing of Dakota half-breed scrip of which she was entitled to a share. Perhaps advised by Martha Brown, Sibley bought Helen small gifts, and in 1855, at the time of her fourteenth birthday, he gave her a melodeon. It may have been shortly after this that he sent her east for a year or two of better schooling than could be had in St. Paul.[2]

Their relationship must have been well known in the small community, and although it was apparently an embarrassment to Sarah, it was no political or social liability to Sibley himself. Mixed-blood children were common among frontier traders, army men, and government agents, and the only remarkable thing in Sibley's case was his acknowledgment and support of Helen. Like the Brown family, she attended the Jackson Street Methodist Church and was a favorite among the young people there. During a civic celebration in 1858 the tall, dark-eyed seventeen-year-old was one of thirty-three young women selected to represent the states of the Union on a float that paraded through the streets of St. Paul. Behind it in a carriage with other dignitaries rode her father. In listing the participants, the *Daily Minnesotian* identified Miss Delaware without further comment as Helen Sibley.[3]

During his years in Congress Sibley had expanded the scope of his writing ventures. He prepared a description of the Minnesota country that was published by the Washington *Union* in 1850 and reprinted as a promotional flyer. It was also reprinted in the first volume of *Annals* published by the Minnesota Historical Society. In December of the same year he sent to his friend Porter at the *Spirit of the Times* what he described as "a part of a letter in the French language appended to a public document." Its author was the Reverend

The Sibley House at Mendota as sketched by Augusta Sibley

Georges-Antoine Belcourt, a missionary priest at Pembina who gave a detailed account of the buffalo hunts organized by his Métis parishioners. Sibley, who knew and corresponded with Belcourt, had translated the piece. It appeared in Porter's publication the next month. While in Washington Sibley also worked with the Smithsonian Institution toward publication in 1852 of a grammar and dictionary of the Dakota language compiled by the missionaries. At about the same time he wrote a short memoir of his friend Joseph Nicollet for the Historical Society and revised two of his earlier articles from the *Spirit of the Times* for inclusion in a book of advice on field sports—hunting and shooting—for young readers. Both were published in 1853.[4]

Nearly six years passed before Sibley sent anything more to Porter, but in 1856 he received a letter from the editor announcing a new publication called *Porter's Spirit of the Times* and soliciting contributions from "Hal." It struck a nostalgic chord, and within a month Sibley sent off another essay. Far from being an account of earlier adventures, however, this was a passionate attack on the growing new practice of market hunting "which, unless soon repressed, will result in the extinction of the game of America." His pen dripped indignation as he also denounced those who "sport with the lives of little birds

Helen Hastings Sibley, from a portrait published in the St. Paul Dispatch, *October 1908*

merely to gratify a propensity for useless shedding of blood, and who crawl stealthily upon a covey of grouse or bevy of quail, which are huddling closely together on a fence-rail, on a cold December day, merely to boast of having massacred a dozen of his shivering and unsuspecting prey at a single shot."[5]

With a note of melancholy he reported that although buffalo and elk still roamed in Minnesota, "they are gradually retiring before the avalanche of white settlers who are precipitating themselves upon us." As for the Indians: "Turn to the history of the Six Nations, and of the other bands whose graves are numberless on both sides of the Alleghanies and you will need but little aid from the imagination." It was, he said, the old story of broken treaties and betrayed promises, and the Dakota "can look for no redress of their grievances on this side of the 'spirit land.'"

The same year saw the first of two long reminiscences that Sibley wrote for the Minnesota Historical Society. Invited to give the annual address in the winter of 1856, he delivered a lengthy paper, mostly devoted to incidents and personalities recollected from his own early years on the Upper Mississippi. In concluding he hinted that he intended to expand the work and incorporate accounts from others as well as himself. He made a beginning the following winter, when he interviewed Jack Frazer, drawing out stories of the man's early years as a Dakota hunter and warrior of Wacouta's band. One of these tales he sent as his last contribution to Porter's publication, but the rest remained in his files for a decade.[6]

For Henry Sibley as well as for Minnesota, the four years he had spent in Congress marked a great divide. Already surveyors were busy in the oak savannas, woodlands, and prairies. Two hundred years of border society—a middle ground between Native American and European—was being swept aside almost overnight. Sibley's livelihood, his youth, and his keenest pleasures had been part of that world, and when he turned to reminiscence and history, his style took on tones of both nostalgia and self-justification. He used the occasion of his address to the Historical Society for a vigorous defense of fur traders "who have been charged with fraud and villainy of every conceivable description." He himself had felt those charges in the form of political attacks, and, like others, he may have sensed not only the passing of an older society, but the denial of its very existence across the cultural chasm that divided it from the new Minnesota.[7]

Although there were times when, viewed from middle age, the march of progress seemed headed toward an alien landscape, Sibley was poised to take full advantage of the new era he had worked so hard to bring about. The amount of treaty money remaining to him after all his obligations had been paid was no bonanza.[8] Yet it left him relatively free of debt and well situated for making money in land and other businesses of the thriving new territory. He already owned some real estate in St. Paul and St. Anthony and had modest investments in pine timber, lumbering, and steamboats. As he once more admitted to Trowbridge, however, his success in accumulating a fortune had not been "flattering." Fred Sibley, in a moment of discouragement with managing business affairs and employees at Mendota, may have pointed to one factor in this. "Your character for generosity," he told his brother, "stands so high among all . . . that it will be an expensive matter to sustain it here."[9]

Land speculation was the great obsession of Minnesotans both high and low in the mid-1850s. Triggered by the opening of the vast country west of the

Mississippi, it was further stimulated in 1855, when Congress gave military-bounty land warrants to veterans of the Mexican War and similar warrants (called half-breed scrip) to mixed-bloods in exchange for land claims based on treaties with the Dakota and Ojibwe tribes. The speculative frenzy ended abruptly in the late summer of 1857 with a nationwide panic and depression that wiped out inflated land values and left Minnesota and other frontier areas virtually without circulating money for a few months.

Like his associates, Sibley invested in land, and like other leading men in the territory, he also served as an agent for capitalists in older communities who sought to cash in on the soaring profits. Sibley's principal client was Pierre Chouteau, Jr. The relationship established in the fur trade, in the legal contest with Rice, and in the struggle over treaty claims was extended to land ventures. Although the Sioux and Minnesota Outfits continued to exist until 1855, their whole business by then was in real estate and townsite development. Thus Sibley's largest claims were made with the Chouteau Company as a silent partner, and from 1855 to 1859 he drew a salary as manager of its Minnesota land holdings.[10]

The Dakota treaties had not yet been ratified when the partners informally staked out extensive claims at Traverse des Sioux and made plans for platting a town. For nearly a hundred years the Traverse had been a trading station and a key point in the transportation network of the fur trade, and Sibley was clearly convinced that it would continue to develop as a commercial center. Although mistaken, he was not alone. In late 1851 and through 1852 his employees there were as much occupied with fending off competing land claims made by Madison Sweetser and others as they were with the Indian trade. By the next year the settlement was prospering from government business that accompanied construction of the new Fort Ridgely near the

Dakota reservation. Sibley built a warehouse at Traverse des Sioux, and in 1854 a train of 180 Red River carts arrived, sent by Kittson from Pembina. The same year, however, saw the platting of the nearby town of St. Peter, which soon became a formidable trade rival.[11]

Another potential townsite on which Sibley had his eye was Oliver's Grove, opposite the mouth of the St. Croix. It was at a junction point for river traffic, and a break in the steep bluffs that lined the western bank of the Mississippi promised

Sibley as governor, 1859

easy access for stage roads and steel rails. Also recommending the location were mill sites along the nearby Vermillion River. Hence, in partnership with Alexis Bailly and his son Henry, and with Alexander Faribault, Sibley platted the town of Hastings in 1853. According to tradition, it was named for him in a drawing of lots among the proprietors.[12]

Closest to his heart, if not his pocketbook, was the land at Mendota. It was still a part of the Fort Snelling military reservation and owned by the U.S. government. With the removal of the Dakota, however, there was little to justify the fort itself, much less the large expanse of land around it. As early as 1850 Sibley had drafted a bill that would have reduced the reservation to one square mile, but it failed in the Senate. He tried again with more success in 1852, following in his second bill the recommendations for a boundary that had been made by the fort's commander. A clause in the law allowed 320 acres at Mendota to be platted as a town and claims entered under the existing law governing townsites. Thus by the spring of 1853 the town of Mendota was incorporated and in June Sibley had a surveyor busy laying out lots. The plat was formally entered in 1854, and from then until 1857 Mendota served as the seat of Dakota County.[13]

The most controversial part of the military reservation was not Mendota but the valuable land on the west bank at the Falls of St. Anthony, already staked out by a number of farsighted squatters. At first Congress declined to let them simply "prove up" their nonlegal claims and decreed that the land be sold at public auction. Two years later, however, the lawmakers retreated before concentrated lobbying and gave away what was to become the center of downtown Minneapolis at the regular government price of $1.25 an acre.[14]

One of those who benefited was Congressman Robert Smith of Illinois. Through connections at the War Department he had been granted possession of the government mill at the falls, and early in 1853, Sibley received a letter from him. Smith's associate in the enterprise, Henry Rice, had suggested that they cut Sibley in with a one-third interest, and Smith accordingly was inviting him to join. Already burned in one partnership with Rice, Sibley declined the offer and contented himself with a tract of land on the east side above the falls that he purchased from the Métis trader and guide Pierre Bottineau.[15]

As white men carved up the land and jockeyed for possession of its riches, the Dakota were slowly making their way toward the area designated for them along the Minnesota River. Although the tribe still had no assurance that they could occupy the reservation permanently, Governor Gorman had directed them to move, and the new occupants of their previous homes were adding other forms of persuasion. At Red Wing the Dakota village mysteriously burned while the band was absent on a hunt. Sibley tried to intervene on behalf of the small Wahpekute band, telling Gorman that some of them wanted to live beside the Cannon River and adopt the ways of white men, but he was apparently unsuccessful.[16]

The payments to traders and mixed-bloods, along with government expenses charged by Ramsey to the subsistence fund had so depleted it that the Dakota were in urgent need of their first annuities, due in July 1853. Not until November, after they were assembled at the reservation, was a partial payment made. Since none of the promised housing, roads, or other improvements had appeared, the bands scattered again to their old localities for a winter of hunting and meager subsistence.[17]

Hoping to mend relations with the Mdewakanton and achieve some solution for the tenuous status of the reservation, Gorman took Little Crow with him to Washington in the spring of 1854. Sibley, who had other business in the capital at the same time, probably encountered them there and may have added his own influence toward passage of a bill by the Senate that would have established a permanent home for the tribe in the Minnesota River valley. The measure failed in the House, however, and the Dakota continued to occupy their reservation solely at the pleasure of the President.[18]

Another bill in which Sibley had a keen interest had been introduced by Rice early that spring and was passed in July 1854. It settled the much-troubled situation of the so-called Half-Breed Tract along Lake Pepin, which had been addressed without success by treaties signed in 1841, 1849, and 1851. Congress agreed to the simple solution of dividing the land among claimants and exchanging it for land warrants (scrip) applicable anywhere in the public domain. The implementation was watched carefully by leading Dakota mixed-bloods in Minnesota, who held a meeting at Hastings the following summer and appointed Sibley, Bailly, and Faribault to represent them.[19]

One key figure in this implementation was former Illinois senator James Shields. A flamboyant military man and frontier politician who had once challenged Abraham Lincoln to a duel, Shields was an intimate friend of Stephen Douglas. Following his defeat for reelection, he had secured through Douglas an appointment with the federal land office to handle distribution of the half-breed claims. Shields also plunged into large-scale land speculation in southern Minnesota, working with Faribault to found the town of that name, and promoting Irish immigration to the area. Sibley and Shields, both close to Douglas, had been acquainted in Washington, and after Shields moved to Minnesota they developed a brief but active business and political relationship that went well beyond the question of half-breed scrip and the interests of the mixed-blood community.[20]

Sibley had hoped to phase out his trade with the Indians and terminate the Sioux Outfit in 1852, but it took longer than he had expected. Not until 1855 was the business finally closed. By then his associates McLeod and Brown had turned to land speculation. Brown had become proprietor of the town of Henderson and McLeod would soon found Glencoe. Both were serving in the territorial legislature, as were Kittson and Joe Rolette, son of Sibley's former partner. The latter pair made the long trip from Pembina by dogsled for the legislative sessions. In 1854, Kittson moved to St. Paul and joined with Forbes in buying Sibley's St. Paul Outfit, which the two men continued to operate as a supply house for the Indian trade. Borup meanwhile had joined with his former partner, Charles Oakes, to open St. Paul's first bank, and Fred Sibley, who had virtually managed the Sioux Outfit for four years, left Minnesota in the spring of 1854 and returned to Detroit.[21]

Among Sibley's new ventures at this time was a short stint as a newspaper owner. It was motivated more by politics than profit. In the summer of 1852 Goodhue, who was still an erratic but faithful supporter, had died. After the *Pioneer* had floundered for nearly six months, Sibley joined with Joe Brown to ensure that the paper would continue as a Democratic voice independent of both Robertson and the Rice faction. Sibley stayed in the background while Brown moved smoothly into the role of editor. When Brown was a boy he had been briefly apprenticed to a printer, and his versatile talents proved fully equal to yet another career.[22]

As editor, Brown maintained the paper's nominally nonpartisan position through 1853, but by early 1854 his business affairs at Henderson drew him away from St. Paul. On the fervent recommendation of Ben C. Eastman, a congressman from Wisconsin and close political friend, Sibley arranged with a young New Yorker named Earle S. Goodrich to run the paper in partnership with himself and Brown. Goodrich immediately expanded the *Pioneer* and turned it from a weekly into Minnesota's first daily. Sibley underwrote the cost of new equipment and waited none too patiently while Goodrich shopped in the East for a steam-driven press and the paper itself, without hands-on leadership, went steadily downhill. Once back in St. Paul, Goodrich improved the paper but continued to demand more cash for expansion. In October 1854, Brown withdrew from the partnership and Sibley's disposable resources began to run low.[23]

The following summer, in the midst of another election campaign, Rice's deeper pockets prevailed. Already owning the *Democrat*, he bought both Goodrich and the *Pioneer*, merging the two papers as the *Pioneer and Democrat* and leaving the Sibley faction without a newspaper. Indignant and apologetic, Sibley's friend Eastman wrote that he hoped the devil would catch the traitor Goodrich "and take him to his hottest hell."[24]

Hell, Sibley may have reflected, might be no warmer than Minnesota politics at that point. But at least hell had no railroads. If iron rails were bringing a new era of progress, they also carried a freight of corruption that made the claims and political influence of Indian traders look trivial.

As early as 1850 railroads had begun to assume a role in national politics. In September of that year Stephen Douglas secured for the state of Illinois the first grant of federal land for subsidizing and promoting a railroad. The recipient Illinois Central was at the heart of a developing network with connections reaching north, south, and west. In the years that followed it became a potent political influence, and it was one link among the group of lawmakers who supported ratification of the Dakota treaties. The precedent of granting federal land for railroad construction also signaled for the country a new era of corporate organization and pyramiding financial and economic power. For frontier promoters it promised endless opportunities and another surge of westward expansion. As this scene unfolded, Minnesota stood at center stage.[25]

Less than three months after the historic Illinois Central grant, Sibley was planning to seek a similar one for his own territory. The next grant went to the state of Missouri, but by the summer of 1851 Goodhue's lyrical vision for the land just acquired from the Dakota included a train that "comes thundering across the bridge into Saint Paul, fifteen hours from Saint Louis, on the way to Lake Superior." The long struggle over treaty ratification delayed the train, but in 1853 the territory's legislature chartered no less than five railroad corporations, all eager for government subsidy.[26]

The managers of the Illinois Central system, however, had their own plans. Douglas and others were already promoting a northern terminus for the network at the head of Lake Superior and had brought into their townsite and railroad schemes both Robertson and Rice. From his new vantage point as territorial delegate, Rice launched a land-grant bill in Congress, and early in 1854 a squad of attorneys and lobbyists descended on St. Paul to secure a railroad charter from the legislature. Their line, the Minnesota and Northwestern, was to run from the present site of Duluth through St. Paul to the Iowa border. From there it would extend to Dubuque and connect with a branch of the Illinois Central.[27]

It was a moment of shifting loyalties and realignments. Politicians from all factions were interested in the road. Joe Brown proved accommodating and introduced the proposal into the upper house but apparently had no financial stake in the enterprise. Sibley remained on the sidelines, although his close associates, Steele and Borup, were both among the incorporators. Ramsey, also an incorporator, was later named a director, and his continued involvement with the Minnesota and Northwestern led to a growing alliance with Rice and an aloofness toward Sibley. Gorman, the new Democratic governor, was no friend of either Robertson or Rice, and he was cool to the enterprise but unwilling to stand in the way of the Illinois Central juggernaut.

Many legislators resented the charter provision that any land grant made to the territory would vest in that corporation with no further action required. In effect, it handed such federal subsidies directly to the company without limitations or conditions imposed by the territory. There were numerous objections, but the measure was rammed through only hours before the legislature adjourned. Gorman hesitated, but besieged by a milling mob around the Capitol, he signed it, at the same time issuing a public protest. Sibley was still ambivalent, balancing his distrust of Robertson and Rice against the rising railroad fever throughout the territory and his loyalty to Douglas.[28]

In Congress Rice's land-grant bill ran into objections over the cozy arrangement with the Minnesota and Northwestern. Representative Elihu B. Washburne of Galena opposed it along with the owners of several lines in competition with the Illinois Central, including the Chicago and Rock Island and the Michigan Southern. Sibley's friend Ben Eastman was annoyed because the influence of Douglas had moved the bill ahead of land grants for Wisconsin, in which Eastman was interested. The measure quickly died.

Called on to use his influence on behalf of the grant, Sibley agreed, provided he was allowed to draft a new bill. In doing so he worded it carefully to prevent any existing company from laying claim to the land. Perhaps at Sibley's suggestion also, Hugh Tyler, veteran of the treaty struggle, was recruited to lobby for the measure. At some point during the spring, probably when Sibley was in Washington just before the rewritten bill was submitted to Congress, he and Tyler had a friendly discussion with George W. Billings, the chief lobbyist for the Illinois Central. As Tyler later recalled it, Billings pointed out that two very small changes in wording would make it possible for the Minnesota and Northwestern to receive the grant. Sibley replied that opponents of the previous bill would see through the device. Billings pressed further and suggested smoothly that the changes could be made without the knowledge of such opponents. Sibley balked again, and the matter was dropped.[29]

The new bill passed the House without amendments, was approved by the Senate, and was signed by the president on June 29, 1854. Two days later the incorporators of the Minnesota and Northwestern met in New York, elected officers, and blandly accepted the grant. Rice was present and wrote triumphantly to tell Ramsey of his election to the board and plans to have the line surveyed immediately.[30]

While Minnesota celebrated the news, Sibley, astounded, examined the bill as reported in the papers and found that the changes suggested by Billings had indeed been made. Those behind the Minnesota and Northwestern were apparently confident that, with the grant already secured, he would hardly dare to derail the federal subsidy along with the territory's first railroad. They were mistaken; the smell of fraud was too strong. Sibley immediately wrote to Washburne and Eastman. Still not certain that the papers had printed the law correctly, he outlined the situation to Washburne (whom he apparently trusted more than Eastman) and asked him to "trace out the original bill in my handwriting as it passed the House, and find how so material alterations could be made upon the engrossment."[31]

The whistle had been blown. Investigation showed that two small but crucial changes had appeared in the bill after it had passed the House. Although the clerk of the House protested that it was an innocent error, and no one was ever prosecuted, the Minnesota land grant was immediately repealed. "I think," Washburne told Sibley, "they would have taken my life could they have had a fair chance." And Rice wrote sarcastically to Ramsey: "I think the scamps that have disappointed such patriots as Sibley and Gorman should be made to feel hemp." More soberly, he added: "The sole object is to get this left an open question so that some aspirants can feather their own nests and control the political complexion of the territory and future state."[32]

Sibley himself was already laying plans for a return to active politics, since it was clear that with its charter still intact and backed by the power of the Illinois Central system, the Minnesota and Northwestern would refuse to die quietly. Running for the legislature may have been urged by Brown, for in a letter to "My Old Friend" written in September to arrange strategy, Sibley observed: "Now that you have got me in, you must get me safely out." To do so was not difficult, although the supporters of the railroad, realizing that the next battle would be in the legislature, made every effort to ensure that it was "safe."[33]

Elected in October 1854, Sibley took a seat in the territorial House. There he stubbornly upheld an unpopular minority position against repeated attempts by the railroad's friends to renew its charter, extend its life, and influence Congress in its favor. His efforts were supported by Gorman with several vetoes and opposed by all the pressure that Ramsey and Rice could bring to bear. During this time no tracks were laid, and in the panic and depression of 1857 the company's prospects collapsed along with the rest of the frontier economy.[34]

Minnesota's long and turbulent romance with railroads was only beginning however. Ironically, the same summer that had seen the Minnesota and Northwestern scandal also witnessed a history-making celebration sponsored by the Rock Island line, which had laid the first tracks to the Mississippi. Hundreds of notable people, including ex-President Millard Fillmore, went by train from Chicago and embarked on steamboats for a "grand excursion" up the river to St. Paul. For one day in June 1854, the territory's small capital had basked in a moment of glory, and its leading clergyman, the Reverend Edward D. Neill, had expounded from the pulpit on the virtues of railroads, concluding that they were "invaluable aids in the promotion of pure and undefiled religion."[35]

· 11 ·

Schism and Statehood

$\mathcal{T}$HE PROMISE that railroads would bring a revolutionary era of shrinking distance and vast prosperity had led Stephen Douglas to hope that they might bind the country into an economic unit and defuse the crisis over slavery. With federal land grants gaining acceptance and railroads poised to cross the Mississippi, he ventured in May 1854 to push through Congress the Kansas-Nebraska Act. It struck down existing limits to the spread of slavery and left to the vote of settlers in those two territories the decision on whether to become free or slave states. Instead of uniting the country, however, the results polarized it. Neither the steel tracks nor the interlocking interests of the new corporate businessmen who built them could bridge the moral rift that was driving the country apart.[1]

Only a year later the political scene in Minnesota was already responding to new national tensions and sweeping changes. For settlers pouring into southern Minnesota from the eastern states and from Europe, the personal feuds that had dominated politics in the territory were irrelevant. No Whig organization really existed in Minnesota, and the burning issue of slavery immediately drew non-Democrats to the new Republican Party.

In March 1855 a group of self-styled "Republicans" meeting in St. Anthony called for a convention to be held in St. Paul in July. There they were to form an organization and make a nomination for territorial delegate. The spot was offered to Ramsey, but though pressed repeatedly, he cautiously declined. His hesitation was not surprising given the radical nature of the platform, which declared slavery a national curse, demanded repeal of the fugitive slave law, and advocated an antiliquor law in Minnesota.[2]

On the same day the territory's Democrats met in a convention that nominated Rice by acclamation and offered no platform. Hopelessly outnumbered, the minority, led by Sibley and Gorman, walked out and convened to nominate David Olmsted. Their platform denounced Rice and declared devotion to "the cardinal doctrines of the party in their purity." Sibley took no public part in the campaign that followed, and the *Pioneer*, edited by Goodrich, confined itself to personal attacks on Rice—until Rice bought the paper a week before election day, after which it abruptly reversed itself. Olmsted, however, came out forthrightly on the issue of slavery, publishing a letter in which he declared it "a great moral and political evil" that should not be allowed to spread beyond the states where it was protected by the Constitution.[3]

With the presidential election of 1856 the lines hardened further. Sibley's old friend and former hunting companion, John C. Fremont, was nominated by the Republicans, but James Buchanan of Pennsylvania won the White House. Buchanan represented the proslavery wing of the Democratic Party, and since his administration controlled all federal patronage, Rice accommodated immediately. In Minnesota Gorman was replaced by a governor more sympathetic to the administration, and the party outsiders, still led by Sibley, came by necessity to be identified with Democrats who opposed the spread of slavery.

In fact, such Democrats included many of Sibley's longtime friends among the mixed-blood population. As early as 1853 some of them had sensed the implicit threat in barriers erected along racial lines. The legislature that year had considered a law to restrict the rights of free blacks and require them to post a bond before being allowed to live in the territory. It was defeated at the last minute by the action of three Métis representatives, including Joe Rolette. To this group of antislavery voters were added new German and Irish immigrants who had no sympathy for the South but were uncomfortable with the moral manifestos and anti-Catholic, nativist leanings of the Republicans.[4]

As the gap widened between free-soilers and slaveholders, Sibley's own noncommittal position of "Jeffersonian Democrat" was being superseded by history. The Douglas doctrine of local option—"squatter sovereignty"—had originated with Lewis Cass during his struggles in 1850 to reach a compromise the nation could live with. Sibley's ties to both men inclined him to accept it, even while the disastrous results were becoming apparent. Although Solomon Sibley had been among the New England settlers of the Old Northwest who had worked to keep Ohio from becoming a slave state, the slowly crystallizing position of his son appears to have been more a response to the times than a result of any longstanding conviction.

Both the schism in national politics and a resurgence of railroad fever overshadowed the prospect of statehood for Minnesota in the fall of 1856. Changing demographics had produced a rough alignment of sectional interests with political parties in the territory. Republican strength was steadily growing in the southeast, while the original triangle between the St. Croix and Mississippi with its established communities and seat of government remained heavily Democratic. Even more solidly so were the lumbering and trading communities scattered in the north. Therefore the shape of the state to be carved out of the huge expanse of Minnesota Territory was critical to both economic and political fortunes. If the state were cut off a few miles north of St. Paul and St. Anthony and extended to the Missouri River, it would hold a majority of Republican voters and it would also leave the commercial and industrial settlements stranded in a corner and tributary to the spreading agricultural domain in the south and west.

On December 24, 1856, Rice introduced in Congress an enabling act in which the proposed state had approximately the present north-south shape. He followed it a few days later with a bill that gave Minnesota its long-awaited second railroad land grant. It specified the routes to which land might be given, and the railroad network thus outlined lent powerful reinforcement to the boundaries set forth in the enabling act. The system the act defined radiated from St. Paul and Minneapolis and extended a long finger to the Canadian border at Pembina. As a concession to the interests of southeastern Minnesota, it included an east-west line from Winona to the Big Sioux River with branches connecting to the Minnesota River valley. In Congress, Rice's bills met stiff opposition, but Stephen Douglas, again acting as Minnesota's powerful patron, used his influence to push them through. The two bills passed within a week of each other early in 1857, and together they put a heavy brake on the drive for an east-west state.[5]

For a while Sibley found himself pulled in conflicting directions on the issue. Although his political fortunes rested with the older communities to the north, his economic interests lay in the south. In 1856 he had joined Shields as a director and principal stockholder of the Minneapolis and Cedar Valley Railroad, chartered by the legislature with a line running through Mendota and Faribault to the Iowa border. Most of Sibley's land holdings lay in southern Minnesota, and there remained the possibility that if Traverse des Sioux could overcome the competition of St. Peter, it might become the capital of an east-west state. It was a hope that he had mentioned to Chouteau some time earlier.[6]

The last push toward an east-west state was an effort in the 1857 Minnesota legislature to move the capital immediately from St. Paul to the Minnesota River valley. Governor Gorman, Sibley's political ally, had become an economic rival, with extensive investments in the town of St. Peter. Already a lame duck destined for replacement by Buchanan, Gorman struck a deal with the Republicans, and an act for removal of the capital to St. Peter passed both houses. Outrage over the measure led Joe Rolette to star in one of the most famous farces of Minnesota politics by disappearing with the engrossed copy of the bill until it was too late for final signature. Sibley took no open part in the contest, but he wrote to his friend LeDuc, "I learn that some men oppose me at H[astings] on the score that I am an east & west line man. I was so if I could have got what I wanted, but despairing of this I stand now on the offer of Congress, line & all."[7]

In a closing act as governor, Gorman called a special session of the legislature in May to implement the enabling act and the federal land grant by providing for a constitutional convention and accepting and regranting the railroad lands. More than two dozen companies had already been chartered by the territorial legislature at various times. The promoters of the principal ones quickly united in a scheme to divide the routes and the accompanying donations of land. Shields had been in Washington at the time the federal bill was drafted, so it was probably no accident that the exact route of the proposed Minneapolis and Cedar Valley line was among those specified for a land grant under that law.[8]

Sibley had not run for reelection to the legislature in the fall of 1856, nor did he join Brown, Shields, and a crowd of others who headed for Washington after the presidential election. The following spring, however, he agreed to become chair of the Minnesota Democratic Party. It was a move to unify the divided Democrats before the rising tide of conflict over which party would frame the state's constitution. With emotions roused by the open warfare going on in Kansas, the election of delegates descended into a name-calling confrontation between "slaveholders" and "nigger lovers." At issue was the status of free blacks in the new state. Republicans favored full citizenship; Democrats opposed it.[9]

Accusations of fraud swirled around the polls, and by July 13, when the convention assembled, it was clear that neither of the partisan groups would

Joseph R. Brown

permit the other to conduct the proceedings. After some jockeying for control, the Democratic members adjourned to another room in the Capitol. On motion of Joe Brown, they unanimously chose Sibley to preside, and after accepting a number of contested delegates, they settled in to the business of framing a state constitution. Meanwhile the Republicans were doing the same thing at the other end of the building.

As a group the Democrats were more experienced in government and less driven by ideology than the Republican delegates. Restrained by Sibley's lofty moderation and parliamentary experience and propelled by

Brown's down-to-earth pragmatism, they made good progress. The task demanded no great imagination, for other state constitutions offered convenient models.

As chair Sibley now and then stepped aside to debate an issue. His positions were generally consistent with his self-image as a follower of Jefferson and his years as a Democrat in the post-Jacksonian West. He was intensely suspicious of banks and their power to issue currency, and he fiercely opposed the jailing of debtors, which he had also managed to defeat while in the territorial legislature. His own clash with the special privileges granted in the charter of the Minnesota and Northwestern Railroad led him to favor general laws to govern impartially the forming of all corporations. He favored strong local government, popular election of judges, and sharp curbs on state power, including two-year terms for officers and strict time limits on legislative sessions. A striking example of his desire to keep government close to the people was his stand on giving school lands directly to the townships in which they were located. To the surprise of many, he argued passionately: "I do not want to see every township put under the supervision of a great Central Committee located here in St. Paul."[10]

While suffrage for blacks was an explosive issue, the same question for Indians demanded more delicacy. Not only Sibley and Brown, but other delegates, too, had Indian relatives and mixed-blood children. Therefore mixed-bloods who lived in the white community were granted the rights of citizenship, while Indians who chose to do the same could be certified by a judge. Sibley's main contribution was his insistence that duties as well as rights be equal, and these citizens should therefore be required to serve in the state militia like any others.[11]

Spring that year had been late, with river traffic delayed until May, but the summer saw a record number of steamboat arrivals and a continued tide of immigrants and land speculators. As August 1857 wore on, the capital city was plagued by a minor crime wave, and several whole blocks of its pine-board buildings burned down. Meanwhile, delegates from the two rival conventions passed each other in the halls of St. Paul's four hotels or shared drinks at the bars and pursued off-the-record conversations. Brown and others busily cultivated the idea that a compromise must be reached. Sibley held out for submitting both constitutions to the voters, but before the end of the month he was won over—no doubt by Stephen Douglas.[12]

The Little Giant himself visited St. Paul on August 15 and was saluted with appropriate public ceremonies. In the florid rhetoric of the times, Gorman declared that "Kentucky has had her Clay, Massachusetts her Webster, and Minnesota as a part of the mighty West, claims her Douglas." The Illinois senator briefly addressed the Democratic convention, on which, he said, the eyes of the country were fixed. He also let it be known in personal conversations that failure to reach a compromise document would doom Minnesota's admission as a state.[13]

Only a day or two after Douglas's departure, a conference committee agreed on by the two conventions began its work. By August 27 it had completed a single constitution for the State of Minnesota. Brown was one of the five Democratic members, and he played a key role. Barring blacks from the polls but allowing constitutional amendments to be put to a vote of the people by a simple majority of the legislature compromised the issue of suffrage. On August 28 both conventions adopted the document, including a "schedule" that provided for apportionment of legislative and Congressional districts and for the election of state officers at the same time that the constitution was submitted to the voters. The date was set for October 13, and a board of three canvassers was named—territorial Governor Samuel Medary, Brown for the Democrats, and Republican Thomas J. Galbraith.[14]

On September 9 the Republican Party convention adopted a strong antislavery platform and named a ticket headed by Alexander Ramsey for governor. Although hesitant before, Ramsey no longer held back. The new party had won control of the territorial House in 1856, and the close contest for delegates to the constitutional convention had confirmed Republican strength. More than one former Whig officeholder was drawn in, and the militant younger Republicans found themselves challenged for leadership by conservatives more concerned with votes than radical principles. The Democrats, unified by an agreement that Rice would be supported for the Senate and Sibley for governor, met a week later. They endorsed the Douglas doctrine of popular sovereignty and nominated Sibley by acclamation.

Stephen A. Douglas

Many friends had urged Sibley to take one of the Senate seats himself, but his desire to stay in Minnesota was apparently still strong, and he seems to have clung to the naive notion that office-holding was about governing rather than influence and spoils. Rice never forgot the latter principle, and from his place in Washington he continued to "take care" of his fellow Minnesotans. In 1857 these included both Joe Brown and Franklin Steele. Thus in the years immediately ahead, two of Sibley's warmest friends and supporters became separated from him, politically and to some degree personally.

The campaign lasted less than a month but was bitter. Given their history as former allies, both Ramsey and Sibley left personal attacks and furious language to the party newspaper editors—Republican Thomas Foster of the *Minnesotian* and Earle Goodrich of the *Pioneer and Democrat*. They also left most of the campaigning to others, although Ramsey spoke in settlements up the Mississippi as far as Sauk Rapids and made a swing through the Minnesota River valley. Sibley had less need for campaigning, since nearly every officeholder in the existing territory was Democratic and could be relied on to advance the cause in his own district.

Advancing the cause took many forms that year, and they became more interesting as early election returns revealed an almost even race. Since Republican strength lay in the settled areas, Ramsey seemed ahead at first, but as votes came in from more distant and isolated places, the lead began to alternate. Charges of fraud, already flying on both sides, grew more serious and reached a crescendo in early November after the returns from Pembina were received—316 for Sibley, none for Ramsey.

All votes were first canvassed in counties by the register of deeds, and the result was then forwarded to the board of three state canvassers specified in the constitutional schedule. Counties were nevertheless required to send to the secretary of state all precinct reports along with the poll books. It may have been by privately examining this mass of documents that Brown learned the county canvasses had favored Sibley. Blandly, he proposed that the state board not stop with the county figures but extend its count to include precincts not allowed in the county canvasses. Medary objected that it would take all winter. Galbraith, suspecting a plot, objected also, and Brown's motion was defeated—as he had hoped. The action cost Ramsey a difference of 198 votes and justified the nickname "Joe the Juggler," applied by Brown's political opponents. At last, on December 19, 1857 the board declared Sibley the winner by 240 votes out of 35,340.[15]

It must have been a bittersweet moment when Sibley read Medary's official letter certifying his election as governor of Minnesota. There had been reason to dream of the office for more than fifteen years and his rejection by President Pierce in 1853 was still a fresh memory. Now, however, his paper-thin victory was clouded by fraud, and although it was not yet clear that he and Minnesota would be held in limbo for five months by the Congressional battle over Kansas, the state he proposed to lead already lay flattened by economic disaster.

In the turmoil of the election the territorial newspapers had given little space to a nationwide financial panic triggered in New York on August 24 by failure of the Ohio Life Insurance and Trust Company. Most of the country suffered tight currency and hard times, but in Minnesota, with its uncontrolled speculation and wildly inflated land values, the panic brought immediate and widespread ruin. By the end of October all of St. Paul's banks—including Borup and Oakes—had closed. Some guessed that the city lost nearly half its population. Buildings stood empty and real estate could not be sold at any price. Elsewhere dozens of prospective townsites were abandoned or turned into farm fields, and investors tried desperately to fend off creditors. By winter circulating money had nearly disappeared, and daily business relied on barter or local scrip.[16]

Sibley suffered along with all others, but he had avoided plunging again into debt. Therefore he did not face outright ruin. Traverse des Sioux, already struggling with its rival, St. Peter, immediately faded. The decisive blow came in 1858 when St. Peter secured the county seat. Soon the buildings of Traverse des Sioux were being hauled away to the neighboring town, and Sibley's hopes for monetary return disappeared with them. At Hastings, however, the reverse happened. A well-publicized boomtown had been promoted on the settlement's northern outskirts by Ramsey's brother-in-law, John Nininger, in partnership with Ignatius Donnelly, a young speculator from Philadelphia. Financing for Nininger's town evaporated in the panic, and most of its buildings and population eventually migrated to Hastings.[17]

Hopes for Mendota were still alive also. In partnership with Chouteau, Sibley had erected a sawmill there in 1856, and the Minneapolis and Cedar Valley was poised to build its line through the town. Even the skeptical Dousman had agreed that the railroad "will make the old place walk right ahead." Grading of roadbeds and laying of tracks had come to an abrupt halt, however, when the panic tightened its grip. As with a number of Minnesota railroads, stock had been issued to the promoters without requiring payment, and cash for actual building was dependent on borrowing until government lands could be acquired and sold.[18]

The schedule appended to the constitution called for the new legislature to meet on December 2. Its first business was to name two U.S. senators, one for a full six years and the other for a term that would expire in 1859. Democrats held a majority, so the real decision was made in the Democratic caucus. No one challenged Rice for the full term, but a dispute over the other one resulted in the unexpected election of James Shields.

On the national scene the gulf was already widening between the president and Douglas. Gorman, the obvious free-soil candidate for the second

Senate seat, was never popular with Minnesota Democrats, and even less so after his attempt to move the capital. His support trailed behind that of Franklin Steele, who had strong ties to Buchanan and the southern wing of the party. Those ties rested not only on family and political roots in Buchanan's section of Pennsylvania, but also upon a recent favor. Just a few months earlier in 1857 Steele had acquired Fort Snelling and all of its remaining military reservation for $90,000 in a private, unannounced sale facilitated by Rice and by Buchanan's secretary of war.[19]

For the Douglas forces the compromise choice was Shields, an outsider to Minnesota politics, yet well connected in Washington. Sibley, having no vote on the matter, could avoid any public commitment, but it seems likely that he backed the swing to Shields. Although Rice assured Anna Steele, "I am satisfied that Mr. Sibley was for your husband," Steele himself recalled receiving no help at all from his brother-in-law. Nine months later, his anger increased. At that time a special election to choose a successor to Shields was being urged by Democratic politicians. Before adjourning in August 1858, the legislature had decreed that no further sessions would be held until December 1859, many months after the Senator's term had expired. Steele was by then the leading candidate to replace Shields, but Sibley, as governor, refused to declare the need for an election. His hopes dashed again, Steele was furious.[20]

As the winter wore on it seemed that Minnesota's admission would be delayed indefinitely. Since Medary still held the office of territorial governor, Sibley officially remained in Mendota. The legislators, hesitant at first about their legal status, became bolder as the weeks went by. In March 1858 they agreed to submit to the voters two amendments to the constitution. One simply vented their frustration by unilaterally declaring Minnesota a state; the other responded to the overwhelming demand that something be done to get the promised railroads rolling. At an election on April 15, Minnesota voters adopted both.[21]

The railroad amendment authorized the state to issue bonds to the amount of five million dollars and exchange them for mortgage bonds of the companies that had received land grants. This presumed that the state bonds would sell to eastern investors who might hesitate to risk their money in unbuilt railroads. Actual issuing of the state bonds to railroad companies was to proceed in tandem with completion of roadbeds and transfer of the title to public land.

The amendment never became a party issue, since both groups were split on it. Among the Democrats, Rice, Brown, and Steele all supported the measure; Gorman opposed it, and Sibley made no public statements. Whether or not his silence masked opposition, his growing uneasiness over the scheme was apparent. Again he found himself in an ambiguous position. Not only were his political friends and business associates promoting it; he himself had a financial interest in its adoption, and he was keenly aware of the perceived conflict between this and his role as governor-elect. After the amendment had passed, he debated the propriety of resigning his position as a director of the Minneapolis and Cedar Valley railroad.[22]

On May 11, 1858, Congress passed the bill for admission of Minnesota as the 32nd state, and on May 24, Sibley and the other state officers elected five

Minnesota newspapers celebrated statehood with banner headings. This appeared in the Winona Times, *May 15, 1858*

months earlier were sworn in without fanfare. The new governor immediately called the legislature back into session—this time legally—and gave his inaugural address on June 3. In opening he voiced at length Minnesota's (and his own) righteous indignation over the long delay in admission. Next he addressed some unfinished business from the recent election.[23]

In the course of debates over admission, a Republican congressman had alleged that the new state's governor held office fraudulently. With the tone of injured honor that so often crept into his public statements, Sibley now demanded a full investigation, for "God knows that I am not so wedded to office as to accept any position at the expense of the purity of the ballot box." In fact Ramsey, although making no formal charges, had been spreading the word in Washington during the past winter that he had been "cyphered out." Thus challenged by Sibley, he asked through his attorney to examine the voting records, but he never followed up on the request, nor did others. Both parties, it seemed, preferred to let the issue die.[24]

Sibley went on to call for strict economy in government and careful regulation of banks, which were "at best, but a necessary evil." He congratulated the state on the generous grants of school and university lands that had been conveyed in the enabling act. In a sharp departure from his former sentiments in favor of local control, he in effect cautioned the lawmakers to keep their hands off—a veiled warning that he later followed up with a pocket veto to a bill that would have turned the school lands over to township governments.[25]

The university's lands were already encumbered. Chartered in 1851, the frontier institution proclaimed the territory's aspirations to higher education, but it consisted of little more than a hope and a few preparatory classes. Sibley, named to the original board of regents, had been a dogged supporter, along with Steele, who had donated a site for the first building. By 1858 a second building had been erected, financed by bonds that were secured by a mortgage on the university land grant.[26]

The new governor's warning to the legislators on economy was not motivated simply by principle. The state's treasury was empty, although the legislature of the previous spring had authorized borrowing to the limit allowed by the constitution—$250,000. Accordingly, as soon as bonds could be printed, Sibley and the state treasurer set out for New York to raise the money. In this they were successful, although Sibley was unable, despite his best efforts, to find buyers for the university's bonds.[27]

In regard to the state railroad bonds, the governor promised to demand the strictest accountability from the companies. It was on this question that he encountered the fiercest conflict of his administration. He asked that the mortgage bonds given to the state by the railroads take precedence over all their other debts. An explosion followed. The law was silent on the question of priority to other creditors, and the companies denied his authority to require this degree of security. The new chief justice of the Minnesota Supreme Court, Charles E. Flandrau, refused to give an opinion unless a case were brought, so the Minnesota and Pacific line sued the governor on a writ of mandamus. The court decided that the governor could require no additional restrictions and ordered him to issue the state bonds. Sibley did so under protest and was subsequently attacked from two sides. Rice pronounced it disgraceful that a court order was needed to force him to do his duty; others argued that the court had no jurisdiction over the governor and suggested that only self-interest led him to obey it.[28]

Ignoring the critics in both camps, Sibley went on to fulfill what he saw as his obligation to the state to market the bonds. The effort required a number of weeks in New York during the winter of 1858–59. It netted him little more than a siege of disabling leg pain that Sarah thought was gout and laid to his "living too high" at the St. Nicholas Hotel.[29] Times were still ferociously hard, and the credit of the new state, it seemed, was not much better than that of the railroads.

No trains were yet running by the time Sibley left the governor's office at the end of the year, and the bonds were widely regarded as worthless. In his farewell message, Sibley argued passionately against any thought of repudiation: "Better, far better that we be visited by pestilence or famine, for these are the instruments of God, for which we are not responsible, but our own act in violation of public faith and the pledged honor of the State, would sink Minnesota for all time to come, beneath the contempt and indignation of the civilized world."[30] It was a position he would maintain for nearly thirty years.

One other issue that had been raised by Sibley in his inaugural address was the need for an effective state militia. This was prompted by more than a desire for martial display. A year earlier the settlements in southwestern Minnesota had been terrorized by a small band of outlaw Dakota who had separated years before from the main tribe. The killing of isolated farmers near Spirit Lake and along the Des Moines River was followed by months of futile pursuit and unwarranted government threats to the rest of the tribe. These efforts had only demonstrated the inability of the U.S. Army and the Indian Department to cope with the situation. Even more recently, just a week before Sibley spoke, a fierce skirmish had occurred at Shakopee between a group of Dakota and a war party of Ojibwe. No Europeans were involved, but alarm spread wildly, and the legislators promptly gave Sibley his militia.[31]

During the territorial years there had been persistent indignation at the presence of Dakota hunters far from their reservation. The Indians, however, had little choice but to seek game and other food where they could find it. Sibley's lament about broken treaties and betrayed promises in his article for Porter was only too true. Through the mid-1850s the roads, houses, and other improvements on the reservation still lagged; Congress failed to appropriate money to meet treaty payments in full; and delivery of supplies was inadequate and nearly always late. Meanwhile as settlements moved closer to the reservation and even encroached on it, tension grew. Following the events at Spirit Lake in 1857, the attitude of white Minnesotans turned ugly. "We have plenty of young men who would like no better fun than a good Indian hunt," observed one St. Paul editor.[32]

In the summer of that year Flandrau, the government agent for the Dakota, was appointed to the territorial Supreme Court and a few months later elected chief justice of the new state. Joe Brown—probably with Rice's help—succeeded him as agent. Brown's tenure, along with a renewed missionary effort, brought rapid change. He knew the Dakota, and he knew how to work the system at the Indian Office. Despite his history as a trader, speculator, and notorious whiskey seller, Brown accepted the policy laid out by the missionaries and implemented it effectively. Homes were built, fields were plowed, and the Upper and Lower Sioux Agencies, which served the two divisions of the tribe, began to take on the look of small villages, with government warehouses, blacksmith shops, mills, and schools.[33]

This very progress, however, polarized the Dakota. Led by the older chiefs, Wabasha and Wacouta, a large part of the tribe recognized the inevitable need for adapting and, now that they had the chance, moved quickly to do so. Traditionalists, along with many of the younger men who saw change threatening their honor as hunters and warriors, fiercely opposed the Indian farmers who adopted European clothing, schooling, and in some cases Christianity. Traditional attitudes were reinforced by frequent contact with Yankton and Yanktonais tribesmen, who still lived as free buffalo hunters in the Missouri River valley. Soon the young men began to form soldiers lodges. Although these were based on the temporary form of policing organization adopted for hunting and warfare, they took on a new and more permanent cast as a secret network of militants pledged to upholding the tribe's ancient rituals and social customs.[34]

Early in 1858 Brown and the Indian Office also acted to clarify the uncertain legal status of the reservation. A group of chiefs and head men taken to Washington signed a treaty in June that year by which the Dakota gave up the half of their reservation that lay north of the Minnesota River and agreed to allotment of individual, privately owned farms from the remaining land.

As the pressure against ancient communal customs and group identities thus increased, so did tension within the tribe. Hostility toward farmer Indians escalated into harassment, destruction of property, and frequent threats of violence. Some of the anger in the soldiers lodges also spilled over onto the barns and livestock of settlers who were hurriedly staking claims to the ceded lands just north of the river.[35]

This was the situation late in 1858 when Sibley moved to organize the new militia. He created four divisions and assigned them to various areas of the state. To command the critical westernmost division he appointed Brown, with a rank of major general. Conscious, perhaps, of the widening gulf between himself and his friend of many years, Brown responded with an outpouring of emotion. The commission, he wrote, gave him satisfaction, but he valued it most for the man it came from. Sibley's testimonial of confidence, he concluded, gave him more satisfaction than "a far greater act from other sources" could ever produce.[36]

Neither Brown nor the rest of the militia was called upon to discipline the Dakota while Sibley was governor. It was instead white citizens of Wright County who posed the state's first serious challenge to law and order. This occurred in April 1859 when a settler named Jackson, accused but later acquitted of murdering a neighbor, was lynched by a mob with the apparent collusion of the Wright County sheriff. In July one of the alleged leaders of the mob was arrested in Hennepin County. The man was returned to Wright County, but Sibley asked the state's attorney general to go to Monticello and conduct the prosecution himself. Before the trial ended another mob rescued the prisoner and made threats that sent the attorney general hurrying back to St. Paul. Faced with this blatant defiance of the state's authority, the governor declared Wright County guilty of insurrection and sent three companies of militia to restore order.[37]

Even with this persuasion, the county authorities were clearly reluctant to enforce the law, but by the time Sibley arrived at Monticello himself several men had been arrested. After receiving written assurances from the district attorney and the sheriff that others would be sought, Sibley sent the troops home and declared a victory over border ruffianism. Although the court eventually released the suspects for lack of evidence and the action was widely ridiculed in the newspapers as the "Wright County War," the governor was satisfied. "One great object I had in view," he said, "was to demonstrate at this early period of her history, that the State had not only the will but the power to put down all combinations to resist the law."[38]

Nothing was more deeply embedded in Henry Sibley than respect for law. Everything in his background and character demanded that the processes of justice in a civilized society be followed, both in form and substance. Although his term as governor was truncated and generally lacklustre, in this case it set a lasting stamp on Minnesota. Mob violence certainly occurred, but it proved rare, and lynch law never became an accepted way of life. Largely on this basis, an informal evaluation of the state's governors by a group of historians and political scientists in 1966 placed Sibley seventh among the top fifteen—and first among those who had served only a single term.[39]

· 12 ·

Widening Rifts

LTHOUGH SIBLEY, AS GOVERNOR, was urged by many friends to run for a second term, he decided firmly against it. Because of the delay in the transition from territory to state, it was almost certain that the legislators elected in the fall of 1858 would never actually serve. Nevertheless, the Republicans had conducted an earnest campaign and had taken both houses. The trend was clear, and rather than try a rematch with Ramsey, Sibley declined nomination in favor of George L. Becker. A lawyer and former St. Paul mayor, Becker had earned the party's support when, as one of three Democratic congressmen elected in 1857, he had withdrawn after it proved that the census of the new state justified only two. In 1859, however, the portent of a rising Republican tide proved accurate, and Becker lost to Ramsey by a decisive vote that ended ten years of Democratic control.[1]

Sibley, meanwhile, turned his eyes toward a wider horizon. In 1860 Minnesota Democrats for the first time would have a voice at the party's national convention—and never had it seemed more crucial. Across the growing chasm over slavery that divided the nation, the one remaining bridge between

General View of St. Paul, 1857

South and North was the Democratic Party with its proslavery and free-soil wings. Its presidential candidate was to be named in Charleston, South Carolina, late in April. Minnesota selected the state's eight delegates at a meeting held on January 12.[2]

In Minnesota, as in the other northwestern states, Douglas was by 1860 the overwhelming choice of Democratic voters, but the division among Minnesota party leaders continued. Now a minority in the party, those who identified in varying degrees with Rice held clear of endorsing Douglas. Rice apparently had no real convictions on the subject of slavery, but both before and after statehood the notable patronage that he and his associates had enjoyed under the Buchanan administration tied them to the "National Democrats"— the southern wing of the party. Joe Brown remained one of them, as did Franklin Steele.

Gorman and Robertson, Democratic warhorses, led the charge for Douglas, while Sibley, following his usual political style, stood apart and gave an appearance of remaining above the strife. He may have had a hand in engineering a prearranged set of compromise resolutions that Becker introduced and attributed to Shields. The resolutions supported the free-soil position and endorsed Douglas but retreated from calling for a unit rule binding the delegates to vote for him. They were ultimately accepted after debate that lasted until two in the morning. Those at the meeting chose four avowed Douglas delegates, three from the opposition, and Sibley. In seeking the appointment he again angered friends of Steele, who felt that their candidate had been shouldered aside.[3]

The role played by Sibley in St. Paul foreshadowed his actions throughout the tumultuous conventions in Charleston and later in Baltimore. Although consistently working for Douglas, he used every opportunity to achieve compromise and forestall a sectional split in the party. His opponents among Minnesota Democrats may have read his instinct for the middle of the road as a signal that he could be persuaded away from the Douglas wing. Before the delegates assembled in Charleston, Rice, working through Becker, intimated that he would use all his influence to secure the ex-governor a high place in Washington. "Nothing," Becker told Sibley, "would be more gratifying for me than to see you at the head of the War or Interior Department."[4]

In Charleston Sibley sought and secured a seat on the credentials committee. During the struggle over a platform, the Minnesota delegation divided its votes in the first stages but united as a block in favor of the version finally adopted, which was a simple reaffirmation of the document agreed to by the party four years earlier. At this point six southern states withdrew from the convention. The next crucial vote was to require a two-thirds majority for a presidential nomination. On this, Minnesota's three uncommitted members split from the Douglas supporters, who fiercely opposed it. After fifty-seven ballots Douglas had still not achieved a two-thirds vote, and the fragmented convention adjourned to reassemble at Baltimore six weeks later.[5]

Again in Baltimore Sibley served on the credentials committee. This time the decisions it made were more critical, since some of the southern states had elected (or reelected) delegates to attend the convention in Baltimore. In a few states rival meetings had been held and there were two sets of delegates demanding admission—seceders and free-soilers. Sibley himself was apparently responsible for suggesting one or two compromise solutions, but like the majority of the committee, he was determined to make the nomination of Douglas possible. The final report, delivered after four days of work, was adopted by the convention and prompted six states to walk out—this time including California and Oregon. The main convention then went on to name Douglas as the Democratic candidate, while the southern wing met in another building to nominate John C. Breckinridge of Kentucky.

Minnesota's three uncommitted delegates joined the Breckinridge convention and returned home prepared to campaign against Douglas. Steele united with the delegates and Rice in a public letter stating support for Breckinridge, thus making the political gulf between himself and his brother-in-law unmistakable. Sibley, meanwhile, had been honored in Washington at the organizing meeting of the Democratic National Committee and had accepted a position on it representing Minnesota. The chair of the committee was the financier August Belmont, a dedicated supporter of Douglas.[6]

The Douglas campaign in Minnesota was launched at a convention held in St. Paul on August 22. When Sibley arrived halfway through the day's proceedings, his presence was announced, and he was conducted to the platform with three cheers. Thanking the convention, he seated himself amid hearty applause. Then and throughout the election he occupied the symbolic chair of elder statesman. Leaving the active campaigning to Gorman and others, he worked to raise money from eastern sources, for it was still scarce in Minnesota.[7]

The Breckinridge men posed little threat, for their base of voters was small, and although they controlled a number of local newspapers, the powerful voice of the *Pioneer and Democrat,* by then owned as well as edited by Earle Goodrich, was strong for Douglas and the conservative forces of national unity. As Goodrich reflected in one editorial: "While the Douglas men in the South are contending for the Union, in the North the Democratic Party upon the platform of Non-Intervention is engaged in battling Black Republicanism. This contest involves the fate of the Union." No doubt Sibley agreed.

But the center could not hold. Fresh from their triumph of the year before, the Republicans carried the state for Lincoln.[8]

As he watched the country prepare to tear itself apart, Sibley also dealt with an intensely private loss. In November 1859 his daughter Helen had married Dr. Sylvester J. Sawyer, a physician who had boarded briefly with the William Brown family in St. Paul and was hoping to establish a practice in Wisconsin. Sibley, then still governor, had attended the simple wedding in the Browns' home and had given away the eighteen-year-old bride.[9]

The couple moved to Milwaukee, where they rented a small house and reported themselves happy in married life and as a part of the local Methodist community. They hoped that Sibley would stop there on his return from Charleston in May, and Helen wanted to learn the address of her uncle, Fred Sibley, in order that she might write to him. Later that month Sawyer bought another physician's house and practice in Racine County and they moved to the country. There on September 4 Helen gave birth to a baby girl. Already ill, she died two days later of scarlet fever, and a week afterward the child died also. Sibley expressed keen sorrow when he heard the news, and Sawyer told the Browns: "He has been very kind, both before and since Helen's death."[10]

Sarah's attitude toward Helen had apparently bordered on hostility. Whether or not death softened it, little more was said about the young woman, and as years passed, her very existence was nearly forgotten by the St. Paul community. Among the Dakota, however, Sibley's blood tie to their people was remembered, and the story is told that on at least one occasion many years later, a group of them reminded him of it in asking his help.[11]

The death of Sibley's first grandchild followed by only a few days the birth of another son, Charles Frederick. Sarah also had been dangerously ill that summer when in early July, seven months pregnant, she was stricken with pleurisy and pneumonia and remained in critical condition for nearly a month. Weakened, no doubt, by the additional drain of childbirth, she recovered slowly. Painful attacks continued through the winter and into the spring. Even in the following fall she admitted that she was "not right well yet." Possibly to assist with the household, Sibley's sister Sarah spent the summer of 1861 at Mendota, and she took seventeen-year-old Gussie to Detroit with her in the fall.[12]

Like Sibley's political life, his wife's social life had come to revolve around St. Paul and its growing corps of elite families—the Ramseys, the van Ettens, the Niningers, and others. Sarah's brother John lived there as well as her sister Abbie Potts. As early as the spring of 1859 she had told a friend that "Mr. S." was "quite in the notion" of building a house in St. Paul and moving there the following winter, but apparently he changed his mind. By 1861 Sarah's lingering illness had only increased her growing discontent with the isolation of Mendota. Staring out at the first snowfall in November, she wrote to her sister Rachel, whose soldier husband was stationed in Louisville, "Oh! how lonely and dreary it is.... Mendota is so dull compared to Louisville."[13]

During Sibley's term as governor Sarah had risen to her role as the state's first lady and had supplied local leadership for a civic cause that drew many American women out of their concentrated domesticity. That cause was the preservation of Mount Vernon. Initiated by a South Carolina woman in 1853 as a gesture of patriotic veneration, the idea quickly spread throughout the country and became a demonstration against the forces of disunion. The focus on Washington's home and family life made it acceptable as an object of female activity, and Mount Vernon's historic significance made it a symbol of national unity. Soon a small army of "lady managers" was raising money in local communities, North, South, and as far west as Minnesota.[14]

Solicited by the Mount Vernon Association, Sarah agreed to organize the effort, sending a circular to local newspapers and contacting as many as seventy-five women whom she thought would be influential and active in communities throughout the state. To mark Washington's birthday and benefit the cause they invited the orator Edward Everett, who was touring the country as a champion of the effort, to present his popular lecture on "The Character of Washington," at the new St. Paul Mercantile Library. The event not only produced seventy dollars for the association but served as an admirable showcase for the new uniforms of the St. Paul Pioneer Guard and for the governor's resplendent dress uniform as commander-in-chief of the state militia.[15]

In Minnesota, as elsewhere, some abolitionists objected to the southern origins of the movement and declined to support a historic property maintained by slave labor. One was Ann Loomis North, wife of John North, founder of Northfield and a promoter with Sibley of the Cedar Valley Railroad. Like her husband, Ann North was a fervent abolitionist, and she found it impossible to accept Sarah's invitation to join the corps of fund-raisers. Others, like the ladies of Stillwater, which was an abolitionist stronghold, preferred to avoid the issue by giving the money directly to Everett himself.

Mary Bronson LeDuc, wife of Sibley's Hastings associate and a close friend of Sarah, had no such reservations. To her Sarah wrote: "Send me as much money as you can rake and scrape, put on as bold and impudent [a] face as possible, and perhaps you will find another lady willing to assist you." Mary complied, and two months later her husband told Sibley that "Mrs. LeD. is just now exercised upon the Mt. Vernon Association quest."[16] The result of her efforts and those of others were disappointing, however, for in 1859 money was still painfully scarce in Minnesota. By October 1860, when Sibley himself wrote to the head of the Association to tell her that Sarah was too ill to continue at her post, time was running out on efforts to draw the country together. Not even the ties of a shared history could prevent the dissolution of the Union.

In the lull that preceded the reality of secession, Minnesota began to recover from the effects of the panic. A bumper crop in 1860 lifted spirits and helped to revive the state's economy, and at the end of August a telegraph line finally reached St. Paul. Boosters of all parties glowed that fall at the words of William H. Seward. Visiting the state to campaign for Lincoln, the New York senator predicted that "the ultimate central seat of power of the North American people" would be in Minnesota. A few days later, the first state agricultural fair was held at Fort Snelling, and Sibley was called on to say some words about the changes he had seen in his twenty-five-year residence across the river.[17]

The harvest was less bountiful in 1861, but by then high prices and a booming wheat market were bringing a wave of wartime prosperity. As steamboats unloaded their cargoes at St. Paul, the levee was lined with mowers, reapers, cultivators, and other examples of the new horse-drawn farm machinery. Although no longer promoting townsites, Sibley continued to invest selectively in land on behalf of both himself and Chouteau. He also worked with the St. Louis firm to secure payment by the government of some claims against the Indian bands of the Upper Missouri. Railroad building had been suspended by the panic, and in March 1861 the legislature foreclosed on the companies that had received public lands and cancelled their charters. The Minneapolis and Cedar Valley line was rechartered as the Minneapolis, Faribault, and Cedar Valley. The names of Sibley and Shields dropped from the list of directors, while those of LeDuc and North appeared. The most significant addition was Erastus Corning, president of the New York Central.[18]

In the anxious weeks between the secession of the southern states and the beginning of hostilities at Fort Sumter, Minnesota Democrats had continued to call for "some peaceful adjustment," while the editor of the Republican *Minnesotian* thundered "THERE MUST BE BLOOD-LETTING." A variety of compromise solutions were proposed by Douglas and other national leaders. With the coming of war, however, the Democratic Party hurried to repudiate disunion and proclaim support for the nation and its government. Douglas led the way, but his sudden death on June 3, 1861, deprived the northern Democrats of leadership. St Paul mourned him with ceremonies worthy of a president, and Sibley was among the honorary pallbearers.[19]

Across the land communities and even families found themselves on opposing sides. The Sibleys were no exception. About her niece, Mary Steele, Sarah wrote: "She is a queer one still, [and] is a hot secessionist when she can get anyone to hear her, which is very seldom." Meanwhile, their brother Frank, whose sympathies had been similar to those of Mary, made no objection when Governor Ramsey took over Fort Snelling for the state and reactivated it as a recruitment and training center for volunteer troops.[20]

The old fort, which had been nearly deserted since 1854, when its garrison was transferred to Fort Ridgely, was once again humming with activity in the fall of 1861. The Sibleys had seen three regiments board steamboats on their way to the South, and Sarah wrote: "There are still six or eight hundred men in the fort, which gives this place quite a lively appearance. Poor fellows, it is rather a sad sight to see them go off, perhaps never to return."[21]

Sibley himself saw friends and associates take commissions one by one. Gorman was named colonel of the First Minnesota Volunteers, and Robertson busied himself recruiting a second regiment, which he hoped to command. Shields resumed his rank of general, earned in the Mexican War, and LeDuc later secured an appointment with the Quartermaster Corps.

Sibley never sought a commission. A brother, a brother-in-law, and many of his closest friends were graduates of West Point, and his ties had been long and intimate with the pre–Civil War army of occupation that was spread so thinly across the trans-Mississippi West. Yet he himself was not a military man, and apparently at the age of fifty he had no wish to become one. Many of the officers who had come and gone at Fort Snelling over the years were now serving with the Confederate Army. No doubt he foresaw the river of blood that would fill the chasm between the states, and he held to a conviction that the carnage might have been avoided.

In the late summer of 1861 Earle Goodrich of the *Pioneer and Democrat* launched a movement for the Minnesota Democratic Party to self-destruct. "The necessities of the Government, induced by the war," he wrote, "overshadow, swallow up, and extinguish all mere party platforms." Several days later the paper published a long list of Minnesota Democrats calling for a "Union" convention to be held on September 5. The intention was apparently to draw together all parties, but the move was undercut by the Republicans, who held their own convention the day before, renominating their state officers and endorsing a platform that called for outright confiscation of all property, including slaves, in the Confederate states. Joined at the last minute by a few antiabolition Republicans, the Unionists named a ticket of little-known political newcomers who withdrew two weeks later. A sparsely attended

Democratic convention made nominations that were ignored by Goodrich's *Pioneer and Democrat.*[22]

Sibley's name, along with those of Brown, Rice, Robertson, and Steele, was notably absent from the list of Union Party backers. Although he had run twice as a nonpartisan candidate a decade earlier, times had changed, and Minnesota was no longer a territory dependent on federal favor. What he regarded as a radical and uncompromising Republican Party now controlled the state, and its more extreme members were openly calling for a scorched-earth policy toward the South. "We must make rebellion synonymous with desolation; and the track of our armies must be as a shining track of ruin," declared Minnesota's young lieutenant governor, Ignatius Donnelly.[23] Even in the shadow of national emergency Sibley clearly felt the need for an organized opposition.

The first year of war saw few successes for the Union Army and mounting criticism of the Lincoln administration, both from Democrats and from abolitionist Republicans. By July 2, 1862, when Minnesota Democrats met to nominate candidates for Congress, opposition had congealed, and the party presented a united force. Sibley chaired the convention and played a major role in preparing a hard-hitting list of resolutions that condemned secession and abolitionism as "twin heresies, producing only hatred, strife, and bloodshed." The resolutions went on to denounce the Republicans for heavy-handed confiscation of property and suspension of civil liberties, as well as for corruption, extravagance, and incompetence in conducting the war.[24]

Republican zeal for appointments to office had been notable all across the country in 1861, but nowhere was it more evident than in Minnesota's Indian affairs. Already notorious for corruption, the Indian Office was well known as a place to make an easy fortune. Thus Democrats were summarily turned out and Republicans named, regardless of experience or competence. Early in 1861 the Dakota saw Joe Brown replaced as their agent by Thomas J. Galbraith, a stubborn man with a drinking habit and contempt for Indians. The results turned a tense situation into a disaster.

When Galbraith arrived at the Lower Agency in May to take up his new duties, he found boiling resentment over the treaty signed in 1858. Two years had passed before it was ratified, and during that time settlers crowded into what had been reservation land across the Minnesota River, partly cutting off Dakota access to former hunting grounds to the north and east. Assured that a fair price would be paid, the Dakota had left the exact sum to be named by the Senate. A fair price, according to Agent Brown was $5.00 per acre; the Senate Committee on Indian Affairs recommended $1.25; the Senate as a whole fixed on thirty cents. Expecting an adequate sum, the Dakota had agreed to pay their debts to the traders then doing business on the reservation. During the two-year delay, those debts continued to climb, and by the time the meager treaty money arrived in 1861, the lower bands found that all of it was paid directly to the traders.[25]

Meanwhile the rift within the tribe continued to widen, and Galbraith's policies hastened the process. He openly favored the farmers, both with annuity money and in other ways. Anger mounted among young members of the soldiers lodges in both the upper and lower bands. Continuing to meet in secret, they dominated and intimidated others and helped to stimulate a revival of traditional spiritual practices in opposition to the missionaries. Among the upper bands many farmers left their fields in fear for their lives, and troops were needed to keep the peace at the annuity payment in 1861. A poor corn crop that year was followed by a severe winter and a spring of grim hunger. Rumors circulated that the embattled U.S. government would be unable to make its promised payments.[26]

Some supplies arrived that spring when navigation opened in 1862, and government warehouses at the two agencies were partly stocked. The cash annuities, however, were delayed, week after week. Traders also had supplies on hand, but they refused to extend more credit, fearful that Indian anger would prevent their payment from the annuity money. As tension mounted, Galbraith summoned troops and waited. At last, early in August, an armed confrontation with some five hundred Sisseton and Wahpeton forced him to open the warehouse at the Upper Agency. Their demands for food met, the Dakota dispersed, and the troops headed back to Fort Ripley.

Among the lower bands there was less hunger and open hostility, but no less anger. The young zealots of the soldiers lodge shared with each other their fury and frustration, but leadership was lacking—and so were voices of moderation. The erosion of traditional roles and social institutions under reservation conditions weakened the influence of even the most respected chiefs. Several of them had joined the farmers, and others remained silent. The women of the tribe, who in a strong communal society could speak with a unified voice, were also silenced by separation onto family farmsteads and division caused by missionary teachings.

The ground was shifting elsewhere, too. The Great White Father no longer commanded monolithic authority. News of defeat and stalemate on southern battlefields circulated among the bands, carried by literate mixed-bloods and government employees. In fact Galbraith himself had been busy recruiting volunteers from among the many mixed-blood men on the reservation for a corps of scouts and sharpshooters to aid the Union Army. On August 16 he left the Lower Agency, headed for Fort Snelling with his small force of "Renville Rangers."

The next day four young Mdewakanton men returning from a hunting expedition north of the Minnesota River began to dispute their relative bravery and daring. The stakes escalated, until at last, in a show of bravado, they shot four white settlers. Then fleeing to their village, which was a stronghold of the soldiers lodge, they begged for protection. Intense discussions followed, centering on the undoubted fact that the entire band would be punished for the crime. Others were called in, and there was a rising wave of sentiment in favor of immediate war. At last, in the middle of the night, they decided to appeal to Little Crow.

Taoyateduta, who had defied threats of death to sign the treaty of Mendota, had also been a leader in negotiating the 1858 treaty. His readiness to deal with the government despite its repeated betrayal of solemn agreements had damaged his prestige with the tribe. Nevertheless, he was the one leader who retained credibility with both groups among the divided Mdewakanton. Although speaking some English, living in a government-built house, and willing to wear European clothing on occasion, he clung strongly to Dakota religious beliefs and resisted becoming a farmer. His ambivalence was symbolized by a tall tipi standing beside the brick house in which his family lived.

It was in this tipi that an agonizing confrontation took place in the predawn hours of August 18, 1862. After listening to the story of the young men and the harangues of their supporters, Little Crow blackened his face as if in mourning and covered his head. At last someone hurled an accusation of cowardice. Springing to his feet, the chief retorted with a powerful recital of the utter hopelessness of war against the whites. Then he concluded: "Braves, you are little children—you are fools. You will die like the rabbits when the hungry wolves hunt them in January.—Taoyateduta is not a coward: he will die with you."[27]

Little Crow

· 13 ·

Terror in the Valley

*T*HE SUN WAS LOW IN THE WEST on August 19, 1862, when Governor Alexander Ramsey found himself standing before the Sibley house at Mendota. Notified at midday by an urgent message from Fort Snelling that there was trouble at the Lower Agency, he had climbed into a buggy and driven at once to the fort. There he learned the appalling news that not only had the agency been sacked and most of its inhabitants killed, but that a detachment of troops sent from Fort Ridgely had been ambushed and nearly wiped out, along with the fort's commander. Clearly he was faced with more than a passing Indian scare—and at a time when most of the state's able-bodied men were being drafted for service in the South. He ordered the officer in charge to pull together the recruits on hand and collect what arms and equipment were available. Then he crossed the river to Mendota and sought out Sibley.[1]

Thirteen years had passed since the two men had first met on that spot. The stocky young ex-congressman from Pennsylvania had developed gray sideburns and the beginnings of a paunch. The frontier trader was still erect

Alexander Ramsey in the 1860s

Sibley circa 1863

and lean, but his hair had thinned, and the years of politics and public office had stamped a crease of worry between his eyebrows. No doubt those changes were far from their minds at the moment, but the shock that brought them face to face may have stirred recollections of other times—of treaty tables and tents, of anxious conferences by candlelight, and of facing down the fury of Dakota men who knew they had been manipulated. Now, a decade later, the outcome of their work loomed before them, although its tragic dimensions were still unclear.

As usual, Ramsey was blunt. He wanted Sibley to take command of an expedition against the Indians. By then Sibley could be equally blunt. Would he have complete charge, he asked, or would he be second-guessed by army men and politicians? Ramsey assured him that there would be no interference, and Sibley accepted the assignment. Back in St. Paul that night, the governor penned a letter to Sibley appointing him commander of the "Indian expedition" with the rank of colonel in the state militia and directed that four companies of recruits for the not-yet-organized Sixth Minnesota Regiment be placed under him, ready to leave Fort Snelling immediately. Meanwhile Sibley packed his saddlebags.[2]

Next morning the crowd of raw recruits boarded a small steamboat that had been sent up from St. Paul, and Sibley checked the supplies. He found no tents, no camping equipment, no cooked rations, and only part of the ammunition needed. Firing off a letter to Ramsey, he detailed a quartermaster to round up the essentials and went on with the men to Shakopee, where he scoured the country for horses and wagons. Next day he detached a company of men to march west by way of Glencoe and meet him at Fort Ridgely. The rest of the force pushed on to Belle Plaine, with Sibley personally attending to a multitude of problems, "for a greener set of men were never got together."[3]

At Belle Plaine Sibley began to sense the extent of the panic that had gripped the western settlements. He was also handed an urgent note directed to Ramsey from Charles Flandrau. The judge and former Indian agent, who made his home at Traverse des Sioux, had been aroused at four in the morning of August 19 by a messenger from New Ulm. Gathering together a hundred volunteers at neighboring St. Peter, he had set out for the small German settlement up the Minnesota River, where the party arrived late that night. He would do what he could, the note said, to organize a defense.[4]

Sibley hastily recalled the detachment he had sent to Glencoe, and on August 22 with 225 men and wagons made his way along a rutted road through the deep forest known as the "big woods," reaching St. Peter after dark. At daybreak he sent some 120 men to aid Flandrau and waited anxiously for the company from Glencoe and for a promised force of additional volunteers.

Most of all he needed horses, but he also needed firearms and ammunition. Knowing that the U.S. quartermaster had a supply of Springfield muskets, he told Ramsey that if red tape was in the way, "cut it with the bayonets of a corporal's guard."[5]

Meanwhile Sibley did what he could to organize food and shelter for the fleeing settlers and to create some order from the straggling mob of young recruits and civilian volunteers that passed for troops. He may have been heartened by finding Alex Faribault and Faribault's brother-in-law Stephen H. Fowler, a veteran of the Mexican War, with a small party of armed and mounted men from the Cannon River valley, as well as by the appearance of William Forbes from St. Paul. Faribault and Forbes, once his trusted clerks, now became his military aides. Another addition to his immediate staff was Joe Brown, who had learned the news on his way back from a business trip to the East. In a fever of anxiety for his family, whom he had left at their new home near the Upper Agency, Brown had dashed on immediately to join Sibley.[6]

With each hour in St. Peter the full danger and horror of the situation became plainer. Warriors from the Dakota soldiers lodges had fanned out across the countryside, attacking whole families of settlers without warning. Refugees poured in from miles around, some simply terrified, but others with stark tales of tragedy. And there were the hacked bodies, a few with signs of deliberate mutilation. Looking at them, Sibley may have recalled with sickening vividness his first encounter with tribal warfare at Kaposia. The pent-up rage of the Dakota could have had no clearer statement, and it roused a matching rage in himself that he hardly knew how to handle. "Oh, the fiends, the devils in human shape!" he wrote to Sarah, "my heart is hardened against them beyond any touch of mercy." And he told Ramsey that he would fire upon a flag of truce: "The day for compromise of any kind has passed."[7]

The movements of the enemy and the status of forces farther up the Minnesota valley were also becoming clearer. Jack Frazer had fled to Fort Ridgely from his farm near Wacouta's village. A day later the seasoned sixty-year-old hunter had slipped past the Dakota around the fort and made his way to St. Peter. The fort, he told Sibley, was holding out. Indian agent Thomas Galbraith with his little force of Renville Rangers had reached it on the 19th, and a company of the Fifth Minnesota Infantry that had departed for Fort Ripley on the Upper Mississippi had been recalled. Its commander was now directing the defense of the fort and of more than 250 women and children gathered there.[8]

Frazer could also tell Sibley for the first time that Little Crow was leading the Dakota and that he had assembled a large force near Fort Ridgely. On August 22 that force made a determined assault on the unwalled fort. They were turned back, mainly through the effective use of three small cannon. The fact that many of the Dakota had then departed for New Ulm became apparent on the 24th, when news reached Sibley that the town had been attacked the day before and partially burned. Flandrau had led the townspeople in a successful defense, but clearly the place had to be evacuated. The men that had been sent by Sibley arrived in time to help guard the long column of wagons and refugees as they made their sad way across the prairies to Mankato.

On August 25 Minnesota Lieutenant Governor Ignatius Donnelly arrived in St. Peter with dispatches from Ramsey and instructions to urge that Sibley move ahead with greater speed. Donnelly found a confused scene of scattered tents, half-uniformed men, small groups of mounted volunteers riding around aimlessly, the occasional roll of drums, and periodic bursts of gunfire. "I can now see why great bodies move slowly," he wrote. "The wonder is that bodies of militiamen move at all." He estimated that the town held about 3,000 refugees, with another 2,000 camped along the road from Mankato. They, too, impeded movement by their need for help and their terrified pleading that the troops not desert them.[9]

There was no occasion to demand more speed, Donnelly concluded. With forces at last gathered and amounting to more than 1,200 men, Sibley was already planning to advance next day to the relief of Fort Ridgely. In preparation he organized his "expedition" into three segments. Recruits for the Sixth Minnesota (none of whom had yet been mustered into the U.S. Army) he placed under command of William Crooks, the West Point-trained son of Ramsay Crooks. A second regiment of foot soldiers was formed from the remaining crowd of unmounted civilian volunteers and placed under Fowler. A contentious collection of some 300 mounted volunteers was given to Samuel McPhail, who had had similar experience in the Mexican War and in Missouri during 1861. About 150 of them, mostly men from Hennepin County, refused to recognize McPhail's authority (or Sibley's) and threatened to mutiny. After several confrontations they took off for Fort Ridgely in advance of the main column and later claimed the glory of having been first to relieve the beleaguered garrison.[10]

Sibley still had no provisions, but he was confident of living off the stock and gardens of abandoned farms on the three-day march. What bothered him more was a continuing shortage of ammunition and his tenuous control over the civilian volunteers, who were his only mounted men. He was keenly aware that he commanded the sole organized force standing between the Mississippi and what might be the whole Dakota nation in arms to the west. Although he repeatedly boasted that they could whip "the savages," he suspected privately that his untrained men would panic at any surprise attack, and he therefore refused to advance at night.[11]

While Sibley struggled with the brutal realities of war in the Minnesota River valley, Ramsey was fighting a different war in St. Paul. After slashing red tape to forward supplies and men, his next objective was getting the attention of the U.S. government. It was no easy feat. Washington was fixated on the Virginia front and the tragic drama just then taking shape at Second Manassas. Secretary of War Edwin M. Stanton did little more than shrug and insist that the draft of men for the Union Army continue despite Indian depredations.

Ramsey then appealed to Lincoln. "Half the population of the state are fugitives," he wired. "It is absolutely impossible that we should proceed.... No one not here can conceive the panic in the state." Lincoln responded tersely: "Yours received. Attend to the Indians. If the draft cannot proceed of course it will not proceed."[12]

In regard to panic, Ramsey had not exaggerated. Ignorance both about the Dakota and about distances in the country fed the fear of newcomers along the Mississippi. Even at Mendota there was an alarm, and Sarah Sibley called on the governor for protection. Her husband, learning of it while he was at St. Peter, was less than sympathetic. "Well, did I ever!" he exclaimed. "You are just as safe there as if you were in New York City." Later, having no doubt received her reply, he wrote more gently: "Only in case my column should be defeated and destroyed need you feel any alarm. Until that happens, which I by no means intend shall occur, you may rest securely."[13]

The genuine threat in the Minnesota River valley was compounded by a conviction that the Ojibwe were about to descend from the north. For a time that fear seemed reasonable enough. Like the Dakota, the Ojibwe bands of the Upper Mississippi and Leech Lake had been promised by treaty many things that never materialized. They also detested their agent, Lucius Walker, who apparently suffered from paranoid delusions. Hole-in-the-Day, chief of the Gull Lake Ojibwe and principal spokesman for the Mississippi bands, had, like Little Crow, been to Washington and was well aware of the Union reverses in the war with the South. He also seems to have had current information on what was happening among the Dakota.

Although the Ojibwe were far from joining their bitter enemies in a war against the whites, Hole-in-the-Day was quite ready to use the situation for the advantage of his own people. Joined by a group from the Pillager Band at Leech Lake, he made threats and warlike gestures that sent missionaries and settlers fleeing from the area around Crow Wing and Gull Lake to nearby Fort Ripley at the same time the Dakota were attacking New Ulm and Fort

Ridgely. Immediately a wave of alarm spread through the northern settlements, from Duluth to the St. Croix River valley and from St. Cloud to the outskirts of St. Paul.

At the same time there were newspaper reports of white men—presumably Confederate agents—having circulated among the Indians. This was confirmed, in the view of the writer, by the scope of the war, which showed evidence of more intelligence than he thought Indians capable of. A Republican paper also hinted darkly that Democratic politicians with southern sympathies had deliberately stirred up hostility among the Indians.[14]

Conspiracy theories paled, however, before the glare of public hatred directed at the Dakota and all Indians. On August 30 Thomas M. Newson, former editor of the *St. Paul Times* and a leading local citizen, published a long letter in which he called for "a war of extermination" against the Dakota, every one of whom should be hunted down like a poisonous reptile. He bewailed the patience and endurance with which, he said, whites had worked for years to teach and uplift the Indians and the "partiality of our State in granting them the right of suffrage to the exclusion of the free intelligent black."[15]

Genocide was also on the mind of Jane Grey Swisshelm, the vitriolic editor of the *St. Cloud Democrat.* "Do not wait to be hunted," she urged the men of St. Cloud. "Exterminate the wild beasts. Never let it be said that whole settlements were given up by Anglo Saxons to a few thousand lousy, lazy savages." In St. Paul the flames were fanned further by gruesomely explicit accounts of mutilated corpses and Indian barbarities, which were later found to be greatly exaggerated.[16]

Ramsey called a special session of the legislature to deal with the crisis. It convened on September 9, and in his opening address the governor made it clear that the policy of the state was wholesale slaughter of the Dakota. "If any shall escape extinction," he said, "the wretched remnant must be driven beyond our borders." He was only a little more restrained with the Winnebago, who had taken no part in the conflict. They, too, were to be expelled from the state, for no Indians could be tolerated in the rich agricultural domain of southern Minnesota.[17]

Having reached Fort Ridgely on August 29, Sibley also talked fiercely in dispatches and letters of driving the Dakota "across the Missouri or to the devil," but his first act was to load his supply wagons with the women and children who had taken refuge at the fort and send them to safety. Some were still coming in, for he noted that another woman and five children had "straggled into camp in a most pitiable condition." Most of the refugees had nothing but the ragged clothes they stood in, and he hoped that public charity would care for them in St. Paul. "God knows what is to become of them," he told Sarah. "If you could only hear one tithe of the stories told by these poor people, you would be horrified."[18]

Another pressing need was to bury those who had been slain in the early onslaught at the Lower Agency and Redwood Ferry. On August 31 he sent out a detachment of 150 men to perform that duty, to rebuild the ferry, and to reconnoiter the area. He was still uncertain as to the whereabouts of Little Crow with the main Dakota force, and pursuit was postponed, since he was short of cartridges and expected supplies and reinforcements within a day or two. As a result he lost more than half his mounted contingent. Irked by military discipline and chafing at having no chance to "hunt Indians," many, led by the rebellious party that had ridden ahead to the fort, left and returned home. Along the way they justified their desertion with bitter complaints about Sibley's caution and excessive delay.[19]

Almost immediately the need for caution was underscored by the worst disaster of the campaign. Sibley had entrusted the burial detachment and reconnaissance duties to Brown, sending along a company of infantry and a small force of mounted volunteers. Knowing his friend's occasional propensity for rashness, Sibley had warned him particularly about the danger of ambush and of camping where trees or gullies might provide cover for an enemy approach. Nevertheless, after two days with no sign of Indians, Brown divided the party, and when it was reunited at a campsite chosen by the young captain of the infantry company, neither Brown, Alex Faribault, nor Jack Frazer, all of whom were present, objected that the spot was near the head of a wooded ravine known as Birch Coulee.[20]

In the silence before dawn on September 2, sentries fifteen miles away at Fort Ridgely detected the sound of distant rifle fire. Sibley at once sent out McPhail with some 240 men and two cannon, keeping the remainder of his force on the alert. McPhail reached Birch Coulee but was stopped by Indians hidden in the forested gully. Ignorant of the enemy numbers and fearing that he would be surrounded, McPhail sent word back to the fort for help. Sibley and his entire force arrived a little after midnight but waited until daylight to advance. The Dakota resisted for a while but withdrew as cannon fire raked the woods. An hour before noon Sibley, pushing out ahead of his own column of troops, rode into the camp.[21]

It was a grisly sight. The attack had been a nearly complete surprise. From the cover of nearby trees and tall grass, the Dakota had been within easy gunshot, while the troops were sheltered only by the wagons they had brought, the carcasses of some ninety dead horses, and hastily dug foxholes. Thirteen already lay dead and 47 were wounded, more or less seriously. They had been without food or water for thirty-six hours and their ammunition was almost gone. The smell of decaying flesh—both horses and men—hung heavy in the air. Sibley found Brown with a bullet wound in his neck, but Faribault and Frazer were unhurt. "These Indians," he told Sarah, "fight like devils; no one has seen anything like it."[22]

Back at Fort Ridgely, the colonel had occasion to realize that he was no longer the young Hal, accustomed to long hours in the saddle and bivouacking on the prairie. He was dirty, stiff, and in a daze of exhaustion. He was also angry and sick at heart. Letters from friends made it clear that the scornful tales carried by deserting volunteers had created impatience and anger throughout the settlements to the east. There was also more than a touch of political animosity. Not only his ability to lead, but also his will to fight the Dakota was called into question. The caustic pen of editor Swisshelm described him as "the State undertaker, with his company of grave-diggers and ferry-boat builders."[23]

Always proud and easily stung by criticism, Sibley immediately sent his resignation to Ramsey, saying that he would be happy to leave as soon as a replacement could be found. To Sarah he huffed: "It is hard indeed, while we are fighting and doing our best, to have a set of ninnies and poltroons abusing us at home." Yet he was clearly also torn by weariness and a longing to go home himself. "The responsibilities of my position are so great," he wrote "that I can't hardly sleep at all." And again: "I am nearly worn out with night watching and the labor necessary to get the material I have to work with into condition for a campaign."[24]

The battle of Birch Coulee as imagined by artist Anton Gág

Some comfort came from the support of that very material. Officers and men repeatedly begged him not to quit and voiced their confidence in him. The expedition's chaplain and interpreter, Stephen Riggs, also defended him. What Sibley lacked in enterprise as a field commander, he made up as a tireless administrator with solid concern for his troops. He never ceased nagging the state authorities for adequate supplies of food, clothing, and blankets to replace those given to refugees. He also badgered Ramsey to find a means of getting the men mustered in, so that they might receive the bonuses due them and be assured of pensions for their widows. Suspecting—with reason—that every movement of his force was closely watched and surprise attack a constant threat, he personally made the round of sleepy sentries at night before throwing himself down. Therefore, as he told Sarah, what rest he got "has been without undressing ever since I left Mendota."[25]

The attack at Birch Coulee carried the conflict to a new stage. Attached to a stake on the abandoned battlefield, Sibley left a note addressed to Little Crow. As he had anticipated, it was picked up immediately and carried to the chief. Three days later he received an answer, delivered under a flag of truce by two young mixed-bloods. The letter revealed for the first time that Little Crow was holding a large number of white women and children as prisoners, while the two messengers, who were both well known to Sibley, brought the news that most of the mixed-bloods were virtually captives also.

The presence of hostages complicated the situation for Sibley, raising yet another barrier to immediate pursuit of the enemy. "I must use what craft I possess," he told Sarah, "to get these poor creatures out of the possession of the red devils." Little Crow clearly wanted to parley, but Sibley refused to talk until the prisoners were freed. Nevertheless, the exchange of notes continued.[26]

This contact with the enemy, combined with reports from two Christian converts who had deserted the Indian camp, bringing a few prisoners with them, led gradually to a clearer picture of what had happened. The attacks on isolated settlements, as well as the battles at New Ulm and Fort Ridgely, had been carried out by warriors of the lower bands, mainly the Mdewakanton. Little Crow and leaders of the soldiers lodge no doubt had hoped that they would be joined by the upper bands and perhaps even by the distant Yankton. Some young men of the Wahpeton and Sisseton followed Little Crow, taking part in the destruction of the Upper Agency and in attacking Fort Abercrombie on the Red River. The leaders of those bands, however, stood aside from the conflict along with most of their people. They also saw to it that the agency personnel and traders, along with the nearby missionaries, were allowed to reach safety.

The farmer Indians of the lower bands had found themselves in an impossible position. Already shunned with fundamentalist fury by the more traditional tribesmen, they feared outright attack if they resisted joining in the war. At the same time, they knew they could expect no mercy from the enraged Indian-hating whites. As one young Mdewakanton woman recalled: "Like a destructive storm, the war struck suddenly and spread rapidly. Everything was confusion. It was difficult to know who was friend and who was foe."[27]

After the setbacks at New Ulm and Fort Ridgely, Little Crow tried to unite his forces and moved his people away from the scene of hostilities to a point near the mouth of the Chippewa River. All of the lower Dakota followed, camping now in territory that belonged to the upper bands. Before long, friction developed over the role of the mixed-bloods, the treatment of the captives, and the pillaged goods from agency warehouses and traders' stores. Those opposing Little Crow's militant young soldiers consolidated into a distinct "peace" group, which was joined by farmer Indians and a number of others from the upper bands.

This new cohesion of the antiwar elements of the tribe became apparent to Sibley when he received a note secretly delivered by Little Crow's mixed-blood go-betweens. It carried the names of Wabasha and Taopi, the latter a leader of the farmers, who claimed that they and their people had opposed the war and were kept in Little Crow's camp only through threats of death. They desired to surrender and would bring along all the prisoners they could secure if Sibley would name a place. The commander assured them that he would punish murderers but would not injure the innocent. He planned to march within three days, he said, and would receive them if they approached his force on the open prairie under a flag of truce. Still not wholly united, and torn between fear of Little Crow's soldiers and distrust of the advancing white army, the leaders of the peace party made no immediate response.

"They want to play 'good Indian,'" Sibley mused, "but they must separate from the 'unclean thing' or share the same fate." The ancient Biblical truth cut both ways, of course. Eleven years earlier he himself had warned Congress that its unclean policy of betrayal and genocide would lead to war. The reality of that war, however, with all its horror and hysteria, left no distance for moral reflection.[28]

The sobering news of Birch Coulee and of the large number of captives held by Little Crow muted the public clamor for immediate action. At the same time the trickle of aid reaching Sibley was beginning to swell. On September 2 some companies of the newly recruited Seventh Regiment had arrived, and twelve days later an even more welcome addition came with 250 men of the Third Minnesota. That regiment had been surrendered at Murfreesboro, and the men had been exchanged by the Confederates on condition of no longer fighting the South. Experienced troops, they introduced an element of military discipline to Sibley's force of raw recruits. Ammunition and clothing were also coming through—but no horses.

In St. Paul, too, things were moving ahead. Yielding to Ramsey's frantic demands for help, the national administration created a military Department of the Northwest and on September 6 assigned to it Major General John Pope, who was highly dispensable to the Union Army after his defeat at Second Manassas. Pope at once confirmed Ramsey's claims of urgency. "You have no idea," he wrote from St. Paul to his superiors in Washington, "of the terrible destruction already done and of the panic everywhere in Wisconsin and Minnesota. Unless very prompt steps are taken these states will be half depopulated before the winter begins." To Sibley he sent a complimentary and reassuring letter, and the commander's long reply suggests his genuine relief in at last having a structure of military authority to back him up.[29]

On September 18 Sibley started moving his force across the Minnesota River, intending to advance up the southwest or right bank. He had 1,450 men and five light artillery pieces. After the numerous desertions and the slaughter of horses at Birch Coulee, only 27 men were mounted and those were mostly occupied with herding the cattle in the supply train. He had barely ten days' supply of bread and feared that if he did not meet the Indians soon, he would have to withdraw on that account. He need not have worried, however. Little Crow's mounted scouts were keeping close watch of his movements, and the Dakota were preparing to advance.[30]

Four days later Sibley's force camped on the prairie beside a small lake, expecting the next day to cross the wooded valley of the Yellow Medicine River and reach what remained of the Upper Agency. The Dakota meanwhile were planning a surprise attack at the edge of the valley, and warriors placed themselves on three sides of the route by which the column would march. A little after dawn, before the camp was broken, a few veterans from the Third Minnesota formed an unauthorized foraging party to visit a nearby abandoned farm. Their route led directly through the Dakota line, and the Indians were forced to open fire at once. The rest of the Third Minnesota, without orders, rushed to aid their comrades, and Sibley had some trouble in getting the men to retire before they were surrounded. In the meantime the whole force had rallied, and after two hours of fighting, the Dakota withdrew, heavily outnumbered, overpowered by artillery fire, and leaving dead and wounded behind.

The Battle of Wood Lake, as the engagement came to be called, was decisive. Little Crow retreated to his main camp, only to find that in his absence the prisoners had been seized by the "peace" faction, who were prepared to defend them by force. The defeated militants had little choice. Gathering together their families and belongings, they turned defiantly to the north and west, leaving the Minnesota River valley forever. Winter loomed ahead on the unforgiving plains, and as Little Crow had predicted, they would be hunted like rabbits.

On September 26 Sibley and his force arrived at the Dakota encampment near the mouth of the Chippewa River. He estimated that it held about 150 lodges of Indians and mixed-bloods, all of whom now proclaimed their friendship for the whites. There were also more than a hundred captives. He surrounded the camp and entered with a few officers, demanding the surrender of the prisoners. They were immediately brought forward. "The poor creatures cried for joy at their deliverance from the loathsome bondage in which they had been kept for weeks," he wrote. "They all clustered close around our little group, as if they feared that attempts would be made to keep them in custody."[31]

Then and later Sibley stated his belief that most of the women had been repeatedly raped. He admitted to Sarah, however, that not every one of them had suffered. Several reported that they had been treated kindly, and one had preferred her Indian captor to her white husband. Sibley did not mention her name, but she was probably the wife of Dr. John Wakefield, the physician at the Upper Agency. Appalled at the offhand announcement by officers that all the Dakota men would promptly be hanged, Sarah Wakefield fiercely defended the man who had saved her life and whom she knew only as "Chaska"—the Dakota term for a first-born son. Her insistence must have been unsettling to Sibley, for he mentioned her several times, concluding: "A pretty specimen of a white woman she is, truly!"[32]

In contrast, Sibley witnessed at least one happy reunion when the prisoners were freed. Brown, torn with anxiety, had ridden along with the troops despite his wound. He found his wife and children safe among the mixed-blood captives and learned how the spirited Susan Brown had saved her own family members and several others from threatened death by warning that her Sisseton relatives would punish any injury to her or to those under her protection.[33]

The headquarters of the expedition was now established at what Sibley immediately named "Camp Release." He could not pursue Little Crow without mounted troops. Those Wahpeton and Sisseton who had remained aloof from the hostilities were in their villages farther west, protesting their anger at Little Crow and their desire for peace. The captives, provided with what comforts his men could give them, were ready to depart for Fort Ridgely. Sibley felt that his job was done, and his first act was to request that he be relieved of command and allowed to return home. He repeated this a day or two later, citing illness and concern about his business affairs. "He ought to go home," his friend Riggs observed, "for he is suffering much with rheumatism." Sibley's own dispatches must have crossed paths on the way with one headed up the valley from St. Paul. It announced that he had been made a brigadier general in the U.S. Army.[34]

With this appointment Sibley's situation changed markedly. No longer was he the volunteer leader of an ad hoc expedition summoned to enforce the law in a state emergency. He was now a part of the Union Army, involved in one sector of the Civil War. Unsought by himself, he had acquired a military career and the rank of general. His primary responsibility was no longer to the state, but to the nation. As awareness of this new status sank in, his attitude began to change. Sarah noticed it immediately, and accused him of becoming enamored with military life. He protested, of course, that he was much more attached to "a certain wife of mine, who I hope soon to rejoin." Nevertheless, she was right; the ground had shifted.[35]

Sibley as a brigadier general, taken in the winter of 1862

attached to "a certain wife of mine, who I hope soon to rejoin." Nevertheless, she was right; the ground had shifted.[35]

Before news of the appointment arrived, Sibley had already begun to address the problem of his "friendly" prisoners and the rising crescendo of demands for wholesale revenge. With only a vague sense of the situation but a keen awareness of public outcry, Pope instructed him to treat all Dakota "as maniacs or wild beasts, and by no means as people with whom treaties or compromises can be made." The rules of war, in other words, did not apply. Meanwhile, solely on his own authority, Sibley had created a military commission of five officers to conduct trials of the men whom he suspected of participating in hostilities.

Drum-head justice it was, as Sibley freely admitted, yet his ingrained sense of legal propriety demanded some color of law, even in the disposal of those deemed maniacs and wild beasts.[36]

Military commissions had been first used in the Mexican War and later in the South where martial law prevailed and the army policed both civilians and its own troops. No one, however, had declared martial law in Minnesota. Moreover there was deep division as to the status of the Dakota. Were they an enemy nation engaged in war, or were they a criminal element of the state's own population? Without doubt the Dakota considered themselves a sovereign nation, and just as certainly most Minnesotans, including Henry Sibley, viewed them as wards and dependents of the Great White Father. For nearly twenty years Sibley himself had urged ending what he considered the fiction of sovereignty along with the treaty system. Like the missionaries, the Quakers, and other "friends of the Indian," he had consistently called for making the Dakota subject to U.S. law and eventually welcoming them to citizenship. Nevertheless, their status as a separate people remained enshrined in federal policy.[37]

The issue of sovereignty aside, the unannounced and widespread slaughter of civilians—probably more than five hundred—had foreclosed the possibility of simple amnesty. Although the military commission had no legal jurisdiction, and Sibley had no authority to create it, the device offered a practical alternative to peremptory executions. State courts were far distant and would have been overwhelmed by the volume of cases. Moreover, they would have been grossly prejudiced and besieged by murderous mobs. In its isolated tent on the prairie, the commission listened to brief testimony translated by Riggs, who served as principal interpreter, and made swift, often arbitrary decisions. Sibley reviewed each sentence and approved nearly all. The simple criterion of guilt was evidence of "voluntary participation" in hostilities. As Sibley later explained, the commission did not inquire into the degree of guilt in most cases. That made verdicts easy, since many of the accused freely admitted their participation, while denying personal crimes. Thus the proceedings were conducted with dizzying speed, and most of the accused were sentenced to death.[38]

At first Sibley planned to execute the condemned immediately, but two things stopped him. One was a well-justified doubt of his authority to do so— a doubt that grew more serious with his new status as a U.S. Army officer. Had he remained a state militiaman, little question would have been raised. A second consideration was the fact that immediate hangings would deter the small groups of Dakota who were still coming in to surrender. Some had initially followed Little Crow, and others had simply scattered to the prairies.

Faced with the approach of winter and scant sympathy from tribesmen to the west, while assured by Sibley that only the guilty would be punished, many were deciding to risk the mercy of the Great Father.

Whether or not Sibley's own passion for bloody retaliation had cooled, voices in St. Paul were already accusing him of shielding the Indians. He and his closest aides were, they pointed out, either related to the Dakota or had lived among them. One who doubted Sibley's resolve was Flandrau. According to Riggs, the judge had urged Sibley to kill all Dakota—men, women, and children. Years later Flandrau recalled receiving a dispatch from Sibley announcing immediate execution of the condemned warriors. On it the judge had written angrily: "He says he will, but he won't do it." Pope, impatient at the slow pace of punishment, ordered that all the prisoners be sent to Fort Snelling. Sibley doubted the feasibility of the plan, but he was content to turn over the job of conducting hangings.[39]

In preparation for the move, the troops entered the Indian camp, disarmed all, and separated out the able-bodied men, placing them under close guard along with those already condemned, who were being kept in chains. During this maneuver, Sibley himself went to some of the Dakota lodges to issue the orders. There his heart threatened to betray him. "The poor women's wailings when separated from their husbands, fathers, and sons are piteous indeed," he wrote "Poor wretches, they are objects of pity notwithstanding the enormities perpetrated." As if to justify the stern measures and reinforce his anger, he added that among the things recovered from the lodges were daguerreotypes of white families, who were presumably dead, and the fresh scalp of a young girl.[40]

Just as Sibley was preparing to start with his prisoners on the long march to Fort Snelling, he received from Pope a countermanding order. He decided, nevertheless, to move the entire operation to the Lower Agency. Supplies had become a desperate problem as the number of prisoners mounted toward two thousand, and Sibley had already sent half of them, with part of his troops, to the Upper Agency, where some potatoes and corn were still unharvested in the fields of farmer Indians. More crops would be available at the Lower Agency, and from there communication would be easier. By October 25 the trek was completed, and all were settled at what was universally dubbed "Camp Sibley," although the general himself declined to use the name officially.[41]

There the military commission resumed its work, and the number of condemned increased steadily. Sibley, as before, reviewed each case and passed judgment on the final sentence. "This power of life and death is an awful thing to exercise," he confessed to Sarah, "and when I think of more than three hundred human beings subject to that power, lodged in my hands, it makes me shudder." He declared his intention to do full justice, but no more, even though the papers were pronouncing him too lenient. He still expected to carry out executions as soon as the commission had finished its work. Pope, however, who had been urging Sibley on, realized belatedly that the exercise of the death sentence rested solely with their commander-in-chief. Thus the "awful thing" was suddenly lifted from Sibley's shoulders and placed on those of Abraham Lincoln.[42]

By November 5, 1862, the commission had sentenced 307 men to death and 16 to prison. Another 69 were judged innocent. To the anger of most Minnesotans, Lincoln did not immediately approve executions but asked to see the records of the commission. With more delay in prospect and cold winds already carrying a hint of snow at the Lower Agency, Sibley disbanded the camp and divided the prisoners, sending the condemned men to a location near Mankato and the women, children, old people, and "good" Indians on to Fort Snelling. When Chaplain Riggs, who shared Sibley's tent, asked permission to accompany the latter group, Sibley denied it, perhaps only half joking as he declared that both of them would freeze, since neither man had blankets enough to stay warm alone. Persisting, Riggs pleaded that he did not want to witness the executions. He was told that he must stand by his commander "to the bitter end."[43]

A new threat now appeared—this time from the fury of returning settlers and townspeople in the Minnesota River valley. As the line of wagons and carts carrying the convicts approached New Ulm, a fierce mob attacked the column with pitchforks, hatchets, clubs, and stones. Despite the flanking line of troops, they seriously injured some fifteen of the manacled prisoners. Not wanting to fire on the crowd, which included women and children, Sibley at last ordered them driven back with a bayonet charge and detoured the column around the town. He also arrested some twenty men, who were forced to march a dozen miles with the troops and then set free after a sharp lecture on respect for the law and the flag. As for the women, Sibley commented: "The Dutch she devils!—They were as fierce as tigresses."[44]

Much the same treatment met the four-mile long procession of Dakota families—mostly on foot—as it trudged on down the valley to Fort Snelling. Of the 1,600 who arrived there, more than a hundred were mixed-bloods who had already been held captive by the hostile Dakota. Of the rest only about 150 were men, all of whom had been found innocent of taking any part in the war and some of whom had helped to save white lives. The rest were women and children. Passing through settlements, many were attacked and beaten despite the efforts of their guards. In one case scalding water was thrown from an up-per-story window upon a cart loaded with old people and young children. In another case a nursing infant was snatched from its mother and dashed to its death. The Dakota carefully hid the graves of those who died along the way, knowing that if found the bodies would be desecrated.[45]

Sibley himself remained in Mankato, awaiting developments. The quar-ters were more comfortable, but tension was high and so were problems with discipline. Whiskey was available, and despite the general's best efforts drunkenness persisted among the troops. Some of them also harassed the small group of Dakota women who had been brought along to cook for the prisoners. In response to complaints, Sibley one night ordered a surprise ar-rest of all soldiers found in the Indian tents. To his intense embarrassment the dragnet turned up his assistant adjutant general, Joe Brown. Although Brown insisted that he was simply protecting the women in a relative's tent, the snickering spread throughout the camp.[46]

Pope had already let it be known that he expected to be transferred and that Sibley would be left in charge of the Minnesota district. Rumors flew that

Execution of 38 Dakota at Mankato, December 26, 1862

Senator Henry Rice would be made a major general and be placed over the entire department of the Northwest. Sarah apparently shared the indignation voiced by political friends of Sibley at such a move, but Sibley himself accepted the prospect with equanimity. He would rather serve under a fellow Minnesotan than a stranger, he said, for in that case "I know I should be allowed to do pretty much as I pleased." The honor given him in promotion from a private citizen to a brigadier general was greater, he felt, than any that could be accorded Rice.[47]

As it turned out, Pope remained in charge of the Northwest with headquarters in Wisconsin, while Sibley took command of the Minnesota district on November 25. His new headquarters were in St. Paul, and thus he was at last able to go home, leaving Colonel Stephen Miller to manage affairs at Mankato. No doubt to Sarah's joy, Sibley also arranged at once to move his family from Mendota to the capital city.

Resentment over the delay in executing the 307 condemned Indians continued building throughout the state. Pope, Ramsey, Senator Morton Wilkinson, and Minnesota's two congressmen all appealed to Lincoln to hasten the wholesale hanging. They warned of a mass uprising and indiscriminate massacre of the Dakota if the guilty ones should be pardoned. Sibley remained silent but stood by his original decisions in passing the death sentence. On December 6 Lincoln dispatched an order with the names of 39 Dakota to be hanged and telling Sibley to hold the other prisoners pending further instructions, "taking care that they neither escape nor are subjected to any unlawful violence."[48]

The president's orders were followed. Of all men, Sibley was the least likely to condone mob action. Warned by his experience at New Ulm, he took seriously the rumors of a widespread conspiracy to attack the stockade holding the prisoners at Mankato. Miller, alerted in advance to one attempt, was able to suppress it with a show of force. Sibley then authorized him to declare martial law and sent him all the troops he asked for, although remaining dubious that the men, who were drawn from Minnesota regiments, could be depended upon "in the last resort."[49]

It did not come to that. On December 26, 1862, the largest mass execution in U.S. history took place without further disturbance. After the spectacle of 38 enemy warriors hanged on a single scaffold, Minnesotans contented themselves with demanding that all Indians be removed from the state—or at least from the southern part of it. Their thirst for revenge may have been partially slaked by knowledge that a bill was moving through Congress that called for abrogation of all treaties with the Dakota. A million acres of former reservation lands, not only belonging to the Dakota but also to the unoffending Winnebago, would soon be open to white ownership.

· 14 ·

Revenge on the Plains

$\mathscr{P}$OSSIBLY THE MOST UNPOPULAR MAN IN THE STATE during the winter of 1862–63 was the Reverend Henry B. Whipple, Episcopal bishop of Minnesota, who was widely credited with having influenced Lincoln to spare the majority of the condemned Dakota. Whipple had been in Minnesota only three years, but in that time he had become deeply interested in missions to the Indians, both Dakota and Ojibwe, and incensed at the corruption he found in the government's Indian Department. He had chosen the town of Faribault as the seat of his diocese and had become a close friend of Alexander Faribault, whom he called "one of the kindest men I have ever known." Whipple and Sibley had, of course, met, but not until the aftermath of the conflict did they become well acquainted.[1]

As early as December 1862 several of the missionaries were questioning the action of the military commission and the speed with which the trials had been conducted. They included Riggs, who had felt private misgivings throughout the process, telling his wife at one point, "I should not like to have my life set upon by this Commission." Whipple went even further, arguing in published letters that the Dakota had been a deeply wronged people and that many of them had taken a reluctant part in the war. In public Sibley maintained a stoic silence, swallowing his humiliation when Lincoln overruled 270 of his sentences. His attempt at legal process had, in fact, pleased no one. While Whipple maintained that the civilized world could not justify putting surrendered enemies on trial, Senator Morton Wilkinson was declaring to Congress that Sibley "ought to have killed every one of the Indians as he came to them." The general was left with little choice but to stonewall the whole question.[2]

Nevertheless Sibley was clearly disturbed over the moral issues raised by his friends and by the ambiguities of his own position. In ongoing private correspondence with Whipple he strained hard to justify his actions. When the bishop objected to hanging men who had come in under a flag of truce, Sibley insisted that he had made it perfectly clear that the guilty would be punished. He argued that those who resisted his police action had made themselves willing accessories to mass murder. "A great public crime has been committed," he told Whipple, "not by wild Indians who did not know better, but by men who have had advantages, some of religious teachings." He himself had been forced, he said, to turn his back on long associations and even "personal attachment" to some of the condemned. Duty demanded it, for the hard fact that every one of them deserved capital punishment was a thing of which "I have no more doubt than I have of my own existence."[3]

Most Minnesotans would have agreed fervently, but, unlike Sibley, they drew little distinction between the guilty and innocent. All were Indians. Those at Fort Snelling were enclosed in a stockade on the bottomlands below the fort, where they were kept until spring. Neighboring whites harassed them and also harassed the missionaries whose continuing ministry brought about a wave of religious conversions that swept not only the camp at Fort Snelling, but also the men still imprisoned at Mankato. On May 4 and 5, 1863, the Dakota at Fort Snelling were crowded like cattle onto two steamboats and began their journey into exile at a desolate place named Crow Creek on the Upper Missouri. As the strains of their hymn-singing rose from the boats, the citizens of St. Paul pelted them with a farewell volley of stones.

Before this forced deportation took place, the question had arisen of how to aid the handful of mixed-bloods and Indians who had actively assisted the whites and had saved many lives at the risk of their own. They, too, were homeless and destitute, and they were welcome neither among their own people nor in white communities. On this problem Sibley and Whipple were in agreement and worked closely together. The general used his military authority to provide for many of them, hiring the men as scouts and sending them with their families to Big Stone Lake on the state's western border. There they were supplied with rations and army protection. Although unpaid, the men could earn money by hunting and trapping when not on active duty.[4]

For those who declined this arrangement, the problem was more difficult. Sibley intervened with the Indian Department to prevent their deportation, but outside of the army he had no access to government funds. "I have done the best I could for them," he told Whipple, but the time for their claims to be recognized "is not <u>now</u>, as you will very readily appreciate." They were, in fact, in constant danger, since the state had placed a bounty on Dakota scalps and citizens were encouraged to murder Indians on sight. Sibley gave shelter to some of them at Mendota, where he set aside town lots for their use. Faribault did the same with his land in the Cannon River valley. There a few Dakota families, protected by the influence of Bishop Whipple, eked out a living through farmwork and hunting.[5]

·   ·   ·

Politically, as Ramsey and Sibley may have sensed at the beginning of the conflict, the war against the Dakota once more drew them together in mutual support. As in the early 1850s, Ramsey's course was simple and pragmatic: conquest, preferably at the least possible cost to the U.S. government and its citizens. Sibley's role was again more complicated. He accepted conquest as divinely ordained and his duty to the country as a sacred obligation. Nevertheless his own human sympathy, his awareness of government duplicity, and his love for the land and its vanishing past left him with a divided heart and a troubled conscience.

Behind the public rhetoric calling for punishment of the hostile Dakota and protection of Minnesota's pioneers, there were powerful political and economic forces pushing to carry the war onto the northern plains. Since 1858 nearly all of the supplies and goods shipped west by the Hudson's Bay Company had traveled over the trails established in the 1840s by Sibley's agent Norman Kittson and by the Métis traders of the Red River. In 1859 those routes had been augmented by a steamboat on the river. It was commanded by Kittson himself, who was now the American representative of his former British competitor. This international traffic was a growing pillar of St. Paul's commerce. In addition, gold had been discovered in Montana, and wagon trains of eager prospectors were already rolling from Minnesota across Dakota Territory. Moreover, the route for a future transcontinental railroad had long since been laid out from Lake Superior westward. As Sibley had foretold in 1850, the Indians of the plains were encircled as by a ring of fire—and now the Dakota had lit the match.[6]

The election in the fall of 1862 had sent Ignatius Donnelly to Congress and enough Republicans to the legislature to assure that a Republican would succeed Henry Rice, whose term in the Senate ended in the spring of 1863. Over stiff opposition from the more radical wing of the party, Ramsey was chosen. He remained in the governor's office, however, until July 1863. Meanwhile Sibley endured harassment and humiliation when the Senate denied his appointment as brigadier general early in March. The outcome had been foreseen, since there was an effort to limit the swelling number of Union Army generals, and neither of Minnesota's senators was any friend of Sibley.

As senator-elect, Ramsey tried unsuccessfully to have the question of Sibley's appointment reconsidered, and the Minnesota legislature, anticipating the rejection, had already adopted a joint resolution supporting the new general. Some fifty St. Paul businessmen also signed a letter urging him to accept the reappointment that President Lincoln promptly offered. In a characteristically stiff and self-deprecating letter, Sibley assured them that he would. Part of this broad-based support for him reflected new friendships that had been formed in the field. Many of the officers who served under Sibley in 1862 and again in 1863 were Republicans. They included such influential party figures as William R. Marshall and Stephen Miller. Both future Minnesota governors, these men leaned toward Ramsey's wing of the party and became strong personal if not political allies of Sibley.[7]

Harassment continued, however. Senators Rice and Wilkinson, political opponents of each other but united in their enmity to Sibley, secured from the secretary of war an order to raise an independent force of mounted Indian fighters. It was to be organized and commanded by Edwin A. C. Hatch, an old friend and longtime associate of Rice in the Winnebago trade. Recruiting of volunteers for Hatch's Independent Battalion of Cavalry began in July 1863 to the intense annoyance of Generals Pope and Sibley. Its announced purpose was to protect Minnesota settlers while the regular army forces were engaged in a major offensive on the Dakota plains.[8]

The Minnesota border had been relatively quiet throughout the winter of 1862–63. Most of the Dakota, including the Sisseton and Wahpeton as well as Little Crow with his shrinking band of followers, had withdrawn to the north and west, camping near Devils Lake and in the Turtle Mountains. No one doubted, however, that with the coming of spring there would be renewed guerrilla warfare along the broken line of settlements reaching from St. Cloud to Fort Abercrombie on the Red River and south into Iowa.

While Pope busied himself with planning grand strategies to crush the main body of Indians, Sibley faced constant demands to provide for the safety of isolated farms and villages in the western part of his own state. The more venturesome settlers had begun to return to their homes, and as early as April sudden raids and surprise attacks by the Dakota were reported. Sibley divided his troops and assigned small detachments to patrol a line of posts established at the larger settlements from Sauk Centre south to Paynesville and Fort Ridgely, then on to Madelia and Fairmont. In addition Sibley was under pressure to guard the stage road that had been opened in 1859 to Fort Abercrombie, and, of course, to protect the wagon trains and steamboat shipments of the Hudson's Bay Company.[9]

The offensive planned by Pope involved a pincer movement against the hostile Dakota. One force, under Sibley, would march to the Missouri River by way of Devils Lake, driving the Indians before it. A force under General Alfred Sully, which would come up the Missouri by steamboat, would cut off their escape. The two armies were to meet and presumably annihilate the Dakota somewhere along the Upper Missouri.

Throughout the spring months of 1863 Sibley organized men, supplies, and transportation for the expedition with his usual exhaustive attention to

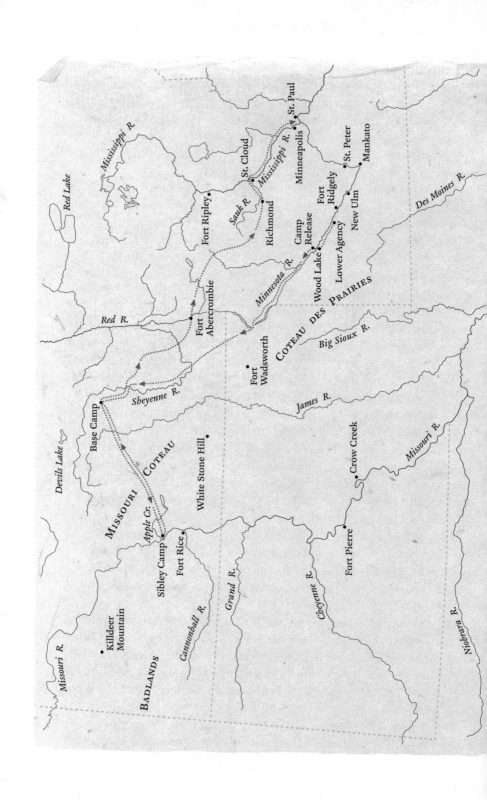

detail. Hundreds of barrels were ordered to carry hardtack—barrels that would later prove poorly made and given to bursting when hauled over rough ground. With an acute labor shortage in Minnesota, Sibley asked for 260 "contraband" slaves from St. Louis to serve as drivers for some 300 six-mule teams that would pull supply wagons and other equipment. The result was more than the general had bargained for. The first group of forty men, who arrived on a barge towed by the steamboat "Northerner," was accompanied by 10 women and 26 children. Hastily Sibley wired Pope, "What shall I do with families of contrabands sent up?" After being turned away angrily from the levee at St. Paul, the barge with its passengers went on to Fort Snelling. There is no record of what Sibley did with the families, but it is possible that the women were given employment at the fort as laundresses.[10]

On June 10 Sibley formally took command of the small army that he had assembled at Camp Pope near the mouth of the Redwood River. Riggs again served as interpreter and chaplain, and Forbes was commissary. Joe Brown was guide and leader of the scouts, while Sibley also had hired the Métis guide Pierre Bottineau, who knew the country north to Pembina and west to the Upper Missouri. Among the general's aides were young Captain Douglass Pope, a nephew of Sibley's commander, and Lieutenant Frederick J. H. Beever, scion of a wealthy English family, who had been educated at Oxford and had drifted around the world from one military adventure to another. Anticipating a need to pursue hostile Indians into British territory, the general had sought permission to cross the 49th parallel—a request that was emphatically denied.[11]

There were about 3,300 troops, including infantry, cavalry, and scouts, plus a battery of eight artillery pieces. This number was matched by nearly as many teamsters, herders, and other civilian employees. When at last the march commenced on June 16, the line stretched out for five miles, including the supply wagons and a herd of cattle to serve as beef on the hoof.[12]

For Sibley himself the campaign started with heartbreak. Three days after arriving at Camp Pope he received news that his seven-year-old daughter Mary had died. The gentle little girl was clearly a favorite of her father, for throughout the summer he was haunted by thoughts of "my dear lamblike little Mamie." Added to his grief was concern for his wife, who, pregnant again, was left alone to bury a third one of their children. He waited anxiously to hear from her before the expedition started, and on three successive days he noted "No letter from Sarah."[13]

He was still in a somber mood as the expedition passed the sites of the Wood Lake battle and Camp Release, already sinking into history. There was

opposite: *The Minnesota Valley and Dakota plains in 1862 and 1863, showing the route of Sibley's expedition to the Missouri*

something strange and solemn, he reflected, in how the sudden explosion of violence just ten months earlier had set into relentless motion a "war of races." Perhaps he also wondered at the irony of events that placed himself at the head of an army snaking its way west "like a huge serpent" to annihilate the Dakota.[14]

A season of severe drought was already under way. Blistering heat had delayed their start, smoke was in the air, and grass fires threatened them several times. Ten days' march brought them to the valley between Big Stone Lake and Lake Traverse, near the old trading station that had been Sibley's farthest outpost in 1835. There they stopped for two days to give the footsore men and weary beasts a rest and to repair wagons and barrels.

The massive supply train needed for the long cross-country march demanded much of Sibley's attention. Most of the mules brought from Missouri were young and unbroken, and the troops found daily entertainment in watching the drivers struggle to hitch them to the wagons. Runaways were a constant threat, and, as one correspondent to the *Pioneer* noted, with "wild mules, wild Irishmen, wild Missourians, and contrabands" the general "has his hands full to obtain anything like system."[15]

The pause also provided an occasion for a more general shakedown. Sibley enforced discipline on stragglers, traced the source of some illicit whiskey, and ordered the burial of Indian remains that his men had scattered about, threatening severe punishment for desecration of graves. He also settled some petty quarrels among his officers. With a flash of exasperated humor, he appointed three colonels to determine what were necks and shanks in issuing beef. On June 30 he sent a detachment north to Fort Abercrombie for supplies and led the main column westward, up out of the Minnesota River valley and onto the Dakota plains.

Four days' march to the northwest under a searing sun took them to the big bend of the Sheyenne River, where they were to rendezvous with the column from Abercrombie. Smoke and dust had thickened and so had grasshoppers, clouds of them glistening and filling the air, looking to Sibley like snowflakes. Horses and mules threatened to give out in the heat, while fires and insect swarms caused worry about finding forage on the journey ahead.

The green valley of the Sheyenne, reached on July 4, was a welcome relief. There they made camp beside the river, with plenty of wood, water, and grass, while the officers gathered to celebrate the day with toasts to President Lincoln and other dignitaries. The wagon train with supplies did not arrive for five days, but in the meantime mail and dispatches came through with messengers from Fort Abercrombie. The messengers also brought St. Paul papers telling of Lee's advance into Pennsylvania. News that the Civil War was reaching a climax only added to Sibley's gloom. He prayed that God would soon end "the unnatural brutal war" and reunite the country.[16]

Even more alarming was word that his ten-year-old son Frank was ill. Although the boy's condition was said not to be serious, a terrible foreboding seized Sibley. It threw him into a state of depression accompanied by vivid and agonizing dreams that persisted throughout the campaign.

Despite this dark frame of mind, he took daily note of the wild beauty of the country as they moved north along the Sheyenne. Buffalo were becoming common. They also saw elk and an occasional antelope, but hunting was strictly forbidden. The sound of gunshots was reserved as warning of a hostile presence.

Crossing the Sheyenne on July 16, they took a more westerly route and two days later made camp thirty-five miles southeast of Devils Lake. The spot was two miles from Lake Jessie, where Nicollet and Fremont had camped in 1839, and which Fremont had named for Jessie Benton, his future wife. There they encountered a small party of gold seekers who were determined to reach Montana despite the obvious dangers. As Sibley was inspecting the campsite near the muddy margin of a small lake, his horse fell, wrenching the general's leg and leaving him with a lame knee and hip. Though painful, the blow was nothing compared to one he received the next day, when mail from Fort Abercrombie caught up with them. It brought the news of Frank's death.[17]

July 19 was a Sunday, and as was the usual custom, they stayed in camp, resting men and mules and observing the Sabbath. It was also the occasion for implementing a change of plans. Two days earlier they had met Métis hunters who reported that the Indians were no longer near Devils Lake but had divided into several bands and were moving toward the Missouri. Sibley proposed to establish a base camp and leave there some of the cumbersome supply train, along with the slower troops. The rest of the expedition would push ahead with greater speed in pursuit of the Dakota.

Accordingly the next day the pared-down force started a rapid march west toward the James River. Sibley, after a sleepless night, rode in an ambulance wagon, nursing his crippled leg along with torturing thoughts of his dead children and his grieving wife. "Two more wretched days than the last past I have never experienced," he wrote.[18]

They camped that night within two miles of a large hunting brigade of Métis from Pembina, who sent a delegation of a hundred mounted men to greet them. The spokesman was their priest, the Reverend Alexis Andre, who made a formal speech in French, thanking the United States for sending troops to chastise the Dakota. The Indians were, he declared, as much enemies of the Métis as of the Americans. In closing he wished them victory in the battle that all anticipated would soon take place. Sibley replied briefly and then translated the substance of the message for his officers. Despite their declared enmity for the Dakota, these *gens libres* of the plains were in regular touch with the Indians, and Sibley tried through them to send a message to the Sisseton chief Standing Buffalo, who in 1862 had indicated his friendship for the whites.

The next day Sibley's men crossed the James and two more days' march to the southwest took them to the higher, broken ground of the Missouri Coteau. On July 24, as they neared a hill called the Big Mound, the scouts brought word that a large Dakota camp was close by. Sibley ordered the wagons to be circled on the shore of a small, brackish lake and earthworks were thrown up. Meanwhile several of the scouts had been able to contact their relatives among the Dakota. The messages they brought back were mixed. Standing Buffalo wanted to hold a council with Sibley some said, but others warned of an immediate attack.

Clearly the Dakota were still divided. Any hopes Sibley might have had for engineering a peaceful surrender were dashed when the militants seized the initiative. A group of Indians appeared on the hill and began to hold a conversation with some of the scouts, but when one of the regimental surgeons rode up to join them, a young warrior suddenly shot and killed him. The others fled, and Sibley, after a brief wait to see if Standing Buffalo would appear, ordered an advance.

The battle of Big Mound was wholly one-sided. Outnumbered and short of guns and ammunition, the Dakota men could only try to hold off the troops while their families frantically broke camp, loaded supplies, and fled.

A number of warriors were slain, and as night fell, the rest joined the flight, pursued by Sibley's cavalry under Colonel McPhail.

With the main body of his troops exhausted from the long day of marching and fighting, Sibley made camp and sent his aide Beever with a message telling McPhail not to risk ambush but to hold his position until the rest of the force caught up. Somehow the message was misunderstood, and to the general's dismay McPhail returned, appearing with his men just as the others were about to

Standing Buffalo

march forward and join him. Thus the opportunity for a follow-up to the victory was lost, and Sibley was spared the onus of harrying and slaughtering a crowd of fleeing women and children. The expedition took a day to recoup and to bury its three casualties, and on July 26 the soldiers resumed their dogged march on the trail of the Indians.

The Dakota themselves were slowed by the presence of their families and the effort to salvage their supplies. Along the way they were forced to abandon many things. Sibley's troops found buffalo robes, dried meat, kettles, and other things the fleeing Indians had discarded to lighten their load. They also found one old woman who had been unable to keep up the pace and later an unarmed Teton youth asleep in the grass. They took him to the general, who could determine no clear explanation for his presence but eventually released him on the promise that he would take a message to his father that the Teton should remain at peace.

Clearly Sibley thought he was still on the trail of Sisseton and Wahpeton, along with some hostile Mdewakanton. According to later Indian accounts, the two former groups, including Standing Buffalo and his followers, separated from the others during or immediately after the battle at Big Mound and fled northward to the British border. The party that Sibley followed was said to have been led by the outlawed Wahpekute Inkpaduta and to have included Teton and some Yankton.[19]

Whatever their identity, the men had meanwhile circled back and tried again to hold off the pursuers. A brief attack was followed by skirmishing through most of the afternoon on July 26. One cavalryman was shot as he tried to saber a wounded warrior. Nine Indians were slain, and to Sibley's indignation, all were scalped. He could do little about it, since his own state was rewarding the practice. "Shame upon such brutality," he wrote. "God's image should not be thus mistreated and disfigured." Two days later, at a place known as Stony Lake, the enemy made a more determined stand, but once again they were unsuccessful. With troops ahead and on the flanks to protect the supply wagons, the column kept moving steadily forward and suffered no casualties.[20]

On the 29th they crossed Apple Creek and reached the Missouri. It was already plain that the Indians had made their escape across the river—but not without cost. More than a hundred abandoned wagons and carts loaded with goods were left in the thick woods that lined the bank. Without boats Sibley could not follow, and there was no sign of General Sully and his force.

They made camp on a tableland well away from the wooded river bottom, where Dakota skirmishers continued to swarm. That night the Indians set fire to the prairie around the camp and captured several mules. More disturbing to Sibley was the loss of Lieutenant Beever, who had gone the day before with a message to one of the officers and had failed to return. His body was found by a detachment sent to burn the wagons and other belongings left by the Indians on the riverbank. The young Englishman's burial affected the general deeply and brought back haunting anxieties for his own family. "Another bereavement," he wrote, "would go far to upset my reason."[21]

Meanwhile the scouts had been talking with the enemy across the river. They confirmed what had been rumored earlier—that Little Crow with a small party had returned to the Minnesota River valley and had there met with death. On the far side of the Missouri, however, the Dakota remained defiant. Sibley sent up rockets in the faint hope of signaling Sully, but as supplies dwindled and as men and mules began to wilt in temperatures that climbed above a hundred degrees each day, he knew he could not wait. On July 31 he ordered a dress parade, and, with proper formality and all the pomp his weary, sweating troops could summon, he declared victory. "The campaign has been a complete success," he told the men. "You have marched nearly six hundred miles from St. Paul, and the powerful bands of the Dakotas . . . have succumbed to your valor and discipline and sought safety in flight." The next day they started homeward.[22]

The return march was uneventful. On the day that Sibley's force reached Fort Abercrombie, Sully, delayed by low water on the Missouri, finally left his advanced post above Fort Pierre. A week later he reached the mouth of Apple Creek, where Sibley had camped. The Indians meanwhile had recrossed the Missouri and were again hunting buffalo in the James River valley. There, on September 4, Sully found them near a place called White Stone Hill. While his advance column parleyed with the leaders, he brought up his full force and swept through the camp without warning. More than 200 were slain, including many women, children, and old people. Some 150 prisoners were then marched across the scorching plains to join their relatives deported from Minnesota. At Crow Creek Joe Brown's son Samuel, who was serving as a government interpreter, talked with the survivors and wrote indignantly to his father of the indiscriminate killing. The battle of White Stone Hill, he concluded, "was a perfect massacre." Thus Sully achieved the famous victory that had eluded Sibley.[23]

When the returning expedition reached Richmond on the Sauk River, they met Ramsey, who was bound westward to make a treaty with the Red Lake and Pembina Ojibwe that would nail down U.S. control of the Red River valley. Among members of the treaty-making party was Ramsey's spokesman and supporter, Joseph A. Wheelock, the editor of the St. Paul *Press*. He sent to his readers a vivid description of the expedition's camp with its neat rows of white tents and its sun-browned veterans, busy preparing supper. In a headquarters tent at the center, marked by a large flag, he found Sibley, looking tanned and thinner, his face deeply lined by private sorrow, but still "full of his work, and intent only on that."[24]

Noting that the campaign had been made with remarkably little loss of life to either the army men or their animals, Wheelock acknowledged: "As a triumph of organizing and business skill that march and return across the dry, parched plains is probably without a parallel in history." Then he added, "But that is all. Praise must stop there. General Sibley is not a soldier." Most later historians have agreed. Even Sibley himself said so repeatedly, although his statements have the ring of mere formal disclaimers. He was indeed no soldier. He had neither the ruthlessness of a Sully, the savagery of a Chivington, nor the bravado of a Custer.

Without a massacre to his credit, the general again faced abuse from his political foes, some of whom had loudly predicted the expedition's failure. "The hour for striking the avenging blow had arrived," fumed the editor of the Minneapolis *State Atlas*, "but *the blow was not struck*. It was stayed by treason or cowardice on the part of H. H. Sibley." And speaking for the Rice faction among Democrats, the *Pioneer* declared that Hatch's new independent battalion of Indian fighters would finish off any Dakota who escaped Sully, "who alone seems to show the desire or capacity to whip them."[25]

Recruitment for Hatch's Battalion was going slowly, however. The original concept of a freewheeling volunteer force to hunt down Indians along the border was quashed by Pope's angry objections, and when three companies had at last been formed and equipped at Fort Snelling, Sibley assigned them to Pembina. It was the equivalent of a station in Siberia, and the resemblance became stronger as they struggled northward through November blizzards.[26]

The same early blizzards struck a detachment of Sibley's own troops as they escorted an emergency supply train headed westward from Mankato to Crow Creek on the Missouri. Drought, poor planning, and wholesale theft by Indian Department officials had resulted in starvation among the deported Dakota and Winnebago. Instead of sending supplies up the Missouri, the Minnesota superintendent of Indian affairs, Clark W. Thompson, opted for an untried overland route that he hoped would prove the feasibility of travel from Minnesota into Dakota Territory—and incidentally benefit St. Paul contractors, who had an oversupply of condemned pork and flour. The relief train finally reached Crow Creek on December 2, 1863, but it brought too little and came too late for many of the dying Indian prisoners. The spectacle of incompetence and brazen corruption no doubt helped to persuade Sibley that, for the time at least, only the army could be entrusted with Indian affairs on the plains.[27]

It was a hard winter everywhere. Fearing a new attack from Hatch's Battalion, the Sisseton and Wahpeton withdrew to the north and west and were wintering on the Souris and Upper Assiniboine Rivers. The hostile Mdewakanton, less accustomed to the open plains, gathered in the Turtle Mountains on the international border. At last, led by the chiefs Shakopee and Medicine Bottle, they approached the British settlement at Fort Garry, asking for aid.[28]

With none of Her Majesty's troops on hand to protect them, citizens there were apprehensive and nervous. The governor, an officer of the Hudson's Bay Company, would have been happy for the help of Hatch's Battalion, but he had no authority to invite American troops onto British soil. After some weeks of tension and an indignant protest from Sibley that the British were providing the enemy with food and ammunition, private citizens, contacted by some of Hatch's officers, took things into their own hands. In a clandestine operation, they invited the two Dakota leaders to a council, drugged them, and transported them across the border to Pembina.[29]

With Shakopee and Medicine Bottle in custody, a number of their starving followers surrendered to the Americans. Others moved westward and settled permanently in British territory. Since giving permission was easier than driving them out, the Hudson's Bay Company and Her Majesty's government reluctantly agreed. The two captured chiefs were sent to Fort Snelling, and after a long delay resulting in part from questions about their illegal entrapment, they were tried by a military commission and sentenced to hanging.[30]

Sibley's appointment as a brigadier general passed the Senate in March 1864 with strong support from Ramsey and Donnelly and without opposition from Wilkinson. As it was being considered, the general himself traveled to Milwaukee to confer with Pope and Sully about plans for the coming summer. Pope's strategy called for an all-out assault on the Indians west of the Missouri, along with military protection for parties of gold-seekers and the establishment of a new line of forts on the Dakota plains. Sibley had favored concentrating on Minnesota and was only too happy to leave the western campaigning to Sully. He was delegated, nevertheless, to build a fort on the James River and send a contingent of Minnesota troops to join Sully on the Missouri.[31]

The location that Sibley chose for the new Fort Wadsworth was not on the James but at the western edge of the Coteau des Prairies. To supply it, he laid out a military road from St. Cloud and Sauk Centre. The Minnesota brigade of Sully's force, commanded by Colonel Minor T. Thomas, left Fort Ridgely on June 7, 1864, accompanied by nearly 300 emigrants bound for the gold fields of Montana. Without a long detour toward Devils Lake, the march across Dakota was shorter than in 1863, and the rendezvous at the Missouri was successful.[32]

Sully established Fort Rice at the mouth of the Cannonball River, a few miles below where Sibley had waited the year before. Having heard of a large encampment of mixed Dakota and western Indians a few days' march to the northwest, he sought them out. There, at Killdeer Mountain, he destroyed the camp and its winter store of food and other supplies with the same cold efficiency he had shown at Whitestone Hill. Indians of all ages and genders were slain, and no prisoners were taken. Joined by the emigrant train, Sully then made a difficult march through the badlands of western Dakota to the Yellowstone and returned by way of the Missouri.[33]

As Sibley continued through the rest of 1864 and 1865 with the largely routine chores of administering a military department, his attention was never far from the scattered groups of Sisseton and Wahpeton who had taken little or no part in the war. Deprived of their rights under former treaties, they were literally without legal status of any kind. The general had scarcely reached St. Paul after his 1863 expedition when he received a letter from Father Andre in Pembina. The priest reported that a council had been held there at which representatives of Standing Buffalo's people and other upper Dakota bands had reaffirmed their peaceful intentions toward both Métis and whites. While praising Sibley's humanity in the treatment of Indian women and children, Andre probably overstated the case in declaring: "Your course has inspired them with an entire confidence in you."[34]

In his efforts to find a way by which these battered refugees could return to a peaceable life, Sibley worked closely with Joe Brown, whose ties by marriage to the Sisseton provided a bridge of sorts. As early as the fall of 1863 he had sent Brown to the Red River valley in a vain attempt to parley with Standing Buffalo. As the general's "special military agent," Brown continued to supervise the corps of Indian and mixed-blood scouts and to provide information on enemy movements. At the same time he sought to establish communication and trust with Dakota people who in the eyes of higher military authorities did not exist.[35]

Although Brown was formally responsible to the young commanding officers at Fort Abercrombie and later at Fort Wadsworth, his lengthy reports were clearly intended for Sibley's eyes. Often they were supplemented by private letters, and he received some orders directly from St. Paul. A man less patient and canny might have found the situation impossible. Brown had long been accustomed to working with the general, but on one occasion he noted that his "perceptive organs were not equal to the task" of distinguishing the limits and directions of his authority. Sometimes, perhaps, he recalled his position at Traverse des Sioux in 1835, when Sibley had instructed him to defer to Joseph Renville, yet at the same time to ensure that the post made a profit.[36]

Working now with another Renville—old Joseph's nephew Gabriel, who was also the half-brother of his own wife, Susan—Brown welcomed a steady trickle of Dakota families who arrived throughout the fall of 1864 and the spring of 1865 at the camp maintained by the scouts on the James River. Although some of the headmen sought voluntarily to declare their loyalty to the United States, the army officially regarded them simply as prisoners. Early in February 1865, Pope issued arbitrary instructions restricting their contact with whites and defining the areas to which various Indian groups on the plains should be confined. The order aroused Brown's keen sense of the absurd. In his response to Sibley he noted that Pope had made no mention of the considerable mixed-blood and Métis population, asking pointedly if the commander had determined whether they were Indian or white. He also commented dryly that since Pope permitted no Indians east of the Red River, he presumed the Ojibwe to be white.[37]

The growing assemblage of Sisseton and Wahpeton survived at first by hunting and on supplies funneled out by Brown from Fort Wadsworth. Told to plant crops, they argued that the ground near the James River was poor and the location exposed to hostile attacks. Brown pleaded with Sibley to let them go to their former homes on the shores of Lake Traverse where they could fish as well as farm, and although this violated Pope's order, Sibley and his subordinate officers apparently looked the other way. Thus while reformers, army commanders, lawmakers, and Indian agents battled each other over a "final solution" to the Indian problem, the upper bands of Dakota quietly determined their own future.[38]

Slowly it was dawning on the country that the accelerating and costly war on the plains was linked to a dysfunctional Indian policy. Reformers like Whipple had pointed this out for years, but in 1864 both politicians and military officers joined the chorus. General Pope, exasperated at Indian Office interference with his military operations, submitted a plan to the War Department. Its keystone was an end to the national policy of treaty-making. Indians should become in law, he said, what they were in fact—wards of the government—and their custody should be entrusted to the War Department. He recommended that tribes who had not adopted agriculture be concentrated on the northern plains, which the general considered unfit for white settlement anyway. There, under permanent surveillance by the army they would be forced to remain peaceful, but otherwise they should be left to themselves to die or adapt.[39]

Pointedly nudged by Pope late in 1864, Sibley seconded his commander's call for an end to the treaty system and restoration of Indian affairs to the War Department. Whereas formerly he had favored separating the Dakota into small communities surrounded by white settlers, he now saw no solution but to concentrate the hostile groups on a large reserve, supervised by the army and far from white vengeance and interference. The country near Devils Lake was his recommendation. It was, he believed, suited for agriculture, yet unlikely to attract white settlers "for half a century to come."[40]

Before sending his recommendations to headquarters, Sibley discussed them privately with Whipple. The bishop, who was already working with the Indian Office toward consolidating the Ojibwe on a single remote reservation, responded cordially, although he favored the Coteau des Prairie instead of Devils Lake for the Dakota—a place that Sibley feared would be politically unacceptable. Wherever located, both men advocated an agricultural colony, and Whipple promised Sibley he would "second your efforts."[41]

As the Civil War drew toward a close at Appomattox in the spring of 1865, Sibley was nursing anger and disappointment at what he considered another slight to his military service. In December Pope had passed him over for promotion, while recommending that Sully be raised to the rank of major general. Whether the preference rested on Sully's record at slaying Indians or on the fact that he, unlike Sibley, was a career military man, Sibley felt it was unfair and he set forth his displeasure in a long letter to Pope. He also appealed to Ramsey and other political friends, none of whom was able to help him.[42]

News of the fall of Richmond reached St. Paul just before noon on Tuesday, April 4, and the town exploded with pent-up joy. Sibley, Gorman, and other dignitaries made impromptu speeches to a crowd gathered at the International Hotel, and the rest of the week was absorbed in preparations for a grand celebration. As the top commander in Minnesota, Sibley directed most of the arrangements, but if this relatively pleasant duty lightened his mood, events of early May soon darkened it again.

On May 2, five members of a family living near Mankato in the Blue Earth valley were murdered by a party of five or six mixed-bloods led by an army deserter who had heard that a large sum of money was in the house. When captured, the leader tried to deflect suspicion by claiming that nine bands of hostile Dakota were lurking in the neighborhood, and once again panic swept the frontier. No Indians were found, the prisoner, a mixed-blood named John Campbell, was promptly lynched, and all but one of his companions were slain on the Coteau by Brown's scouts. Nevertheless, newspapers proclaimed a new Indian outbreak, and race hatred flared so hotly that the aging missionary, Dr. Thomas S. Williamson, was warned by a mob to leave Mankato after delivering a sermon sympathetic to the friendly Dakota.[43]

Again the "howlers," as Sibley called them in private correspondence, were in full cry. A writer for the *Press* questioned not only Sibley's ability, but also his commitment to protecting frontier settlers because of his "lenient policy in disposing of Indian prisoners." Less restrained, the editor of the Faribault *Central Republican* attacked "the blundering incompetency, or worse, of this immaculate hero." Defending himself, Sibley wrote a letter to the *Press* on May 5, pointing out that no amount of military force could keep out small parties of desperate marauders and reminding readers that his wholesale death sentences had been overruled in 1862.[44]

Despite Minnesota's hysteria, however, hostilities had nearly ceased, even on the northern plains. The country as a whole, weary of war, was willing to support peaceful overtures to the tribes, and the new civil government of Dakota Territory, created in 1861 but long overshadowed by military campaigns, was asserting itself. Governor Newton Edmunds, who had been appointed by Lincoln in 1863, had come west from New York State by way of Michigan, where he had known Sibley's brother, Alexander. A quiet man, Edmunds was more interested in business than politics and was determined to promote settlement in the new territory. For that, peace was necessary. Working with the Indian Office, he had already outmaneuvered General Pope, had secured an appropriation from Congress, and was poised to make a treaty with those of the western bands who were willing to parley.[45]

Pope insisted on yet another summer of campaigning and sent Sully to root out hostile Dakota said to be gathering at Devils Lake and along the British border. None were found. Humiliated by the failure, Pope turned on Sibley, telling him in an angry telegram that his "spies and scouts" had "simply lied." Pope also informed Sibley brusquely of his appointment as a military representative on a commission to treat with Indians of the Upper Missouri. On August 15 a letter from Secretary of the Interior James Harlan confirmed the news that Sibley would be a member of Governor Edmunds' treaty-making party along with his new immediate commander, General Samuel R. Curtis.[46]

Reduction and reorganization of the Union Army, along with a new administration and the restored political ascendancy of the Indian Office, were producing confusion and conflict. Edmunds, in his role as superintendent of Indian affairs in Dakota Territory, recommended sending the Sisseton "prisoners" near Fort Wadsworth to Crow Creek. In an urgent appeal to Curtis, Sibley pointed out again that the Sisseton had never been hostile and were almost certain to clash with those Dakota who had initiated war in 1862. In regard to the proposed treaty, he also warned Curtis that the season was too late for assembling the scattered western bands and suggested that the council be postponed to the following summer so careful preparations could be made.[47]

The voice of experience fell on deaf ears, and Sibley was ordered to meet the other commissioners at Sioux City on September 10. Traveling overland, he arrived on the appointed day but learned that those coming from the east had been delayed and that travel up the Missouri would be hindered by low water. While waiting, he busied himself with studying Harlan's instructions to the commissioners and drafting preliminary articles of the treaty, which would involve declarations of peace but no land purchases.[48]

United at length in Yankton, the commissioners proceeded upriver toward Fort Sully. On the way Sibley, accompanied by Curtis, stopped to visit the prison camp at Crow Creek. There they distributed extra blankets and a few other supplies. They found conditions somewhat less grim than in previous years. The Winnebago had departed on their own initiative to join the Omaha tribe, who had invited them to share a reservation in Nebraska. Some thousand Dakota, mostly women, children, and old people remained at Crow Creek, their destiny still undecided. Even government agents, however, were beginning to admit that the site was inhospitable and unsuited to farming. The following year would see the Dakota transferred to the mouth of the Niobrara River in Nebraska and reunited with their husbands and fathers, who were released from imprisonment at Fort Davenport.[49]

Sibley's warning to the treaty commissioners proved correct. It was October before they reached Fort Sully, and few of the Teton or Yanktonais appeared. Several bands that had already indicated willingness to make peace signed agreements, and further negotiations were postponed until spring. By mid-November Sibley was back in St. Paul.[50]

As early as July the general had let it be known that he intended to leave military service, and, as before, he received many expressions of loyalty and regret from his subordinates. Nevertheless, writing to Secretary of War Stanton from Sioux City, he resigned his commission and requested an appointment as brevet major general. This was granted on November 29, 1865, and ratified by the Senate in April. Because of his continuing service on what was now known as the North Western Indian Commission, however, he was not immediately mustered out.[51]

The commission members met at the Indian Office in Washington during the winter of 1865–66 and broadened their strategy. Sibley was chosen to lead a group assigned to negotiate at Fort Laramie with the Brule, Oglalla, Arapaho, and Cheyenne. The rest, under Edmunds, were to finish their work on the Upper Missouri at Fort Rice. Perhaps because his own real interest was in the fate of the Dakota bands, or perhaps because he was simply weary of the whole thing, Sibley resigned from the commission in April.[52] By then, he was fifty-five years old.

Meanwhile, he had been steadily pleading the cause of the Sisseton and Wahpeton, including the restoration of their annuities. Brown suggested his own appointment as a special agent of the Indian Office to gather and conduct to Fort Rice "all the refugee Indians that can be persuaded to make peace." Sibley immediately had Brown hired, but he was not able to get the food, ammunition, and other supplies needed. Another difficulty arose when the new commander at Fort Abercrombie quarreled with Gabriel Renville and demanded his arrest, even suggesting in a confidential note to the authorities at Fort Wadsworth that some sentinel be found to shoot the mixed-blood leader "by accident." Since Renville was the acknowledged spokesman of both the Sisseton and Wahpeton, he was a key figure to any negotiation. Brown again appealed to Sibley.[53]

In the end the persistence of the two men won out, and a delegation from the upper Dakota bands went to Fort Rice. The commissioners, however, were less sympathetic than Sibley had hoped. They turned a cold shoulder when, encouraged by Brown and Renville, the Sisseton and Wahpeton took a hard line and insisted on their full treaty rights. No progress was made. Brown, for his part, fumed at the character of the commissioners, and although he wished that Sibley had been present, he did not wonder at the general's decision to resign.[54]

Negotiations held the following winter in Washington were more successful. The treaty rights of the two bands were acknowledged, although Congress refused to reinstate their annuities. Those who were willing to become farmers secured the home they wanted on the west shore of Lake Traverse and at the head of the Coteau. Others, some of whom still lived by hunting on the plains, were assigned a reservation at Devils Lake, beside the new Fort Totten. Brown meanwhile had moved his family to the south end of Lake Traverse, where he founded the town of Brown's Valley and devoted much of his time to working for and with his wife's people. They needed assistance, for the year 1867 found them hovering on the edge of starvation, without tools for farming or government support of any kind.[55]

Sibley was not officially mustered out until the summer of 1866, more than a year after the close of the Civil War and when he was fifty-five years old. His final promotion, however, had effectively ended his career as a soldier. To some extent that promotion compensated for its earlier denial, although brevet promotions were nearly universal among Union Army officers at the close of the war. His hypersensitivity to perceived slights had increased through years of public attacks on his character and competence in a military role he had never sought. Some of that sensitivity would cling for the remainder of his life, although the honors heaped on him in later years no doubt went far to soothe the pain.

· 15 ·

The Conscience of the State

AR FROM CHECKING THE TIDE OF GROWTH and change that Stephen Douglas and others had sensed in the 1850s, the four years of war had seen it swell into a flood that was engulfing the continent. The plains around Devils Lake that Sibley thought so remote in 1864 were being settled within less than a decade, and by 1875 the population of Minnesota itself had grown nearly two and a half times since 1860. Yet the war had shattered thousands of lives and destroyed whole communities. In its aftermath an undertone of melancholy haunted the nation.

The Sibley family was not immune to the pervasive sense of loss. The two children buried in 1863 had been joined by a third in 1864. Alexander Hastings, born to Sarah in January, died in August, and Sarah's mother, Mary Steele, went to her grave a month later. Meanwhile Sarah herself struggled with depression as well as failing health and took little pleasure in the family's elegant new home at 417 Woodward Street in St. Paul's fashionable Lower Town. Two years later, between repeated bouts of painful pleurisy, she had yet another child, prompting her brother-in-law, General Richard W. Johnson, to write to Sibley: "Don't you think it is high time to put a stop to these regular arrivals?" There is no record of the response.[1]

Alfred Brush, born in July 1866, was only fifteen months old when a disastrous accident nearly destroyed the house and took a further toll on the health and spirits of the family. A dinner party had ended on the evening of November 14, 1867, and the Sibleys had just seen the last guests out the door when they heard a crash followed by piercing screams from the second floor. Dashing up the stairs, Sibley was greeted by a servant girl enveloped in flames from a kerosene lamp that had apparently exploded in her hands. Running to the nearest bedroom, he clawed frantically at the bedding for something heavy enough to smother the fire. Sixteen-year-old Sallie Sibley, just behind her father on the stairway, shrank away in fear, but Augusta stepped forward, and the desperate young woman threw herself into Gussie's arms.

Seared by the flaming oil, and with her dress burning, Gussie disengaged herself and with the help of Sallie and her mother, tried to put out the fire in her own clothes. Sibley, meanwhile, returned and threw a blanket over the first victim. The flames, towering two or three feet above her head, were so fierce that he was badly scorched in the effort to smother them. As he turned to the nursery, where the fire had started, Gussie announced, in an even voice, "Pa, I believe I'm burning up." Seizing a pitcher of water that stood on a washstand, he poured it over her and telling her to lie on the floor, rolled her in a rug.

By then servants and neighbors were arriving, and with some difficulty the fire was put out. There were a few minutes of deadly fear over the fate of the baby, who could not be found, but it proved that his nurse had snatched him in her arms and fled to a neighbor's house. Maggie Murphy, the young servant, was burned beyond recognition and died in agony several hours later. Friends and well-wishers who called the next day found Sibley with his hands heavily bandaged and most of his hair and mustache singed away. He was still profoundly shaken by the horror he had witnessed.[2]

Gussie was severely burned on her shoulders and arms, and for several months there was question about her complete recovery. She was restored to health, however, by the following September when she married Captain Dou-

Sibley's home at 417 Woodward Street in St. Paul's Lower Town

glass Pope, Sibley's former aide de camp, who had been stationed at Fort Snelling during the war's closing years. At twenty-four, Gussie seems to have been a mainstay of the family, and her departure with her soldier husband left an aching void. Sarah was too ill to attend the brief early-morning ceremony, and it was, Anna Steele observed, a sad wedding. "You don't know how much I miss her," Sarah told Mary LeDuc, some months later, advising her friend to hold onto her daughters as long as she could, and "at any rate, don't let them look at an officer."[3]

During the winter of 1868–69 Sarah had her hands full with two-and-a-half-year-old Alfred, who "rules this house, or would like to." In May 1869 she was stricken again with pneumonia, and after a week's illness died at the age of forty-six. Thus Sibley was left to face the future in a half-empty mansion, with an eighteen-year-old daughter and two young sons, Freddie only eight, and Allie, not yet three.[4]

After being relieved of military responsibility, the general had returned to business affairs and also to recording his own reminiscences and those of others. In the years 1866 and 1867 he published his work on Jack Frazer as a series of articles in the *Pioneer*, prefacing it with an apologetic reference to the recent Indian war and his reluctance "to make public any sketches in which the Dakotas have borne a prominent part." He was confident, nevertheless, that it would "not be lacking in interest, or in a certain sort of value." Frazer himself fell ill the next year, and his wife wrote to Sibley about Jack's desire to see his friend and her own need for money "to get him a few things while he is sick." In 1869 Frazer died, and Sibley paid for a tombstone to mark his grave.[5]

Early in 1867 the general had been elected to a three-year term as president of the Minnesota Historical Society. During this period he began the task of expanding his reminiscences, bolstering his own memories with facts and recollections gathered from friends. The work was completed in 1873. A year earlier he had also published a final sporting article, appropriately titled "Sports of By-Gone Days," and by the end of the decade he had written a number of individual sketches and memoirs for the Historical Society, which appeared when Volume 3 of its *Collections* was compiled in 1880. In that year he was again elected president of the Society and continued in the position until his death.[6]

An equally long period of responsibility for another institution he had helped to found began in 1868, with his appointment as a regent of the University of Minnesota. One of his first duties was to join in selecting a new president. His own nomination for the post was his brother-in-law, Richard

Johnson, who had just moved with his family to St. Paul. When no support developed for Johnson, Sibley united with the other regents in appointing William W. Folwell, who served for the next fifteen years. The general continued as a regent until his death in 1891.[7]

One of the memoirs Sibley wrote honored Hercules Dousman. Said to have been Wisconsin's first millionaire, Dousman was suddenly stricken in September 1868 while sitting in the garden of his mansion at Prairie du Chien. He and Sibley were still bound together by business and financial ties along with almost forty years of friendship. The families continued to visit occasionally, and Sibley corresponded with Dousman's son, whom he addressed with a touch of nostalgia as "Mon Cher Louis," and with whom he also maintained a close business relationship.[8]

An even sharper blow came two years later with the equally sudden death of Joseph R. Brown in November 1870. Brown had spent much of his time since 1867 lobbying in Washington for Dakota treaty rights and raising funds in New York for a "steam wagon," which he hoped would provide a cheaper alternative to railroads on the open plains. He died in a New York hotel.

The news brought an outpouring of public recollections. As one St. Paul politician later commented, Brown had been "the best abused man in the country." In the end, however, few of the many men he had outwitted held any enmity. The hard-bitten newspaperman, Earle Goodrich, recalled the first and last words he had heard from Brown: "'Why. God bless you! Come in!'—at St. Paul, in 1854, and 'God bless you! Good night!' at New York, in 1870... . And between these two have been blessings numberless, but no curses."[9]

Sibley arranged for a special train to carry mourners from St. Paul to the funeral at Henderson, and when business took him east a few days later, he accepted an appointment as special administrator of the estate to help the family with legal matters in New York. At Brown's graveside he spoke briefly and from the heart, concluding, "And now, my old and tried friend, I leave you to your long and lonely sleep. Peace to your ashes." His words moved many to tears. To history, however, Sibley left no memoir of Brown, although he had known the man better than any of those who wrote their recollections. Brown, on his part, had once told Sibley that he was "The man with whom I had less reserve, and whose good opinion I have always valued beyond that of any other living."[10]

Just two weeks after Brown's death, the *Pioneer* published a lengthy commentary by him on U.S. Indian policy. In it he advocated eliminating tribal influence and initiating a program of personal rewards and individual incentives that he compared (revealingly) to the rearing of children. Writing the piece may have been suggested by a sea change in the country's policy that he had already witnessed. The new direction was in line with what Brown and Sibley had long advocated, but the influence behind it came from Whipple and other powerful reformers who had the ear of President Ulysses S. Grant. With the creation of an independent Board of Indian Commissioners in April 1869, the country had at last shouldered the "white man's burden" of educating, civilizing, Christianizing, and assimilating American Indians—or, as their descendants have put it bitterly, of saving the person and killing the Indian.[11]

The work of the North Western Indian Commission, from which Sibley resigned in 1866, had been doomed to failure by the unchecked rush of gold seekers into the northern Rockies. This led to the slaying of Captain William Fetterman and his command of eighty soldiers in December 1866 by northern tribesmen on the Bozeman Trail. Along with new hostilities on the southern plains, it resulted in yet another public cry for military action. A peace commission formed in the summer of 1867 fared no better. Its chief military representative, General William T. Sherman, had visited Minnesota and conferred with Sibley. Their meeting resulted in a warm personal friendship but led to no breakthrough in Indian policy. Although the commission first recommended measures leading toward assimilation and civilian control of Indian affairs, it reversed itself a year later.[12]

Sibley stayed on the periphery of these national events, but in the spring of 1869 he was once more deeply enmeshed in the affairs of the Sisseton and Wahpeton. Through the grim winter of 1867–68 he had used what influence he possessed with the Indian Office and the army to secure emergency relief for the starving families at Lake Traverse and Devils Lake. Meantime Whipple had been lobbying Congress for more substantial aid. The bishop was successful, and in the spring of 1868 the lawmakers appropriated $30,000 made payable to Whipple. His jubilation evaporated when he learned that the

money would stay in the treasury unless he himself purchased supplies and distributed them to the Indians.[13]

Without an office or a staff, and with only grudging help from the Indian agent and army officers at Forts Wadsworth and Totten, the bishop found it an overwhelming task. Nevertheless, hiring Dr. Jared W. Daniels to work with the Dakota, he began purchasing supplies and arranging for wagons to haul them. In November 1868 he visited Lake Traverse, where he found that "words would fail me to describe the abject misery." On the way, however, he was caught

Bishop Henry B. Whipple

in a blizzard and suffered exposure that left him with a lingering illness. In March 1869, Congress appropriated another $60,000, again designated for Whipple. He visited the reservation once more in July, but, unable to continue the work, he turned to his friend Sibley, who had assisted him through the spring. In October 1869, when the bishop left for southern France to recover his health, Sibley assumed management of the whole project.[14]

Neither Whipple nor Sibley charged the government for their services, using what stipends they might have claimed to pay Daniels, who remained at Lake Traverse. The regular government agent there, having no money to implement his own program, found himself in an awkward position, and in August 1869 he was officially replaced by Daniels. By December Sibley could see the need for additional money, and he wrote to both the secretary of the interior and the Indian Office, urging another appropriation by Congress, for "the Indians are doing so well and seem so anxious to assimilate themselves" that failing to support them would be a tragedy. He secured only $10,000. By April 1870 the previous appropriations had been expended, and Sibley was urging his friend General Winfield S. Hancock to order the commander at Fort Totten to continue issuing provisions to the Indians at Devils Lake until new funds became available.[15]

Whipple returned that summer. "I am ashamed of myself," he wrote to Sibley, "when I think of your labors to save me. May God reward you for I never can." Meanwhile Sibley's old friend William H. Forbes had been appointed as the first civilian agent at Devils Lake, and Daniels was compiling a glowing report to the Indian office on agricultural improvements and farming efforts at Lake Traverse.[16]

There was inherent irony in the fact that reformers pinned their hopes for the future of Indian people on agriculture just when American farmers became locked in a losing battle with the country's new industrial economy. As the decade of the 1870s opened, railroad corporations were stirring anger across the agricultural Midwest by charging exorbitant rates and discriminating to the benefit of favored customers. In Minnesota, nature also brought dire hardship to settlers, most of whom had far greater advantages than their Indian neighbors.

Prairie fires in 1871 cut a wide swath across the state's western counties, destroying crops, livestock, and even many farm buildings. Hailstorms that same year compounded the damage and left many farmers without reserves to start over. Although government assistance was still regarded as an unconscionable and perhaps unconstitutional interference with Providence and the marketplace, Christians were enjoined to charity. As pleas for relief poured in from county after county along with heart-wrenching stories of hunger and suffering, Governor Horace Austin called on individuals and churches to supply food and used clothing. Some railroads, already under political attack and mindful that their business depended on rural prosperity, volunteered free transportation of relief supplies, while the legislature reluctantly appropriated money for seed grain to be distributed to carefully screened farmers.[17]

Disaster on an even larger scale appeared in 1873 when clouds of grasshoppers swept from the Dakota plains across the southwestern corner of Minnesota, devouring crops in their path. Sibley, who continued to have a financial interest in southern Minnesota land and railroads, was a director of the St. Paul and Sioux City line. It ran through the heart of the affected area, and largely in response to his efforts, the company that fall investigated the need for relief in the communities it served. On December 22 Sibley presented to the St. Paul Chamber of Commerce an appeal from Cottonwood County and set in motion a sweeping campaign to raise private funds for feeding and clothing destitute families in southwestern Minnesota and northwestern Iowa. He himself headed an "executive committee" to approach well-heeled members of the business community and he wrote personally to directors and out-of-state stockholders of the railroad. The effort produced more than $6,000, plus carloads of much-needed clothing, bedding, food, and firewood contributed by less prosperous citizens.[18]

To the grasshopper damage had been added falling prices for farm products, when, in September 1873, the banking house of Jay Cooke and Company failed, plunging the country into depression. Cooke's failure also halted construction of the Northern Pacific Railroad, which had turned Duluth into an overnight boomtown and had carried prosperity across northern Minnesota. Faced with hard times and declining tax revenue, both the new governor, Cushman K. Davis, and the legislators reacted grudgingly to Sibley's urging that the state provide more aid to needy settlers. Limited appropriations both for direct relief and seed grain were made on the assumption that the emergency would end when new crops came in.[19]

By early summer it became clear that the worst was still ahead. Eggs laid the previous year had hatched, and millions of new grasshoppers spread the scourge even farther across Minnesota. Reluctant to call the legislature into special session, Governor Davis appealed to county governments in the more populous parts of the state to fund new relief efforts. Some complied and others refused. Ramsey County, prodded vigorously by both Sibley and the governor, led the way with a contribution of $5,000. People would die, Sibley told the commissioners flatly, if the county did not respond.

Supplemented by gifts from individuals and from organizations like the Grange and the White Earth band of Ojibwe Indians, this novel public-private partnership raised a sum of nearly $19,000. Davis asked Sibley to administer its distribution, aided by a committee of prominent citizens. One of them was John S. Pillsbury of Minneapolis, with whom Sibley formed a lasting friendship. Following the governor's directions, they worked exclusively through county commissioners in the stricken areas—a policy that Sibley later questioned. The job kept him busy throughout the fall of 1874, and he reported to the legislature in January 1875, accounting for the money with his usual meticulous care. No compensation for his work was offered or expected.

In concluding his report Sibley declared that at least $100,000 for relief and another $50,000 for seed grain were needed to prevent destitute settlers from giving up and moving elsewhere. Neither Davis nor the legislators agreed. Of $20,000 appropriated for relief, only half was distributed, largely because farmers were required to swear that they possessed no property whatsoever. Since even a cow or a team of horses disqualified them, few would consent to take the help. The legislature, however, created a joint committee on frontier relief, and although suspicion remained strong that relief to grasshopper victims would erode the moral fiber of recipients, appropriations for aid in destroying the insects continued until the invasion ended in 1877.[20]

Long before finishing his work on grasshopper relief, Sibley had once again become deeply involved in Indian affairs. The "peace" policy initiated by President Grant in 1869 was followed in 1871 by a clause in the Indian appropriation act that put an end to the recognition of tribes as independent na-

Minnesota farmers fighting grasshoppers in the 1870s

tions and therefore to treaty-making. Thus Indians became officially wards of the government, forbidden to practice their religions and subject to confinement on reservations and to compulsory education.[21]

The administration implemented the policy not only through a national commission of reform leaders, but by employing missionaries and other church representatives as agents on reservations across the country. Although efforts were made to distribute the offices evenly among the leading religious denominations, rivalry and disputes became common. At Lake Traverse the longtime work of Presbyterians Riggs and Williamson among the upper bands of Dakota justified their claim to control the reservation at the expense of Episcopalian Jared Daniels. Opposition to the heavy-handed rule of the missionaries and their converts soon developed. It was led by Gabriel Renville, and with Brown gone, Renville turned to Sibley for advice and support. At Devils Lake the Indian Department appealed to Sibley for help in finding a suitable Catholic agent, and the general may have been instrumental in securing the removal of an unfortunate choice made in 1875.[22]

In the summer of 1874 Sibley agreed tentatively to serve on the national Board of Indian Commissioners, provided that he would not be called upon "to expend much time and labor." He seems already to have doubted his ability to continue, probably because of his new responsibility for the distribution of state grasshopper relief. Friends, however, ranging from Secretary of the Interior Columbus Delano to Forbes at Devils Lake, urged the importance to the Indians of his presence on the commission.[23]

He served through the fall, but facing the need for exhausting trips to Washington and a barrage of complaints and requests from agents in his own area, he resigned in January 1875, voicing his "fervent desire" that the commission might succeed in "saving the remnant of the Indian tribes from threatened extinction." He also promised that anything he could do as an individual "will be cheerfully performed." Apparently the Indian Office took him at his word, since pleas for advice and assistance as well as appeals for him to attend meetings of the board continued throughout the next two years, and he maintained informal supervision over affairs at Lake Traverse and at Devils Lake, where Forbes, ill for nearly a year, died in July 1875.[24]

The disaster at the Little Big Horn in June 1876, shocked Minnesota, for Custer's men had been stationed at Fort Snelling before being ordered west. In a letter of sympathy to Louis Dousman, whose wife's brother had fallen there, Sibley noted that the "calamity . . . has produced a profound sensation in this City, where so many of the officers were personally known." As a result new cries went up throughout the West for avenging Custer and exterminating the Lakota. Whipple and other reformers defended the peace policy, and the bishop was among those sent to negotiate with the hostile Indians. "Day by day we are praying for wisdom," he told Sibley in a letter written at the Red Cloud Agency on September 18. Whipple urged that Sibley be included on the Sioux Treaty Commission when it met in Washington. The general was invited, and although he declined to serve, he sent a lengthy letter. In it he reviewed the record of broken promises and government betrayal that had led "very many friendly Sioux to band together for mutual protection against attack."[25]

This was Sibley's last formal statement on the nation's Indian policy. He referred again to his speech of 1850 in Congress and once more called for the extension of U.S. laws to all Indian people, along with individual land allotment and full citizenship. Allotment in particular was the direction in which many supporters of the peace policy were already looking. Meanwhile, under President Rutherford B. Hayes, who took office at the end of 1876, churches withdrew from their special role in Indian affairs, and Sibley, along with others, found that he had virtually no influence with the new administration.[26]

The aging general's last involvement with Indian affairs began in May 1881 when he received a letter from the Ojibwe chief White Cloud at the White Earth Reservation. Two months earlier Congress had yielded to persistent lobbying from Minnesota businessmen who sought improvement of navigation on the Mississippi River and—equally important—the regulation of the power supply for mills at the Falls of St. Anthony. The suggested solution was to construct a series of federal dams that would turn the headwaters lakes into reservoirs and control the flow of water in the river. In appropriating money for the purpose Congress had included a sum to pay for incidental damage to Indian property.[27]

Ojibwe people had lived for generations along the shores of Lake Winnibigoshish and Leech Lake. They had been given the land by treaty. Now they faced permanent flooding of their homes, their sacred spots, their farms, wild rice and cranberry beds, sugar bushes, and fine stands of timber. It was a devastating blow to their communities and livelihood for which no sum of money could compensate them. White Cloud warned of trouble and asked for Sibley's advice in dealing with the government.

In the following fall representatives of the Interior Department visited the reservation, estimated damages, and offered the tribe $15,000. The leaders refused the money and denied permission for construction of the dams on tribal property. There were no further negotiations, but in the spring of 1882 teams of surveyors and timber cutters arrived to begin work. Angry Ojibwe threatened to drive them away, and rumors spread of a possible Indian war. Again White Cloud, who had been designated as spokesman for the tribe, wrote to Sibley. He had told the government men, he said, "that we wished an understanding with the Great Father.... We have waited patiently until my people did not know what to think."[28]

In a letter to the *Pioneer* Sibley assured alarmed citizens that the Ojibwe chiefs would do all possible to prevent trouble, and he blamed the tension on the failure of Washington authorities to get the tribe's consent or to offer adequate payment. In reply a government attorney told him bluntly that Ojibwe consent could never be obtained "if they were in their right minds," and that the government had no choice but to go ahead without it. After a troubled summer, Bishop Whipple persuaded the Department of the Interior to appoint a commission to negotiate with the tribe, and Sibley was made its chairman. Winter weather prevented travel to the remote area, and by the spring of 1883 Sibley had become too ill to serve. His resignation put an end to any effective work by the commission, and no payment was made to the Ojibwe until 1887 as a part of government efforts to move all the bands to White Earth. By then four dams had been completed without the consent or compensation of the tribe. Homes, villages, gardens, and burial grounds were under water, and hundreds of people had been displaced.[29]

Of all the public questions to which Sibley devoted his later years, the unfinished business of the state railroad bonds was the one with which his fellow Minnesotans most identified him. As governor he had issued the bonds, and he felt a need for justification that drove him to an almost obsessive pursuit of the matter throughout two decades. Reared in a world of relative equality and individual ownership, he remained fixated on the simple moral necessity of repaying a debt and recognized no new dimensions of the issue in a complex world of increasing privilege, power, corporate ownership, and public subsidy.

Of the $5 million authorized in 1858, only a little over $2.25 million had been issued. All of the railroads had defaulted by 1860, and Ramsey, as governor, foreclosed on their land grants, at the same time proposing that the state redeem its bonds. The idea met with swift rejection, and instead the voters adopted another constitutional amendment that required that any plan for repayment be submitted to a public referendum.[30]

In 1866 with the war over and railroad building once again high on Minnesota's agenda, Governor William R. Marshall returned to the question. The state had received a windfall from the U.S. government consisting of 500,000 acres of internal improvement lands, and the time seemed propitious for redemption. Since the bonds had for years been selling at a small fraction of their face value, Marshall appointed a commission to locate the owners and determine what they had paid. The survey revealed that the largest block was held by a contractor from Cleveland, Ohio, who had constructed roadbeds for a price that the commission determined was more than three times the normal cost. He claimed payment at the face value of the bonds. The legislature agreed and submitted a redemption plan to the voters. They defeated it resoundingly.

Already Sibley's sense of personal responsbility had been stirred by his friend Dousman, who owned bonds issued to the Minneapolis and Cedar Valley Railroad, of which Sibley had been a director. Dousman wrote that he "bought them for the reason that they were signed by you as Governor of the State" and "there is nothing on the face of the Bonds to show that the payment is contingent on the good faith or rascality of the companies." Sibley was further roused by frequent Republican claims that the bonds had been issued fraudulently by a Democratic administration and were no true obligation of the state. He took this as a direct attack on his own honor. In newspaper articles and public addresses his abhorrence of repudiation took him to new heights of impassioned rhetoric.[31]

A referendum held in 1870 approved a plan that would have redeemed the bonds at approximately 25 percent of their face value, but it was rejected by a majority of the bondholders. That fall Sibley ran for the legislature on the sole platform of paying Minnesota's honest debts. St. Paul was, as always, a Democratic stronghold, and his friends and neighbors sent him to the statehouse. There on February 8, 1871, he delivered a celebrated speech in which he reviewed the history of the bonds and concluded that if it were not for his confidence that the voters would ultimately meet their obligation, he would move to a place where he and his children would no longer "be subjected to the intolerable shame and humiliation of being citizens of a repudiating state." His fellow legislators dutifully agreed on a plan and submitted it to the voters. At a special election in May 1871 payment was again defeated.[32]

The bondholders next went the route of legal action, suing the railroads, since they could not sue the state. Both the Minnesota Supreme Court and the U.S. Supreme Court denied their claims, but the judges of both courts took the opportunity to lecture the state on its moral duty. Stirred by the condemnation of the courts, several Minnesota church bodies made public statements calling upon the voters to honor their just debts. Leading clergymen, including Whipple, added their voices.[33]

In 1876 Sibley's friend Pillsbury became governor, and throughout his three terms he continued to struggle with the problem. At his urging, in 1877 and again in 1878, the legislature adopted plans to exchange the bonds for new state obligations or for land. Both were defeated in statewide referenda.

The bonds were to come due in 1883, and time was running out. There was little Sibley could do, but he did not remain idle. From his position with the St. Paul Chamber of Commerce, he launched a petition in May 1880 to the state conventions of both the Democratic and Republican parties, again urging the moral necessity of paying the bonds.[34]

It was becoming apparent by then that Minnesota voters, many of whom associated the bonds with the oppressive power of railroad corporations, would not be moved. Therefore during Pillsbury's last year in office an elaborate scheme was hatched to bypass the people. The legislature of 1881 created a special tribunal to judge the validity of the constitutional amendment of 1860 that required a popular vote on the bond redemption. The judges were handpicked, but after some intricate legal maneuvering, the Minnesota Supreme Court itself overruled the 1860 amendment as contrary to the original constitution of the state. With the voters out of the loop, the way was thus open for a special session of the legislature, called by Pillsbury in October 1881 to exchange the infamous railroad bonds for new "adjustment bonds."

As these events were taking shape, Sibley wrote to Charles Trowbridge in Detroit: "My trust is that my life may be spared long enough to see the surrender and destruction of the dishonored bonds, which for more than twenty years have borne upon their face my official signature." His wish was granted. Three years later, with hyperbole common to the times, Cushman Davis declared of Sibley: "The instructive impulses of his magnificent integrity have wiped clean every stain from the escutcheon of his beloved state."[35]

· 16 ·

Larger than Life

ENRY SIBLEY TURNED SIXTY in February 1871. The preceding decade had left its marks upon him. Photographs taken at the time show a face that looks haggard and pinched. One sees plainly the hardship and anguish of war, the deaths of three children, the injury and scarring of Gussie in the terrible fire, and the long illness and death of Sarah. Added to these were the repeated need to defend himself against public attack and the recent loss of his friends Dousman and Brown. His eyes stare out with the stern defiance of a survivor.

A survivor he continued to be. Postwar Minnesota was poised for expansion, and business opportunities abounded. The 1870s and 1880s saw Minneapolis and St. Paul together become the industrial, commercial, and financial hub for a region that stretched to the Rockies on the west and across the Canadian border to the north. Fortunes were made in milling, railroads, and lumber. At the Falls of St. Anthony, sawmills, dominant in the 1870s, were overshadowed by state-of-the-art flour mills in the 1880s. Franklin Steele, despite his early start there, was quickly surpassed in wealth and power by the Washburns and the Pillsburys.

But it was railroads that were still shaping the face and future of Minnesota. The land grants they received ultimately covered a fifth of the state's area, and the destinies of towns and cities rested on them. By 1867 steel rails provided a year-round, all-weather connection through Iowa to the rest of the country, and in 1872 a direct line up the Mississippi from the East reached St. Paul. Two years earlier rail service had been opened to the head of Lake Superior, where Duluth, a new boomtown fostered by financier Jay Cooke and his Northern Pacific Railway, threatened briefly to eclipse the cities on the Mississippi

Sibley in 1870

as the transportation center of the region. Cooke's venture collapsed, however, and a young St. Paul freight agent named James J. Hill emerged from his warehouse beside the lower levee to become the "empire builder" of northwestern railroading.

Sibley's strongest personal and political ties after leaving Mendota linked him to St. Paul, and he contented himself with building the city's infrastructure, engaging in only a few ventures that reached beyond it. In 1867 he became president of the St. Paul Gas Light Company, a post that he continued to hold until his death. It was a modest, stable business, with an office just a fifteen-minute walk from his home, and it demanded only a fraction of his time. Others invested in it were Dousman's son Louis, Norman Kittson, and Aaron J. Goodrich, whom Sibley had known for nearly twenty years as one of Minnesota's first territorial judges.[1]

Also during the late 1860s the general took a role in expanding the city's financial institutions. Banking was no longer the "necessary evil" that he had scorned in the 1850s. The National Banking Acts in 1863 and 1864 had reorganized the country's banking system, eliminated the practice of floating "wildcat" notes, and established a sound national currency. In 1867 Sibley participated in organizing a savings bank, and in 1869 he joined with Kittson, Hill, and Henry P. Upham to form the City Bank of St. Paul. He served as president until it merged in 1873 with the First National, of which he continued to be a director throughout his life. In 1869 he also became a director of the Minnesota Mutual Life Insurance Company.[2]

During Sibley's years in pre-territorial Minnesota, business had been almost indivisible from civic responsibility. Out of that experience came an assumption that the business community had a positive obligation to provide for the city's improvement and social welfare. When he took the lead in reestablishing the St. Paul Chamber of Commerce in December 1866, he saw it as an instrument for public and charitable projects more than boosterism. Aside from the Chamber of Commerce, which he repeatedly served as president, he gave his own time to still other civic causes, including the inspection of the city's schools in 1867 and 1868, and the acquisition of Como Park in 1872. The year 1882 found him discussing with other civic leaders the need for "a school in St. Paul where young ladies could finish their education instead of being sent to Vassar and other eastern colleges."[3]

Reports of gold at Lake Vermilion in 1865 drew the general's interest toward the far north for a short time. He was president of the Minnesota Gold Mining Company while the brief excitement lasted, and the business took him on at least one trip to Duluth. He was accompanied by General William T. Sherman, who was much impressed with the commercial possibilities of the Lake Superior country. Little or no gold was found, and the iron that did exist on the Vermilion Range was still too remote for profitable mining. By 1870 Sibley had written off the whole venture as "unsuccessful."[4]

In the same region Sibley's brother Alexander soon had better luck, acquiring Canadian rights to a mine on Silver Islet, just off Thunder Bay in Lake Superior. The veins of silver extending under the lake proved extremely rich, and profits were on the order of several hundred per cent. It is unclear whether Sibley himself invested in the mine, but he made several trips to see it. In the summer of 1873 he was accompanied by Lathrop E. Reed, vice president of the City Bank, and he wrote a lengthy letter to the *Pioneer*, describing the massive coffer dams and cribs that had been built to keep the mine from being flooded. He also touted the island as a tourist mecca, and he himself made another visit in the summer of 1875 that was apparently for pleasure and family reunion rather than business. On that trip he was accompanied by his own three children, Sallie, Fred, and Allie, as well as by their cousin Charlie, the son of Abbie Potts.[5]

The only other mineral in which Sibley took an interest was coal. His gas company was by far the largest consumer of coal in Minnesota, and shipping it from the East was expensive. Most of it came by way of Lake Superior, and the main supplier was Hill, whose firm of Hill, Griggs, and Company was beginning to control much of the state's high-grade fuel business. Sibley was trying to free the gas company from a heavy load of debt and to expand its services. Therefore he constantly sought ways to lower its largest item of cost. Learning that there were deposits of coal along the Missouri, he visited Bismarck in 1873 to explore the potential for mining it. Apparently, however, he decided not to invest.[6]

That year the Northern Pacific tracks had reached the Missouri, and the trip took Sibley by train over the same plains that his army had trudged across exactly ten years earlier. The panic and depression of 1873 ended further railroad construction for some time. Just ten more years, however, found the general at a St. Paul banquet held in September 1883 to honor Henry Villard and to celebrate his completion of the first northern transcontinental line. Seated that day at the same head table with Sibley and other notables was Jim Hill.

Hill's journey to dominance in the railroad world had started with dispatching freight for the Hudson's Bay Company and others along the routes pioneered in the 1840s by Sibley and Kittson. In the mid-1860s Kittson, then serving as U.S. agent for the British company, contracted with Hill to handle the shipment of goods from St. Paul to Georgetown on the Red River, where they were loaded on a company steamboat and dispatched to Fort Garry. After Hill acquired a steamboat of his own and mounted competition, he and

Kittson united in the Red River Transportation Company, which, for six years monopolized the shipment of goods and people to the expanding settlements in the new territory of Manitoba.[7]

Hill, meanwhile, with the backing of Canadian financiers, was maneuvering to gain control of the St. Paul and Pacific Railroad, which had collapsed in the depression of 1873. In 1878 he succeeded, bringing Kittson along as his partner. Renaming the company the St. Paul, Minneapolis, and Manitoba, he extended its main line to the Canadian border rather than westward. Thus the company acquired a rich land grant in the Red River valley and a lucrative connection with the new Canadian Pacific Railroad. It soon became the major funnel feeding grain from the Dakota and Manitoba wheat fields into the mills of Minneapolis.

Kittson was in the habit of consulting Sibley, his old friend and continuing business associate, about major investments. Later he admitted that his decision to join the hard-driving Hill in the great gamble of acquiring the St. Paul and Pacific had been an exception. He had feared, he said, that Sibley would advise against it.[8]

Sibley's own railroad investments seem to have been an extension of his earlier interest in the Minneapolis and Cedar Valley along with land and

St. Paul celebrated completion of the Northern Pacific's line to the West Coast in 1883 with this welcoming arch.

townsites in southern Minnesota. As early as May 1865 he joined Rice and Steele in becoming a director of the Minnesota Valley Railroad, later to be named the St. Paul and Sioux City. His treaty-making trip to the Missouri that fall had given him a chance to look over the route as well as the proposed terminus. He liked what he saw, and the company remained the principal focus of his railroad activity. It built no empires, but it became known as one of the state's best-run lines, and to Sibley it brought none of the financial woes that overtook his friend William LeDuc, who had linked his fortunes to the ambitious but unsuccessful Hastings and Dakota Railroad.[9]

After Sarah's death Gussie and her husband, Douglass Pope, returned to St. Paul, and they must have remained with Sibley during much of the next two years. Their first child, Alice Sibley Pope, was born in St. Paul in the spring of 1871. By the time they left, the general had formed a new and lasting domestic arrangement.[10]

Partly, no doubt, through Sibley's influence, Sarah's brother-in-law and his own good friend, Thomas Potts, had held the post of surgeon at Fort Snelling through most of the war. In 1866 he became city physician of St. Paul, but financial problems soon overwhelmed him. In a desperate effort to establish a new medical practice that would support his family, Potts set out for Duluth in January 1870. As yet the boomtown at the head of Lake Superior was little more than a railroad construction camp, so Abbie and their four children remained in St. Paul. Potts sent money when he could and visited occasionally.[11]

Before many months had passed, letters from Potts were directed in care of the general, and it seems clear that Sibley had come to the rescue of the family. Abbie, for her part, managed the combined households, served as the general's hostess, and kept an eye on his two young boys. Harry, the oldest Potts son and Sibley's namesake, found work in one of his uncle's business enterprises. He was apparently a worry to his father, who wrote during one of Sibley's business trips, "I hope while his uncle is gone Harry will spend most of his time at home, that is during the evenings." Later he told Abbie fretfully that Harry might be able to get a better paying position in Duluth, "but he would have to <u>work</u>."[12]

Nearly three years later, when depression and the collapse of the Northern Pacific left Duluth almost depopulated, Potts returned to St. Paul. His health, however, had already been failing when he headed north, and he died in October 1874. The family was still in mourning the following January, when the two daughters, Mary and Abbie, were married in a double ceremony, Abbie to Charles W. McIntyre, and Mary to a rising young railroad financier named Crawford Livingston. The wedding was held in the big house on Woodward Street, and Sibley stood in place of their father. It followed only two weeks after Sibley's own daughter Sallie married Elbert A. Young, a St. Paul wholesale merchant.[13]

The city's gossips waited impatiently through the next fifteen years for yet another wedding to be announced, but it never was. Abbie Potts continued to act as Sibley's housekeeper and hostess, and she also became his nurse after he began to have periodic attacks of intense pain, possibly caused by a stomach ulcer or gallstones. Their relationship was tender and affectionate. He wrote to her regularly when away from St. Paul. "You do not know how much I miss you, especially when during the hours of a long night, the enemy is gnawing at my vitals," he said in 1877, while on one of his many trips east. As time went by and they both grew older, she accompanied him on winter travels to warmer climates and health spas.[14]

By that time the house was again lively with the voices of young children. Douglass Pope died suddenly in 1880, and Gussie with her three daughters moved permanently to St. Paul. "My large house is now pretty well filled," Sibley told Charles Trowbridge, "but I am thankful that I can give a home to my distressed daughter and her children." Other grandchildren must soon have frequented the house also, for Sallie lived with her husband and their family just across the street. Young Fred, meanwhile, held a position at the First National Bank where he was, his father said, "very attentive to business," and Alfred was at school in Racine, Wisconsin.[15]

The death of Franklin Steele in September 1880 no doubt caused Sibley to reflect once more on the passage of time and the loss of old friends. He had seen little of his brother-in-law in recent years, for Steele had spent much of his time in Washington, where his wife Anna had moved some years earlier. Other members of the Steele family continued to be part of Sibley's circle in St. Paul, including Dr. John Steele, and Rachel and Richard Johnson.[16]

Faced with a choice after they left Mendota, Sibley and his family opted to attend St. Paul's Episcopal Church in the capital city. His own upbringing as an Episcopalian no doubt played a role, along with the resolute anti-Catholicism of local Presbyterian leaders—an attitude for which Sibley had no sympathy. It seems likely, however, that the general was also influenced by his growing friendship with Whipple. He apparently held reservations about the practice of charging for pews, for Whipple assured him that all churches in the diocese with the exception of St. Paul's were "free." Although Sibley attended regularly and served as a vestryman of the parish for the rest of his life, he did not become a communicant until his final days. The reason, as he explained to Fletcher Williams in 1877, was that "I am not sectarian," and "prefer to turn to the pages of sacred writ for guidance." At one point in his later life he committed to paper some withering verses in which he compared the simple faith and unadorned church of "Then" with the cushioned pews and fashionably indifferent congregation of "Now."[17]

Like Sibley himself, Minnesota's Democratic Party survived, although it won no statewide elections in the postwar years. Old loyalties were strong, and communities with solid blocks of Catholic voters remained Democratic. The most notable was St. Paul, where a large German population and an influential Irish minority continued the Democratic tradition begun by French-Canadian settlers in the 1850s. They were aided by support from leading businessmen like Kittson, Sibley, and especially Hill, whose Irish wife was a devout Catholic.[18]

Political issues in the 1870s and 1880s were largely economic, and genuine opposition on those issues was left to a series of insurgent movements and third parties willing to challenge the growing power of railroad corporations and the milling industry. Their spokesman was Ignatius Donnelly, who split violently with established leaders of the Republican Party during a bitter election in 1868. Irish but not Catholic, originally a Democrat but converted to the radical antislavery cause, Donnelly was a prophetic maverick who drew support from dissenting elements in both parties.[19]

Sibley's interest in politics continued to be keen, but his only ventures at office-seeking were his 1871 service in the legislature on the issue of the state railroad bonds and a nominal candidacy for Congress in 1880. The latter was a reaction to a fiercely fought congressional election in 1878. Donnelly that year had run in opposition to the Republican mill owner William D. Washburn in the state's third district, which included both Minneapolis and St. Paul. With support from St. Paul, he captured the nomination of the Democratic Party, along with that of his own Greenback organization. His narrow defeat, though contested on the basis of documented fraud, left the Democrats in disarray, and when Sibley was nominated by acclamation two years later, it was more a statement that the old guard had regained control of the party than an effort to elect a candidate. With his usual show of reluctance, Sibley assented to it. He did not campaign actively, but he confided to Trowbridge that although the Democrats were heavily outnumbered in the district, he expected a substantial crossover vote from Republican friends.[20]

As the decade of the 1880s advanced, prosperity returned and Minnesota along with the rest of the country began to look backward with ever-greater confidence and self-congratulation. The frontier era had closed. A continent had been conquered and its people destroyed or subdued. But there were also premonitions of great change in the country, along with nostalgia for a simpler past.

Anniversaries and founders loomed large. As president of the Historical Society, Sibley prepared a paper for the bicentennial observance of Louis Hennepin's historic visit to the Falls of St. Anthony. Four years later, he himself became the subject of an anniversary celebration. On October 28, 1884, just fifty years after his arrival at Mendota, he was feted at a brilliant banquet in St. Paul's Metropolitan Hotel, where the principal speaker was Cushman Davis, then Minnesota's most acclaimed orator. It was the first in a long series of honors. In 1885 he was elected President of the Minnesota Club; in 1888 he received an honorary degree of doctor of laws from Princeton University, and in the same year he was made a commander of the Loyal Legion. There was even a proposal to erect a statue of him on Pilot Knob.[21]

Minnesota had found—or created—its heroic and spotless pioneer image. The substance of that myth and its implied messages were caught by Henry A. Castle in verses composed for the occasion of Sibley's installation as a commander of the Loyal Legion:[22]

> *In mettled youth the stalwart pioneer*
> *Who strode the forests; scaled the dizzy steep;*
> *Taught the swart savage justice to revere,*
> *and ploughed the path of empire wide and deep*
>
> *In early manhood builder of the state—*
> *A leader and a master, laying down*
> *The rod and rifle for the realm sedate*
> *Of legislator—and the civic crown.*
>
> *In life's ripe prime the soldier, whose strong arm*
> *To periled thousands wrought deliverance,*
> *Whose cool and prudent prowess quelled alarm*
> *As quailed the foe before his angry glance.*

The romantic rhetoric was exaggerated beyond what Sibley himself might have written, but his own hand had helped to sketch the portrait. The first outlines had been drawn by Hal in the *Spirit of the Times*, and the background had been fleshed out in the general's many reminiscences and memoirs. Yet he had flinched before the task of writing for himself the life story of Castle's "first and noblest Minnesotian." Already he was tired, and he was, above all, a private person, who kept his own emotions and doubts closely hidden from public view. Having come face to face with the inevitable need for glossing over memories and evading facts, he left the job to others.

One eager volunteer was a young Presbyterian clergyman named Nathaniel West, a neighbor and admirer of the aging general. Whatever his credentials for writing history, West lacked both talent and judgment. The authorized biography he produced is largely a compilation of Sibley's own notes and published writings along with official documents and correspondence—all of it heavily larded with fawning flattery and classical allusions. West's book was printed in 1889, and the distribution was limited—perhaps intentionally.

Few of Sibley's contemporaries remained alive by then. One of them was the farmer-missionary Samuel Pond, whose sharply honest perceptions were not enfeebled by age. The two old men exchanged letters. Pond reflected on their shared loneliness and the loss not only of friends, but of an entire world: "From Lake Pepin to Lac Traverse, from Rock [Roque] to Frenier, they are gone—all gone—gone to oblivion: for who knows that they were ever here? They have not been succeeded by their children, but supplanted by strangers, some of them by strangers from beyond the sea."[23]

In his reply Sibley was more preoccupied with judgments and justifications: "In this, the evening of my life, my efforts, for more than forty years, to induce the government to change its Indian policy, and to do justice to that race, although unsuccessful, are a source of consolation to me." That he still struggled with misgivings and perhaps regrets is suggested by the fact that in West's compendium of his public achievements there is no mention of the two treaties that were his greatest contribution to ploughing the "path of empire." They are buried in silence.

One Sunday afternoon a few months before Sibley's death his minister called to see why the old gentleman had been absent from church. Sibley was seated in his study, head in hands. Failing to rise with his usual formal courtesy, he said in apology: "I have been thinking over my life and have decided that it is well nigh a failure." Surprised and probably somewhat amused, the clergyman asked who, then, could possibly be judged a success. "I am nearing the end of my course," Sibley

Sibley in the 1880s

shrugged, "and as I look back, the only thing that gives me real satisfaction is the little good I have done. And I have neglected so many opportunities."[24]

He closed the books on February 18, 1891, two days short of eighty years. In his last letter, penned six weeks earlier, the writing is firm and readable, the words clear and coherent.

The general was buried in St. Paul's Oakland Cemetery with religious services but no military fanfare. While he rested there, his heroic pioneer image marched on to loom larger with passing years. In a lengthy memoir published early in the 1890s, J. Fletcher Williams, Secretary of the Historical Society, gave an account of Sibley's career that was more factual and succinct than West's but with a few romantic touches of its own. Soon after the turn of the century a new dimension was added. James H. Baker, who had been a colonel under Sibley in the campaign of 1863, wrote a series of biographical essays on Minnesota's governors. In describing the first in the honored line, he proclaimed: "As Washington stands for the infant nation, so Sibley stands for our infant state. He is the bright consummate flower of our earlier days."[25]

Baker's work, published in 1908, no doubt helped to inspire members of the Minnesota Chapter of the Daughters of the American Revolution to rescue the old stone house at Mendota. The women may have been unaware of

The Sibley House Historic Site in Mendota

Sarah Sibley's earlier efforts to aid in preserving Washington's home, but with determination and hard work worthy of their predecessors, they acquired and restored the vacant building, which Williams had described with considerable exaggeration as once having had "all the appointments of a manorial mansion or estate." When opening the house as a historic shrine in 1910, the women of the DAR hailed it as "the Mount Vernon of Minnesota."[26]

At about this time Sibley's life and the large collection of business and personal papers he had bequeathed to the Minnesota Historical Society began to receive attention from the academic community. In the 1890s Wisconsin historian Frederick Jackson Turner advanced the idea that American society had been uniquely shaped by the presence of its westward moving frontier. The concept precisely matched the temper of the times. It conformed to the compelling new worldviews of evolution, both biological and social, and it pictured the frontier as a progression of stages, moving from savagery to civilization.

One of Turner's graduate students, Wilson P. Shortridge, believed that Sibley and the varied roles he played over time in the Upper Mississippi valley aptly modeled his mentor's famous thesis. "If the West be thought of as a period rather than a place, then the study of a limited area which passed through the successive stages in the evolution of society on the frontier should be typical of what was repeated over and over again in the conquest and settlement of the continent," Shortridge argued. In articles, a dissertation, and later in a book, he sought to show that Minnesota's development and Sibley's life within it had indeed followed the path laid out by Turner— hunting and trapping, barter, agricultural settlement, organized government, commercial centers, and industry. Shortridge's work, titled *The Transition of a Typical Frontier with Illustrations from the Life of Henry Hastings Sibley* and published in 1919, focused on the thesis rather than the man. Sibley appears as the one-dimensional public image of a frontiersman who both led the way and adapted while the area progressed from what historians still conceived as "wilderness" into a fully developed state.[27]

There is more depth and perspective in the treatment given Sibley a little later by William Watts Folwell in his classic *History of Minnesota*, the four volumes of which were published in 1921, 1924, 1926, and 1930. Folwell had known the general personally for many years and the two had worked closely during Folwell's tenure as president of the university and Sibley's as a regent. Although he attempted no full-length portrait, his composite picture of Sibley was the most balanced one yet achieved. Influenced by Folwell and also venerating Turner, Theodore C. Blegen went on to hold up Sibley as a literary figure and an example of culture on the frontier. Between 1927 and 1950 he edited with introductions several pieces from the *Spirit of the Times*, as well as the unfinished autobiography and the series of essays on Jack Frazer.

Meanwhile popular history had also discovered Minnesota's "princely pioneer" (as Baker had called him). In 1929 he became the hero of a romantic novel. Although disguised with blond hair, blue eyes, and a Boston accent, Sibley's image is instantly recognizable as Jasper Page in *Early Candlelight*, by Minnesota author Maud Hart Lovelace. There he stands as the benevolent embodiment of Anglo-American culture in the racially and ethnically diverse community around early Fort Snelling. Forty years later the durable image of the "border baronet" reappeared as one of Roger Kennedy's *Men on the Moving Frontier*. Kennedy echoed Lovelace in concluding that Sibley was "a romantic refugee from puritanism," whose "happiest years were spent among the Indians in a wilderness."[28]

By the end of the 1980s the idea that the western frontier was a unique experience and a defining condition of the country's character had been dismissed by most scholars. The end of colonialism and growing globalization had thrown a glaring light on the assumption that the United States was an exception, standing outside the currents of world history. In 1992 historians William Cronon, George Miles, and Jay Gitlin were writing: "We can best know the history of the American West if we read it as a chapter in the much larger history of European colonialism."[29]

Led by historians like David Thelen and Howard R. Lamar, comparative history gained ground through the '90s, especially in relation to frontiers and borders. Studies of the differing frontier experiences in Canada and Mexico cast further doubt on Turner's thesis, and the concept of "frontier" itself as a definite stage in the evolution of society yielded to viewing it as a process or meeting place, where connections, choices, and the emergence of new forms and solutions were at least as important as conquest. These included biological as well as social elements, for environmental historians soon pointed out the ecological and cultural impact of plants and animals that accompanied human migrations—as in the case of the horse on the northern plains.[30]

Also in the late-twentieth century, the growing power and self-determination of former colonial peoples throughout the world was felt among Native Americans. Dakota scholars and activists pulled from the shadows Sibley's part in the treaties of 1851 and the conflict of 1862. Again he became a controversial figure, this time as a symbol of racism and as a perpetrator of injustice and oppression. Building on the widely repeated myth that he had made a fortune in the fur trade, they denounced him as a two-faced exploiter.[31]

Each version of Sibley's image, including the shadow side, has elements of truth, yet behind it remains a complex and deeply human individual who spent a long lifetime on a series of frontiers and responded to profound and rapid changes in the world around him. If any lesson can be learned, it is the inseparability of individuals from their times and from the assumptions and pressures of the society in which they have lived. Some swim with the current, some struggle against it, and some have divided hearts.

NOTES

Notes for Chapter 1

1. Blegen, ed., *Unfinished Autobiography of Henry Hastings Sibley* (henceforth cited as Blegen, *UA*), 8. A manuscript copy of this is in the Henry H. Sibley Papers (henceforth cited as Sibley Papers) and may also be found on Roll 32 in the microfilm edition. All citations here are to the published work.

2. Ross and Catlin, *Landmarks of Wayne County and Detroit*, 364; Palmer, *Early Days in Detroit*, 814; Bates, in *Michigan Pioneer and Historical Collections* (henceforth cited as *MPHC*) 22:324 (quotation).

3. Certificate from Rhode Island College, December 29, 1793; certificate of admission to the bar of Rhode Island, April 11, 1797; Philip Amidon to Jacob Amidon, May 1, 1797; letter of recommendation by Judge David Howell, May 21, 1797 (quotation), all in the Solomon Sibley Papers.

4. For the genealogy of the Sibley family, see West, *Henry Hastings Sibley*, 2-35.

5. Letter of recommendation from Joseph Gilman, July 25, 1797; license to practice law in the Northwest Territory, September 9, 1797; Benjamin I. Gilman to Solomon Sibley, February 18, 1798, all in the Solomon Sibley Papers. According to evidence in his papers, Sibley remained in Marietta about four months, and then moved back up the Ohio to Wellsburg, Virginia (then called Charleston), where he lived through the winter and spring of 1798. He went directly from there to Detroit.

6. Return J. Meigs to Sibley, April 9, 1798, Solomon Sibley Papers; Bond, *The Foundations of Ohio*, 421.

7. An excellent picture of this period in Detroit is found in Bald, *Detroit's First American Decade*.

8. Joseph Gilman to Sibley, August 23, 1798; Arthur St. Clair, Jr., to Sibley, July 16, 1798, in Solomon Sibley Papers.

9. Bald, *Detroit's First American Decade*, 139, 142-45; Bond, *Foundations of Ohio*, 470-75.

10. Sibley to Hastings, April 15, 1802, Solomon Sibley Papers. West's statement (*Sibley*, 33) that Solomon studied law under William Hastings of Boston is not supported by evidence in Sibley's papers. Documents there suggest that he studied in Mendon, Massachusetts, under Seth Hastings, who later (1801-07) became a U.S. congressman, and who maintained a lifelong friendship and correspondence with the judge. It was presumably in honor of Seth Hastings that Solomon named his second son.

11. Bald, *Detroit's First American Decade*, 160-61, 188-90, 197.

12. Sibley to Abbey and Mary Russell, August 16, 1798, Solomon Sibley Papers.

13. Sibley to Abbey and Mary Russell, June 26, 1799, Solomon Sibley Papers.

14. Bald, *Detroit's First American Decade*, 161; Earl Sproat to Sibley, November 6, 1799; Ebenezer Sproat to Sibley, November 29, 1799; Paul Fearing to Sibley, March 4, 1801 (quotation); Zenas Kimberley to Sibley, May 28, 1801, Solomon Sibley Papers.

15. Blegen, *UA*, 8.

16. Henry H. Sibley to Elizabeth F. Ellet, July 1, 1852, Sibley Papers.

17. Ellet, *Pioneer Women of the West*, 215-17. For comments on Sarah Sibley's spirit and sense of humor, see Jonathan P. Sheldon to Solomon Sibley, January 21, 1821, Solomon Sibley Papers; Bates, in *MPHC* 22:401.

18. Blegen, *UA*, 8.

19. Hildreth, *Early Pioneer Settlers*, 120-64.

20. Hildreth, *Early Pioneer Settlers*, 230-35.

21. Hildreth, *Early Pioneer Settlers*, 223, 235-37; Hildreth, *Pioneer History*, 204-6.

22. Hildreth, *Early Pioneer Settlers*, 237-39. The story of American conquest in the Ohio valley is told in a number of sources. For a recent account, see White, *The Middle Ground*, 413-517.

23. Ellet, *Pioneer Women of the West*, 215-18.

24. Ellet, *Pioneer Women of the West*, 221-22. The birth of the Sibleys' fourth child is alluded to in a letter to Solomon from James Abbott, June 12, 1813, in the Solomon Sibley Papers.

25. Sarah to Solomon, January 8, 22, 1823, Solomon Sibley Papers.

26. Sarah to Solomon, December 15, 1822.

27. Sarah to Solomon, February 6, 13, and 28, 1822. James McCloskey was cashier of the Bank of Michigan.

28. Sarah to Solomon, December 21, 1821.

29. Sarah to Solomon, February 13, 1822.

30. Sarah to Solomon, December 21, 1821; February 6, 1822; Ebenezer S. Sibley to Solomon, February 7, 1821. There were eight Sibley children. After Mary, born in Marietta in 1813, came Augusta, Alexander, Sarah, and Frederick. Apparently there were also two who died in early infancy. Of several published lists, none are in total agreement and none seems to be fully accurate or complete. See West, *Sibley*, 35; Burton, ed., and Burton, comp., *Proceedings of the Land Board*, 158 (n.p.); Burton, Stocking, and Miller, eds., *City of Detroit*, 2:1397.

31. Blegen, *UA*, 9.

32. Trowbridge, in *MPHC* 4:474; West, *Sibley*, 34.

33. Woodford, *Lewis Cass*, 120 .

34. Parkins, *Historical Geography of Detroit*, 140, 143-45, 172-74.

35. Woodford, *Lewis Cass*, 129; Smith, *James Duane Doty*, 11.

36. For the Brush family, see Burton,

Stocking, and Miller, eds., *City of Detroit*, 2:1361; Bald, *Detroit's First American Decade*, 139, 191. Apparently young Edmund Brush gave Solomon considerable worry. See, for example, Andrew G. Whitney to Solomon, November 23, 1821; Sarah to Solomon, February 28, 1822; letter from Edmund Brush filed among undated papers for the year 1823, Solomon Sibley Papers.

37. Burton, ed., and Burton, comp., *Proceedings of the Land Board*, 164, 214; James Abbott to Solomon Sibley, May 27, June 12 and 20, 1813; Affidavit of Sibley, June 21, 1813, in the Solomon Sibley Papers; Bates, in *MPHC* 22:306.

38. Burton, Stocking, and Miller, eds., *City of Detroit*, 2:1532; Burton, ed., and Burton, comp., *Proceedings of the Land Board*, 174, 228; Kinzie, *Wau-bun*, 151-54; Robert A. Kinzie to Henry Sibley, December 28, 1824; March 27, 1828, in the Sibley Papers.

39. Schoolcraft, *Narrative Journal of Travels*. For biographical data on Schoolcraft here and below, see Freeman, "Henry Rowe Schoolcraft."

40. Woodford, *Lewis Cass*, 202, 219. Trowbridge's journal of the expedition, along with a biographical sketch of the author by Ralph H. Brown, was published in *Minnesota History* for June, September, and December 1942. See Brown, ed., 23:126-48, 233-52, 328-48. See also Campbell, in *MPHC* 6:478-91.

41. Doty's career is fully covered in Smith, *James Duane Doty*.

42. Woodford, *Lewis Cass*, 115-18, 124, 167. The quotation from Woodbridge is in Smith, *Doty*, 33.

43. In addition to holding the posts of congressional delegate, judge, and district attorney, Solomon Sibley also served under Cass as territorial auditor, as a trustee of the City of Detroit, and as a treaty commissioner in negotiations with several Indian tribes in 1821. In 1827 he became Michigan's chief justice.

44. For an analysis of Cass's impact on U.S. Indian policy, see Prucha, *Lewis Cass and American Indian Policy*. An account of the various treaties Cass negotiated is in Comfort, *Lewis Cass and the Indian Treaties*.

45. Prucha, *Lewis Cass and American In-*

dian Policy, 11; Lavender, *The Fist in the Wilderness,* 262, 291.

46. Woodford, *Lewis Cass,* 151; Cass, in *North American Review,* 24:391.

47. Quoted in Prucha, *Lewis Cass and American Indian Policy,* 8.

48. Gilpin, *The Territory of Michigan,* 122; Comfort, *Lewis Cass and the Indian Treaties,* 43; Prucha, *Lewis Cass and American Indian Policy,* 8, 14.

Notes for Chapter 2

1. Blegen, *UA,* 9.

2. Solomon Sibley to John C. Calhoun, December 15, 1822, in the Solomon Sibley Papers; Blegen, *UA,* 9.

3. Austin E. Wing to Solomon Sibley, December 22, 1827; Sibley to Wing, January 30, 1828, in the Solomon Sibley Papers.

4. Freeman, "Henry Rowe Schoolcraft," 99, 112-13.

5. Blegen, *UA,* 10.

6. Bayliss, Bayliss, and Quaife, *River of Destiny,* 81-95.

7. Bayliss, Bayliss, and Quaife, *River of Destiny,* 88; Chapman, in *MPHC* 32:305-53; Schoolcraft, in *MPHC* 36:53-86.

8. Sibley to Trowbridge, October 11, 1828, in the Sibley Papers; Schoolcraft, in *MPHC* 36:84-86; Blegen, *UA,* 10.

9. Blegen, *UA,* 10.

10. Chapman, in *MPHC* 32:307, 309; Jonas K. Greenough to Sibley, November 30, 1830, Sibley Papers.

11. James L. Schoolcraft to Sibley, July 7 [1829]; Greenough to Sibley, November 30, 1830, Sibley Papers.

12. Blegen, *UA,* 10.

13. Blegen, *UA,* 16.

14. Trowbridge, and Heydenburk, both in *MPHC* 3:52-61.

15. Hubbard, *The Autobiography of Gurdon Saltonstall Hubbard,* 75-80. Stuart's letters in both the Sibley Papers and the American Fur Company Papers are often notable for their articulate expression and humor.

16. Lavender, *Fist in the Wilderness,* 316. A comprehensive account of the development and influence of the Mackinac mission and its school is in Keith Widder, *Battle for the Soul.*

17. Wood, *Historic Mackinac,* 1:399-407; Trowbridge, in *MPHC* 3:55.

18. Sibley to Trowbridge, July 21, 1829, Sibley Papers.

19. Sibley to Trowbridge, July 21, 1829; testimonial letter, April 28, 1830, Sibley Papers.

20. Contract, dated September 4, 1830, Sibley Papers. In his autobiography Sibley gives his date of first employment with American Fur as June 1, 1829, making no distinction between the temporary summer job and his later permanent position.

21. Blegen, *UA,* 18.

22. Wood, *Historic Mackinac,* 1:399-407; Freeman, "Schoolcraft," 140-42, 154-56; Janet White, in *Michigan History* 32:340-51.

23. Wood, *Historic Mackinac,* 1:401; William T. Boutwell to Sibley, June 19, 1832; Frederick Ayer to Sibley, May 2, 1835; Eunice O. Osmer to Sibley, November 12, 1834, April 18, 1835, Sibley Papers.

24. West, *Henry Hastings Sibley,* 62.

25. Wood, *Historic Mackinac,* 1:90; Heydenburk, in *MPHC* 3:58; Baird, in *Wisconsin Historical Collections* (henceforth cited as *WHC*) 14:46 (quotation); McDowell, in *Michigan History* 56:271-86.

26. The extensive literature of the fur trade has viewed it from a succession of perspectives, all perceptibly related to the context of the times. First treated as an instrument of national destiny, it was later studied as a seed ground for business empires. In the mid-twentieth century historians were popularizing the folkways and humble heroism of the workers who literally carried it upon their backs. (See Grace Lee Nute, *The Voyageur.*) By the end of the century a new interest in the roles of women and indigenous peoples led to viewing the fur trade as an example of the interplay and accommodation of contrasting cultures. (See Richard White, *The Middle Ground,* Carolyn Gilman, et. al., *Where Two Worlds Meet,* and also the work of Sylvia Van Kirk, Jennifer S. H. Brown, Jacqueline Peterson, and Keith Widder.)

27. Blegen, *UA,* 12, 13.

28. Lockwood, in *WHC* 2:110-12.

29. Blegen, *UA,* 18.

30. Blegen, *UA,* 18-22.

31. Blegen, *UA*, 22; Ellet, *Pioneer Women of the West*, 222.

32. Lavender, *Fist in the Wilderness*, 319-25, 377-81.

33. Gilman, in *Wisconsin Magazine of History* 58:16.

34. Gilman, in *Wisconsin Magazine of History* 58:13-15, 17.

35. Gilman, in *Wisconsin Magazine of History* 58:17; Gilman, in *Minnesota History* 42:137-39.

36. Gilman, in *Minnesota History* 42:136.

37. Glimpses of the relationship between Rolette and the management of American Fur can be found in the Mackinac Letter Books.

38. Crooks to James Abbott, September 9, 1821; Crooks to Samuel Abbott, October 1, 1821, Mackinac Letter Books.

39. Correspondence with Rolette in the Mackinac Letter Books contains repeated references to his supplying bullets and lead.

40. Blegen, *UA*, 24.

41. Lavender, *Fist in the Wilderness*, 412-14.

42. Blegen, *UA*, 25.

Notes for Chapter 3

1. The best account of Crooks's career is to be found in Lavender, *Fist in the Wilderness*, which is virtually a business biography of him. He and Sibley remained in regular contact until Crooks's death in 1859.

2. Blegen, *UA*, 25.

3. See Sibley's commission as justice of the peace, June 29, 1832; Sibley to Nancy and Kate Dousman, March 25, 1833, Sibley Papers. For Robert Stuart's high estimate of Hercules Dousman, see Stuart to Crooks, August 18, 1827, Mackinac Letter Books.

4. Blegen, *UA*, 26.

5. A copy of the contract is in the Hercules L. Dousman Papers, in the Minnesota Historical Society (henceforth cited as MHS). The original is owned by the Newberry Library, Chicago.

6. Contract dated September 2, 1825, between Alexis Bailly and Joseph Rolette; "Recapitulation of Furs & Peltries rec' from Uppr Mississippi Outfit, 1833," dated August 15, 1834; Bailly to Joseph P. Bailly, March 2, 1835 (typewritten copy), all in the

Alexis Bailly Papers (henceforth cited as the Bailly Papers).

7. Taliaferro, in *Minnesota Historical Collections* (henceforth cited as *MHC*), 6:189-255; Lavender, *Fist in the Wilderness*, 371-72.

8. Rolette to Crooks, September 18, 1834, American Fur Company Papers.

9. Bliss to Bailly, September 20, 24, 1834, Bailly Papers.

10. Blegen, *UA*, 27.

11. Scanlan, *Prairie du Chien*, 195.

12. Contract between Joseph Rolette and Murdoch Cameron, April 20, 1805, photocopy in the MHS, original in the notary records of James A. Gray, National Archives of Quebec at Montreal; Scanlan, *Prairie du Chien*, 105, 189; Lockwood, in *WHC* 2:132, 173-75; Brisbois, in *WHC* 9:293-94.

13. Dessloch, in *Famous Wisconsin Women* 2:4-10. Jane Dousman's life and romance with Hercules Dousman have been fictionalized in two novels by August Derleth, *Bright Journey* and *The House on the Mound*.

14. Kinzie, *Wau-bun*; Crooks to Rolette, January 12, 1835; January 7, 1836, American Fur Company Papers. Correspondence with Rolette in the Mackinac Letter Books contains frequent references to his family connections and especially to his brothers Hypolite and Laurent. For the latter, see also Parker, ed., *Recollections of Philander Prescott*, 150; *WHC* 20:197n.

15. Parker, ed., *Recollections*, 129; Brisbois, in *WHC* 9:294.

16. Anderson, in *WHC* 9:180-81; Fonda, in *WHC* 5:237; Grignon, in *WHC* 3:279.

17. Dousman to Crooks, October 14, 1834, American Fur Company Papers; Sibley to Crooks, November 1, 1834, Sibley Papers.

18. Blegen, *UA*, 27.

19. Blegen, *UA*, 28-29.

20. Bowers, *The Old Bailly Homestead*; Bailly, "The French-Canadian Background of a Minnesota Pioneer—Alexis Bailly," Bailly Papers; Baird, in *WHC* 14:43. Bailly's familiarity with law, current events, and languages are apparent from a scanning of his papers.

21. Sibley, in *MHC* 1:383. The story of the Fort William trip was told in a reminiscent account by Bailly, which is quoted in Manitoba, Historical and Scientific Society, *Transactions* No. 33:4.

22. Included in Bailly's papers is an "Account against Red River Expedition for Joseph Rolette," which lists "Goods Supplied Mr. Alexis Bailly at the Forks—1821." Authorization from Colonel Josiah Snelling for Bailly to build "a warehouse, or store, and a house for his own residence" on the military reservation, April 13, 1825, is in the Sibley Papers.

23. Bible records from the Bailly family; Alexis Bailly to Joseph B. Bailly, March 2, 1835, (typewritten copy) in the Bailly Papers.

24. Blegen, *UA*, 29.

25. Blegen, *UA*, 30; Sibley to Crooks, November 1, 1834, Sibley Papers.

26. Sibley to Crooks, November 1, 1834; Crooks to Sibley, December 19, 1834; Crooks to Rolette, December 20, 1834, American Fur Company Papers.

27. Rolette to Crooks, January 20, 1835, American Fur Company Papers.

28. Crooks to Sibley, December 19, 1834; Crooks to Samuel Abbott, December 20, 1834, American Fur Company Papers.

Notes for Chapter 4

1. Goodmans, *Joseph R. Brown*, 113; draft of a letter from Joseph R. Brown to Lewis Cass, June 17, 1836, Sibley Papers.

2. Brown to Cass, June 17, 1836; Parker, ed., *Recollections of Philander Prescott*, 47, 80, 153.

3. The Dakota, also called Santee, are the eastern division of the broad alliance known as Sioux. Other major groups are the Yankton-Yanktonais and the Lakota. The standard history of the Dakota is Meyer, *History of the Santee Sioux*. For a more ethnographic perspective, see Gibbon, *The Sioux*. The evolving relationship of Euro-American traders with the tribe is dealt with in Anderson, *Kinsmen of Another Kind*.

4. Lawrence Taliaferro, "Annual Census of the Indians within the Agency at St. Peters - Upper Mississippi - for the information of the Department - giving a list of the

Chiefs & head men - the Names of tribes & usual location," September 1, 1834, handwritten copy in the Sibley Papers; Lettermann, *From Whole Log To No Log*, 80.

5. Taliaferro's census of 1834; Lettermann, *From Whole Log To No Log*, 100–9.

6. Blegen, *Minnesota*, 146–48.

7. Folwell, *Minnesota*, 1:136; Kappler, ed., *Indian Affairs, Laws and Treaties*, 2:305–9).

8. Lettermann, *From Whole Log To No Log*, 93, 97.

9. Taliaferro's census of 1834.

10. The Sibley Papers contain voluminous records of the sutler's store while under Sibley's management. The account given here is based on Prucha, in *Minnesota History* 40:22–31. Se also correspondence in the American Fur Company Papers, especially Sibley to Crooks, November 1, 1834, February 28, 1835, June 27, 1837, and January 10, 1838.

11. Patterson, in *Minnesota History* 40:79–81.

12. Gilman, in *Minnesota History* 42:127–29.

13. Blegen, *UA*, 35, 36; Sibley to Crooks, December 31, 1834; Rolette to Crooks, January 20, 1835, American Fur Company Papers; Joseph Renville to Sibley, February 22, 1835, Sibley Papers; Bernard W. Brisbois to Alexis Bailly, May 10, 1835, Bailly Papers.

14. Sibley to Sarah Whipple Sibley, August 1, 1835, photocopy in Sibley Papers, original in Solomon Sibley Papers.

15. Sibley, in *MHC* 3:168–77.

16. Sibley, in *MHC* 3:177–79; Folwell, *Minnesota*, 1:437; Queripel, in *Minnesota Archaeologist* 36:51–55.

17. Contract with Jean B. Faribault, signed by Sibley and Rolette, July 6, 1835, Sibley Papers.

18. Babcock, in *Minnesota History* 20:259–68.

19. Babcock, in *Minnesota History* 20:259–68.

20. Agreement with Joseph Laframboise, June 28, 1835, Sibley Papers.

21. Biographical information here and below is from Ackermann, in *Minnesota History* 12:231–46.

22. Anderson, *Little Crow*, 41.

23. Contract with Joseph Renville for trade at Lac qui Parle, June 6, 1835, Sibley Papers.

24. On Mooers, see Pond, *Dakota Life in the Upper Midwest, 15-17;* Featherstonhaugh, *Canoe Voyage,* 1:318-20.

25. Agreement with Joseph R. Brown, June 17, 1835, Sibley Papers.

26. Contract with Joseph Renville for trade at Lake Traverse, June 6, 1835, Sibley Papers.

27. Brown to Sibley, September 28, 1835, Sibley Papers.

28. Brown to Sibley, September 28, 1835; January 23, 1836, Sibley Papers.

29. See, for example, Crooks to Sibley, April 18, 1835, American Fur Company Papers.

30. Renville to Sibley, January 8, 1836; Brown to Sibley, May 6, 1836, Sibley Papers.

31. Brown to Sibley, October 4, 1836, Sibley Papers.

32. Brown to Sibley, October 4, 1836; Parker, ed., *Recollections,* 171.

33. Goodmans, *Joseph R. Brown,* 288-91; Brown to Sibley, September 28, 1835; Featherstonhaugh, *Canoe Voyage,* 1:385-87.

34. Blegen, *UA,* 37.

35. Blegen, *UA,* 37.

36. Blegen, *UA,* 38.

37. Gilman, et al., *The Red River Trails;* Brown to Sibley, September 28, 1835; January 3, 1855, Sibley Papers.

38. Sibley to Sarah W. Sibley, August 1, 1835.

39. Blegen, *UA,* 39. Because of Sibley's liaison in the years 1840-41 with a Dakota woman, these passages have on occasion been cited as an example of deliberate falsehood. Although it was clearly not the whole story, the incident as told may well have occurred early in his life at Mendota.

Notes for Chapter 5

1. For shifting expectations and definitions of male success during the early nineteenth century see Kimmel, *Manhood in America.* For social life at Fort Snelling, see Blegen, *UA,* 31.

2. Samuel to Ruth Pond, November 14, 1834, Pond Family Papers.

3. Sibley to Mary Sibley, September 1, 1835; to Fred Sibley, April 11, 1837; February 21, 1838, copies in Sibley Papers.

4. Sibley to Sarah W. Sibley, August 1, 1835; to Solomon Sibley, April 21, 1839; to Fred Sibley, April 21, 1839; to Eliza Trowbridge, January 8, 1840, copies in Sibley Papers; Dousman to Sibley, May 25, 1840, Sibley Papers.

5. Sibley to Sarah W. Sibley, August 1, 1835; West, *Sibley,* 59; Blegen, *UA,* 35. The first new building built by Sibley was a stone warehouse, finished in 1836. Work on his residence, probably started in 1837, may not have been fully completed until 1839. Saved from destruction by the St. Paul chapter of the Daughters of the American Revolution, the Sibley House is preserved as one of the state's premier historic sites. It is now owned by the Minnesota Historical Society. The presence of a black servant, when slavery was practiced frequently although illegally at Fort Snelling, has raised the question of whether Sibley was at this time a slave owner. A note in Volume 2 of his memorandum books, written at some time in the fall of 1837, suggests that Robinson may indeed have been a slave, but that if so, he belonged to Dousman and had been loaned to Sibley.

6. Sibley to Fred Sibley, April 11, 1837, April 21, 1839; Fremont, *Memoir of My Life,* 1:33. Fremont, writing many years later, mistakenly recalled the name of the second dog as "Tiger." Boston, slightly smaller than Lion, had been given to Sibley by Captain Martin Scott. See *Pioneer Press,* May 20, 1894, 16.

7. Sibley to Eliza Trowbridge, January 8, 1840 (quotation); West, *Sibley,* 61; Blegen, in *Minnesota History,* 15:382-94. Sibley to Crooks, September 1, 1834, January 10, 1838, April 6, 1842, American Fur Company Papers; Featherstonhaugh, *Canoe Voyage,* 260. Sibley supplied Featherstonhaugh with a guide for his trip up the Minnesota River in September and October 1835, but the geologist lodged at the fort. Another guest was George Catlin, who visited the fort in July 1835 and returned the next summer to make an expedition to the Pipestone Quarry in what is now southwestern

Minnesota. Sibley was called upon to supply Catlin and his companion with a guide and horses for the trip. In June 1838, Frederick Marryat spent two weeks as a guest in Sibley's house. For Sibley's recollections (and low opinion) of all three, see his reminiscences in *MHC*, 1:392–94.

8. Quoted in Pond, *Two Volunteer Missionaries*, 60.

9. West, *Sibley*, 63; Folwell, *Minnesota*, 1:192. The regulations of the Lake Harriet Mission School, dated August 18, 1836, are in the Sibley Papers.

10. Featherstonhaugh, *Canoe Voyage*, 265; Blegen, *UA*, 32; Pond, *Two Volunteer Missionaries*, 107, 130; for Ogden, see also Sibley to Sarah W. Sibley, March 25, 1840, copy in Sibley Papers.

11. Sibley to Mary Sibley, September 1, 1835.

12. Smith, *History of Wisconsin*, 1:145–48; Kappler, *Laws and Treaties*, 2:493; Goodmans, *Joseph R. Brown*, 145.

13. Crooks to Sibley, February 3, 1838, Sibley Papers.

14. Dousman to Sibley, May 6, 1838, Sibley Papers; Gilman, in *Minnesota History* 42:129; Goodmans, *Joseph R. Brown*, 147.

15. Dousman to Sibley, July 12, September 8, 1838, Sibley Papers; Sibley to Solomon Sibley, April 21, 1839, copy in Sibley Papers. Henry Sibley devoted nearly a page of this letter to defending the company and himself against Stuart's accusations, which had apparently received wide currency in Detroit.

16. Gilman, in *Minnesota History* 4:129; Sibley to Solomon Sibley, December 9, 1838, copy in Sibley Papers.

17. Sibley to Solomon Sibley, April 21, 1839. The Winnebago treaty had granted $200,000 for the payment of debts. See Kappler, *Laws and Treaties*, 2:499.

18. Sibley to Solomon Sibley, July 27, December 16 (quotation), 1839, copies in Sibley Papers.

19. Sibley to C. A. Harris, September 22, 1837, Office of Indian Affairs, Letters Received.

20. Kappler, *Laws and Treaties*, 493; contract with Anderson, January 9, 1837; Anderson to Sibley, October 18, 1837; contract

with Faribault, June 25, 1838, Sibley Papers; Williams, *City of Saint Paul*, 54–56; Holcombe, *Minnesota in Three Centuries*, 2:443. Powers of attorney are in the Sibley Papers for the spring and summer of 1838.

21. Sibley later wrote an account of Frazer's life and adventures in a series of sixteen articles that were published weekly in the *Pioneer*, beginning December 2, 1866. They have been collected in a book with an introduction and annotations. See Blegen and Davidson, eds., *Iron Face*. Marryat is quoted on pp. xiii, xix.

22. Sibley to Mary Sibley, September 1, 1835.

23. Lockwood, in *WHC* 2:150n. (Quoted from Kinzie, *Wau-bun*.)

24. Blegen, *UA*, 14. For an analysis of the distorted image of Minnesota's earlier cultures that Anglo-Americans created, see White, in *Minnesota History* 56:179–97.

25. Boutwell to Sibley, August 13, 1838; Brush to Sibley, September 3, 1838, in Sibley Papers. Sibley expanded on his friendship with Martin Scott in a reminiscent article published years later. See *Forest and Stream*, 5:258 (December 2, 1872).

26. Nicollet's journeys are described in Bray, *Nicollet and His Map*. For Sibley's warm memoir of him, see *MHC* 1:146–56.

27. Accounts of this trip can be found in Sibley's "Early Days of Minnesota," in *MHC* 3:254–58, and Fremont, *Memoirs*, 1:37–38. Both men misstated the date, Fremont recalling it as 1838 and Sibley as 1840. Contemporary accounts are in *Spirit of the Times*, April 16, 1842; April 15, 1843, and June 17, 1843, written by Sibley under the pseudonym "Hal, a Dacotah." A more detailed account, apparently a draft version of one or more of the published articles, was preserved in the Sibley Papers and printed in the *Pioneer Press*, May 20, 1894, 16. The manuscript has since been lost. See also Sibley to Solomon Sibley, November 5, 1839. Black Dog's band and Little Crow's band agreed to accompany the hunters, but the people of the latter left and returned home after a few days.

28. Sibley to Eliza Trowbridge, January 8, 1840, copy in Sibley Papers.

29. Dousman to Sibley, March 31 (quo-

tation), July 7, 1840; Crooks to Dousman and Rolette, June 21, 1840; Sibley to Solomon Sibley, November 5, 1838, December 16, 1839, September 2, 1840 (quotation); Mackenzie to Sibley, August 6, September 22, 1840, all in Sibley Papers.

30. Sibley to Sarah W. Sibley, March 21, 1840; agreement between Joseph Laframboise and A. Faribault, September 24, 1840; Dousman to Forbes, October 13, 1840, SIbley Papers; Sibley, in *MHC* 3:258–61.

31. Dousman to Sibley, April 28, May 25, September 28, 1840, Sibley Papers.

32. Sibley, in *MHC* 3:258–60. An account that covers some of the events of this expedition and describes Dakota hunting customs in greater detail was published by Sibley in 1847. See *Spirit of the Times*, 17:87. For Dakota hunting customs, see also Pond, *Dakota Life*, 43–53.

33. Sibley, in *MHC*, 3:259–65. See also *Spirit of the Times*, November 25, 1843. Sibley's reminiscences are unreliable in a number of details, for he misstated not only the year, but the time of his return, which he recalled as the first of March. Contemporary records show that he was back at St. Peters by January 26, 1841.

34. Whether records of this relationship were systematically destroyed is not altogether clear. Fragmentary references, like the letter from Forbes quoted below, remain in the Sibley Papers. Some of the papers also bear marginal notes by an unidentified person, probably Minnesota Historical Society librarian Return I. Holcombe, who knew Sibley personally. These give the name and identity of the child's mother. (See, for example, Alexis Bailly to Sibley, September 6, 1849.) In the spring Dousman sent a man to the Cedar River to collect traps left there by the Dakota. Among them were fourteen belonging to Bad Hail and his lodge. (Dousman to Sibley, April 27, 1841, Sibley Papers.) Memories, apparently faulty, gave rise to the story that Red Blanket Woman regularly visited the Sibley house with her child and received gifts from Mrs. Sibley. (See D. R. Kennedy to Theodore G. Carter, April 23, 1906, in Carter Papers.) Other evidence suggests that Sarah Sibley remained distant toward both mother and child. (See Sylvester J. Sawyer to William R. Brown, Oct. 4, 1860, Brown Papers.)

35. Forbes to Sibley, February 15, 1842, Sibley Papers.

36. The parish records are now held by the Archdiocese of St. Paul. In Volume 3 of a memorandum book in the Sibley Papers there are notations of payments made for special expenses and gifts purchased for Helen (microfilm roll 17). Sibley applied for half-breed scrip to which Helen Hastings was entitled under an act of 1855, and an affidavit made by Forbes in 1856 gives her age as fourteen and testifies that she is supported by her father, who is not named (No. 135, Sioux Affidavits, Roll of mixed-blood claimants, relinquishment by Lake Pepin half-breed Sioux, in Miscellaneous Reserve Papers, Records of the Bureau of Indian Affairs). Helen Sibley appears as a member of the William R. Brown family in the census of 1850. The age given for her there would also be consistent with a birth date of 1841. A small amount of correspondence from and concerning her is in the William Reynolds Brown Papers in the Minnesota Historical Society. Further information about her, including a portrait, is in an article published in the *Pioneer Press*, October 25, 1908. The unidentified author of the piece may have been Return I. Holcombe. For assistance in reconstructing the story of Helen Sibley, the present author is indebted to Alan R. Woolworth, Sumner Bright, Bruce A. Kohn, and Garneth Peterson, all of whom have generously shared their research.

Notes for Chapter 6

1. Goodmans, *Joseph R. Brown*, 148–52, 160, 187.

2. For the military reservation, see Folwell, *Minnesota*, 1:217–24; Sibley to Crooks, March 1 and September 13, 1841, American Fur Company Papers, Letters Received; Crooks to Sibley, April 23, 1841, American Fur Company Papers, Letters Sent; Sibley to Robert Lucas, February 13, 1841, Sibley Papers. Sibley's first use of the name Mendota occurs in a letter to his mother dated at "Mendota (St. Peters) 13 September 1841."

3. Depositions of Jacques Leferre and François Chevalier, January 26, 1841; warrant for arrest of Jean Baptiste Deniger, February 13, 1841, Sibley Papers. On Baker's estate, see Kenneth Mackenzie to Sibley, April 6, May 27, and June 2, 1841, Sibley Papers.

4. Folsom, *Fifty Years in the Northwest*, 519; Folwell, *Minnesota*, 1:228; Sibley to Crooks, December 21, 1839, American Fur Company Papers; Williams, *City of Saint Paul*, 185-90.

5. Crooks to Dousman, April 19, (copy), Dousman to Sibley, May 10, to Crooks, May 11 (copy) and June 18, 1841, Sibley Papers; Gilman, in *Minnesota History* 42:129.

6. On Doty's career see Smith, *James Duane Doty*.

7. For a full discussion of the negotiation and ultimate defeat of the Doty treaties, see Gilman, in *Journal of the West*.

8. Doty reported the negotiations and defended the terms he had agreed to in three letters addressed to Bell from Mendota on August 4, 9, and 14, 1841. Enclosed with the letters of August 4 and 14 are copies of the two treaties. See Office of Indian Affairs, Letters Received (copies on Microfilm 175, Roll 759). For Wacouta and Wabasha, see Doty to Sibley, August 22, 1841, Sibley Papers.

9. The northern and western borders of the purchase, described in Article 1 of the treaty are vague at best, reflecting the lack of precise landmarks and knowledge of the country. It seems likely, for example, that there was confusion of the Crow Wing with the Crow River. Doty exceeded his instructions in a number of respects. He had been authorized to negotiate for only five million acres and to spend less than $5,000 on all expenses, including gifts. For these limitations, see T. Hartley Crawford, commissioner of Indian Affairs, to Doty, May 10, 1841 (2 letters), Office of Indian Affairs, Letters Sent (copies on Microfilm 298, Roll 30).

10. Crawford to Doty, May 10 (2nd letter); Doty to Bell, August 4; Dousman to Sibley, June 18, 1841.

11. Sibley to Crooks, August 26, 1841, American Fur Company Papers; Doty to Bell, August 9, 1841.

12. Benton to the President, September 14, 1841, Office of Indian Affairs, Letters Received, St. Peters Agency (copy in Microfilm 175, Roll 759). Benton's objections to the treaty, enclosed with this copy of his letter to the President, are dated September 22, 1841.

13. Sibley to Sarah W. Sibley, September 13 and to Solomon Sibley, October 2, 1841, copies in Sibley Papers; Agreement between Chouteau, acting for the American Fur Company, and Rolette, Sibley, and Dousman, October 8, 1841, Dousman Papers (copy in the MHS).

14. Emily Mason to John T. Mason, January 2, 1842, Mason Papers (copy in the MHS).

15. Sibley to Solomon Sibley, March 19, 1842, copy in Sibley Papers; Stuart to Sibley, May 5, 1842, Sibley Papers.

16. Sibley to Crooks, February 2, 1842, American Fur Company Papers; Doty to Sibley, February 28, 1842, Sibley Papers.

17. Sibley to Crooks, February 9 (first quote) and February 11 (second quote), 1842, American Fur Company Papers; Crooks to Sibley, March 21, 1842, Sibley Papers.

18. Sibley to Solomon Sibley, March 19, 1842.

19. Articles of Agreement, February 26, 1842, copy in Sibley Papers, original in Newberry Library; Sibley to Spencer; to Senate; to Congress, March 16, 1842, Sibley Papers.

20. Sibley to Solomon Sibley, March 19, 1842; Crooks to Sibley, March 21, 1842, Sibley Papers.

21. Franklin Steele to Sibley, April 6 (quotation) and April 9, 1842, Sibley Papers.

22. Sibley to William Woodbridge, April 24, 1842, Woodbridge Papers.

23. Michael Brisbois to Sibley, October 3, Dousman to Sibley, October 20 (quotation), and December 28, 1842, Sibley Papers. In fact, the financial situation was better than it appeared, and Crooks ultimately succeeded in paying off all of the company's debts. See David Lavender, *Fist in the Wilderness*, 419.

24. The conflict gave its present name to Battle Creek, on the southeastern edge of

the city of St. Paul. Sibley's own account of it is in his collection of articles, edited by Blegen and Davidson, *Iron Face*, 175–81.

25. Sibley, in *Spirit of the Times*, 18:25.

26. Permits from Amos J. Bruce, Indian Agent, for Sibley and others to travel in Indian country for forty days, September 30, 1842, Sibley Papers. Sibley's account of this expedition appeared in *Spirit of the Times*, April 11, 1846. It was reprinted in *Minnesota History*, 15:382–94 with an introduction and notes by Theodore C. Blegen.

27. West, *Sibley*, 85; Dousman to Sibley, March 22, 1843.

Notes for Chapter 7

1. West, *Sibley*, 85, 426; Williams, *City of St. Paul*, 225n.; Sarah Sibley to Abbie Potts, undated, but ca. summer 1848, Livingston Papers; weddings, births, and deaths are recorded in the Sibley family Bible, Sibley Papers.

2. Sibley to Ramsay Crooks, January 2, 1844, American Fur Company Papers; to Fred Sibley, February 20, 1844, Sibley Papers.

3. Sarah Sibley to Abbie Potts, ca. summer 1848; to Sibley, March 20, 1853, Sibley Papers.

4. Family Bible; Dousman to Sibley, November 25, 1846; Sibley to Charles Trowbridge, September 6, 1847, Sibley Papers.

5. West, *Sibley*, 418. Although Sibley's contemporaries never called him "squire," the title has been half-humorously used by later historians.

6. Holmquist and Brookins, *Minnesota's Major Historic Sites*, 13–15; West, *Sibley*, 90, 413 (quote); Hollinshead, "Reminiscences."

7. McDermott, *Seth Eastman*, 32–48, 66, 68, 77.

8. *Minnesota Pioneer*, May 26, 1849, p. 2. Eastman's daughter Nancy had been born in 1831 when her father was stationed at Fort Snelling as a young lieutenant just out of West Point. She lived with her mother's people. Mary Eastman's sympathy for the Indian did not extend to Africans. A southerner, she was an ardent supporter of slavery.

9. Letter dated January 26, 1844

(quote), Sibley Papers. For a listing and discussion of the articles, see Flanagan, in *Minnesota History* 41:217–28. The translation (from French) was a piece by the Reverend Georges A. Belcourt. Porter later started another periodical, to which Sibley contributed two articles in 1856 and 1857. For the origin of the name "Walker in the Pines," see Blegen and Davidson, eds., *Iron Face*, 144. See also Martin McCleod to Sibley, July 30, 1844, Sibley Papers.

10. *Spirit of the Times* 16:78; Fremont, *Memoirs* 1:33. The portrait of Lion was painted by Charles Deas, probably in the summer of 1841. It now hangs in the Sibley House. See Coen, *Painting and Sculpture in Minnesota*, 14.

11. Hollinshead, "Reminiscences"; Sibley, in *Spirit of the Times* 18:66. In 1872 Sibley returned to his memories of this trip as well as the prowess of Lion in a reminiscent article published in *Forest and Stream*.

12. Gilman, in *Minnesota History* 42:130.

13. Gilman, in *Minnesota History* 42:132; Williams, *City of Saint Paul*, 47–49; Rife, in *Minnesota History* 6:226 (quotation); Franklin Steele to Peter Garrioch, January 12, 1841, Sibley Papers.

14. Contract with Steele and Kittson, June 30, 1842; Chouteau Co. to Sibley, July 23, 1842, Sibley Papers.

15. For this and the paragraphs below, see Gilman, in *Minnesota History* 42:130–33; Gilman, et al., *Red River Trails*, 5–7, 10–14.

16. Kittson did in fact use the middle trail in 1850 and again in 1851. See Gilman, et al, *Red River Trails*, 12.

17. Gilman, et al., *Red River Trails*, 13; Alexander Christie to Sibley, May 15 and 21, 1845, and September 10, 1846; Robert Clouston to Sibley, October 3, 1846; Duncan Finlayson to Sibley, June 22, 1847, Sibley Papers.

18. Letters from Alexis Bailly, December 16, 1844; Louis Provençalle, December 20, 1844; Joseph Laframboise, October 1, 1845 and February 24, 1849, Sibley Papers.

19. Eastman, *Dahcotah*, 137 (quotation). For references to hunger among the western bands, see letters from McLeod and Kittson to Sibley throughout the years 1846–51.

20. Sibley, in *MHC* 3:252; Anderson, *Little Crow*, 32–45.

21. Anderson, *Little Crow*, 35n., 36–45. Anderson argues that Sibley was mistaken in the identity of the son addressed by Big Thunder, since Taoyateduta, living in Lac qui Parle, was unlikely to have been present at his father's death. Sibley was closely acquainted with the Kaposia band and both he and Faribault spent time hunting with Taoyateduta (see Anderson, 37). It seems improbable that both men would have been confused. Trading, annuity payments, and other activities no doubt brought Taoyateduta back to the Mississippi quite regularly. For a reference to his trade with the western bands, see McLeod to Sibley, January 29, 1846. There he is already referred to as "Little Crow."

22. Anderson, *Little Crow*, 46–53.

23. See, for example, letters from Stephen R. Riggs, February 26, 1844; from Riggs, Thomas Williamson, and Samuel Pond, September 13, 1845; from Gideon Pond, November 25, 1848; Sibley to Gideon Pond, February 7, 1849 (quotation); undated partial draft of article on Indian tribes of the Northwest, all in Sibley Papers. The extension of U.S. laws would have implied an end to the sovereignty of Indian tribes and therefore to the treaty system, although Sibley never directly acknowledged this.

24. Folwell, *Minnesota*, 1:310. Dousman signed as a witness to the treaty, which was concluded in Washington.

25. Letters from Dousman, November 25. Forbes, December 8, 1846, Sibley Papers; Sibley, in *MHC* 1:394. Also evidence of his presence in Washington is a note from Jessie Benton Fremont, February 21, 1847, Sibley Papers. A copy of the Winnebago treaty is in the Sibley Papers.

26. Sibley to Trowbridge, September 6, 1847, copy in Sibley Papers.

27. For this and the paragraph below, see Gilman, in *Minnesota History* 42:132–37.

28. Contract with St. Croix and Snake River Ojibwe, dated March 13, 1837; Warren to Sibley, March 13, 1837, August 18, 1838, April 23, 1840 and June 18, 1841; Dousman to Sibley, September 22, 1838,

May 25, 1840 and January 17, 1845 (quote), Sibley Papers.

29. Folwell, *Minnesota*, 1:225; Gilman, in *Minnesota History* 42:139; Williams, *Saint Paul*, 173. Beginning in 1838, many of Dousman's frequent letters to Sibley include information on steamboats in which they held an interest.

30. Gilman, in *Minnesota History* 42:132, 139.

31. Goodmans, *Joseph R. Brown*, provides a full-length portrait of the man. His activities during the 1840s are described in Chapters VII, VIII, and IX.

32. Agreement with Brown, September 28, 1846, Sibley Papers. For earlier dealings, see Goodmans, *Joseph R. Brown*, 218, 225–31, 241–43.

33. Sibley to Trowbridge, September 6, 1847, copy in Sibley Papers.

Notes for Chapter 8

1. Folwell, *Minnesota*, 1:486–95.

2. For a detailed discussion of the political maneuvering that resulted in the creation of Minnesota Territory, see Lass, in *Minnesota History* 50:309–20 and 55:267–79. See also, Goodmans, *Joseph R. Brown*, 247–55, 267–83. This and the following paragraphs rest on these sources. According to his own recollection, Sibley's discussions with Martin included the name of the new territory. See his reminiscences in *MHC* 1:394.

3. Dousman to Sibley, January 28, 1848, Sibley Papers.

4. See, for example, John McKusick to Sibley, April 22, 1847, Sibley Papers.

5. Dodge to Sibley, June 8, 1848, Sibley Papers; Williams, *City of St. Paul*, 197. There are numerous letters from Lambert in the Sibley Papers for 1848 and 1849.

6. Folwell, *Minnesota*, 1:225.

7. Hollinshead, "Reminiscences."

8. The full "founding story" of Minnesota, with generous credit to Sibley, is told in Folwell, *Minnesota*, 1:241–47. The speech was among the first documents printed for posterity by the newly formed Minnesota Historical Society two years later. See *MHC* 1:47–54.

9. Folwell, *Minnesota*, 1:242; Sibley to

Gideon Pond, December 6, 1848 (quotation), February 7, 1849, Sibley Papers.

10. Owens, "Political History of Minnesota," 33. Folwell and other historians may have overestimated Sibley's generosity in moving the capital to St. Paul. In 1849 he owned no land at Mendota and could not legally have acquired any.

11. West, *Sibley*, 130.

12. Lambert's description was written for the first issue of the *Minnesota Pioneer* and is reprinted in Williams, *City of St. Paul*, 206. Elihu B. Washburne to Sibley, May 6 (quotation); Kenneth Mackenzie to Sibley, June 14, 1849, Sibley Papers.

13. A printed copy of the address, without date, is among the Sibley Papers. In the microfilm edition it is filed at the beginning of June (Roll 5, Frame 688–92), but correspondence indicates that it was issued around the end of April. For Goodhue and his press, see Williams, *City of St. Paul*, 210.

14. Ramsey Diary, May 2, 3, and 8–27, 1849, Alexander Ramsey Papers.

15. Urevig, ed., in *Minnesota History* 35:353–54; Dousman to Sibley, May 29, 1849, Sibley Papers. Anna Ramsey had been acquainted with the Steele family in Pennsylvania. See Ramsey to John Speel, June 5, 1849, Ramsey Papers.

16. Sibley to Charles Trowbridge, July 11, 1849, Sibley Letter Book. The story of the Ramsey/Sibley friendship has been somewhat exaggerated. Throughout the 1850s it appears to have cooled, although they became allies again after 1862.

17. Williams, *City of St. Paul*, 186–89, 223; Folwell, *Minnesota*, 1:367; Forbes to Sibley, November 30, 1848; Lambert to Sibley, January 13; Jacob W. Bass to Sibley, January 28, 1849, Sibley Papers; Rice to Chouteau, June 2, 1849, copy in Washington County District Court, File No. A1785 1/2.

18. Williams, *City of St. Paul*, 188, 189; Lambert to Thomas Potts, February 13, 1849 Sibley Papers; Sibley to Chouteau, June 25, 1849, Sibley Letter Book; Rice to Dousman, September 29, 1848, Hercules L. Dousman Papers, originals in State Historical Society of Wisconsin and microfilm copy in the MHS.

19. Williams, *St. Paul*, 223; Sibley to

Chouteau (private), June 20, 1849, Sibley Letter Book.

20. Sibley to Chouteau, June 25, 1849, Sibley Letter Book; Rice to Sibley, June 30; Chouteau to Sibley, July 12, 1849, Sibley Papers.

21. Gilman, in *Minnesota History* 42:134; Rice to Chouteau, June 2, 1849; Sibley to Chouteau, August 8, 1849, Sibley Letter Book. In planning to leave La Pointe, Borup was no doubt anticipating the decision made in Washington the following winter to remove all Ojibwe bands from Wisconsin into northern Minnesota, where access to them would be via the Mississippi and not through Lake Superior.

22. Sibley to Chouteau, August 8 (first quotation); Chouteau to Sibley, September 3; Sibley to Chouteau, September 5 (second quotation), 1849, Sibley Letter Book.

23. Borup to Sibley, September 9, Sibley Papers; Sibley to Chouteau, September 12, Sibley Letter Book; Sibley to Borup, September 12, 1849, Sibley Letter Book; Borup to Sibley, undated, Sibley Papers.

24. Gilman, in *Minnesota History* 42:135; Rice and David Olmsted to Chouteau and W. G. and G. W. Ewing, September 26, 1849, Rice Letter Book. On the Ewings, see Trennert, *Indian Traders on the Middle Border*.

25. Sire to Sibley, October 9, 1849, Sibley Papers; Sibley to Chouteau, October 10, 1849, Sibley Letter Book. A recitation of the complaint against Rice and the terms of the settlement agreement are in File No. A1785 1/2, Washington County District Court records. With this settlement, litigation ceased for a time. In the spring of 1851, however, Chouteau filed suit on behalf of himself and Sibley. They claimed that Rice had obtained their agreement through misrepresentation and fraud. In the next four years the case moved through a tangle of legal technicalities and was appealed three times to the Minnesota Supreme Court. The last action recorded was appointment of a referee on April 3, 1855. The course of the litigation can be followed through File No. A1785 1/2, Washington County District Court records, and in *Minnesota Reports*, July 1851, 8–23; July 1852, 83–97; January 1854, 166–69.

26. Rice to Dousman, October 16, 1849, Dousman Papers, copy in the MHS. A copy is also in the Rice Letter Book. Dousman had come to St. Paul at the end of September on business related to a possible Dakota treaty. See Rice to Chouteau, September 28, 1849, Rice Letter Book.

27. *Minnesota Pioneer*, October 25, 1849.

28. Brown to Sibley, December 21; Potts to Sibley, December 21, 1849, Sibley Papers; Ramsey Diary, November 9, 1849, Ramsey Papers.

29. Sibley to Fred Sibley, August 10; to Forbes, November 12; Forbes to Sibley, December 21; Borup to Chouteau, December 6 and 21 (quote), 1849; Faribault to Sibley, January 21, 1850; all in Sibley Papers. Fred Sibley did not arrive in Minnesota until the spring of 1850.

30. Petitioners included Sibley's brother Sproat, who asked the delegate to use his influence with the army to prevent a threatened transfer (E. S. Sibley to Sibley, January 14 and 26, 1850). There are numerous letters from Goodhue, Forbes, Faribault, Potts, and other Minnesota friends in the Sibley Papers for the winter and spring of 1850. See especially, Forbes to Sibley, December 21; Joseph Mosher to Sibley, December 25; Potts to Sibley, December 21, 1849, January 15 and April 17, 1850. Sibley had apparently been a strong influence toward sobriety for both Forbes and Mosher.

31. Removal was based on the treaties of 1837 and 1842. Under the first the Ojibwe had been given the right to hunt and fish on ceded land "at the pleasure of the President." Under the second, they ceded their remaining land along the south shore of Lake Superior, trusting the verbal assurances of treaty commissioner Robert Stuart that they would not be forced to move. For political maneuvering to secure the removal order, see White, "The Regional Context of the Removal Order of 1850," Section 4.

32. Sibley to Ramsey, February 9; Ramsey to Sibley, April 27, 1850, Sibley Papers. On Cass and his role in the Compromise of 1850, see Klunder, *Lewis Cass*, 241–53.

33. Sibley to Ramsey, March 27, 1850, Ramsey Papers; Charles Trowbridge to Sib-

ley, April 15; Sibley to Subcommittee of Indian Affairs, May 18, 1850, Sibley Papers; Rice to Dousman, December 6, 1849, January 8, 21, and 23, 1850, Dousman Papers.

34. On complaints regarding the Winnebago, see *Minnesota Chronicle and Register*, February 2, 1850 (clipping in Sibley Papers); Orlando Brown to Sibley, with enclosures, February 2; Sire to Sibley, February 10; Ramsey to Sibley, April 10, 1850, Sibley Papers.

35. Ramsey to Sibley, April 27, 1850, Sibley Papers. Both Ramsey and Sibley had known that Rice was seeking the contract, but neither had anticipated his success in getting it. See Rice to Ramsey, March 19; Sibley to Ramsey, March 22, 1850, Ramsey Papers.

36. Sibley to Subcommittee of Indian Affairs, May 18; to Fred Sibley (telegram), May 16; Fred Sibley to Sibley, May 19; Potts to Sibley, May 29, 1850, Sibley Papers.

37. The Winnebago contract and its outcome are fully discussed in Folwell, *Minnesota*, 1:311–17. See also copy of letter from Olmsted to Chouteau Co., June 2; Ramsey to Sibley, June 3; Olmsted to Sibley, June 4, 1850, Sibley Papers.

38. A copy of the broadside, "An Address by the Hon. Hal. Squibble," is in the Sibley Papers under date of April 1. For the campaign and election, see Folwell, *Minnesota*, 1:369–72. Folwell suggests that Mitchell's nomination was in part a payback for his help to Rice in getting the Winnebago contract.

39. Brown made a flying visit to Washington in July and helped lay out the strategy for the campaign. See Brown to Sibley, May 31; Forbes to Sibley, July 11; Fred Sibley to Sibley (with postscript by Brown), August 11, 1850, Sibley Papers. For Goodhue's role, see Hage, *Newspapers on the Minnesota Frontier*, 31–34. For the vote by communities, see Folwell, *Minnesota*, 1:372n.

Notes for Chapter 9

1. Sibley to Riggs, August 11; to Commissioners of the American Board, September 3, 1849, Sibley Letter Book. He expressed many of the same convictions three months earlier in connection with his

newspaper review of Mary Eastman's book.

2. Folwell, *Minnesota*, 1:254, 268-72.

3. Sibley to Ramsey, September 13 and 23, 1849, Sibley Letter Book.

4. Folwell, *Minnesota*, 1:273-75, 323-25. The mixed-blood treaty was never ratified, despite Sibley's best efforts at persuading Congress.

5. McLeod to Sibley, January 3, 1850, Sibley Papers.

6. McLeod to Sibley January 3 and February 10; Ramsey to Orlando Brown, February 22, with enclosures; Brown to Sibley, March 22; Fred Sibley to Sibley, May 29, 1850, all in Sibley Papers.

7. Sibley to Pond, May 13, 1850; to Riggs, August 11, 1849, Sibley Papers. Sibley described Indian commissioner Orlando Brown as "a good natured sort of a man, very indolent, knows nothing about Indians, and likes his glass of brandy."

8. A printed copy of the speech is in the Sibley Papers. There is also a copy in the pamphlet collection of the MHS.

9. Fred Sibley to Sibley, September 25, Joseph Sire to Sibley, October 12, 1850. On October 19 Ramsey noted in his diary that however late the season, if he received instructions from the Indian Office, he would try to make a treaty, "For the people are impatient. They want the country."

10. Sibley to Chouteau, November 3, 1850, Sibley Papers; Rice to Dousman, December 23, 1850, Dousman Papers; Office of Indian Affairs, *Annual Report*, 1851, p. 423. Ramsey also minimized the number of dead. For the full story of this tragedy, see White, "The Regional Context of the Removal Order of 1850," Section 6.

11. Sibley to Chouteau, November 3, 1850, Sibley Letter Book; Fred Sibley to Sibley, November 24 and December 16, 1850, January 28, 1851, Sibley Papers.

12. The intricate political machinations surrounding the Dakota treaties of 1851 from beginning to end have been the subject of several historical studies. The most extensive is in Folwell, *Minnesota*, 1:266-304, 462-70. See also Kane, in *Minnesota History* 32:65-80. The history of the Ewings is in Trennert, *Indian Traders on the Middle Border*.

See especially 177-80, 184-86, 191, 193. See also George W. Ewing to Sibley, September 24, 1849, January 13, 1850, Sibley Papers. Olmsted had traded exclusively with the Winnebago.

13. Here and below, see Folwell, *Minnesota*, 1:276, 277n; Trennert, *Indian Traders on the Middle Border*, 158-60.

14. Kane, in *Minnesota History* 32:69; Sibley to Ramsey, February 9, 1851, Ramsey Papers.

15. McLeod to Sibley, April 22 and 26, 1851, Sibley Papers.

16. Sibley to Chouteau, November 3, 1850; *Minnesota Pioneer*, July 3, 1851.

17. The best descriptions of events at the treaty-making are in the *Minnesota Pioneer*, July 3-August 7, and in the diary kept by Mayer. A second artist, Ashton White, was an official of the Indian office. See Heilbron, ed., *With Pen and Pencil on the Frontier*, 145-202. No Indian accounts have been preserved.

18. James McClure to Sibley, February 14; Samuel M. Plummer to Sibley, December 9, 1838. See also Huggan, in *MHC*.

19. Sibley testimony, *Ramsey Investigation Report*, 215.

20. McLeod later remarked that there had been mismanagement of the Indians and too much of what looked like bribery (see letter to Fred Sibley, December 20, 1851, Sibley Papers). This may suggest that Brown's methods were more heavy-handed.

21. The initial offer, as reported by Goodhue, included an annuity of $25,000 to $30,000 for a period of thirty or forty years and a lump sum for subsistence, removal and "to arrange their affairs," of "say $125,000 or $130,000." See *Minnesota Pioneer*, August 7, 1851. The final settlement, approximately twice as large, was much closer to Sibley's consistent recommendation of ten cents per acre. There is no record of what role traders, missionaries, or mixed-bloods played in putting the counteroffer into writing and in assisting with the negotiations.

22. For complete terms of the treaty, see Kappler, *Laws and Treaties*, 2:588-90.

23. Two copies of this paper are in the

Sibley Papers under date of July 23, 1851. The amounts listed, both for traders and mixed-blood families, total a little over $210,000.

24. Sibley testimony, *Ramsey Investigation Report*, 214; Folwell, *Minnesota*, 1:283. Chute is quoted by Kane, in *Minnesota History* 32:74.

25. Sibley testimony, *Ramsey Investigation Report*, 211.

26. *Pioneer*, August 7, 1851.

27. Here and below, see Folwell, *Minnesota*, 1:284-87; Kane in *Minnesota History* 32:76; Anderson, *Little Crow*, 61-64.

28. To Borup, August 8, 1851, Sibley Letter Book. In the Mendota treaty a separate clause was included relating to the mixed-bloods, since they had already received a tract of land under the treaty of 1830. For its terms, see Kappler, *Laws and Treaties*, 2:591-93. A copy of the traders paper signed by the Wahpekute is in the Sibley Papers under date of August 5, 1851. The total payment to Sibley promised by the Dakota in the traders papers and agreed to orally by the Mdewakanton was $134,950.

29. *Pioneer*, August 7, 1851; *Democrat*, July 29, 1851.

30. To Dr. J. B. Blake, September 6, 1851, Sibley Letter Book; Anderson, *Little Crow*, 65. See also Sibley to Luke Lea, August 31, 1851, Letter Book.

31. To Borup, August 7, 1851, Sibley Letter Book.

32. To Borup, September 17; to Joseph Laframboise, October 6; to McLeod, October 6; to E. S. Sibley, October 8; to Kittson, October 9, 1851, all in Sibley Letter Book. He also recorded the incident of the hymn in the family Bible along with the date of his son's death.

33. Sibley to Dousman, October 31; to Chouteau, November 1, 1851, Letter Book; Dousman to Sibley, November 4, 1851, Sibley Papers; Rice to Dousman, October 15, November 7, 1851, Dousman Papers.

34. Sibley to Sarah A. Sibley, September 7, 1851, Sibley Letter Book.

35. McLeod to Fred Sibley, November 15 and December 13, 1851, Sibley Papers. The activities of Sweetser were described at length by Folwell, 1:288-304, but at the

time of his writing, the involvement of the Ewings could only be conjectured. Their papers were later added to the collections of the Indiana State Library, and microfilm copies of letters relevant to Minnesota activities are in the MHS. The account here and below is based on Kane, in *Minnesota History*, and on Trennert, *Indian Traders on the Middle Border*, 172, 177-80.

36. Folwell, *Minnesota*, 1:290-92.

37. Ramsey to Sibley, April 25; Sibley to Dodge, May 3, 1852, Sibley Papers; Sibley to Ramsey, May 10, 1852, Ramsey Papers.

38. Sibley to Ramsey, May 10, 1852; Wabasha quoted in Anderson, *Little Crow*, 66.

39. Dousman to Sibley, September 20, 1852, Sibley Papers; Sibley to Borup, September 30, 1852, Sibley Letter Book. When later questioned under oath, Dousman refused to answer concerning the Rice contract (*Ramsey Investigation Report*, 288). Here and below see Folwell, *Minnesota*, 1:293-95.

40. Folwell, *Minnesota*, 1:297-99.

41. Folwell, *Minnesota*, 1:299-302.

42. Tyler received 15 percent from the money paid by the upper bands and 12 percent from the Mdewakanton funds. Sibley voluntarily added another 10 percent from the $90,000 paid by the Wahpekute. In total, Tyler collected $55,250.

43. Although Sweetser posed as a friend of the Indians, he had told both Dousman and Borup that he would cooperate with them for a price of $30,000. His correspondence with the Ewings also reveals his true position.

44. Hage, *Newspapers on the Minnesota Frontier*, 40-45.

45. In his history, Folwell devoted a separate essay to the investigation. See *Minnesota*, 1:464-66 (Appendix 8).

46. *Ramsey Investigation Report*, 72, 73.

47. Sibley to Ben C. Eastman, June 17 and September 25; to William G. LeDuc, August 2; to Augustus C. Dodge, August 7; to R. McClelland, Secretary of the Interior, October 17; to Lewis Cass, October 22; to Charles Trowbridge, October 22, 1853, all in Sibley Letter Book. The Senate's statement is quoted in Folwell, *Minnesota*,

1:469. Immediately after the Senate's action, Ramsey demanded that Sibley and the other traders pay him $5,000 "for his sacrifices, loss of time, expeditions, etc." His insistence, in Sibley's words, was "beyond the bounds of delicacy." See Sibley to Dousman, May 28, 1854, Sibley Letter Book. Apparently some such payment was made, but the amount is unknown. See Ramsey diary, April 26 and May 8, 1854, Ramsey Papers. The incident may have increased the growing coolness between Sibley and Ramsey in the years that followed.

48. Dousman is quoted by Fred Sibley in a letter to him, July 5, 1853, Sibley Letter Book.

Notes for Chapter 10

1. Sibley to William H. Forbes, June 1, to Hercules Dousman, August 1, to Henry M. Rice, October 2, 1853, Sibley Letter Book. Letters from Dr. Thomas Potts frequently mention the trouble with Augusta's eyes, for which he was providing medical care.

2. *Dispatch*, October 25, 1908; Ledger, p. 38, William R. Brown Papers; Entries for December 1, 1852, August 21, 1855, Miscellaneous Account Book, vol. 3, Sibley Papers. The fact of Helen's schooling was recorded by Folwell in the notes of an interview held with Return I. Holcombe. See 84:119, Folwell Papers.

3. *Dispatch*, October 25, 1908; *Minnesotian*, September 3, 1858.

4. Sibley's letter to Porter and Belcourt's article are both in the *Spirit of the Times*, 20:546. Sibley's interest in the Dakota language is reflected by the presence among his papers of several lexicons and vocabulary lists compiled by missionaries and traders. See also a letter from Joseph Henry, Director of the Smithsonian, April 5, 1853.

5. William T. Porter to Sibley, July 24, 1856, Sibley Papers. The article quoted appeared under the title "Game in the West," in *Porter's Spirit of the Times*, 1:126. It was reprinted in *Minnesota History* 18:415–19.

6. Letter from E. D. Neill, December 3, 1855. The address appeared in the *Pioneer and Democrat* and was later published under the title "Reminiscences: Historical and Personal" in Volume 1 of *MHC*. A partial manuscript copy, filed in the Sibley Papers under date of February 1, 1856, contains a more specific statement of his future plans. For Frazer, see Blegen and Davidson, eds., *Iron Face*, xxi. What later became the fourth in the series of Frazer's tales appeared under the title "The Three Dakotas," in *Porter's Spirit of the Times*, January 31, 1857.

7. Quotation in *MHC* 1:379; Gabriel Franchere to Sibley, February 18, 1856, Sibley Papers. See also White, in *Minnesota History* 56:180–83.

8. Exact amounts are impossible to determine from the undated and incomplete records available. One memorandum in Sibley's handwriting, apparently written in late 1852, indicates a total of $246,000 received by him from "Sioux money." (This must have included money passed on to him by traders and mixed-blood people who were in his debt, plus amounts collected on behalf of his own mixed-blood daughter.) Of this sum, $181,283 is recorded as paid to the Chouteau Company, $26,404 to Ramsay Crooks on behalf of the American Fur Company, $15,411 to a bank in Galena for repayment of a loan, and $9,000 to Hugh Tyler. The remaining balance of $13,902 may have been still further reduced by payments to Rice and later Ramsey, of which there is no record. See "H.H. Sibley in a/c with Sioux Money" filed under date of November 1, 1852, in the Sibley Papers.

9. Sibley to Trowbridge, August 24, 1851, Sibley Letter Book; Fred Sibley to Sibley, February 17, 1851, Sibley Papers. An undated and undocumented estimate of the net worth of several territorial figures was made by Return I. Holcombe. He named Rice as "easily the wealthiest man in the territory" at $40,000, followed by Steele and Borup. He guessed that Sibley and Joseph R. Brown were worth "perhaps $10,000 each." Holcombe, *Minnesota in Three Centuries*, 2:423.

10. Sibley's land dealings in partnership with Chouteau can be followed in his correspondence for 1853–55 (especially Letter Books 90 and 91) and in the ledgers of the

Sioux Outfit, especially volume 50. Articles of agreement dated September 1, 1855, distributing the assets of the Sioux and Minnesota Outfits and placing Sibley on salary as Chouteau's agent are at the end of volume 50. Additional records are in the Chouteau Papers. Fur trade ledgers TT, VV, and WW contain numerous entries, and pp. 40 and 41 of WW show the settlement of September 1855. (Microfilm copies in MHS.) See also Pierre Chouteau, Jr., to John B. Sarpy, January 18, Sibley to Chouteau Co., July 23, to Pierre Chouteau, Jr., July 31, 1856; to Chouteau Co., April 27, 1858; October 22 and November 12, 1859, in Missouri Historical Society, St. Louis.

11. See correspondence of Fred Sibley with McLeod and Duncan R. Kennedy in late 1851 and 1852, Sibley Letter Book; Joseph A. Sire to Sibley, November 23, 1851, Sibley Papers. A map of the initial townsite is in the Sibley Papers under date of January 1, 1852. For the later years see Hughes, *Old Traverse des Sioux*, 102-5, and correspondence in Sibley Letter Books for 1855, 1856, and 1857.

12. Curtiss-Wedge, ed., *Dakota and Goodhue Counties*, 1:230-36; Upham, *Geographic Names*, 165. In the summer of 1854 Faribault sold his share of Hastings to William G. LeDuc, a St. Paul lawyer and bookseller, for $4,000. Sibley to Borup, June 17, to Fred Sibley, July 3, 1854, Sibley Letter Book. A plat of Hastings is in the Sibley Papers under date of January 1, 1853.

13. Fred Sibley to Sibley, February 26, 1853; John Wilson, Commissioner of U.S. Land Office, to Sibley, July 6, 1854, Sibley Papers; Sibley to William H. Forbes, June 1, 1853, Sibley Letter Book; Curtiss-Wedge, ed., *Dakota and Goodhue Counties*, 157-60.

14. On the sale of the Fort Snelling military reservation, see Folwell, *Minnesota*, 422-34. Sibley tried but was unsuccessful in securing belated compensation for the settlers who had been forced off the military reservation in 1839. For an appeal by one of them, see letter from Joseph R. Brown, November 25, 1850, Sibley Papers.

15. Smith to Sibley, February 1, 1853, Sibley Papers.

16. Sibley to Gorman, March 24, 1854, Sibley Letter Book.

17. Meyer, *Santee Sioux*, 89-92.

18. Anderson, *Little Crow*, 69-73; George W. Manypenny to Sibley, April 12, 1854, Sibley Papers.

19. Folwell, *Minnesota*, 1:324, 482-86; Sibley, Bailly, and Faribault to George W. Manypenny, July 25, 1855, Sibley Letter Book; Thomas A. Hendrick to Sibley, Bailly, and Faribault, August 24, 1855.

20. *Dictionary of American Biography*, 9:106; Shields to Sibley, October 5, 1855, February 23, November 20, and December 23, 1856, January 12, 1857, Sibley Papers.

21. Williams, *City of St. Paul*, 41, 48, 390; Upham, *Minnesota Geographic Names*, 316, 382; Sibley to Charles Trowbridge, July 3, 1854, Sibley Letterbook. Sibley himself was a silent investor in the bank of Borup and Oakes, as was Alexander Faribault. See Sibley to Borup, January 11, 1854, Sibley Letter Book; agreement dated January 30, 1854, Sibley Papers.

22. Hage, *Newspapers on the Minnesota Frontier*, 39; Sibley to Henrietta Goodhue, October 31, 1853, Sibley Letter Book.

23. Hage, *Newspapers on the Minnesota Frontier*, 46-52, 56; Sibley to Eastman, March 12; to E. S. Goodrich, March 12 and July 23 1854, Sibley Letter Book; *Pioneer*, October 4, 1854. Sibley's investment came ultimately to $6,500. See satisfaction of mortgage on the *Pioneer*, July 22, 1859, Sibley Papers.

24. Hage, *Newspapers on the Minnesota Frontier*, 57-59; Eastman to Sibley, October 19, 1855.

25. For a full discussion of the vision held by Douglas, see chapter on "The Great Superior Scheme: Continental Ambitions in Townsites, Railroads, and Politics," in Cohen, *Business and Politics*. Folwell also devotes a chapter to the "Railroad Miscarriage" in *Minnesota*, 1:327-50.

26. Dousman to Sibley, December 8, 1850, Sibley Papers; *Pioneer*, July 31, 1851; Folwell, *Minnesota*, 1:329.

27. Here and below, see Folwell, *Minnesota*, 1:329-32; Cohen, *Business and Politics*, 160, 175-77, 182-84.

28. Murray, in *MHC* 12:125; Sibley to

Eastman, March 12, 1854, Sibley Letter Book.

29. Tyler to Sibley, August 1, 1854, Sibley Papers.

30. Rice to Ramsey, July 4, 1854, Ramsey Papers.

31. Sibley to Washburne; to Eastman, July 16, 1854, Sibley Letter Book.

32. Washburne to Sibley, August 18, 1854, Sibley Papers; Rice to Ramsey, July 24, 1854, Ramsey Papers. Although Rice's complicity in the fraud was widely suspected, it was never established.

33. Sibley to Brown, September 20, 1854.

34. Folwell gives a detailed account of the long contest with the Minnesota and Northwestern in both the legislature and the courts. The corporation maintained that according to the terms of its charter the land grant had already been accepted and could not be repealed by Congress. Repeatedly successful in the Minnesota courts, this claim was ultimately defeated in the U.S. Supreme Court—but not until 1862. See Folwell, *Minnesota*, 1:340-50; West, *Sibley*, 216-22.

35. Williams, *City of Saint Paul*, 352; *Minnesotian*, June 14, 1854.

Notes for Chapter 11

1. See Cohen, *Business and Politics*, 173. Cohen concludes (p. 239): "The irony of Douglas's career lay in his pursuit of the politics of vested interests before the interests had been vested."

2. *Minnesotian*, April 4, July 27, 1855.

3. *Minnesotian*, July 28, 1855; *Pioneer*, September 3, 1855.

4. The political maneuvering around the so-called "Black-law" was recalled by Robert Watson, an abolitionist legislator from Washington County. See his *Notes on the Early Settlement of Cottage Grove and Vicinity*, [18]. For the German position, see *Pioneer*, August 23, 1855.

5. Anderson, *History of the Constitution*, 46-60; Folwell, *Minnesota*, 1:390-93; 2:38n.

6. Saby, in *MHC* 15:11; Bradley B. Meeker to Sibley, January 10, 1856; Shields

to Sibley, January 12, 1857, Sibley Papers; Sibley to Chouteau, February 13, 1855, Sibley Letter Book.

7. Folwell, *Minnesota*, 1:382-87; Sibley to LeDuc, May 21, 1857, LeDuc Papers.

8. Folwell, *Minnesota*, 2:39-41.

9. George L. Becker to Sibley, March 26, 1857, Sibley Papers. Unless otherwise noted, the account of the constitutional convention here and below is based on Folwell, *Minnesota*, 1:396-421.

10. For Sibley's positions on various questions, see Minnesota Constitutional Convention (Democratic), *Debates and Proceedings* as follows: corporation laws, 124-29; militia service, 150-52; time limit on legislative sessions, 255-65; opposition to four-year term for governor, 376; limit on state debts, 395; banks, 411; powers of cities and counties, 473-76; election of judges, 507-9; debtors, 362, Folwell, *Minnesota*, 1:381. For his statement on school lands, see Owens, "Political History of Minnesota," 441.

11. *Debates and Proceedings*, 150-52.

12. Williams, *City of St. Paul*, 365, 374, 376, 379.

13. *Pioneer and Democrat*, August 16, 1857; Owens, "Political History of Minnesota," 446.

14. The "schedule" was incorporated in sections 16, 17, and 18 of the Constitution. See Anderson, *Constitution of Minnesota*, 133. For the account of the election here and below, see Folwell, *Minnesota*, 2:1-4; Ramsey Diary, entries for September and October 1857, Ramsey Papers. Charges and counter charges can be followed in the St. Paul newspapers for the months of October, November, and December. There is an almost complete gap in the Sibley correspondence for the late summer and fall of 1857.

15. Hall, *Observations ... of Political Contests in Minnesota*, 48-50.

16. Williams, *City of St. Paul*, 379-81.

17. Hughes, *Old Traverse des Sioux*, 10; Brainard, in *Minnesota History* 13:127-51.

18. Contract with Franklin Steele and Eli Pettijohn, February 19, 1856; Dousman to Sibley, June 3, 1857, Sibley Papers; Saby in *MHC* 15:19. In a lesser speculation, S

ley had also become a proprietor of the town of Breckenridge, proposed Minnesota terminus of the Minnesota and Pacific Railway. See letters of August 20 and September 22, 1858, Sibley Papers.

19. Karstad, "Political Party Alignments in Minnesota, 1854-1860," 136. Folwell cites evidence that Steele blamed Rice for deserting him in the 1857 election (*Minnesota*, 2:8), but a year later Steele was apparently reconciled with Rice and angry at Sibley. (J. J. Noah to Sibley, November 24, 1858, Sibley Papers.) On the notorious sweetheart deal by which Steele acquired Fort Snelling, see Folwell, *Minnesota* 1:503-13.

20. Sibley to LeDuc, December 19, 1857, LeDuc Papers; Rice to Anna Steele, August 29, 1858, Franklin Steele Papers; Rice to Sibley, June 22, 1858, Noah to Sibley, November 24, 1858, Sibley Papers. Owens, "Political History of Minnesota," 496.

21. Here and below, see Folwell, *Minnesota*, 2:4-8, 37-48.

22. John W. North to Sibley, May 24, 1858, Sibley Papers.

23. Minnesota, *Senate Journal*, 1857-58, p. 372-79.

24. *Senate Journal*, 1857-58, p. 374; Dousman to Sibley, April 12, 1858 (Ramsey quotation); David Cooper to Minnesota Secretary of State, June 21, 1858 (copy), Sibley Papers.

25. *Senate Journal*, 1857-58, p. 375, 376; Folwell, *Minnesota*, 2:33. Sibley's turnaround on the school lands issue may have been related to a plan for township organization adopted early in 1857 that he strongly opposed. See *Senate Journal*, 1859-60, p. 17.

26. Gilfillan, in *MHC* 12:56-59. Still a regent in 1856, Sibley had voted against the second building and the issuing of bonds.

27. *Senate Journal*, 1857-58, p. 421, 448; *House Journal*, 1857-58, p. 856; Isaac Atwater to Sibley, August 2, 11, and 23, September 28, November 30, 1858; Rice to Sibley, July 24, 1858; Ramsay Crooks to Sibley, September 4, 1858, Sibley Papers.

28. Folwell, *Minnesota*, 2:49-51. Sibley, perhaps foreseeing legal action and intending to argue the case himself, had ob-

tained admission to the Minnesota bar. See certification of admission to practice law before the Supreme Court of Minnesota, July 13, 1858, Sibley Papers.

29. Sarah Sibley to Mary LeDuc, March 18, 1859, William G. LeDuc Papers, Minnesota Historical Society. Her description suggests not gout, but possibly a pinched sciatic nerve.

30. *Senate Journal*, 1859-60, p. 11-15; John W. North to Sibley, December 2 and 4; Shields to Sibley, December 28, 1858, Sibley Papers.

31. Folwell, *Minnesota*, 2:24-26, 400-15; Meyer, *Santee Sioux*, 97-101.

32. Meyer, *Santee Sioux*, 92-96, 100-2, quotation, 102.

33. Meyer, *Santee Sioux*, 95-97, 102; Anderson, *Little Crow*, 107.

34. Meyer, *Santee Sioux*, 103, 107; Anderson, *Little Crow*, 108-11.

35. Meyer, *Santee Sioux*, 103-105; Folwell, *Minnesota*, 2:218-20.

36. Folwell, *Minnesota*, 2:27, 28n; Brown to Sibley, December 11, 1858, Sibley Papers.

37. *Senate Journal*, 1859-60, p. 23. See also Trenerry, *Murder in Minnesota*, 13-24.

38. *Senate Journal*, 1859-60, p. 24. The governors' records in the State Archives contain a letter to Sibley from his secretary, William F. Wheeler, describing the arrival of the troops in Monticello. They also include many financial records resulting from the action.

39. Another consideration mentioned in Sibley's favor was the administrative care and competence with which he organized and launched the mechanisms of state government. See Fridley, "Evaluation of Governors," 2, 12.

Notes for Chapter 12

1. Karstad, "Political Party Alignments in Minnesota, 1854-1860," 159-61. On Becker, see Williams, *City of St. Paul*, 250-53. He had been a law partner of Edmund Rice, brother of Henry.

2. The proceedings of the meeting are reported in the *Pioneer and Democrat*, January 13, 1860. See also Jorstad, "Minnesota's Role," in *Minnesota History* 37:45-47.

3. John H. Stevens to Franklin Steele, January 13, 1860, Steele Papers.

4. Becker to Sibley, February 11, 1860, Sibley Papers. Later that year the anti-Douglas editor of the *Henderson Democrat* stated that Sibley had been elected as a delegate uncommitted to Douglas and accused him of "infamously treacherous" conduct. See *Pioneer and Democrat,* June 15, 1860.

5. Here and below, see Jorstad, in *Minnesota History* 37:48-51.

6. *Pioneer and Democrat,* June 30 and July 3, 1860.

7. *Pioneer and Democrat,* August 23, 1860; C. C. Andrews to Sibley, August 27, 1860; August Belmont to Sibley, September 11, 1860, Sibley Papers.

8. *Pioneer and Democrat,* June 10, 1860.

9. *Dispatch,* October 25, 1908; S. J. Sawyer to William R. Brown, October 4, 1860, Brown Papers.

10. S. J. Sawyer to Brown, November 16, 1859; April 16, June 28, September 8, September 19, and October 4, 1860; January 21, 1861 (quote); Helen Sawyer to Brown, December 8, 1859, Brown Papers. Descendants of the Browns recall a letter from Sibley in which he described Helen's death as "A sad ending to an episode that should never have been." Personal communication, Loren Johnson to the author. See also a file memorandum on Sibley by Lee Anderson, June 6, 1972, MHS Archives. The letter has never been located.

11. Sawyer to Brown, October 4, 1860; *Dispatch,* October 25, 1908. Holcombe told Folwell that he had seen some of Helen's letters in the possession of Augusta Sibley Pope (Gussie) and that Mrs. Pope said Helen was her half-sister. See interview in Folwell Papers, 84:119.

12. Sibley to LeDuc, July 23, 1860; January 3 and March 23, 1861, LeDuc Papers; Sarah Sibley to Rachel Steele Johnson, November 18, 1861 (quotation), Sibley Papers. See also Grabitske, in *Midwest Open Air Museums Magazine.*

13. Sarah Sibley to Mary LeDuc, March 13, 1859, LeDuc Papers; to Rachel Johnson, November 18, 1861, Sibley Papers.

14. For the Mount Vernon Ladies Asso-

ciation and its political meanings, see West, *Domesticating History.*

15. For Sarah Sibley's activities on behalf of the Mount Vernon Association, see Grabitske, "First Lady of Preservation," in *Minnesota History* 58:407-16. Everett himself was unable to come, and a substitute gave the speech in Washington.

16. Sarah Sibley to Mary LeDuc, March 13, 1859, LeDuc Papers; LeDuc to Sibley, May 12, 1859, Sibley Papers.

17. *Pioneer and Democrat,* September 2, 19, and 27, 1860. For Seward, see also Blegen, in *Minnesota History* 8:151-61.

18. Chouteau Company to Sibley, August 22, 1860 (with enclosure); memorandum of agreement with Earle S. Goodrich, November 22, 1860; Goodrich to Sibley, March 6, 1861; Rice to Sibley, April 26, 1861; list of property owned by Chouteau Company in Dakota County, January 16, 1861; Act for re-chartering the Minneapolis and Cedar Valley Railroad, March 8, 1861, all in Sibley Papers.

19. Zorn, in *Mississippi Valley Historical Review.*

20. Sarah to Rachel, November 18, 1861; Folwell, 1:514.

21. Sarah to Rachel, November 18, 1861.

22. *Pioneer and Democrat,* August 1 (quotation), August 10-September 10, 1861; Owens, "Political History of Minnesota," 595-607.

23. Quoted in Folwell, *Minnesota,* 2:334.

24. *Pioneer and Democrat,* July 3, 1862. An undated and fragmentary draft of "Democratic Resolutions," written by several hands, including Sibley's, is filed in the Sibley Papers under date of January 1, 1861.

25. Folwell, *Minnesota,* 2:218, 393-400; Anderson, *Little Crow,* 110-13. The amount paid the lower bands was $96,000 for 320,000 acres. The Sisseton and Wahpeton received $170,880 for 569,600 acres. On Indian Office corruption in Minnesota see Nichols, *Lincoln and the Indians* 150-53.

26. Here and below, see Folwell, *Minnesota,* 2:228-36; Anderson, *Little Crow* 116-29.

27. Anderson and Woolworth, eds, *Through Dakota Eyes,* 39-42.

Notes for Chapter 13

1. Much has been published about the Dakota conflict of 1862. Standard historical accounts are in volume 2 of Folwell's *History of Minnesota* and Carley, *The Dakota War of 1862*. These have been supplemented by Anderson and Woolworth, eds., *Through Dakota Eyes*. The most recent of many popular books is Schultz, *Over the Earth I Come*. Official dispatches and documents are compiled in *Minnesota in the Civil and Indian Wars 1861-1865*, Vol. 2. Sibley's papers contain his order book for the campaign of 1862 and extracts from a series of letters written to his wife. Although addressed to Sarah Sibley, the letters were clearly intended also for a wider audience, probably including family members and close friends. That Sibley himself viewed them as a historical record is indicated by the fact that the extracts, copied in his own hand, were given to the Minnesota Historical Society along with the actual letters. Return I. Holcombe, the Society's librarian, compared the extracts and originals for accuracy, adding a few passages and several entire letters that he felt had been overlooked. The originals, along with Sarah's letters and all other family correspondence were then returned to the family. These extracts are cited below as "Sibley to Sarah."

2. West, *Sibley*, 254; *Civil and Indian Wars*, 2:165.

3. *Civil and Indian Wars*, 2:193; Sibley to Sarah, August 21 (quotation).

4. *Civil and Indian Wars*, 2:195; Fridley, in *Minnesota History* 38:116.

5. Sibley to Sarah, August 22; *Civil and Indian Wars*, 2:196 (quotation), 197.

6. *Press*, August 23; Brown to Ramsey, August 22, 1862, Joseph R. Brown and Samuel J. Brown Papers. Through most of the campaign Sibley shared a tent with Brown, Fowler, and the missionary Stephen Riggs, who joined the expedition on September 1. See Riggs to Mary Riggs, September 8 and November 5, 1862, Riggs Letters.

7. Sibley to Sarah, August 24; *Civil and Indian Wars*, 2:198, 200 (quotation).

8. Sibley to Sarah, August 24.

9. Donnelly's reports to Ramsey were published in the *Press*, August 23, 28 (quotation), and September 2, 1862.

10. More battles were fought years afterward by aging patriots than during the actual Dakota conflict. For the battle over who relieved Fort Ridgely, see Folwell, *Minnesota*, 2:383-86.

11. Sibley to Sarah, August 25 and 28; *Civil and Indian Wars*, 2:200.

12. *Civil and Indian Wars*, 2:200, 201.

13. Donnelly, in *Press*, August 27; Sibley to Sarah, August 24 and September 2.

14. *Press*, August 24, 1862.

15. *Press*, August 30, 1862.

16. *St. Cloud Democrat*, September 4; *Press*, September 3, 1862.

17. *Press*, September 10, 1862.

18. Sibley to Sarah, August 28, 30, and 31.

19. Sibley to Sarah, August 31 and September 17; *Civil and Indian Wars*, 2:219; Folwell, *Minnesota*, 2:386.

20. Exactly who was in command at Birch Coulee became the subject of a battle mounted in the 1890s by Hiram P. Grant, the captain of the infantry company. (See Folwell, *Minnesota*, 2:386-91.) Sibley's official reports and private letters are all clear that he appointed Brown, but some historians have suggested that this was a fiction intended to establish the civilian status of the burial party and save Sibley the embarrassment of a military defeat. (See, for example, Schultz, *Over the Earth*, 201.) There are several objections to the theory: (1) There was no clear distinction between civilian and military in the force under Sibley. (2) Brown still held a commission in the state militia and was no more a civilian than Sibley himself. (3) A fiasco blamed on an inexperienced young officer could hardly have been more embarrassing to Sibley than one caused by his well-known friend and political crony.

21. Sibley to Sarah, September 2 and 4; *Civil and Indian Wars*, 2:212-23.

22. Sibley to Sarah, September 4; Samuel J. Brown, in *Brown's Valley Reporter*, September 8, 1887.

23. Sibley to Sarah, September 4; *St. Cloud Democrat*, September 11, 1862. The

largest group of disgusted volunteers was from Hennepin County—a Republican stronghold—and Swisshelm was an ardent abolitionist and radical Republican. Another Republican, Horace Austin, scolded Ramsey for appointing a rival who had been elected "on the strength of Indian votes" and decried Sibley's "imbecility." (See Folwell, *Minnesota*, 2:176n.)

24. Sibley to Sarah, September 5 and 7.

25. Sibley to Sarah, September 12 and 17 (quotation), 1862; *Civil and Indian Wars*, 2:230; Riggs to Ramsey, in *Civil and Indian Wars*, 2:226.

26. Sibley to Sarah, September 10, 1862. The full correspondence of Sibley with Little Crow and others is reproduced in West, *Sibley*, 262-65.

27. Esther Wakeman in *Through Dakota Eyes*, 55.

28. Sibley to Sarah, September 17.

29. *Civil and Indian Wars*, 2:232 (quotation), 234-36.

30. *Civil and Indian Wars*, 2:235.

31. Sibley to Sarah, September 27.

32. Sibley to Sarah, September 27 and 28, October 10. For a full account of Sarah Wakefield's captivity, see Namias, *White Captives*, 204-61.

33. Sibley to Sarah, September 27; Samuel J. Brown in *Through Dakota Eyes*, 74.

34. Sibley to Sarah, September 27; Riggs to Mary Riggs, October 6, 1862, Riggs Letters; *Civil and Indian Wars*, 2:255, 256, 258.

35. Sibley to Sarah, October 25. "Mr. Sibley is flattered a good deal," the watchful Riggs observed, "But I don't discover any particular increase of self esteem." Riggs to Mary Riggs, October 17, 1862, Riggs Letters.

36. *Civil and Indian Wars*, 2:256, 257 (quotation).

37. For an in-depth discussion of the Dakota trials and their legal aspects, see Chomsky, in *Stanford Law Review*.

38. Chomsky, in *Stanford Law Review*, 54. The actual number of settlers slain in the first days of the war is not known. It has been estimated at anywhere from 250 to 1,000.

39. Sibley to Sarah, October 11; Riggs to Mary Riggs, October 17 and 25 1862, Riggs

Letters. Flandrau's words were recalled (with quite a different sentiment) in 1884. They are quoted in Folwell, *Minnesota*, 3:163.

40. Sibley to Sarah, October 13, 17. Sibley was furious after learning that some of his own men had scalped Indian bodies after the battle at Wood Lake. See General Order Number 53, Order Book, Volume 103, Sibley Papers.

41. Sibley to Sarah, October 25.

42. Sibley to Sarah, October 17.

43. Riggs to Mary Riggs, November 5, 1862, Riggs Letters.

44. Sibley to Sarah, November 12; West, *Sibley*, 280; George Crooks, in *Through Dakota Eyes*, 262.

45. Folwell, Minnesota, 2:252; Samuel J. Brown and Good Star Woman, in *Through Dakota Eyes*, 227, 263; Angela Cavender Wilson, in Mihesuah, ed., *Natives and Academics*, 31-33.

46. Riggs to Mary Riggs, November 11, 1862, Riggs Letters. In the same letter Riggs reported stories circulating in the town that Sibley himself had three Dakota wives and several children.

47. Folwell, *Minnesota*, 2:188; Sibley to Sarah, November 3.

48. A copy of the order, in Lincoln's handwriting, is owned by the Minnesota Historical Society. See Jane S. Davis, in *Minnesota History* 41:117-25. Essentially, Lincoln took the position that the Dakota were prisoners of war and allowed the execution only of those for whom the trial records showed actual crimes. One of the 39 received a last-minute reprieve. Sibley defended his own position in letters to Bishop Henry B. Whipple and to the Department of the Interior. (See Chomsky, in *Stanford Law Review*, 54.)

49. *Civil and Indian Wars*, 2:291.

Notes for Chapter 14

1. Whipple, *Lights and Shadows*, 132 (quotation).

2. Folwell, *Minnesota*, 2:208, 297-99 Riggs to Mary Riggs, October 15 (quota tion), November 3, 1862, Riggs Letters Nichols, *Lincoln and the Indians*, 110.

3. Whipple to Sibley, March 7, 1863

Sibley to Whipple, December 7, 1862 (first quotation); March 11, 1863 (final quotation), all in Whipple Papers.

4. List of scouts dated May 5, 1863, Sibley Papers; Sibley to Whipple, October 15, 1863, February 17, 1864, in Whipple Papers; accounts of Gabriel and Victor Renville in *Through Dakota Eyes*, 273–78.

5. Sibley to Whipple, September 26, October 15, 1863, February 17, 1864; George H. Spencer to Whipple, May 11, 1863, February 13, 1864; Taopi to Whipple, May 4, 1864, all in Whipple Papers; Folwell, *Minnesota*, 2:263.

6. Gilman et al., *The Red River Trails*, 20–24. The first trains of gold seekers had traveled to Montana in the early summer of 1862. See White, ed., *Ho! for the Gold Fields*, 23–72.

7. West, *Sibley*, 297–301, 335–37; Folwell, *Minnesota*, 2:186n.

8. Folwell, *Minnesota*, 2:289–91; Williams, *City of St. Paul*, 192.

9. See Babcock, in *Minnesota History* 38:274–86; *Civil and Indian Wars*, 2:294–96.

10. *Press*, May 6, 1863; University of Illinois, *Mereness Calendar*, 12:239, 242 (quotation).

11. Sibley to Brown, May 18, 1863, J. R. Brown Papers; *Pioneer*, July 18, 1863; Neill, ed., *Glimpses of the Nation's Struggle*, 180; University of Illinois, *Mereness Calendar*, 12:244. Sibley's staff is listed by Wright in *North Dakota History* 29:296. On Pope, see Cozzens, *John Pope*, 148, 204; on Beever, see *Press*, August 15, 1863.

12. Folwell, *Minnesota*, 2:266, 267n.; Wright, in *North Dakota History* 29:296.

13. Sibley Diary, June 13 (quotation), 14 and 15, 1863. Sibley Papers. This daily record of the 1863 campaign is apparently the only diary that Sibley ever kept. Unless otherwise noted, details of the expedition are from this source.

14. Diary, June 17 (quotations).

15. Neill, ed., *Glimpses of the Nation's Struggle*, 179; *Pioneer*, July 18, 1863.

16. Diary, July 10 (quotation).

17. For the gold seekers, who were led by James Liberty Fisk, see White, ed., *Ho! for the Gold Fields*, 79. This camp was about two

miles south of present Binford, North Dakota. The expedition crossed the Sheyenne where state highway 26 now bridges it, at the town of Sibley. The fatal illness of the two children was not identified. It may have been either diphtheria or scarlet fever. Frank was earlier reported to have had a sore throat.

18. Diary, July 20 (quotation)

19. Folwell, *Minnesota*, 2:429.

20. Diary, July 26 (quotation). For a summary of the military action based on many first-hand accounts, see Folwell, *Minnesota*, 2:269–76. The number of Indians engaged is unknown, and estimates at the time were probably exaggerated. Sibley guessed that the final attack involved up to 2,500 Dakota. The number of Indians known to have been slain was only 44, but Sibley guessed the actual number at between 120 and 150.

21. Diary, July 31 (quotation).

22. "General Sibley's Order," in *Press*, August 15, 1863.

23. Josephy, *The Civil War in the American West*, 143–46; Samuel J. Brown to Joseph R. Brown, November 13, 1863, J. R. Brown Papers.

24. *Press*, September 12, 1863. The *Press*, though Republican, was owned by Marshall and thus relatively friendly to Sibley.

25. *State Atlas* (Minneapolis), September 23; *Pioneer* as quoted in *State Atlas*, September 30, 1863.

26. Folwell, *Minnesota*, 2:290; Gluek, in *Minnesota History* 34:319.

27. Lass, in *Minnesota History* 39:227–40; Samuel J. Brown to Joseph R. Brown, November 23, 1863, January 6, 1864; Sibley to J. R. Brown (private), December 4, 1863, J. R. Brown Papers.

28. J. R. Brown to Sibley, December 10, 1863, Sibley Papers; to Samuel Brown, December 13, 1863, to his daughter, January 14, 1864, J. R. Brown Papers; Gluek, in *Minnesota History* 34:320.

29. Folwell, *Minnesota*, 2:443; Gluek, in *Minnesota History* 34:321–24; *Civil and Indian Wars*, 2:545; Sibley to Pope, January 20, 1864, Sibley Papers.

30. Folwell, *Minnesota*, 2:445–48. Brown, who was at Pembina and the Red

River settlement during these events, reported in a letter to one of his daughters that twenty or more Dakota children had been "sold" to Red River settlers to save them from starvation (February 13, 1864, J. R. Brown Papers).

31. See correspondence in the Sibley Papers from Ramsey, Donnelly, and others in January, February, and March 1864. A copy of Sibley's commission is filed under date of March 23; *Civil and Indian Wars,* 2:524.

32. *Civil and Indian Wars,* 2:525; Gilman, et al., *The Red River Trails,* 70; White, ed., *Ho! For the Gold Fields,* 107.

33. Kingsbury, in *MHC* 8:449-52.

34. Andre to Sibley, August 25, 1863, Sibley Papers.

35. J. R. Brown to Samuel Brown, October 23, orders to J. R. Brown, November 21, 1863; J. R. Brown to Gabriel Renville, January 31, 1864, J. R. Brown Papers; J. R. Brown to Sibley, November 26, 29, December 5, 8, and 10, 1863, Sibley Papers.

36. J. R. Brown to Sibley, September 8 (quotation), 16, October 18, 1864, Sibley Papers; Brown to Major Robert Rose, commanding at Fort Wadsworth, December 9, 1864, Brown Papers.

37. J. R. Brown to Sibley, December 18, 1864, Sibley Papers; Brown to Rose, January 2, 9, Pope to Sibley (copy), February 1, Brown to Captain A. S. Everest, temporary commander at Fort Wadsworth, February 24, 1865, J. R. Brown Papers.

38. J. R. Brown to Everest, February 7, 28, to Rose, May 1, 1865, J. R. Brown Papers.

39. Pope to Sibley, with enclosed copy of letter from Sully, June 30, 1864, Sibley Papers; Nichols, *Lincoln and the Indians,* 150-53; Ellis, *General Pope and U.S. Indian Policy,* 40-48.

40. Pope to Sibley, November 23, 1864, Sibley Papers. Sibley's response to Pope's prodding is printed in *War of the Rebellion, Official Records,* Series 1, Volume 41, Part 4, 710. He concluded the letter by comparing U.S. Indian policy with what he considered the more firm and honorable British policy. His suggestion concerning Minnesota Indians and the observation on Devils Lake is printed in Series 1, Volume 41, Part 2, 676.

41. Sibley to Whipple, July 25, August 15, August 23, 1864, Whipple Papers; Whipple to Sibley, July 27 (quotation), August 11, 1864, Sibley Papers. Whipple's support was not to be discounted, since General Henry W. Halleck, chief of staff in Washington, was the bishop's cousin and close friend. In 1864 reformers, including Whipple, had not yet taken a stand against military control of Indian affairs, as they did several years later. See Mardock, *Reformers and the American Indian,* 19-22.

42. Sibley to Pope (copy), December 10, Ramsey to Sibley, December 13 and 26, Pope to Sibley, December 29, 1864, Sibley Papers.

43. Folwell, *Minnesota,* 2:346-50; *Press,* May 5, 1865; J. R. Brown to Rose, May 16, 1865, J. R. Brown Papers.

44. *Press,* May 5 (quotation) and 6, 1865; *Central Republican,* May 17, 1865.

45. For an account of Edmunds's role and the antagonism between the army and civil authorities, see Lamar, *Dakota Territory,* 102-7. Edmunds to Sibley, September 20, 1865, Sibley Papers.

46. Pope to Sibley, August (no day), 1865; James Harlan to Sibley, August 15, 1865.

47. Curtis to Sibley, June 18, July 12, 1865; Sibley to Curtis (extract), July 28, 1865.

48. Harlan to Sibley (telegram), August 30, 1865; Sibley to Harlan, September 11, 1865. A printed copy of the instructions and three treaty articles in Sibley's writing are also in the Sibley Papers.

49. John P. Williamson to Samuel J. Brown, December 6, 1865, J. R. Brown Papers; Meyer, *Santee Sioux,* 155-58; Office of Indian Affairs, *Report,* 1865, 25-27; 1866, 44-46.

50. Lamar, *Dakota Territory,* 106; Office of Indian Affairs, *Report,* 1865, 28.

51. Sibley to Stanton, September 12, 1865, Sibley Papers. All other correspondence concerning his promotion and mustering out is reproduced in West, *Sibley,* 339-40.

52. D. N. Cooley, Commissioner of Indian Affairs, to Sibley, April 28, Sibley to Cooley, May 2, 1866, Sibley Papers.

53. Brown to Sibley, March 16 (quotation), April 7, 12, 16, and May 5 (quoted word); General J. M. Corse to Sibley, March 27; Sibley to Brown (copy) April 16; Cooley to Sibley, May 2, 1866, Sibley Papers.

54. Office of Indian Affairs, *Report*, 1866, 46, 48; Brown to Sibley, August 20, 1866, Sibley Papers.

55. Meyer, *Santee Sioux*, 199-201, 220-22. An extended account of the case of the Sisseton and Wahpeton claims, which was not concluded until 1908, is in Folwell, *Minnesota*, 2:418-37.

Notes for Chapter 15

1. Grabitske, "Sarah Jane," in *Midwest Open Air Museums Magazine*, 27. Johnson to Sibley, August 31, 1866, Sibley Papers.

2. The *Pioneer* of November 16, 1867, carried a detailed account of the tragedy.

3. *Pioneer*, May 22, 1869; Anna Barney Steele Journal, September 19, 1868; Sarah to Mary LeDuc, April 30, 1869, LeDuc Papers. Pope had chosen to make his career with the peacetime army after the war, but he resigned his commission in 1871. Whether the Sibleys had personal objections to him is not known.

4. Sarah to Mary LeDuc, April 30, 1869; *Pioneer*, May 22, *Minneapolis Tribune*, May 22, 1869.

5. Blegen and Davidson, eds. *Iron Face*, xx-xxi; Jane Frazer to Sibley, October 24, 1868, Sibley Papers.

6. J. Fletcher Williams to Sibley, January 22, 1867; Williams in *MHC* 6:297-302. Letters in the Sibley Papers from Augustin Ravoux, December 15, 1866; Alexander Faribault, April 20, 1867; Gideon Pond, July 14, 1868; and Edward D. Neill, November 17, 1868, show his efforts to collect material for the reminiscences. Sibley wrote memoirs of Faribault, John Other Day, the Reverend John Mattocks, Gideon Pond, and Hercules Dousman. The piece on Faribault was begun at the time of the old trader's death, part of it appearing as an article in the *Pioneer and Democrat*, August 26, 1860. The sporting piece was apparently solicited by the editor of *Forest and Stream*, a successor to Porter's publications.

7. Johnson was appointed instead to the chair of military science and mathematics, which he soon left to devote himself to business. See Buck, ed., *William Watts Folwell*, 186.

8. Photocopies of twenty-seven letters written by Sibley to Louis Dousman from 1868 to 1882 are in the possession of the author; originals are in the State Historical Society of Wisconsin. Henceforth they are cited as Louis Dousman correspondence.

9. The first quotation is in Gilfillan, in *MHC* 9:179. For Goodrich, see his memoir of Brown in *MHC* 3:204.

10. *Pioneer*, November 18, 1870; J[ohn]. A. Reed to Angus Brown, December 1, 1870; undated, unsigned draft of letter to Reed; Robert Rose to Samuel J. Brown, December 23, 1870, all in J. R. Brown Papers; Brown to Sibley, December 11, 1858, Sibley Papers. A brief record of Sibley's funeral address is in West, *Sibley*, 405, but since the *Pioneer* reported it as "extemporaneous," he may have composed the written version later.

11. *Pioneer*, November 23, 1870. For Indian policy in these years, see Prucha, *Indian Policy in Crisis*, 16-69.

12. Sherman to Sibley, June 23, August 1, 1866, November 25, 1867, Sibley Papers.

13. Meyer, *Santee Sioux*, 200, 220; Benjamin Thompson to Sibley, January 5, Brown to Sibley, February 11, 1868; Sibley Papers; Brown to Whipple, August 3, 1868, Whipple to Orville H. Browning, Secretary of the Interior, August 17, 1868, Browning to Whipple, August 20, 1868, Whipple Papers. This appropriation is not mentioned In the Indian Office *Report* for 1868, possibly because it was funneled through the U.S. Treasury and not through the Indian Office.

14. Whipple, *Lights and Shadows*, 285-93; Whipple to Sibley, enclosing power of attorney, October 5, 1869, Ely S. Parker to Sibley, October 20, 1869, Sibley Papers; Office of Indian Affairs, *Report*, 1869, 29, 326-29. Beginning as early as April there are numerous letters in Sibley's papers relating to relief of the Dakota, many of them addressed to Whipple.

15. Office of Indian Affairs, *Report*, 1869, 320-25; Sibley to J. D. Cox, December 19, to

Ely S. Parker, December 19 (quotation), 1869; to General W. S. Hancock, April 22; from Whipple, July 4, August 10, 1870, Sibley Papers.

16. Whipple to Sibley, August 10, 1870 (quotation); Henry Belland to Sibley, August 6, 1870; Office of Indian Affairs, *Report*, 1870, 225-27.

17. Fite, in *Minnesota History*, 37:204-6; Atkins, *Harvest of Grief*, 44-46, 58. State relief in the form of seed grain was declared unconstitutional by the Kansas Supreme Court in 1875 but was apparently not challenged in Minnesota until the 1890s. It was upheld by the North Dakota Supreme Court in 1890 and by Minnesota in 1898. See Abbott, *Public Assistance: American Principles and Policies*, 1:12-15.

18. Stephen Miller to Sibley, November 8, December 22, Minutes of St. Paul Chamber of Commerce, December 22, 1873; undated list of stockholder donations, filed under date of January 1, 1874, Sibley Papers; *Pioneer*, December 23, 24, 25, 27, 28, 30, 1873; Atkins, *Harvest of Grief*, 60, 67.

19. Here and below, see Atkins, *Harvest of Grief*, 68-78; Folwell, *Minnesota*, 3:97-110. Correspondence and financial records concerning the disbursement of grasshopper relief funds fill an entire roll of microfilm in the Sibley Papers.

20. Atkins, *Harvest of Grief*, 79-81; Trenerry, in *Minnesota History* 36:56-60.

21. Prucha, *Indian Policy in Crisis*, 40, 69.

22. Meyer, *Santee Sioux*, 200-12, 231; letters from Riggs, May 4, 1871, from Renville, February 6, 1875; from J. Q Smith, July 30, 1875, Sibley Papers. Sibley's papers contain frequent correspondence about conditions and appointments at both the Sisseton and Devils Lake reservations throughout the years from 1875 to 1880.

23. Appointment to Board of Indian Commissioners, July 10, letters from Delano, July 17, and Forbes, July 26, 1874. Sibley Papers; Sibley to Abbie Potts, July 17, 1874 (quotation), Livingston Papers.

24. Sibley to Clinton B. Fisk, January 9, 1875. "It is pretty fatiguing to ride 1200 or 1500 miles without stopping," he told Abbie Potts. (See letter of November 20, 1874,

Livingston Papers.) Correspondence with various Indian Office officials and the Board of Commissioners appears in the Sibley Papers for the winter of 1874 and throughout 1875 and 1876. For his continuing responsibility regarding the Devils Lake and Sisseton reservations, see especially letters dated May 10, 25, and 28, June 4, 19, and 22, July 30, November 8, 1875.

25. Sibley to Louis Dousman, July 8, 1876, Louis Dousman correspondence; letters from Whipple, September 18, October 1; from George W. Manypenny, November 23, 1876, Sibley Papers. Sibley's statement, directed to Manypenny, was printed as part of the Board of Indian Commissioners, *Annual Report* for 1876 (Washington, 1877).

26. Mardock, *Reformers and the American Indian*, 144-46, 157-59. Sibley's loss of influence in Indian affairs is clear in the courteous but perfunctory acknowledgments he received from Secretary of the Interior Carl Schurz and in his failure, despite efforts that continued through 1879, to have a small band of Yanktonais under Drifting Goose attached to the Sisseton reservation. (See letters of October 20, December 19, 1877; January 17 and 28, August 13, 1878; February 12, June 26, 1879, all in Sibley Papers.)

27. White Cloud to Sibley, May 19, 1881; Folwell, *Minnesota*, 4:209-11.

28. White Cloud to Sibley, May 11, 1882.

29. *Pioneer*, May 13, 1882, p. 3; Thomas Simpson to Sibley, May 13; White Cloud to Sibley, June 15, 1882; undated speech of White Cloud; Sibley to Flat Mouth, April 28, May 5, 1883, Sibley Papers.

30. Here and below, see Folwell, *Minnesota*, 3:418-41. The list of bondholders compiled in 1866 along with comments by the commission is in an appendix to the Minnesota *House Journal* for 1881.

31. Dousman to Sibley, January 31, 1867, Sibley Papers. Dousman's bonds must have been among the 435 unaccounted for in 1866, since he told Sibley he had not learned of the survey in time to report them. For an example of Sibley's prickly reaction to Republican charges, see his exchange of letters with Senator James R. McMillan, April 12, 15, 20, 1881, Sibley Papers. See also West, *Sibley*, 345-54.

32. Here and below, see Folwell's detailed account of the redemption of the railroad bonds in *Minnesota*, 3:418–41.

33. Whipple to Sibley, February 8, 1877, Sibley Papers. The letter is clearly intended for public distribution.

34. A copy of the petition in Sibley's writing is in the Sibley Papers under date of May 17, 1880.

35. Sibley to Trowbridge, February 24, 1881, copy in Sibley Papers microfilm edition. Davis is quoted in *Folwell*, 3:163.

Notes for Chapter 16

1. A general statement of the St. Paul Gas Light Company from May 1, 1867, to February 18, 1868, is in the Louis Dousman correspondence. Many of these letters bear the company's letterhead and report on its business. See also Goodrich to Sibley, March 31, 1884, Sibley Papers.

2. Letters of April 4 and 11, 1867, June 14, December 8, 1869, Sibley Papers; *Press*, April 30, 1869; Sibley to Louis Dousman on City Bank letterhead, March 13, April 2, 27, September 23, 1872, Louis Dousman correspondence; Williams, in *MHC* 6:294, 295.

3. Williams, *City of St. Paul*, 426; Williams, in *MHC* 6:294, 296, 297; *Pioneer Press*, January 17 (quotation), October 13, 1882. One of Sibley's final efforts with the St. Paul Chamber of Commerce was to supply relief for victims of an earthquake in Charleston, South Carolina. See correspondence for September 1886 in the Sibley Papers.

4. Stock certificate of the Minnesota Gold Mining Company, Richard M. Eames Papers, Minnesota Historical Society; W. T. Sherman to Sibley, June 23, 1866; letters of June 23, December 21, 1867, March 13, 1870, Sibley Papers.

5. *Pioneer*, September 3, 1873, p. 2; July 12, 1878, p. 7. Sibley to Abbie Potts, August 26, 1873, July 28, August 3, 6, 1875, Livingston Papers. Today Silver Islet is a part of Ontario's Sibley Provincial Park.

6. Letters from J. B. McGevin, May 14, William P. Carlin, June 15, William B. O'Donoghue, June 21, 1873, Sibley Papers; Martin, *James J. Hill*, 94–96. Sibley's corre-

spondence with Louis Dousman about the business of the gas company reveals his constant attention to the cost of coal.

7. Here and below, see Martin, *James J. Hill*, 68–83, 121–73.

8. Clipping from *Fergus Falls Weekly Journal*, May 17, 1888, in MHS Scrapbooks, 9:57. This source, containing an obituary of Kittson and an interview with Sibley, reports that Sibley held Kittson's full power of attorney in later years.

9. *Press*, May 4, 1865; Bishop, in *MHC* 10:399–415 (St. Paul, 1905). In 1881 the St. Paul and Sioux City merged with two lines in northwestern Wisconsin to become the Chicago, St. Paul, Minneapolis, and Omaha. The following year it came under control of the Chicago & North Western system, where it operated with semi-independence for many years. See Grant, in *Minnesota History* 57:190–210. For the Hastings and Dakota, see William G. LeDuc, "Railroad Reminiscences," in the LeDuc Papers. An indication of Sibley's financial standing is a list of assessments for personal property in Ramsey County, published in the *Pioneer Press* for July 21, 1882. Sibley owned a modest $6,885, compared with $50,000 each for Kittson and Hill, $20,000 for brewer Theodore Hamm, and more than $10,000 for many others.

10. Numerous letters in both the Sibley and Livingston Papers refer to the presence of Gussie and Captain Pope in St. Paul. In late 1869 Pope was apparently helping Sibley with the task of supplying the Sisseton and Wahpeton. See Sibley to Jared Daniels, December 18, 1869, copied by Pope, Sibley Papers.

11. Potts to Abbie Potts, January 11, 1870. This is the first of many letters in the Livingston Papers from Potts to his wife and various children. Family usage varied in the spelling of Abbie's name. It sometimes appears as "Abby" and occasionally as Abian.

12. Potts to Mary Potts, March 20, to Abbie Potts, March 28, 1870.

13. John M. Lindley, in *Ramsey County History* 34:10–12; Sibley to Louis Dousman, December 30, 1874, Louis Dousman correspondence.

14. Sibley to Abbie Potts, May 5 (quota-

tion), July 12, 1877, Livingston Papers; to Charles F. Sibley, February 16, 1884, Sibley Papers.

15. Sibley to Trowbridge, January 17 (second quote), February 14, June 7 (first quote), 1880, copies in the Sibley Papers microfilm edition. Alfred was apparently unhappy in school and returned home before finishing. In April 1882 he graduated from the St. Paul Business College. See *Pioneer Press*, April 1, 1882, p. 7.

16. *Pioneer Press*, September 11, 1880; Williams, *St. Paul*, 225n. Johnson, like Sibley, was active with the Chamber of Commerce.

17. Whipple to Sibley, December 22, 1865; Williams, in *MHC* 6:304 (quotation); Nathaniel West to Sibley, October 31, 1890, Livingston Papers; West, *Sibley*, 402-4. Sibley raised eyebrows in St. Paul when, during his term as a school inspector, he advocated that the city support Catholic as well as public schools. See Williams, above, 296.

18. For the St. Paul sociopolitical scene, see Wingerd, *Claiming the City*.

19. Gilman, in *Minnesota History* 36:300-8. For Donnelly's political career, see Ridge, *Ignatius Donnelly: Portrait of a Politician*.

20. Sibley to Trowbridge, September 17, 1880, copy in the Sibley microfilm edition.

21. Sibley to Trowbridge, March 19, 1880; Folwell, *Minnesota*, 3:162; Williams, in *MHC* 6:295; *St. Paul Dispatch*, September 2, 1887, 2. The proposal for a statue was apparently part of an unsuccessful effort to promote a residential real estate development on Pilot Knob. See White and Woolworth, "*Oheyawahe* or Pilot Knob," 17-21. Copy in possession of the author.

22. A copy of Castle's verses, and Sibley's address on the occasion are in the Sibley papers, June 6, 1888. See also West, *Sibley*, 374.

23. Pond's letter (January 30, 1889) and Sibley's reply (February 1, 1889), are printed in S. W. Pond, Jr., *Two Volunteer Missionaries*, 246-48.

24. Unidentified newspaper clipping from 1893 in Minnesota Historical Society Scrapbooks, 96:5-6 (M584, roll 27).

25. Baker, *Lives of the Governors*, 103. Before publication in the *MHC*, Williams's essay appeared in the *Pioneer Press*.

26. For an account of the struggle to preserve the house, see Ann Marcaccini and George Woytanowitz in *Minnesota History*. Williams also pointed out that the house was "the first permanent residence, strictly speaking, built in Minnesota," as though urging the need to preserve it. (Quotations, 269.)

27. Shortridge, *Transition of a Typical Frontier*, 111.

28. Kennedy, *Men on the Moving Frontier*, 39, 41. Lovelace's book was acclaimed in Minnesota and became immediately popular. It was reprinted by the University of Minnesota Press in 1949, and a paperback edition was published by the Minnesota Historical Society in 1992 with an introduction by Rhoda R. Gilman.

29. Cronon, Miles, and Gitlin, eds., *Under an Open Sky*, 9.

30. An overview of recent comparative history by Richard W. Slatta appeared in the *Journal of the West*, for Winter 2003. Especially influential in rethinking the nature of the Great Lakes frontier has been Richard White's *The Middle Ground*, published in 1991.

31. Most of the characterizations referred to have been made in oral presentations or in private correspondence, such as personal communications to the author from Angela Cavender Wilson and David Larsen. For a published example, see columnist Nick Coleman in *Pioneer Press Dispatch*, March 4, 1989, sec. A, p. 10.

SELECT BIBLIOGRAPHY

Abbreviations

MHC   *Minnesota Historical Collections*
MHS   Minnesota Historical Society
MPHC   *Michigan Pioneer and Historical Collections*
WHC   *Wisconsin Historical Collections*

Books

Abbott, Edith. *Public Assistance: American Principles and Policies in Five Parts: With Select Documents.* New York: Russell and Russell, 1966.

Anderson, Gary Clayton. *Kinsmen of Another Kind: Dakota-White Relations in the Upper Mississippi Valley.* Lincoln: University of Nebraska Press, 1984.

———. *Little Crow: Spokesman for the Sioux.* St. Paul: Minnesota Historical Society Press, 1986.

Anderson, Gary Clayton, and Alan R. Woolworth, eds. *Through Dakota Eyes: Narrative Accounts of the Minnesota Indian War of 1862.* St. Paul: Minnesota Historical Society Press, 1988.

Anderson, William. *A History of the Constitution of Minnesota.* Minneapolis: University of Minnesota Press, 1921.

Atkins, Annette. *Harvest of Grief.* St. Paul: Minnesota Historical Society Press, 1984.

Baker, James H. *Lives of the Governors of Minnesota,* Vol. 13. St. Paul: MHC, 1908).

Bald, F. Clever. *Detroit's First American Decade 1796-1805.* Ann Arbor: University of Michigan Press, 1948.

Bayliss, Joseph E., Estelle L. Bayliss, and Milo M. Quaife. *River of Destiny: The Saint Marys.* Detroit: Wayne State University Press, 1955.

Blegen, Theodore C. *Minnesota: A History of the State.* Minneapolis: University of Minnesota Press, 1963.

Blegen, Theodore C., and Davidson, Sarah A. *Iron Face: The Adventures of Jack Frazer, Frontier Warrior, Scout, and Hunter.* Chicago: The Caxton Club, 1950.

Bond, Beverley W., Jr. *The Civilization of the Old Northwest: A Study of Political, Social, and Economic Development, 1788-1812.* New York: Macmillan, 1934.

———. *The Foundations of Ohio.* Columbus, Ohio, 1941.

Bowers, John O. *The Old Bailly Homestead.* Gary, Ind.: s.n., 1922.

Bray, Martha Coleman. *Joseph Nicollet and His Map.* Philadelphia: American Philosophical Society, 1980.

Bremer, Richard G. *Indian Agent and Wilderness Scholar: The Life of Henry Rowe Schoolcraft.* Mount Pleasant, Mich.: Central Michigan University, 1987.

Brown, Jennifer S. H. *Strangers in Blood: Fur Trade Company Families in Indian Country.* Vancouver: University of British Columbia Press, 1980.

Buck, Solon J., ed. *William Watts Folwell: The Autobiography and Letters of a Pioneer Culture.* Minneapolis: University of Minnesota Press, 1933.

Burnet, Jacob. *Notes on the Early Settlement of the North-Western Territory.* Cincinnati: Derby, Bradley, & Co., 1847.

Burton, M. Agnes, ed., and Clarence M. Burton, comp. *Proceedings of the Land Board of Detroit.* n.p., 1916.

Burton, Clarence M. William Stocking, and Gordon K. Miller, eds. *The City of Detroit Michigan 1701-1922.* Detroit and Chicago: S. J. Clarke Pub. Co., 1922.

Carley, Kenneth. *The Dakota War of 1862,*

Rev. ed. St. Paul: Minnesota Historical Society Press, 2001.

Cohen, Henry. *Business and Politics in America from the Age of Jackson to the Civil War.* Westport, Conn.: Greenwood Publishing Company, 1971.

Comfort, Benjamin F. *Lewis Cass and the Indian Treaties: A Monograph on the Indian Relations of the Northwest Territory from 1813 to 1831.* Detroit: s.n., 1923.

Cozzens, Peter. *General John Pope: A Life for the Nation.* Champaign: University of Illinois Press, 2000.

Cronon, William, George Miles, and Jay Gitlin, eds. *Under an Open Sky: Rethinking America's Western Past.* New York: W. W. Norton, 1992.

Curtiss-Wedge, Franklyn, ed. *History of Dakota and Goodhue Counties.* Chicago: H. C. Cooper, Jr., and Co., 1910.

Derleth, August. *Bright Journey.* New York: Scribner, 1940.

———. *The House on the Mound.* New York: Duell, Sloan, and Pearce, 1958.

Dictionary of American Biography, vol. 9. New York: Scribner's, 1964.

Eastman, Mrs. Mary. *Dahcotah: Life and Legends of the Sioux Around Fort Snelling,* Reprint ed. Minneapolis: Ross & Haines, Inc., 1962.

Ellet, Mrs. [Elizabeth Fries]. *Pioneer Women of the West.* New York: Charles Scribner, 1852.

Ellis, Richard N. *General Pope and U.S. Indian Policy.* Albuquerque: University of New Mexico Press, 1970.

Featherstonhaugh, George W. *A Canoe Voyage up the Minnay Sotor,* Reprint ed. St. Paul: MHS, 1970.

Folwell, William Watts. *A History of Minnesota,* 4 vols. St. Paul: MHS, 1921, 1924, 1926, 1930.

Fremont, John Charles. *Memoir of My Life,* Vol. 1. Chicago and New York: Belford, Clarke & Co., 1887.

Folsom, W. H. C. *Fifty Years in the Northwest.* St. Paul: Pioneer Press Co., 1888.

Gibbon, Guy. *The Sioux: The Dakota and Lakota Nations.* Malden, Mass.: Blackwell, 2003.

Gilman, Carolyn, Alan R. Woolworth, Douglas A. Birk, and Bruce M. White. *Where

Two Worlds Meet: The Great Lakes Fur Trade. St. Paul: MHS, 1982.

Gilman, Rhoda R., Carolyn Gilman, and Deborah M. Stultz. *The Red River Trails: Oxcart Routes Between St. Paul and the Selkirk Settlement, 1820-1870.* St. Paul: Minnesota Historical Society Press, 1979.

Gilpin, Alec R. *The Territory of Michigan.* East Lansing: Michigan State University Press, 1970.

Goodman, Nancy, and Robert Goodman. *Joseph R. Brown: Adventurer On The Minnesota Frontier, 1820-1849.* Rochester, Minn.: Lone Oak Press, 1996.

Hage, George S. *Newspapers on the Minnesota Frontier 1849-1860.* St. Paul: MHS, 1967.

Hall, Harlan P. *H. P. Hall's Observations: Being More or Less History of Political Contests in Minnesota from 1849 to 1904.* St. Paul: Hall, 1904.

Heilbron, Bertha L., ed. *With Pen and Pencil on the Frontier in 1851: The Diary and Sketches of Frank Blackwell Mayer.* St. Paul: MHS, 1932.

Hildreth, S. P. *Biographical and Historical Memoirs of the Early Pioneer Settlers of Ohio.* Cincinnati: H. W. Derby, 1852.

———. *Pioneer History: Being an Account of the First Examinations of the Ohio Valley, and the Early Settlement of the Northwest Territory.* Cincinnati: H. W. Derby, 1848.

Holcombe, Return I. *Minnesota in Three Centuries,* Vol. 2. New York: Publishing Society of Minnesota, 1908.

Holmquist, June Drenning, and Jean A. Brookins. *Minnesota's Major Historic Sites: A Guide.* St. Paul: MHS, 1972.

Hubbard, Gurdon S. *The Autobiography of Gurdon Saltonstall Hubbard.* Chicago: R. R. Donnelley & Sons Co., 1911.

Hughes, Thomas, *Old Traverse des Sioux,* Reprint ed. St. Peter, Minn.: Nicollet County Historical Society, 1993.

Hulbert, Archer Butler, ed. *The Records of the Original Proceedings of the Ohio Company,* 2 vols. Marietta, Ohio: Marietta Historical Commission, 1917. Introduction, I:xv-cxxxvii.

Josephy, Alvin M., Jr. *The Civil War in the American West.* New York: Knopf, 1991.

Johnson, Ida Amanda. *The Michigan Fur Trade.* Lansing: Michigan Historical Publications. University series, 1919.

Kennedy, Roger. *Men on the Moving Frontier.* Palo Alto, Calif.: American West Publishing Company, 1969.

Kenny, Hamill. *West Virginia Place Names.* Piedmont, W.Va.: The Place Name Press, 1945.

Kimmel, Michael. *Manhood in America: A Cultural History.* New York: Free Press, 1996.

Kinzie, Mrs. John H. [Juliette Augusta]. *Wau-bun, the Early Day in the Northwest.* Philadelphia: J. B. Lippincott & Co., 1873.

Klunder, Willard C. *Lewis Cass and the Politics of Moderation.* Kent, Ohio: Kent State University Press, 1996.

Lamar, Howard Roberts. *Dakota Territory: A Study of Frontier Politics.* Fargo: North Dakota State University, 1997.

Lavender, David, *The Fist in the Wilderness.* Garden City, N.Y.: Doubleday, 1964; reprint ed., Albuquerque: University of New Mexico Press, 1979.

Letterman, Edward J. *From Whole Log To No Log: A History of the Indians Where the Mississippi and the Minnesota Rivers Meet.* Minneapolis: Dillon Press, 1969.

Lovelace, Maud Hart. *Early Candlelight.* St. Paul: Minnesota Historical Society Press, 1992.

Manitoba, Historical and Scientific Society. *Transactions,* No. 3 (1888–89).

Mardock, Robert Winston. *The Reformers and the American Indian.* Columbia: University of Missouri Press, 1971.

Martin, Albro. *James J. Hill and the Opening of the Northwest.* New York: Oxford University Press, 1976.

McDermott, John Francis. *Seth Eastman: Pictorial Historian of the Indian.* Norman: University of Oklahoma Press, 1961.

Meyer, Roy W. *History of the Santee Sioux.* Lincoln: University of Nebraska Press, 1967; rev. ed., 1993.

Namias, June. *White Captives: Gender and Ethnicity on the American Frontier.* Chapel Hill: University of North Carolina Press, 1993.

Neill, Edward D., ed. *Glimpses of the Nation's*

Struggle. St. Paul: St. Paul Book and Stationery Co., 1890.

Nichols, David A. *Lincoln and the Indians: Civil War Policy and Politics.* Columbia: University of Missouri Press, 1978.

Nute, Grace Lee. *The Voyageur.* D. Appleton, 1931; reprint ed., St. Paul: Minnesota Historical Society, 1955.

Palmer, Friend. *Early Days in Detroit.* Detroit: Hunt & June, 1906.

Parker, Donald Dean, ed. *The Recollections of Philander Prescott, Frontiersman of the Old Northwest, 1819–1862.* Lincoln: University of Nebraska Press, 1966.

Parkins, Almon Ernest. *The Historical Geography of Detroit.* Lansing: Michigan Historical Commission, 1918.

Peterson, Jacqueline, and Jennifer S. H. Brown, eds. *Being and Becoming Métis in North America.* Winnepeg: University of Manitoba Press, 1985.

Pond, Samuel W. *Dakota Life in the Upper Midwest.* Reprint ed. St. Paul: Minnesota Historical Society Press, 2002.

Pond, S. W., Jr. *Two Volunteer Missionaries Among the Dakotas.* Congregational Sunday-School and Publishing Society, n.p., 1893.

Prucha, Francis Paul. *American Indian Policy in the Formative Years: The Indian Trade and Intercourse Acts, 1790–1834.* Cambridge: Harvard University Press, 1962.

———. *American Indian Policy in Crisis: Christian Reformers and the Indian, 1865–1900.* Norman: University of Oklahoma Press, 1976.

———. *American Indian Treaties: The History of a Political Anomaly.* Berkeley: University of California Press, 1994.

———. *Lewis Cass and American Indian Policy.* Detroit: Wayne State University Press, 1967.

———. *The Great Father: The United States Government and the American Indians,* 2 vols. Lincoln: University of Nebraska Press, 1984.

Ridge, Martin. *Ignatius Donnelly: Portrait of a Politician.* Chicago: University of Chicago Press, 1962.

Ross, Hamilton Nelson. *La Pointe—Village Outpost.* St. Paul: North Central Pub. Co., 1960.

Ross, Robert B., and George B. Catlin. *Landmarks of Wayne County and Detroit*. Detroit: The Evening News Association, 1898.

Scanlan, Peter Lawrence. *Prairie du Chien: French, British, American*. Menasha, Wis.: s.n., 1937.

Schoolcraft, Henry Rowe, *Narrative Journal of Travels. . . . to the Sources of the Mississippi River in the Year 1820*. Albany, N.Y.: E. & E. Hosford, 1821.

Shortridge, Wilson Porter. *The Transition of a Typical Frontier with Illustrations from the Life of Henry Hastings Sibley*. Menasha, Wis.: George Banta Publishing Co., 1919.

Schultz, Duane. *Over the Earth I Come: The Great Sioux Uprising of 1862*. New York: St. Martin's Press, 1992.

Smith, Alice E., *The History of Wisconsin*. Madison: State Historical Society of Wisconsin, 1973.

Smith, Alice Elizabeth. *James Duane Doty, Frontier Promoter*. Madison: State Historical Society of Wisconsin, 1954.

Summers, Thomas J. *History of Marietta*. Marietta, Ohio: Leader Pub. Co., 1903.

Trenerry, Walter N. *Murder in Minnesota*. St. Paul: MHS, 1962.

Trennert, Robert A., Jr. *Indian Traders on the Middle Border: The House of Ewing, 1827–54*. Lincoln: University of Nebraska Press, 1981.

Upham, Warren G. *Minnesota Geographic Names*, Reprint ed. St. Paul: MHS, 1969.

Van Kirk, Sylvia. *"Many Tender Ties": Women in Fur Trade Society, 1670–1870*. Winnipeg, Manitoba: Watson and Dwyer, 1980.

Watson, Robert. *Notes on the Early Settlement of Cottage Grove and Vicinity*. Northfield, Minn.: s.n., 1924.

West, Nathaniel, D.D. *The Ancestry, Life, and Times of Hon. Henry Hastings Sibley, LL.D.* St. Paul: Pioneer Press, 1889.

West, Patricia. *Domesticating History: The Political Origins of America's House Museums*. Washington, D.C.: Smithsonian Institution Press, 1999.

Whipple, Henry B. *Lights and Shadows of a Long Episcopate*. New York: Macmillan, 1899.

White, Helen M., ed. *Ho! for the Gold Fields: Northern Overland Wagon Trains of the 1860s*. St. Paul: MHS, 1966.

———. *Henry Sibley's First Years at St. Peters or Mendota*. St. Paul: Turnstone Historical Research, 2002.

White, Richard. *The Middle Ground: Indians, Empires, and Republics in the Great Lakes Region, 1650–1815*. New York: Cambridge University Press, 1991.

Widder, Keith R. *Battle for the Soul: Métis Children Encounter Evangelical Protestants at Mackinaw Mission, 1823–1837*. East Lansing: Michigan State University Press, 1999.

Williams, J. Fletcher. *History of the City of St. Paul to 1875*, Reprint ed. St. Paul: Minnesota Historical Society Press, 1983.

Wingerd, Mary Lethert. *Claiming the City: Politics, Faith, and the Power of Place in St. Paul*. Ithaca, N.Y.: Cornell University Press, 2001.

Wittke, Carl, ed. *The History of the State of Ohio*. Columbus, Ohio, 1941, 1942, 1943, 1944.

Wood, Edwin C. *Historic Mackinac*. New York: Macmillan, 1918.

Woodford, Frank B. *Lewis Cass: The Last Jeffersonian*. New Brunswick, N.J.: Rutgers University Press, 1950.

Articles and Chapters

Abel, Annie Heloise. "The History of Events Resulting in Indian Consolidation West of the Mississippi." In *American Historical Association, Annual Report* 1:241–450 (1906).

Ackermann, Gertrude W. "Joseph Renville of Lac qui Parle." In *Minnesota History* 12:231–46 (September 1931).

Anderson, Thomas G. "Personal Narrative of Capt. Thomas G. Anderson." In *WHC* 9:132–206 (1882).

Babcock, Willoughby M. "Louis Provençalle, Fur Trader." In *Minnesota History* 20:259–68 (September 1939).

Baird, Elizabeth Therese. "Reminiscences of Early Days on Mackinac Island." In *WHC* 14:17–64 (1898).

Bates, George C. "By Gones of Detroit," In *MPHC* 22:305–408 (1893).

Bishop, Judson W. "History of the St. Pau

& Sioux City Railroad, 1864–1881." In *MHC* 10:1:399–415 (1905).

Blegen, Theodore C. "Campaigning with Seward in 1860." In *Minnesota History* 8:151–61 (June, 1927).

Blegen, Theodore C., ed. "Henry H. Sibley, Pioneer of Culture and Frontier Author." In *Minnesota History* 15:382–94 (December 1934).

Brainard, Dudley S. "Nininger, a Boom Town of the Fifties." In *Minnesota History* 13:127–51 (June, 1932).

Brisbois, Bernard. "Traditions and Recollections of Prairie du Chien." In *WHC* 9:282–302 (1882).

Brown, Ralph H., ed. "With Cass in the Northwest in 1820: The Journal of Charles C. Trowbridge." In *Minnesota History* 23:126–48, 233–52, 328–48 (June, September, December 1942).

Campbell, James V. "Biographical Sketch of Charles C. Trowbridge." In *MPHC* 6:478–91 (1884).

Cass, Lewis. "Policy and Practice of the United States and Great Britain in Their Treatment of Indians." In *North American Review* (April 1827).

Chapman, Charles H. "The Historic Johnston Family of the 'Soo.'" In *MPHC* 32:305–53 (1903). Includes map of Sault Ste. Marie ca. 1820s and picture of the Johnston house.

Chomsky, Carol. "The United States-Dakota War Trials: A Study in Military Injustice." In *Stanford Law Review* 43:13–98 (November 1990).

Davis, Jane S. "Two Sioux War Orders: A Mystery Unraveled." In *Minnesota History* 41:117–25 (Fall 1968).

Dessloch, Mrs. E. M. "Jane Fisher Dousman." In *Famous Wisconsin Women* 2:4–10 (1972).

Dustin, Fred. "The Treaty of Saginaw, 1819." In *Michigan History Magazine* 4:243–78 (January 1920).

Fite, Gilbert C. "Some Farmers' Accounts of Hardship on the Frontier." In *Minnesota History* 37:204–11 (March 1961).

Flanagan, John T. "Big Game Hunter: Henry H. Sibley" In *Minnesota History* 41:217–28.

Fonda, John H. "Early Reminiscences of Wisconsin" In *WHC* 5:205–84 (1868).

Fridley, Russell W. "Charles E. Flandrau: Attorney at War" In *Minnesota History* 38:116–25 (September 1962).

Gilfillan, Charles D. "The Early Political History of Minnesota" In *MHC* 9:167–80 (1901).

Gilfillan, John B. "History of the University of Minnesota" In *MHC* 12:43–84 (1908).

Gilman, Rhoda R. "The Fur Trade in the Upper Mississippi Valley, 1630–1850." In *Wisconsin Magazine of History* 58:3–18 (Autumn 1974).

——. "Last Days of the Upper Mississippi Fur Trade." In *Minnesota History* 42:123–40 (Winter 1970).

——. "A Northwestern Indian Territory— The Last Voice." In *Journal of the West* 39, no. 1:16–22 (January 2000).

——. "Ramsey, Donnelly, and the Congressional Campaign of 1868." In *Minnesota History* 36:300–8 (December 1959).

Gluek, Alvin C., Jr. "The Sioux Uprising: A Problem in International Relations." In *Minnesota History* 34:317–24 (Winter 1955).

Grabitske, David M. "First Lady of Preservation: Sarah Sibley and the Mount Vernon Ladies Association." In *Minnesota History* 58:407–16 (Winter 2003–04).

——. "Sarah Jane: A Lady's Frontier in Minnesota" In *Midwest Open Air Museums Magazine*, XX, No. 3:20–32 (1999).

Grant, H. Roger. "Minnesota's Good Railroad: The Omaha Road." In *Minnesota History* 57:190–210 (Winter 2000–01).

Grignon, Augustin. "Seventy-two Years' Recollections of Wisconsin." In *WHC* 3:197–295 (1857).

[Heilbron, Bertha L., ed.] "Sibley as a Wild Game Conservationist." In *Minnesota History* 18:415–19 (December 1937).

Heydenburk, Martin. "Incidents in the Life of Robert Stuart." In *MPHC* 3:56–61.

[Huggin, Nancy M.] "Captivity Among the Sioux: The Story of Nancy McClure" In *MHC* 6:438–60 (1894).

Jenks, William L. "The First Bank in Michigan." In *Michigan History* 1:41–62 (July 1917).

Jorstad, Erling. "Minnesota's Role in the Democratic Rift of 1860." In *Minnesota History* 37:45–51 (June 1960).

Jorstad, Erling. "Personal Politics in the Origins of Minnesota's Democratic Party." In *Minnesota History* 36:259–71 (September 1959).

Kane, Lucile M. "The Sioux Treaties and the Traders." In *Minnesota History* 32:65–80 (June 1951).

Kingsbury, David L. "Sully's Expedition Against the Sioux in 1864." In *MHC* 8:449–62 (1898).

Lass, William E. "The Birth of Minnesota." In *Minnesota History* 55:267–79 (Summer 1997).

———. "Minnesota's Separation from Wisconsin: Boundary Making on the Upper Mississippi Frontier." In *Minnesota History* 50:309–20 (Winter 1987).

———. "The 'Moscow Expedition.'" In *Minnesota History* 39:227–40 (Summer 1965).

Lindley, John M. "Crawford Livingston, Chauncey W. Griggs, and Their Roles in St. Paul History." In *Ramsey County History* 34:4–27 (Fall 1999).

Lockwood, James H. "Early Times and Events in Wisconsin." In *WHC* 2:98–196 (1856).

Marcaccini, Ann and George Woytanowitz. "House Work—The DAR at the Sibley House." In *Minnesota History* 55:186–201 (Spring 1997).

McDowell, John E. "Madame La Framboise." In *Michigan History* 56:271–86 (Winter 1972).

Murray, William P. "Recollections of Early Territorial Days and Legislation." In *MHC* 12:103–30 (1908).

Patterson, J. W. "The Post Office in Early Minnesota." In *Minnesota History* 40:79–81 (Summer 1966).

Prucha, Francis Paul. "Army Sutlers and the American Fur Company." In *Minnesota History* 40:22–31 (Spring 1966).

Queripel, Susan. "An Early Nineteenth Century Occupation of Pike Island, Dakota County, Minnesota: Historical Background." In *Minnesota Archaeologist* 36:51–55 (July 1977).

Rife, Clarence W. "Norman W. Kittson: A

Fur-Trader at Pembina." In *Minnesota History* 6:225–52 (September 1925).

Saby, Rasmus S. "Railroad Legislation in Minnesota." In *MHC* 15:1–188 (1915).

Slatta, Richard W. "The Whys and Wherefores of Comparative Frontier History." In *Journal of the West* 42:8–13 (Winter 2003).

Schoolcraft, Henry Rowe. "Memoir of John Johnston." In *MPHC* 36:53–90 (1908).

Taliaferro, Lawrence. "Auto-Biography of Maj. Lawrence Taliaferro." In *MHC* 6:189–255 (1894).

[Thwaites, Reuben G., ed.] "Letter of John Lawe to Josephe Rolette, April 18, 1821." In *WHC* 20:196–98 (1911).

Trenerry, Walter N. "The Minnesota Legislator and the Grasshopper, 1873–1877." In *Minnesota History* 36:56–60 (June 1958).

Trowbridge, C. C. "Detroit in 1819." In *MPHC* 4:471–79.

Trowbridge, Charles C. "Sketch of the Life of Hon. Robert Stuart." In *MPHC* 3:52–56.

Urevig, Frances, ed. "With Governor Ramsey to Minnesota in 1849." In *Minnesota History* 35:352–57 (December 1957).

Voelker, Donald W. "Robert Stuart, A Man Who Meant Business." In *Michigan History Magazine* (September/October 1990).

Webber, William L. "Indian Cession of 1819, Made by the Treaty of Saginaw." In *MPHC* 26:517–34.

White, Bruce M. "The Power of Whiteness: Or, the Life and Times of Joseph Rolette Jr." In *Minnesota History* 56:179–87 (Winter 1998–99).

White, Janet. "William Montague Ferry and the Protestant Mission on Mackinac Island." In *Michigan History* 32:340–51.

Williams, Ephraim S. "The Treaty of Saginaw in the Year 1819." In *MPHC* 7:262–70 (1884).

Williams, J. Fletcher. "Memoir of Joseph R. Brown." In *MHC* 3:201–12 (1880).

———. "Henry Hastings Sibley: A Memoir." In *MHC* 6:264–310 (1894).

Wilson, Angela Cavender. "Grandmother to Granddaughter: Generations of Ora History in a Dakota Family." In Devon A

Mihesuah, ed. *Natives and Academics* (Lincoln: University of Nebraska Press, 1998).

Wright, Dana. "The Sibley Trail of 1863." In *North Dakota History* 29:296 (October 1962).

Zorn, Roman J. "Minnesota Public Opinion and the Secession Controversy, December, 1860—April, 1861." In *Mississippi Valley Historical Review* 36:435-56 (December 1949).

Newspapers
Files of all newspapers cited are in the MHS.

Brown's Valley Reporter (Brown's Valley, Minnesota)
Central Republican (Faribault)
Fergus Falls Weekly Journal (Fergus Falls, Minnesota)
Henderson Democrat (Henderson, Minnesota)
Minneapolis Tribune (Minneapolis)
Minnesota Chronicle and Register (St. Paul)
Minnesota Pioneer (St. Paul)
Minnesotian (St. Paul)
Pioneer (St. Paul)
Pioneer and Democrat (St. Paul)
Pioneer Press (St. Paul)
Press (St. Paul)
St. Cloud Democrat (St. Cloud, Minnesota)
St. Paul Democrat (St. Paul)
St. Paul Dispatch (St. Paul)
State Atlas (Minneapolis)

Government Records
Office of Indian Affairs. *Reports.*

Office of Indian Affairs. Letters Received; Letters Sent. In the National Archives. Microfilm in the MHS.

Kappler, Charles J., comp. and ed. *Indian Affairs: Laws and Treaties,* Second ed. (Washington, D. C., 1904).

Minnesota. Records of the Governors. Henry H. Sibley. In the State Archives.

Minnesota. *House Journal,* 1857-58 (1881).

Minnesota. *Senate Journal,* 1857-58 (1859-60).

Minnesota. *Minnesota in the Civil and Indian Wars* (1892).

Minnesota, Constitutional Convention (Democratic). *Debates and Proceedings* (St. Paul, 1857).

Minnesota. Supreme Court. *Minnesota Reports* (1877 imprint).

United States. *War of the Rebellion, Official Records.*

United States. Senate. *Ramsey Investigation Report* (Serial 699).

University of Illinois. *The Mereness Calendar: Federal Documents on the Upper Mississippi Valley, 1780-1890,* 12 vols. (Boston: G. K. Hall & Co., 1971).

Washington County, district court records. In the Minnesota State Archives.

Unpublished Works
Bailly, Edward C. "The French-Canadian Background of a Minnesota Pioneer— Alexis Bailly." In the MHS.

Freeman, John Finley. "Henry Rowe Schoolcraft." Ph.D. dissertation. Harvard University, 1959. Copy in the MHS. MHS Catalog: Q143/.S37F7.

Fridley, Russell W. "Evaluation of Governors." 1966. In the MHS.

Hollinshead, Ellen Rice. "Reminiscences." In the MHS.

Jorstad, Erling Theodore. "The Life of Henry Hastings Sibley." Ph.D. dissertation. University of Wisconsin, 1957. Copy in the MHS. MHS Catalog: *F605.1/.S56J6.

Karstad, Ruby G. "Political Party Alignments in Minnesota, 1854-1860" M.A. thesis, 1934. Copy in the MHS.

Owens, John P. "Political History of Minnesota." In the MHS.

Steele, Anna Barney. Journal. In the MHS.

White, Bruce M. "The Regional Context of the Removal Order of 1850: A Report Prepared for the Mille Lacs Band of Ojibway, December 1993." Copy in possession of the author.

White, Bruce M., and Alan R. Woolworth. "*Oheyawahe* or Pilot Knob." Copy in possession of the author.

Manuscript Collections
AMERICAN FUR COMPANY
These papers, mostly dating after the reorganization of the firm in 1834, are in the New York Historical Society. Copies of all items cited are on microfilm in the MHS. A helpful guide is Grace Lee Nute,

Calendar of the American Fur Company's Papers (Washington, D.C.: American Historical Association, *Annual Report*, 1945).

BAILLY, ALEXIS

The Bailly Papers are in the MHS.

BROWN, JOSEPH R. AND SAMUEL J.

Mostly dating from after 1862, these papers are in the MHS. Although the bulk of the collection relates to Brown's descendants, they are cited here as J. R. Brown Papers.

BROWN, WILLIAM REYNOLDS

The William R. Brown Papers are in the MHS.

CARTER, THEODORE G.

The Carter Papers are in the MHS.

CHOUTEAU, PIERRE, JR.

Several collections relating to Pierre Chouteau, Jr., and the Chouteau family are In the Missouri Historical Society, St. Louis. Ledgers used here are included in the microfilm publication "Papers of the St. Louis Fur Trade" (University Publications of America), of which the MHS has a copy. They are cited as Chouteau Papers.

DOUSMAN, HERCULES L.

The main collection of Dousman's papers is in the State Historical Society of Wisconsin. Some Dousman documents relating to the American Fur Company are owned by the Newberry Library, Chicago. Copies of correspondence and documents relating to the fur trade in Minnesota, including all items cited here, are in the MHS.

DOUSMAN, LOUIS

Twenty-seven letters from Henry H. Sibley to Hercules L. Dousman, Jr., (Louis), written between 1868 and 1882, were preserved at the Villa Louis in Prairie du Chien. The originals are now in the State Historical Society of Wisconsin. Copies are in the possession of the author. They are cited as Louis Dousman correspondence.

EAMES, RICHARD M.

The Eames Papers are in the MHS.

FOLWELL, WILLIAM WATTS

The Folwell Papers are in the MHS.

LEDUC, WILLIAM GATES

The LeDuc Papers are in the MHS.

LIVINGSTON, CRAWFORD

The Livingston Papers are in the Ramsey County Historical Society, St. Paul, Minnesota.

MACKINAC LETTER BOOKS

Three letter books preserved in the Astor House at Mackinac include fragments of company correspondence between the years 1816 and 1830. The MHS has microfilm copies.

MASON, JOHN T.

The Mason Papers are in the Burton Historical Collection, Detroit Public Library.

POND, FAMILY

The Pond Papers include the letters and papers of Samuel W. and Gideon Pond and their families. In the MHS.

RAMSEY, ALEXANDER

The Ramsey Papers are in the MHS. Like the Sibley Papers, the collection is available in an NHPC microfilm edition with a printed guide.

RICE, HENRY M.

The Rice Papers are in the MHS. They include transcripts of letter books with material dating from June 1848 to November 1849.

RIGGS, STEPHEN R.

A collection of Riggs's letters to his wife, Mary, written during the 1862 campaign, are in the Chippewa County Historical Society, Granite Falls, Minnesota. Typewritten copies are in the MHS.

SIBLEY, SOLOMON

The papers of Solomon Sibley are in the Burton Historical Collection of the Detroit Public Library. Copies of selected correspondence from Henry H. Sibley are in the MHS and are included in the microfilm edition of the Henry H. Sibley Papers.

SIBLEY, HENRY HASTINGS

These papers, owned by the MHS, have formed the core source material for this work. They include correspondence and other documents arranged by date, various account books and ledgers, memorandum books, and letter books. A microfilm edition, produced under the auspices of the National Historical Publications Commission in 1968, includes all but a few recent additions to the collection. Accompanying the thirty-two rolls of microfilm is a printed guide written by Jane Spector Davis.

STEELE, FRANKLIN

The Steele Papers are in the MHS.

WHIPPLE, HENRY B.

The Whipple Papers are in the MHS.

WOODBRIDGE, WILLIAM

The Woodbridge Papers are in the Burton Historical Collection of the Detroit Public Library.

Published Writings of Henry Hastings Sibley
Books

The Unfinished Autobiography of Henry Hastings Sibley Together with a Selection of Hitherto Unpublished Letters from the Thirties. (Minneapolis: Voyageur Press, 1932). The unfinished manuscript of the autobiography was not among the papers given to the MHS by Sibley himself; it was donated in 1924 by his daughter Sarah [Mrs. Elbert A.] Young. Its first publication was in Volume 8 of *Minnesota History*, pp. 329–62 (December 1927), where it appeared with an introduction and notes by Theodore C. Blegen. In 1932 Blegen published it separately as a small book, adding eleven letters written by Sibley to Ramsay Crooks and preserved in the American Fur Company Papers.

Iron Face: The Adventures of Jack Frazer, Frontier Warrior, Scout, and Hunter (Chicago, The Caxton Club, 1950). The sixteen chapters of this book were published as articles in the *St. Paul Pioneer*, where they appeared weekly, beginning December 2, 1866, signed with the pseudonym "Walker in the Pines." In 1950 they were collected in a book under the title *Iron Face*, edited with an introduction and annotations by Theodore C. Blegen and Sarah A. Davidson. A part of the fourth chapter, here entitled "Dark and Bloody Ground," had been printed earlier in *Porter's Spirit of the Times* (January 31, 1857). There it appeared under the title "The Three Dakotas," and some of the personal names had been altered.

Minnesota Historical Collections (MHC)

The *Annals of the Minnesota Historical Society,* 1850–1856, were reprinted in Volume 1 of the *MHC* in 1872. The pages cited here are from a second edition of Volume 1 published in 1902. Volume 3 was published in 1880.

"Description of Minnesota." 1:1–18 (*Annals,* 1850).

"Speech before the Committee on Elections of the House of Representatives, December 22, 1848." 1:19–24 (*Annals,* 1850).

"Memoir of Jean [sic] N. Nicollet." 1:146–56 (*Annals,* 1853).

"Reminiscences: Historical and Personal." 1:374–96.

"Sketch of John Other Day." 3:99–102.

"Memoir of Jean Baptiste Faribault." 3:168–79.

"Memoir of Hercules L. Dousman." 3:192–200.

"Reminiscences of the Early Days of Minnesota." 3:242–81.

"Tribute to Rev. John Mattocks." 3:307–10.

"Tribute to Rev. Gideon H. Pond." 3:364–66.

Spirit of the Times

In writing for this publication and for its successor, *Porter's Spirit of the Times,* Sibley always used the pseudonym "Hal, A Dacotah."

Vol. 12, p. 73 (April 16, 1842). This piece appeared as a letter, without title. It describes Sibley's hunting trip in 1839 with Fremont.

Vol. 13 (April 15, June 17, 1843). "A Hunting Excursion to the Red Cedar," in two parts.

Vol. 13 (Nov. 25, 1843). "Expedition to the Red Cedar With a Large Band."

Vol. 16 (April 11, 1846). "A Buffalo and Elk Hunt in 1842." Reprinted in *Minnesota History* 15:385–94.

Vol. 17 (April 17, 1847). "Hunting in the Western Prairies."

Vol. 18 (March 11, 1848). "Sketches of Indian Warfare."

Vol. 18 (April 1, 1848). "Hunting in the Northwest."

Vol. 20, p. 546 (Jan. 4, 1851). A letter signed by "Hal" introduces Sibley's translation from French of a piece written by Georges-Antoine Belcourt. Two of these articles were reprinted in a book edited by Peter Hawken and titled *Instructions to Young Sportsmen, In All That Relates to Guns and Shooting* (Philadelphia: Blanchard and Lea, 1853).

Porter's Spirit of the Times

Vol. 1, p. 126 (Oct. 25, 1856). "Game in the West." Reprinted in *Minnesota History* 18:415–19.

Vol. 1 (Jan. 31, 1857). "The Three Dacotahs." Also appears as part of chapter 4 in Blegen and Davidson, eds. *Iron Face.*

Forest and Stream

"Sports of By-Gone Days." 5:258 (December 2, 1872). A clipping of this article is in the MHS Scrapbooks, 2:71.

INDEX

Italic page numbers refer to images.

Abbott, James, 14–15, 34
Abbott, Samuel, 34, 46
acculturation of Native Americans, 98, 117; agriculture and, 204–5; Brown on, 213–14; Cass on, 18, 70; communal property as obstacle to, 58, 125; political opposition to Indian policy of "civilization," 82; traditionalists opposition to, 159, 180
agriculture: acculturation and, 204–5; crop failures, 96, 170; Dakota and, 49, 50, 159, 170, 181, 215; droughts and, 96, 196; fair held in Fort Snelling, 167; grasshopper plagues, 216–17, *217*; industrialization and, 215; wheat as crop, 167, 226
Ainse, Pelagie (Mrs. Jean Baptiste Faribault), 53, 78, 84
Aitken, William A., 39, 52, 100
alcohol: temperance organizations, 113; whiskey trade, 40, 47–48, 51, 77, 91–92, 115
American Board of Commissioners for Foreign Missions, 50, 117
American Fur Company: closure of, 84–85; contracts and agreements, 53–54, 67; expansion after 1812, 13; Hudson's Bay Company and, 28, 92–93; Mackinac Island Headquarters, 23–24, *24*; map of region, *33*; monopolies and competition, 28, 31, 48, 51–52, 91–92, 94, 120; organization of, 32, 38–39, 67, 110–11; political influence, 79; treaties of 1837 and, 83
Anderson, Angus, 69
Andre, Alexis, 197–98, 203
annuities: for Dakota, 50, 82, 97, 141, 170, 208; failure to provide, 170; Ojibwe and, 120; Traverse des Sioux treaty and, 126; withheld during treaty

negotiations, 132
Askin, John, 14
Astor, John Jacob, 24, 31, 35
Austin, Horace, 216, 257–58 *n.* 23
Ayer, Frederick and Elizabeth, 63

Bad Hail, 76
Bailly, Alexis, 38–39, 43–46, 52, 81, 140
Bailly, Henry, 140
Bailly, Joseph, 44
Bailly, Lucy Faribault, 44, 46
Baker, Benjamin F., 48, 73, 78
Baker, James H., 232
banks and banking, 26, 142, 151; collapses, 154, 216, 224; regulation of, 157
Barney, Anna (Mrs. Franklin Steele), 84, 155, 211–12, 228
Becker, George L., 162, 163
Beever, Frederick J. H., 195, 198, 199–200
Belcourt, Georges-Antoine, 136–37
Bell, John, 80, 130
Belmont, August, 164
Benton, Jessie (Mrs. John C. Fremont), 83, 197
Benton, Thomas Hart, 82, 83
Big Eagle, 50
Big Mound, Battle of, 198
Big Sandy Lake, 120
Big Stone Lake, 56, 92, 94, 191, 196
Big Thunder, 50, 97
Billings, George W., 144
Bingham, Abel, 22
Birch Coulee battle, 178–79, *179*, 257 *n.* 20
Black Dog village (Mdewakanton Dakota), 48, 50, 71, 85
Blegen, Theodore C., 233–34
Bliss, John, 40
Board of Indian Commissioners, 218
Borup, Charles W. W., 129; banking ven-

275

ILLUSTRATION CREDITS

Pages ii, iii, 21, 36, 37, 41, 45, 47, 49, 55, 57, 64, 69, 78, 89, 93, 108, 109, 111, 123, 124, 139, 150, 152, 156, 162, 171, 172 (right), 179, 184, 188, 198, 211, 214, 217, 223, 226, 231—Minnesota Historical Society

Pages 5 and 13—The Detroit Institute of Arts. Page 5: Chester Harding, *Solomon Sibley* (1822). Gift of the Sibley Estate. Photograph © 1958 The Detroit Institute of Arts. Page 13: Alexander Macomb, *Detroit as Seen from the Canadian Shore in 1821* (1821). Gift of Ernest Newman Stanton, Mrs. Kenneth Taylor White and the Burton Historical Collection in memory of Mrs. Robert Lee Stanton. Photograph © 1995 The Detroit Institute of Arts.

Pages 24 and 26—Courtesy Mackinac State Historic Parks, Michigan

Pages 33, 80, 95, 194—Maps by Matt Kania, St. Paul

Page 126—Francis D. Millet, *The Treaty of Traverse des Sioux*, from the MHS collections

Page 136—MHS/Sibley House Historic Site (SH307). Gift of Mrs. Augusta Ann Sibley Pope.

Page 137—*St. Paul Dispatch* (October 1908), from the MHS collections

Page 172 (left)—MHS/Sibley House Historic Site. From Elsie Pope Rugg's scrapbook (SH 1998.1.1). Gift of Mrs. Janny Rugg Grice.

Page 232—Photo by Joe Michl/MHS